Table of Contents

Chapter 6: Website Design............................. **123**

Chapter 7: Google **171**

How to Use the Internet to
Advertise, Promote, and Market
Your Business or Website —
With Little or No Money

Revised 3rd Edition

By: Bruce C. Brown

Revised By: Lawrence Chan

USE THE INTERNET TO ADVERTISE, PROMOTE, AND ̄ET YOUR BUSINESS OR WEBSITE — WITH LITTLE OR NO ̄NEY REVISED 3RD EDITION

Copyright © 2016 Atlantic Publishing Group, Inc.
1405 SW 6th Avenue • Ocala, Florida 34471 • Phone 800-814-1132 • Fax 352-622-1875
Web site: www.atlantic-pub.com • E-mail: sales@atlantic-pub.com
SAN Number: 268-1250

Library of Congress Cataloging-in-Publication Data

Names: Brown, Bruce C. (Bruce Cameron), 1965-
Title: How to use the Internet to advertise, promote, and market your
   business or web site : with little or no money / by Bruce C. Brown ;
   revised by Lawrence Chan.
Description: REVISED 3rd Edition. | Ocala : Atlantic Publishing Group, Inc.,
   2015. | Revised edition of the author's How to use the Internet to
   advertise, promote, and market your business or website, 2011. | Includes
   bibliographical references and index.
Identifiers: LCCN 2015037917| ISBN 9781601389497 (alk. paper) | ISBN
   1601389493 (alk. paper)
Subjects: LCSH: Internet marketing--Handbooks, manuals, etc. | Internet
   advertising--Handbooks, manuals, etc. | Web sites--Design--Handbooks,
   manuals, etc. | Electronic commerce--Handbooks, manuals, etc.
Classification: LCC HF5415.1265 .B765 2015 | DDC 658.8/72--dc23 LC record available at http://
lccn.loc.gov/2015037917

Printed in the United States

Printed on Recycled Paper

Reduce. Reuse.
RECYCLE.

A decade ago, Atlantic Publishing signed the Green Press Initiative. These guidelines promote environmentally friendly practices, such as using recycled stock and vegetable-based inks, avoiding waste, choosing energy-efficient resources, and promoting a no-pulping policy. We now use 100-percent recycled stock on all our books. The results: in one year, switching to post-consumer recycled stock saved 24 mature trees, 5,000 gallons of water, the equivalent of the total energy used for one home in a year, and the equivalent of the greenhouse gases from one car driven for a year.

Over the years, we have adopted a number of dogs from rescues and shelters. First there was Bear and after he passed, Ginger and Scout. Now, we have Kira, another rescue. They have brought immense joy and love not just into our lives, but into the lives of all who met them.

We want you to know a portion of the profits of this book will be donated in Bear, Ginger and Scout's memory to local animal shelters, parks, conservation organizations, and other individuals and nonprofit organizations in need of assistance.

– Douglas & Sherri Brown,
President & Vice-President of Atlantic Publishing

Dedication

This book is dedicated to my beautiful wife Vonda.
She is my best friend, my soulmate, and my partner for eternity.

In 2014, we moved to Elizabeth City, North Carolina,
because I was transferred in my assignment with the U.S. Coast Guard.
Vonda and I would like to thank our friends at Forest Park Church
in Elizabeth City for welcoming us to your family.
You can find Forest Park Church online at www.fplive.org.

⸻

*"My hands, they're strong / But my knees were far too weak /
To stand in your arms / Without falling to your feet"*
Adele - 'Set Fire to the Rain' (From the Album '21')

⸻

*"Please forgive me for my sins / Yes, I swam dirty waters /
But you pushed me in"*
Adele - 'I'll Be Waiting' (From the Album '21')

⸻

*"You look like a movie / You sound like a song / My God /
This reminds me, of when we were young"*
Adele - 'When We Were Young' (From the Album '25')

Introduction

The very first book I wrote started me on a journey to write more than a dozen books on a variety of topics I felt were relevant and useful to the reader. This book was last revised about four years ago and published in 2011. It is now 2016, and to say that media has evolved would be an understatement. While many of the core strategies, software and technologies mentioned in the second edition are still applicable in a broad sense, they are by their very nature constantly changing with new features.

Technology has changed, social media is stronger than ever, and while many fundamental techniques and strategies have stood the test of time, this edition promises to provide you with a wealth of information designed to help your small business grow and prosper. Times have changed, and it never stops changing in the fast paced world of Internet marketing and promotions.

It was time to dust off this book and ensure that you are still reading information relevant to the current marketing landscape. Establishing, growing, and maintaining your competitive edge in the modern business environment means incorporating multi-level Internet marketing, maintaining a strong Web presence, email advertising, and engaging social media management.

The Internet connects nearly everyone and every business all over the world. Billions of dollars exchange hands over the Web every day. Users search for information from their iPhones®, iPads®, computers, laptops, tablets and thousands of other devices every day — potentially searching for the information, goods, or services your business provides. This book will help you make that connection without the need for significant investment and without the need for a dedicated Web design or marketing staff.

A Web presence is an essential aspect of any business, not just online services or major companies; it is your primary means of communicating and advertising with the consumer market. You must embrace a variety of formats including blogging, email marketing, website design, and social media, just to name just a few.

When you want to research a business, find a new restaurant, shop for new products, compare prices, and make purchasing decisions, you do not do the exhausting job of running to five different businesses in town to compare — you do it all online, usually with a simple query into your favorite search engine. The search engine is the most basic aspect of the Internet experience, and it is going to be the go-to method for people to research your business and services.

Conversely, the Internet allows you to promote, advertise, and market yourself in a cost-efficient manner to a very wide audience. What other marketing tool do you have at your disposal where billions of people have the ability to reach out directly to your business or organization from anywhere in the world? You even have the capability of advertising to all of these potential clients for little to no cost.

You do not need to possess a great deal of Web design knowledge or online experience to use the Internet in an effective manner. After reading this book, you will be able to apply principles and techniques that will empower you to be a leader in the world of online marketing and promotion. The concepts and steps outlined in this book are easy to implement and can be managed at the small business owner level. This book is ideal for someone who does not have an "IT" staff or large marketing and promotion budget. It is perfect for sole proprietors and can certainly teach large corporations a lesson in a "back to basics" approach to low cost marketing and promotion.

The bottom line is that you do not need a professional marketing firm to promote and market your online business. You can do it yourself and put the money you saved from expensive marketing campaigns or expensive website providers towards other business needs.

If you are the owner, proprietor, or manager of a traditional brick and mortar business, you need to be making every effort towards a strong online and social media presence to reach your audience. Antiquated and expensive methods of traditional advertising only reach a small customer base. They are also costly to produce and distribute, and typically fail to generate the return on the investment.

This book will show you how you can use your website, blog, or social media presence to do five key things: (a) advertise current specials, (b) let customers know what products or services are new, (c) provide contact information and directions to your business, (d) provide your customers with additional information, such as how to use your products, and, most importantly, (e) reach a potentially unlimited customer base at little to no cost.

No matter what type of business you have, the possibilities are endless when it comes to what you can do with Internet advertising and online business promotion solutions. While the material covered in this book is constantly changing and evolving with new developments in technology and society, I am confident that the core principles in this book will serve you well for many years to come, and I hope it becomes one of your best, most profitable investments.

This book will help you understand how to create a marketing campaign and how to improve your existing site through proven search engine optimization techniques; we will also cover additional methods that are proven to generate website traffic. To expand on this topic, flip to the end of the book to view additional reading material.

This completely revised, third edition is full of new content designed to help you achieve online success with little to no investment. I was excited to update this book and hope that you find it as useful as others who purchased and used the first and second editions. Here is just some of the recognition the first version of this book received:

- **The National 2007 Indie Excellence Book Awards Business Finalist**

- **2007 Independent Publisher Book Awards Computer/ Internet Bronze**

- **ForeWord Magazine's Book of the Year Awards Finalist**

- **USA Best Books Awards 2007 Business: Marketing & Advertising Finalist**

- **Library Journal: Best Business Book 2006 Marketing/Branding**

Chapter 1

Preparing for Your Exam

Almost everyone is using or accessing the Internet in one way or the other. Computers, laptops, tablets, phones, iPads, game consoles, and even watches can all be connected to the Internet. There are more people using the Internet than there are homes with a landline phone, and the majority of any given population is maintaining some sort of social media presence or personal blog.

Most people visit a website or Facebook® site for the following reasons:

- They want/need information.
- They want/need to make a purchase/donation.
- They want/need to be entertained.
- They want/need to be informed.

All of these purposes were once fulfilled by books, television, and radio, where traditional businesses could previously advertise locally to a relatively small market area. The sheer versatility of information exchange and file sharing online has made the Internet the ultimate all-in-one source for nearly everything. However, that does not mean that you can be lax in how you present yourself online or that you can rely upon a single website or advertising source to get your name out there.

Internet websites are now only the tip of the iceberg; you also have social media networks, apps, and more traditional message boards, which all cater to different audiences. Learning how these audiences differ and how receptive they are to different strategies and brands is just as important as building your own website.

The Internet is very different from other mediums of advertising and marketing in several ways. Not only is the Internet a channel for communication, but it is also a channel for distribution and transactions. There is no other advertising medium that is able to accomplish all these goals at once. With so much interactive information and with such a vast number of resources available at their fingertips, consumers are able to make informed and conscious choices of what they want to buy and how much they are willing to pay, and they have confidence that they are making an informed and educated decision.

This can be a double-edged sword, because customers are constantly being assailed by a wave of information and advertisement from companies just like your own, and they are just as likely to tune out advertisements or stop tracking your business if your strategy is overly aggressive, does not deliver relevant information, is difficult to use, or is not maintained or updated on a regular basis.

Customer loyalty is going to be vital to the success of advertising online. When you gain the loyalty of your customers, you will have them coming back to your website to do business with you. The Ladder of Loyalty concept is simple to understand and is something that you should be striving for, since it ties in all aspects of successful online advertising.

Loyalty has four basic steps that represent all groups of people that may visit your website: prospects, suspects, customers, and advocates. Every potential customer or customer with whom you communicate in some way will be on one of these steps. Where they stand on the Ladder of Loyalty will depend on (1) what visitors know about your business and the products or services that you sell, (2) what customers have bought from you in the past, (3) how frequently customers have bought from you, and (4) how much trust customers have in your business and the products or services that you sell.

A sales and marketing kit will go hand in hand with the marketing strategy you have developed. Assuming you are just starting on the road to developing your strategy, you will have to ask yourself some questions.

- Who or what are your target markets? This should center on a niche market that you may have decided to corner or just products or services you have to sell.

- In what ways do you plan on advertising and promoting your business? You have probably thought about this to some extent and would like to focus in on how you can advertise and promote for free. Many options are on the Internet for use without having to pay hefty (or any) fees, but remember that the most effective strategies are focused toward a specific market, but broadly distributed.

- Are you going to have a central focus of your business promotion? Are you going to target a specific service that you offer with your website design, such as animation or driving traffic to their sites? Like any other form of advertising how you brand yourself is essential. Think about multiple forms of online presence including blogs, website and social media.

- What goals are you trying to reach with your plan? Try setting a goal about the number of responses and the attention that your advertising campaign has brought to your business.

- Are you highlighting your best assets? What you can offer to your future clients? Be sure to put those assets front and center.

Think about your strengths that can benefit your potential clients, and highlight those through your advertising.

- When you are approached with a potential client, what are your plans for responding to them? Do you have a clearly defined way that you would like to follow up? Through email or phone is good, but can you visit their business in person? Communication is critical, even if it is done through email, chat or phone.

- How will you be generating leads on new clients on a consistent basis? Are there resources you can use to build your clientele?

- Will you be keeping a record of how your advertising has been working or not working for your business? You may find that some things work better than others and should be exploited as much as possible. I recommend you try a wide variety of options to promote and grow your business — some may prove ineffective and should be abandoned to allow you to focus on the more productive options.

Effective sales people know how to use the major motivators to promote attention, interest, conviction, and desire. They use motivators to close sales. Learn to use them. Take a few moments to think about successful marketing and how we measure it. At the end of the day, business professionals will test out all manner of methods to measure the effectiveness of their marketing campaign. Each time, however, they miss the mark. People often try inaccurate methods of measuring the success of marketing. Increased sales, for instance, are how you measure the success of your sales, not the success of your marketing campaign. Likewise, increased brand awareness is a measure of the success of your brand agencies and media buyers. Customer satisfaction is a difficult thing to measure, and it only tells you how well your company is performing. Marketing metrics can generally be based upon scientific analysis. Common sense is largely significant in marketing as well. Marketing is about market development, the process of reaching out into new markets, and segments of products and services provided by your business. The objective of your marketing should always be, in the broad sense, to find and tap new markets and segments.

The measurement of marketing needs to be both concrete and objective. You need to evaluate how many new markets and segments you are able to add or strengthen over a period of time, tracking your efforts in an objective manner, usually mathematically, calculating the cost dollar for dollar.

The type of advertising that works best for your company will depend upon numerous factors. In particular, you must take into consideration your target market. Who or what businesses are you going to target to get your best response? Will you stick to Internet advertising, or will that not be enough? What about social media? Do you need a Facebook site? Should you use Twitter™, Vine™, Instagram™, YouTube®, Pinterest, LinkedIn®, and Tumblr? How will you manage all of this? The best approach for your business depends upon the precise nature of your target market, your ability to network and make connections, and how actively you want to go beyond your own network of contacts. Experiment and grow your online and social media presence as your grow your business.

I like to use a restaurant as an example of how promoting online can have a tremendous and positive impact on your business. Let's face it, a restaurant does not specifically need a website, blog or other forms of online marketing to provide its services, but it is strongly recommend to have an online presence; it is critical to be viewed favorably on reviewing platforms such as Yelp or TripAdvisor.

Think about it: when trying to find a new restaurant to dine at, one of the first things we do is check its website and its reviews on the Internet. An online presence allows us to easily get directions to your business and sometimes gives an interesting history or story behind it. This also lets us see the menu, view the photos, read customer reviews, and get a general feel for the place. While most restaurant websites will not post negative reviews on their site, at least it validates that they have some common feedback, and it is a simple enough matter to look for more feedback on other sites. I like to simply look at photos of a restaurant on their website to evaluate their ambiance and atmosphere. Facebook is a great way to get instant feedback on a restaurant (or any business) — are the customers happy? Is it up-to-date and relevant?

If you are a restaurant owner with access and knowledge of online marketing, then you also have access to the feedback customers are giving about your restaurant. They may have concerns or praises about your food or service, which allows you to better tailor your business to your market. You will also be able to respond to any problems as well as offer attractive promotional deals around your most popular products, services, or menu items. You can use Facebook to promote tonight's Happy Hour, featured specials, wine pairings, and more. The opportunities are endless, costs are minimal (to none) and the requisite skills to master social media and websites are also minimal. The only recurring costs may be Web hosting, which can be obtained for under $10 per month (or free in some instances), or you can simply use Facebook, Twitter and other services at no cost at all.

You must promote your website or business and have it entered into search engines before any significant traffic will come your way. The same is true for social media sites. You must establish a presence and promote it heavily to draw in traffic. Social media has the advantage of replication — when people like your Facebook site, it will show up on their friend's news feed. As they like it, more friends may see it, and thus the power of social media marketing. Before you know it, you will have a world of visitors looking at your business.

What is Internet Marketing?

Some business owners believe that posting tweets, updating a business page, and connecting with customers on the Web is a confusing, complicated process that only young people understand. In certain cases, this is true. In a society where technology changes too quickly and news becomes old after five minutes, it is difficult to keep up with the latest trends, especially when marketing your business (and you have been in the game for a long time already).

The Internet is supposed to help you reach new customers more easily, not make it a more difficult process. With a little bit of knowledge and practice, you will share photos, post statuses, and connect with customers within a matter of weeks. The Internet is a personal gateway from the business owner to the customer. It has developed an opportunity for businesses to understand and cater to people's wants and needs more effectively. In a business-booming, constantly competitive world, attracting customers and making a name for yourself is vital — that is why you need to market your business on the Web.

Defining Internet marketing is much more than simply diving into email lists or managing your own Google+™ business account. Internet marketing, also known as online marketing, is a tool that spreads awareness of a company's name on the Web. From subtle messages to social media platforms, Internet marketing strategies vary. It is important to examine your business to know what types of social media platforms and other marketing tools will benefit your business the most.

For example, if you own a retail store, managing a Pinterest account would be a great tool for you. You can post pictures of your store's products and attract customers to either your website or your retail platform. If you are feeling overwhelmed by all the information packed in this book, do not worry. This book will help you to answer questions about Internet marketing, such as where to begin and how to successfully boost your customer audience for little to no money.

Most business owners wonder whether marketing really benefits their company. Within the last few years, the Internet has not only transformed how people interact but also revolutionized the business world. Instead of traditional infomercials, cold phone calls, and printed advertisements, businesses now seek new customers through the Web to boost their revenue. It is an advertising revolution that will not end, and it is time for you to join the bandwagon. If you choose to market your business via social media, emails, or paid advertisements, you will attract more customers, save money (versus traditional advertisement expenses), and broaden your business skills. With just a little bit of perseverance and practice, you will see how easy and cost-effective online marketing is. Once you manage a Facebook business page or learn how to post tweets, you will ditch the newspaper advertisements for good.

Another added bonus is specified target goals and audiences. In regards to traditional advertising, targeting specific groups of audiences was almost impossible to do. You no longer need to waste time and money advertising to the wrong audience; you can now advertise on a national or global level. Instead of having American-based clientele, why not sell your product to a Japanese or German consumer halfway across the world? Once you put your business on the Web, you will open the door to limitless, new possibilities that will expand your business. Using the Internet as a marketing tool is not a fad that will soon fade away. According to a recent study by Search Engine Land, 85 percent of all consumers use the Internet to find local businesses.

From small businesses to large corporations, Internet marketing boosts every type of company, especially social media platforms such as Facebook and Twitter. When it comes to choosing which types of Internet marketing tools to use, you may have no clue where to start — so where should you begin?

There are three different types of Internet marketing platforms to choose from:

1) Web marketing
2) Social media marketing
3) Email marketing

Throughout the course of this book, you will start to understand everything you need to know about these three areas of Internet marketing. There are different advantages to each, but if you want the most effective outcome, try different marketing platforms. Just as every business is unique, so are your Internet marketing tools. What works for some businesses may not work for you. Always be open to try new tactics.

After learning about different types of Internet marketing, it is up to you to decide where to go from here. If you are still unsure about which marketing avenue to pursue, hire an experienced marketer or advertiser to help you get started. It is a great investment for your company. Advertisers know how to brand your company and expand your presence in the best way. Read through technological articles and ask for advice; become informed about Internet marketing and make smart decisions before jumping into the marketing melee.

Spending money

In order to make more money, there are times when you need to spend money, which includes marketing and advertising. However, when it comes to online marketing, prices vary. If you are not willing to do the work yourself, do not have the time to dedicate, or simply wish to try for faster results, there are some Internet marketing services you can pay for, such as:

- Search Engine Optimization (SEO)
- Search Marketing
- Paid Search (Pay-per-click or online advertising)
- Local search visibility
- Mobile optimization
- Social media content development
- Conversion optimization
- Email, SMS, and digital marketing
- Integrated online and offline marketing/advertising

Apart from paying experts and marketing companies to market your business, there are many free ways to advertise your business online. Below are free ways to market your business just as effectively as paying an expert to do it:

- Press releases
- A Google™ Local Business listing
- A niche social media platform
- A Google+ page.

CASE STUDY: PAUL'S PIZZA TRUCK

Who: Paul's Pizza Truck
What: Food Truck (Pizza Specialty)
Where: Nowhere, FL
          (and surrounding area)
Details: New local business with a
          twist (and tight budget)

Meet Paul—the new owner of a pizza business in Nowhere, Florida. At age 30, he's finally made his dream come true: he is opening up the first pizza food truck in town. He plans on officially opening in a month and is willing to commute up to 20 miles near Nowhere for food truck shows and events. Paul wants to advertise on social media for his business but is on a tight budget. Where should he start?

First, let us take a look at Paul's situation:

- Paul has a business that offers unique services: He can travel to customers with his food truck and provide delicious pizza any-time, anywhere.

- He sells pizza and some other gourmet items: his targeted audi-ence ranges from kids to adults; every age group enjoys pizza.

- Paul's Pizza Truck is a new local business: locals may want to try out a new place and support local businesses in their community.

After looking over Paul's services and situation, now we can determine which social media platforms would be best to use. Here are four that he can choose from:

1. **Twitter:** For location updates, Twitter is the perfect social media platform for Paul's Pizza Truck. With Twitter, Paul can send fast updates about where his next events will be, expand his audience by encouraging retweets for free slices of pizza, and include

exclusive information that can only be found on Twitter. Having a Twitter account could greatly boost the pizza truck's audience and bring in business.

2. **Google+:** Having a Google+ page would broaden the pizza truck's local audience very quickly. By encouraging customers to rate and review different pizzas, sharing exclusive information with customers, and giving location updates, Google+ can boost Paul's audience effectively.

3. **Pinterest:** This could be another successful social media platform for Paul. By displaying high-quality pictures on Pinterest and adding short, eye-catching descriptions, Paul could attract people to his website and draw more customers to purchase his pizza slices.

4. **Facebook:** Having a Facebook page would boost Paul's business by posting updates, upcoming events, captivating pictures, and any other enticing media. He can invite his friends to like his page and they can share it with their friends in return.

In a perfect world, Paul would be able to easily manage all four social media platforms himself, and invest into developing a website. If time constraints are too much with the new business, he may opt to focus on just one or two and build over time once he learns how to balance cooking, selling products to customers, and managing his social media accounts.

Let's face it — Internet marketing is a growing trend that is not dying. For some business owners, getting started is the hardest part. You may still be unsure how online marketing works, but taking small steps will bring in new customers, raise awareness of your company, and make you more knowledgeable of the business world. Here are five reasons why you should start marketing your business on the Web:

*   **Gain more customers:** If you do not market your business online (whether it is simply a LinkedIn account or Pandora radio advertisement), then you will lose current and potential customers. A majority of consumers search for goods and services on the Internet either on the go or in the comfort of their home.

If your business is not listed online, then consumers will pick your competition over you because other businesses had an enticing website that attracted them first.

- **Find out what your customers like (or dislike):** Once your business gains social media presence, then you can figure out who your targeted audience is and what they specifically like. Before the Internet boom, businesses took surveys from their customers to find out what new products and services they wanted. Now, you can track customer's likes and dislikes more easily with social media interaction.

- **Build up your business' presence and awareness:** Word-of-mouth advertising will always come in handy, but the Internet will spread your business' presence like wildfire. From social media to banners to Internet searches, your business will pop up when an Internet surfer searches for your type of business. You can also provide as much information about your business as you want on the Internet so potential customers have all the answers right up front.

- **It is the cheapest way to advertise:** Social media accounts are either virtually free or you pay a very small fee for them. TV and newspaper advertising costs double or triple the amount that Internet advertising costs in some scenarios. Even though you need to spend money on advertising in order to gain new customers, limiting the amount you have to spend will benefit you and your business even more.

- **Stand out from the crowd:** While most businesses in your niche are migrating to Internet marketing, get a leg up from the rest and make your business stand out. There are constantly new innovative ways to market on the Internet, and if you stay ahead of the game, then you will bring in more customers than your competition. Always read new business articles and try new marketing strategies. You never know how it will boost your business and make you a better business owner. When it comes to customer relations, utilizing the Internet is the best benefit for your business.

As noted before, let this chapter be a springboard for getting started in regards to Internet marketing and social media platforms. Search the Web for more tips and information to start a social media account, and utilize email marketing. The Internet is meant to be a tool for boosting your business. Take advantage of this free commodity to make your business known.

Strategy Summary

1) **Create your own website.** It is quick, easy, and free.
2) **Read.** Discover what social media platforms, email marketing tactics, and Web marketing tools you want to use.
3) **Set up your social media accounts.** Do not keep putting it off; start today.
4) **Get down to business.** Update statuses, share photos, make events, host contests, and interact with your potential customers.
5) **Study your results.** After a month or two, look over what followers like and dislike. Learn from mistakes and celebrate what has worked for your business.
6) **Repeat.**

Internet marketing is continuously changing. Stay in the know about satisfying your customers and expanding your business.

Chapter 2

Starting Your Online Business

This chapter delves into overall business plans, whether traditional or online, and is a building block for a successful online business venture. An essential step before you begin to design and develop your website is to craft a thought-out marketing plan for your business. A good marketing plan is critical for you to map out your future goals and achieve success. Writing a marketing plan is a fairly straightforward process that requires you to set clear objectives and determine how you will achieve them. This chapter is entirely optional in relation to Web design efforts, but often times, many websites are built and published without a marketing plan, which is a critical mistake. Despite the best of intentions, there are times that a well-conceived website will ultimately fail because of ineffective or nonexistent marketing.

A few resources I highly recommend you spend some time with are your local Chamber of Commerce and your local community college. The Chamber of Commerce exists for the small business. They are your local advocate, cheerleader and supporter. They can host a variety of events to showcase and highlight your business including open houses, business after hours, ribbon cuttings, and much more. They also offer a variety of educational programs designed to help you. As an Ex-Officio Board Member on the Greater Elizabeth City Area Chamber of Commerce in Elizabeth City, NC (**www.elizabethcitychamber.org**), I have personally learned a wealth of information about local businesses, how to be successful, how to market and promote your business, and how to grow your customer base. Our local community college, the College of the Albemarle, operates a Small Business Resource Center that is constantly offering courses of instruction and other events designed to help you become successful and sustain that level of success. You can check out the College of the Albemarle's Small Business Resource Center here (**www.albemarle.edu/sbc**), but I do recommend you contact your local community college.

Upcoming courses at COA include How to Start a New Business, Grant Writing, Is Owning a Small Business Right for You, Going Viral with YouTube for Small Businesses, and LinkedIn Networking Basics for Small Businesses. These are just an example of courses geared towards your success, most of which are very minimal cost or free. My personal thanks to Kelly Thorsby, President of the Greater Elizabeth City Area Chamber of Commerce and Dr. Kandi Deitemeyer, President of the College of the Albemarle, for being such great advocates and supporters of small businesses and entrepreneurship.

A marketing plan must be achievable, realistic, cost-effective, measurable, and flexible. One of the main objectives in developing a marketing plan is to establish your budget. Your marketing plan may consist of:

- Market analysis
- Business objectives
- Marketing strategies
- Steps to achieving business objectives
- A realistic budget
- A realistic timeline

Performing a Market Analysis

You need to be flexible based on your budget, marketplace competition, business objectives, and both internal and external influences. Market analysis helps you determine if there is a need for your supplies or services. Understanding the marketplace, the desire for your products, and your competition will help you better understand how to establish a successful business in a competitive environment.

If there is no need for your products, you will likely fail unless you establish your presence in the marketplace. Likewise, if there is a high level of competition, you must develop a marketing plan that allows you to compete in product, quality, availability, or price. Knowing the marketplace needs and how it is currently serviced is essential in developing your marketing plan. You cannot realistically build your website and just expect customers to find you. Even if you achieve great search engine ranking results, if there is no demand or desire for your products or services, you will fail. Marketplace analysis must be done in advance to ensure there is a viable market for your products or services in the first place.

The following questions will help you perform a basic market analysis:

- What market am I trying to enter?
- What or who is my current competition?
- How successful is my competition?
- What is the market share of my competition?
- Is the market saturated or open?
- What is the market size? Is there room to grow?
- Is there stability in the market, or is it volatile?
- How are my competitors marketing their goods or services?
- What do customers seek in regards to my products?
- What is most valuable to my customers?
- What are customers willing to pay for my products or services?
- What do I offer that my competition does not?
- What effect will the current economy have on my business goals?

You should analyze current or previous marketing strategies as well as those of your competition, both successful and unsuccessful. Understanding failure is as important as understanding success factors. These questions may help you analyze your potential for success in a competitive marketplace:

- Am I offering a new product line, a new service, or a unique product?
- What marketing strategies have I used successfully? What was unsuccessful? Have I used online marketing in the past? What was the success rate or return on investment?
- Have I evaluated the results of previous marketing plans? What was the impact on sales?
- Are we currently using any strategies?
- What strategies are my competitors using?
- How much money is allotted in my current budget? How much am I currently spending? How much was my marketing budget in the past?
- Why would someone choose our product over our competition?
- What do we do to distinguish ourselves from our competition?
- Why would someone trust us more than our competition?
- Who are our customers?
- Where do our customers come from?

You must perform what is known as primary and secondary research. Primary research includes phone interviews, surveys, web-based surveys, and focus groups. Primary research is the most current information available. Secondary research is data that has already been collected for other purposes but may assist you with your market research. Examples of secondary research may be libraries, blogs, or other online resources.

Establishing Business Objectives

Nearly 50 percent of new businesses will fail within four years. This is also true for online businesses; however, they do have some distinct advantages over traditional brick-and-mortar businesses, as well as some overarching challenges. With an online business, you may have fewer employees, less building space, and less overhead. However, without the traditional storefront, you also do not have a physical presence. Instead, you have a virtual presence online through websites or social media platforms such as Facebook. You need to develop a long-term business plan that will map out your path toward success — later on in this chapter, we will take a closer look at how to create a business plan.

To develop your strategic plan, simply organize your goals, objectives, and timelines in a written format. This document is intended to be "living" and can be easily adjusted based on the current operating environment. Even if your business operates online, it still pays to establish a local following, because where you start your business is where you are going to be accessing the majority of your operating resources. You will need to complete your market analysis in order to better prepare your long-term business objectives.

You may be asking, "How can I know what my objectives and timelines are when I don't know how successful I will be in the future?" The point of determining business objectives is not to predict the future, but to establish the desired course of action while setting strategic goals along the way. Your objectives should be attainable and must be measurable so you can evaluate your success in meeting, or failing to meet, these objectives. Ensure that you update your business objectives at least annually, perhaps even semi-annually during your initial operating years.

If you are an existing business, you should first perform a comprehensive evaluation of your current business state. What have you accomplished, and what have you not? Are you profitable or operating at a loss? What and who is your competition? What are the industry trends in relation to your products or services? Use resources to help you research and establish your business objectives, such as the Small Business Administration, which can be found online at **http://dsbs.sba.gov/dsbs/search/dsp_dsbs.cfm**, your local Chamber of Commerce, industry associations, and libraries. Similar research and market analysis must be completed for new online businesses as well.

Document your initial findings and business objectives. Review goals with your employees, as they may provide input or ideas that you have not considered. Ensure that your plan addresses all aspects of your organization such as sales, marketing, human resources, advertising, customer service, and information technology.

Develop a mission statement for your company. A mission statement captures your organization's purpose, customer orientation, and business philosophy. Share your mission statement with both employees and customers, and post it prominently because that will be the core statement and promise you make to both.

Establishing Marketing Strategies

You must establish a clearly defined, written strategy and marketing plan for your online business. Consider all marketing strategies, and implement those that are most relevant to your business operations; offer the most potential for increased customer base and return on investment. Implement and evaluate your marketing strategy as it relates to achieving your corporate business objectives. Some marketing plans may take significant time and investment; think long term, and do not be too quick to change your objectives because you are not meeting the goals in your specified timelines. Be flexible, but allow your marketing strategies time to grow and mature. Your online marketing plan does not need to be overly complex and should not be a time-consuming process, but it is important to map out your objectives, budget, and critical success factors so you can measure and evaluate your success in achieving them. An average marketing plan may be less than a couple of pages in length. It is a map for your company to achieve success on the Internet.

Media exposure is a key component in developing a successful marketing profile and strategy. Your customers will form their opinions, either positive or negative, based on what they hear and see in print, on television, on the radio, or on the Web. Recognizing the importance of media exposure and dedicating resources to promote your online business can boost the sales of your products or services. That positive media exposure is also a major step toward maintaining credibility in your online marketplace and channeling more traffic to your website.

Developing a tactical approach to media exposure should be part of your overall business objectives and marketing plan. There are several things you can do to promote your offline media exposure. These may include:

- Approaching your local Chamber of Commerce and requesting that they write a short article about you and your business. Even if you are an online-only business, local exposure is important. You can then take that article and publish it on your website as another promotional tool or use it in an online e-magazine, or e-zine, campaign. When you do this, make sure to emphasize the unique service or addition your company is making to the community. The Chamber of Commerce tends to get a lot of similar requests and it is worth taking the time to separate your business from the competition that may provide similar services.

- Offering to be a speaker at a seminar or leading a workshop in your area of expertise. This is a great way to gain media exposure that is incredibly positive and is community oriented, thus earning you credibility and trust among potential clients. Circulate your URL and business information at the seminar. Put your website URL, Facebook site, and Twitter account on everything you distribute: flyers, promotional items, business cards, and letterheads. This serves as a key networking opportunity with potential employees and clients, and also as a quick way to establish yourself locally.

- Following up on any correspondence or phone calls from the media with a letter or phone call. Make sure to leave your website URL on their voicemail. This strategy will earn you a reputation as a conscientious, courteous entrepreneur with the media. However, avoid trying to "doctor" the media's voice or articles about you. The media is not there to write you a press release about your own business. It pays to make sure you have a unique brand or niche.

Share your knowledge by writing articles and professional opinions for online publications, and upload them to automated online news and article syndication sites. These syndication sites are perfect for having immediate hotlinks back to your website and other specific landing pages. Remember to include your email or picture in the byline as well as brief biographical information about yourself and your business. The more exposure you generate, the more successful your business will become. Give permission to authors to use your articles in their books, magazines, or other publications and be sure to require them to include a corporate biography and contact information in exchange for the permission.

Develop tactics to make media exposure and coverage work for you. Make media friends wherever and whenever the opportunities present themselves, all in an effort to increase media awareness and promote public relations. You will have to earn media exposure, but the time and effort you expend will be your investment in having a positive public profile both online and offline. Most columnists will give their email address in their byline at the conclusion of their article. Send them a note with your comments and views while offering your expertise as a source for future quotes. Optimize your media exposure whenever possible; the returns for your business will be substantial.

Gaining the trust of your customers is extremely critical in developing a continuing relationship that rewards your online business with repeat customer sales. The one-time sale may boost your immediate sales numbers, but returning customers are what take your business from mediocre to fantastic profits. Your goal is to build quality customer relationships and then maintain them.

Media exposure, both online and offline, opens the door to a potentially long-term relationship with customers by using implied third-party credibility, thus legitimizing you as the expert in your field. Once you attract the prospects, you still have to deliver your goods and/or services and ensure that the customer is completely satisfied. One of the major advantages of using Google marketing tools, for instance, is that the Google name is already equated with trust. Google's reputation is superior, and you can leverage that reputation and trust in your marketing campaigns for your website and of course through other well-established social media sites such as Facebook and Instagram.

Improving Your Public Profile

The more positive your public profile, the more success you will have both online and offline. This is how you gain credibility with your customers. Your public profile is your trademark for success and profits, and your online profile and business rating is critically important to how customers perceive you. Local and state Better Business Bureaus are great organizations to join to obtain positive ratings. Other online business profile ratings services worth considering are **www.resellerratings.com**, **www.epinions. com**, and **www.consumerreports.org**.

Most major cities will have online communities of locals on forums like reddit or social media groups on Facebook. Depending on where your market is placed and what your business objectives are, you are going to want to know what communities are liable to be interested in the services you provide. In more metropolitan locations, being active and receptive in these communities can make or break a local business since locals are much more willing to accept the word of mouth reviews and experiences of their fellows.

Do not underestimate the impact of a review of your business and/or products and services. You must strive to ensure 100 percent customer satisfaction in both service and product quality to ensure you gain only positive reviews for you and your company. Be sure that you are capable of responding to feedback from both your consumers and employees. Being very active on social media and extremely prompt in responding to emails or queries will go a long way toward establishing a positive public profile.

Positioning yourself and becoming an expert in your market takes time, patience, and personal confidence. Just knowing the advantages of effective marketing is half the battle. The combination of media and marketing communicates the benefits and unique aspects of your business, which in turn drives customers to your website. When you establish yourself as an expert in your market, others will be drawn to you for advice, sponsorship, professional opinion and branding — all of which will have dramatic, positive impacts on your online business.

When it comes to sharing your expertise, you goal should be to publish for free, thereby allowing many other organizations, news services, and other publications to distribute your article in return for links back to your website. This becomes a direct product promotion to thousands of potential new customers. There are ways that you can publish a full-page ad promoting yourself and your business without spending a dime.

Contact editors of publications and offer them your press release to add content to their next publication. Many editors are looking for useful and relevant content so they can meet deadlines, but make sure that your press release and business developments can make a palpable change to the local community or else editors can be just as likely to discount your efforts as not newsworthy. Always ensure that you require a corporate biography and full contact information to be published with your articles including website, Twitter and Facebook sites. Target newspapers, magazines, newsletters, websites, and other online publications or apps.

Creativity and Planning

The first step in undertaking a website design or social media project is the planning stage.

With every Web design or social media project you encounter, clarify what exactly is needed to complete the project satisfactorily, defining the precise scope of the project and establishing a program for completing the project over a given period of time.

Defining the audience of a website or your social medial presence is the second and most crucial step. One of the audiences for your website or social medial site is always going to be the group of people your client targets as their primary market. These external visitors might well be targeted through advertising programs, such as pay-per-click marketing. The demographics of that target market group provide you with the basis for your primary audience of external visitors and serves as your first audience reference point.

Also make sure that any website you develop has a clearly marked connection to your social media accounts. While your website will have the bulk of your services and information, it will be your social media that will be the most effective for distributing information about your business developments. Your social media has the power to draw your customers to your website for more detailed information, prompting them to look at your products and services and maybe even to make some purchases.

You should create a profile for your target audience based on general research. Who are the average members of your target audience? Determine what they look like, how old they are, where they live, what they do for a living, how much money they have, and what their hobbies are. This information will help you incorporate an understanding of their specific needs and preferences in the development of your website, blog, social media or other online marketing campaign.

Establishing Your Business Plan

Creating an effective business plan is a two-stage process. First, you need to get a strong handle on the type of business you are becoming involved in. Fact-finding, as you might call it, is going to take some time, so be prepared. You will need to analyze the market you are planning on entering, what is involved in the type of work you are looking to secure, and what potential customers are looking for.

Your business plan should include a summary of your company's mission and objectives. Include a review of the market and an analysis of your place within it. Describe the products and services you are going to offer to customers and explain how you are going to reach out to them. Your business plan will describe your marketing strategy and your sales strategy. It will also describe and analyze the effectiveness of the staff you decide to put together. Not everyone wants a staff to support their business, but it is one more thing to think about.

Once you have a first draft for your business plan, you should have plenty of time to consider which scenarios — good or bad — you are most likely to face with your business as you implement your plans. If you need further assistance in analyzing the general climate for your business, here are some resources to consider:

- The Small Business Administration, at **https://www.sba.gov/ category/navigation-structure/starting-managing-business/ starting-business**
- Nolo®, at **www.nolo.com**
- Palo Alto Software, Inc., at **www.paloalto.com/ps/bp**
- Inc., at **www.inc.com**
- Bplans, at **www.bplans.com**

Most of these online resources provide good reference points for creating a business plan, particularly with a view toward secure financing for the business venture. Nolo is particularly useful for addressing legal issues related to business startups.

A good business plan is one that is regularly updated and altered to reflect changing patterns and objectives of a company and the market in which it operates. Your business plan should help you plan your income and expenses, manage your marketing campaigns, and monitor your sales.

Generally speaking, a business plan should contain the following sections:

- Executive Summary
- Mission Statement

- Company Objectives
- Personal Evaluation of the Business Owner
- Description of Services and Products
- Company Overview (a review of location, personnel, and resources)
- Market Analysis (a review of the business niche and competitors)
- Advertising and Marketing Summaries
- Financial Projections

Before you even think about launching a service or website, you should think long and hard about establishing your business profile and getting the paperwork settled first. If you are establishing a business, you must obtain a license, the necessary permits, and registrations. Consider the precise nature of the business you decide to establish. There are several different business structures to consider: sole proprietorship, partnership, corporation, and limited liability company (LLC). You should consider the pros and cons of these various business structures with input from your attorney and your accountant. In most cases, a sole proprietorship or an LLC is more than adequate for most small business purposes. Here are each of your options:

- The **sole proprietorship** is one of the easiest entities to understand. The status is exactly what it sounds like; it means that you, the business owner, are the only one responsible for your business. The status is simple to set up, and compliance is easy, too. The accounting system you use for a sole proprietorship is straightforward. All of your income and expenses are considered business income and business expenses. There is no reference to a business structure. The major disadvantage of this particular status is the lack of protection offered for either you or your business. You accept full responsibility and the full risk of your business because there is no separate legal structure to protect you. Anyone can sue you, and they can sue you for anything pertaining to your business.

- A **partnership** is fairly similar to the sole proprietorship status except more than one person is involved. You may remain primarily responsible for the business, depending on how you determine to divide up responsibilities with your partner. When you decide to form a partnership, it is crucial that you address the nature of the partnership in all of its intricacies. Think about how profits will be divided and how expenses, including startup costs, will be managed. Partnerships in business are much like marriages in life; without strong foundations and open communication, you will be in trouble. You should plan in advance for the eventual breakdown of your partnership to determine how everything will be divided.

- An **LLC** is usually the best choice for a website design business. An LLC protects your assets like a corporation without the burden of corporate maintenance. This status has become the most popular way to start a business because it offers limited liability to its owners. An LLC is a business entity that has the characteristics of both a corporation and a partnership. With an LLC, you can elect to be taxed as a corporation, or avoid double taxation by choosing to be a "pass-through," or nontaxable, entity. For any legal assistance in developing your business, consider using the cost-effective solutions offered at www.legalzoom.com.

- **Corporations** take you one step further, providing you with protection against potential business problems. If you set up a corporation, you are demonstrating that you do not own the business; that is, your assets are not linked to the business, and you are not responsible for the debts of the business. When you incorporate, you do not actually own your business in the legal sense. You may own all the shares, but technically speaking, you are actually hired by the shareholders of the corporation to manage the business interests, even if the only shareholder is you. It may sound odd, but the major advantage of this structure is that you have considerable protection in the event of legal problems, and you can sell shares to others to generate some good working capital for the expansion of your business.

- A **subchapter S corporation** is a dramatically simplified version of a standard corporation. The paperwork is comparable, but the structure offers the same protections as the corporation structure, along with simplified filing systems.

Employer Identification Numbers & Business Licenses

The first step you should complete is to obtain an Employer Identification Number (EIN), also known as a Federal Tax Identification Number, which is used to identify a business entity. This is typically required for you to obtain a business license in your state and county. The EIN is your permanent number and can be used immediately for most of your business needs, including opening a bank account, applying for business licenses, and filing a tax return by mail. However, no matter how you apply — either by phone, fax, mail, or online — it will take up to two weeks before your EIN becomes part of the IRS' permanent records. You must wait until this occurs before you can file an electronic return, make an electronic payment, or pass an IRS Taxpayer Identification Number matching program. The IRS website will guide you through the process of obtaining an EIN at **www.irs.gov**.

Research and determine the requirements in your state, county, and city for obtaining business licenses, permits, and tax receipts. This information can usually be found on the Internet. If you are the sole proprietor of your business, you will also most likely need to register a fictitious business name, assumed name, or "doing business as" (DBA) name in your state. The following website lists all the requirements and provides links for each state: **www.business.gov/guides/business-law/business-name/dba. html**. You must also check with your county and city. Most will require a county or city business license or tax receipt, and they may also have additional requirements for personal property tax and other important local legalities with which you must comply. Another great recourse for starting your own business is **www.business.gov**.

Finding Your Niche

After determining whether your website will be used for personal or business use, it is time to decide what content, navigation, and features you want to include on your website. Here are some basic questions to get you started:

1. What specific niche are you seeking to fill with your website?
2. How will this website be used to benefit your business?
3. Who is your target audience?
4. What steps should be taken to reach that specific audience?
5. Why should you or a customer even look at or use your website?
6. How will this website be branded to keep its relation to your business?

With business or social media websites, the ultimate goal is to draw visitors in, retain their repeat visits to your site, and grow your customer base. If you are maintaining a business website, you will want to provide additional security measures to protect your visitors from someone who might try to hijack your site for client information or scam your customers without your knowledge. Security is imperative when you are dealing with customers. You own the website, and your customers are putting their trust in your ability to protect them. If someone's information or financial data is hijacked and used illegally due to visiting your website, you might find yourself with serious legal problems, not to mention a severe loss in trust from your customer base.

Your business must be something that you have a passion for, because a website or social media site requires constant updating and maintenance to keep it moving forward. How do you reach a specific audience? Figure out exactly who would benefit from your site and add that to your initial design plan. For example, say you want to publish a magazine of some kind and have determined that your target audience includes people from the ages of 15 to 25. The next step is to decide what type of content will reach your target audience; it is critical, especially with the teen market, to ensure that your Web pages are age-appropriate.

Make sure that the content in your website matches up with what is appropriate for your target age range. Also keep in mind that though parental controls are available, some parents may not consider the possibility that their child might inadvertently be visiting websites that are not appropriate for his or her age group.

Ten Steps Toward Profitable E-Commerce

The following steps can be used as a checklist to ensure that you have everything in place for doing business on the Internet. Once your website is up and running, you will be able to implement low-cost marketing and advertising techniques for promoting and managing your business.

Step one: list goals and ideas

Determine what your goals are concerning your website. Sit down with the people that are going to be helping you so that you can go over your ideas for design, implementation, and promotion. It is important not to discard any of your goals and ideas, no matter how silly and far-fetched they may seem. You want to be as creative as possible to start with, and then you can fine-tune your list by getting rid of those ideas that are not cost effective or are not considered for adoption. This is a good time to do a preliminary projection of your budget, incorporating all the potential costs so that you can set realistic expectations for your online storefront. You will adjust your budget later, after you complete steps 1–4.

Step two: review the products and services you intend to feature online

Take some time to carefully review the products and the services that you are offering on your website. If you are running a restaurant, then you will mostly be providing information about your menu as well as highlighting special online offers and delivery services. If you are trying to buy or sell goods, then you will likely be providing an online store with a shipping service to send your goods abroad.

Things that you should be asking yourself if you plan on providing direct services through your website include the following:

- What are the advantages and disadvantages to your business of selling or advertising your service or products online?
- Are you willing to accept payment online, and, if so, what payment methods?
- What logistics will you have to consider about shipping your product, including cost and method?
- Are you willing to consistently update and maintain your website to reflect current products, market trends, and pricing?

Step three: compare online e-commerce websites

Find sites that are related to your business and take some time to view them. Look at how they promote and advertise similar products or services as well as how each website is laid out and navigated. If a similar website uses a shopping cart for online purchases, try it out, stopping, of course, at the point where you are ready to commit to a purchase. See how smoothly the process works and what can be done to improve the process. A wide range of experience and knowledge of how competitors operate their on-line businesses is valuable information that you can use to get the upper edge on competition.

Step four: determine your target market

Determine what market of consumers you want to target with your website. If you are using your website to promote your brick and mortar business, decide if you are going to be selling your products and services only locally or if you are willing to sell outside of your immediate market area. Since the Internet is global, there are many reasons to promote your website to the national or global marketplace. If you are selling your products or services online, you will need to decide if you are only selling within your own country or if you are going to be an international e-commerce company. It is important to know who your Internet audience is going to be so that you can target them effectively. If you are selling your products internationally, you are going to have to be prepared for some potential language barriers.

Step five: budget

It is important that you have a predetermined budget for your website ahead of time so that you can stay within the guidelines of what you can afford. There are many aspects to your website that you are going to need to take into account. These aspects include the following:

- The development of your website
- Marketing of your website and business
- Customer service and maintenance
- Web hosting
- The cost of a merchant payment system
- Secure server certification
- Domain names
- Search engine submissions
- Any new staff that you may need to hire to maintain your website or to handle the inflow of new business

You want to know where your business costs are going so that you can allocate them appropriately. In most cases, it is not necessary to hire a full-time Web designer. After your initial website design is completed, all you will need is monthly maintenance and updates in most instances. This book is packed with information to help keep these costs as low as possible, so do not become overwhelmed.

Step six: determine your unique selling points

Determine what the unique selling points are going to be for your business. There are many websites on the Internet that are going to be selling the same products and services that you are, and you must separate yourself from the competition. This means that you are going to have to have selling features that will make consumers want to buy from you instead of the next website that they hit. Make a listing of unique selling points that you have currently and those that you are willing to consider for future use. For example, the computer hardware and software industry is very competitive, yet Newegg (**www.newegg.com**) is traditionally the industry leader with superior products, superior customer service, low prices, and one of the finest reputations in the industry. What are their unique selling points, which set them apart from the competition?

Step seven: create a marketing plan

You need to have a solid marketing plan in place so that you know exactly where you want your business to go and how you want to get there. This should be a written plan that you can sit down and read logistically. An online marketing plan should address search engines and techniques for improving a website's visibility on the Internet. There will be more information on how to generate online traffic for your website in Chapter 4.

Step eight: decide on a website structure

Determine what you want the structure of your website to be. This is crucial to implementing your website design plan and integrating how you want your shopping cart to act and perform within your website. Careful planning should be given to the design and structure of your website. Likewise, if you wish to use a blog, or even Facebook, the options become fewer and this process is even more simplified. Again, I recommend that all businesses establish both a robust website and an active, engaging, and updated social media presence.

Step nine: implement online web services

Have all of the services that you are going to need for your website ready to go. This includes Web hosting, a digital certificate, social media, and your completed Web design, which will include detailed descriptions of whatever you are selling (including digital images and pricing, if appropriate). Once you launch your website, ensure that you have ample amounts of product in your inventory ready for sales. Cross link your website with all your other social media sites, link to your Facebook site, and have the Twitter name readily visible.

Step ten: launch your website

This last step marks your entry into the world of e-commerce. Keep in mind that you need to keep a close eye on your website when you first go live so that you can catch any mistakes or areas that need additions or improvements. Listen to customer feedback for potential problem areas or areas for improvement, and encourage friends and relatives to give your site a thorough "shakedown."

By following the above steps, you will be well on your way to a live website for promoting your traditional brick and mortar business or for selling your products and services to the global Internet community. Having all of the above e-commerce concepts in place will ensure that your business is ready to earn you new customers and greater profits. Doing your research and planning will ensure that your e-commerce solution is obtained at the lowest possible financial investment.

Starting an Online Business

Although starting an Internet business is much like starting any other business, there are going to be some significant differences with which you will have to concern yourself. You are going to have to work on building the confidence of your customers by using a variety of techniques, which do not include the face-to-face exchange of a traditional brick and mortar retail store. You will need to clearly convey through your website or social media site that your company has the following attributes:

- Fairness and honesty in its advertising
- Fair prices for products or services
- Superior customer service and satisfaction
- Committment to developing long-term customers

While these aspects certainly apply to any brick and mortar business, the challenge is implementing them widely over the Internet in a successful, but low-cost, solution.

Our goal is to identify the steps required to launch your online business, while ensuring that it is cost effective and that you are marketing your site for the lowest possible cost. First, let's look at the advantages of starting your business online or expanding your traditional business to the Internet.

Start-up costs

Starting an online business requires significantly less capital than a traditional brick and mortar business. In fact, with some careful planning you can start your Internet business with only a few hundred dollars.

You need to keep in mind that there are no get-rich-quick schemes to having an online business; the key to profits is having products people want to buy, and customers must be able to find your website to buy your products. Profits and success come from successful marketing and advertising, which we will help you achieve.

Sales and profits can come from much more than selling products. For restaurants, putting graphical images of their establishment and menus online for prospective patrons to review is a great, low-cost use of the Internet that can directly increase sales without ever selling a product online. The majority of websites do not actually sell any products at all. They simply advertise and market the business, products, or services offered while providing a convenient means of obtaining information for prospective patrons or customers. However, remember that your website is likely going to be the first aspect of your business that most clients are going to look at, so do not be too lax about how much you are willing to spend.

Limitless potential

The Internet has unlimited potential, since it can reach a multitude of consumers, including a wide international audience. Every computer in the world is a potential customer or patron. There is no other method to disseminate your business information to a global audience like the Internet. If a picture is worth a thousand words, a well-designed website with graphics, text, and other information about your business or product is worth infinitely more.

Website design

You can make your online business look extremely professional and experienced by designing a website or social media site that ties together style and content. You can certainly do this yourself or you can also contract a Web design professional or social media specialist, but make sure that it looks polished and professional since your site is going to be the first thing most potential clients look up when they want information about your services.

Developing a Plan for an Online Business

The following steps are a good guideline of what you need to do to start your online business and establish an actionable and sustainable business plan. After following these steps, along with proper Web design and incorporation of the low-cost marketing and advertising solutions in this book, your Internet business will be up and ready for customers to find you. While this section talks mostly about website design, do not discount social media. Embracing social media along with website presence are critical to a well-rounded advertising and marketing campaign. Both can do things the other cannot.

Step one: start with an idea

The first thing that you need to start your online business is an idea that you believe in. This means that you need to have a product or service, a concept of how to sell it, good content ideas for your website, and the belief that you can make it all work. If you do not have all these things in place, you may be wasting your time and money, while setting yourself up for a disappointing failure.

Step two: legal matters

Make sure that you have all the legal information that you need to start your business online. You do not want to find out at a later date that you have overlooked something important. Some of the legalities that you may need to consider include the following.

Incorporate or not?

Find out the legal benefits of incorporating your online business. There are benefits and disadvantages to incorporating your business that include taxes and matters of ownership. Contact a lawyer or tax accountant for more information about incorporating your business. Other options may include sole proprietorship and limited liability corporations.

Copyrights and trademarks

It may not seem like an important factor, but liability issues surrounding intellectual property are something that you will want to consider when you are doing business on the Internet. You can visit the U.S. Copyright Office for more information: **http://www.copyright.gov**.

Contracts and licenses

Make sure that before you sign any contract you know exactly what you are signing and that you understand it fully. If you do not pay attention to contracts and licenses, you could end up being liable for any number of things, such as Web hosting regulations.

There are several contracts that you might need to sign, which include hiring a website designer, a programmer, and/or obtaining a digital certification. You will need a business license, which is typically administered through the local, county, or state government prior to commencing business. Detailed information on how to start a small business may be found at the Small Business Administration website at **http://www.sba.gov** as well as from your local, county, and state governments.

Internet legalities

Make sure that you understand all the legal issues of doing business on the Internet such as the legalities behind obtaining a domain name. This is a dynamic, and often confusing, subject. We found a fantastic reference site (**www.ivanhoffman.com**) sponsored by attorney Ivan Hoffman that contains a vast amount of information related to trademarks, domain names, and e-commerce, as well as articles for Web designers, website owners, and addresses of many other legal concerns surrounding the Internet. Mr. Hoffman's website is a treasure trove of information; I highly recommend you bookmark this website.

Step three: your domain name

An important aspect of your Internet business is having your own domain name. This is a requirement to have your website hosted, and it should uniquely identify your business. The general rule of thumb is that the shorter the domain name, the better, and it should be relevant to your company name, service, or products. If you already have an established corporate name or identity, you should try to base your domain name on that corporate identity. This allows customers to identify your company name with your domain name.

Secure any similar-sounding domain names, as in the example above — Ivan Hoffman's website, **www.ivanhoffman.com**. Your primary domain name should be the domain name that is "hosted," while others may be parked at no additional cost and pointed to the main domain name URL. This allows you to only pay for one hosted domain name but utilize many domain names on the Internet, all directing site visitors to your main hosted site. GoDaddy.com® is a great place to purchase and manage all of your domain names. After years of experience with many other domain name companies, I can assure you that no one beats the quality of service, price, or features that GoDaddy offers.

You can check the availability of domain names, pricing, and even get other suggested domain names based on similarity. I do recommend you invest in your domain name before a different company does. Domain names will cost you a little under $20 per year.

Step four: choosing web hosting

Find a Web company that offers Web hosting; this will improve your on-line presence. You need to find a Web hosting company that is going to be able to provide you with the following things:

- Technical support that is available when you need it
- A website availability that is in excess of 99 percent — you will need this to ensure that when you make changes to your website, the changes will go into effect as soon as possible
- A fast, reliable Internet connection
- Technicians that understand all aspects of e-commerce, including shopping carts and SSL certification
- Compatibility with other providers of e-commerce shopping carts and payment gateways — this is critical as many companies invest in expensive shopping cart software that is rendered useless by Web hosting companies that do not support essential features, such as server side includes, Web scripting, executable files, or other dynamic content.

Take your time when looking for a Web hosting company. You are going to be entrusting a large part of the success of your website to this company. Choose a Web hosting company that has been in business for a long time; there are many start-up Web hosting companies on the Internet that come and go.

One of the most costly things that you will be paying for when you do business on the Internet is your Web hosting service. You want to make sure that you choose a company that is reliable and reputable. There are hundreds of good Web hosting companies out there — based on my past 15 years of experience, I recommend Applied Innovations Inc.® (**www.appliedi.net**) for all Web hosting needs. However, there are many other Web hosting companies out there that offer reasonable pricing with exceptional service, such as HostGator, Liquid Web Hosting, Dream Host Web Hosting, and Hostwinds Web Hosting.

Step five: designing your website

You can design your website yourself, or you can hire a professional to do the job for you. Do you want to spend the time learning how to design an effective website yourself or are you willing to pay the price to have a professional do it for you? There are advantages to both, but if you lack a strong background with computers and design software you will save yourself a lot of time by hiring a professional due to the sheer number of design elements.

There are numerous, high-quality, low-price providers that perform Web design services such as Blue Fountain Media, Maxburst, Bigdrop Inc., and Old City Press. However, if you have the time and really want to make sure your website looks exactly how you imagine, you can do it yourself with the tools we provide in this book.

Often, standard websites are also included in most website hosting packages, so you can use these pre-built sites, input your unique information, and have a website up and running in a matter of hours. However, you run the risk of having your site appear boring or generic, and when you are trying to make yourself stand out in the crowd of competitors, it always pays to be distinct. I will cover more elements of website design in Chapter 6.

Step six: marketing

You will need to develop marketing plans so that you can ensure that potential website visitors can find and navigate your website. Marketing will be discussed more later on in the book; these are some of the topics that we will cover: search engines, pay-per-click (PPC) advertising, keywords and meta tags.

Step seven: interactive websites and updated content

You need to constantly and consistently update your website so that visitors are always seeing new information — your customers want to know what is new and current. Be as creative as you can while still staying within the guidelines of professionalism.

Step eight: your customer database

One of your main tasks when you have an online business is developing and building a customer database. You want to have as many people on your list as you can so that your marketing program reaches a wide range of consumers. This will be absolutely essential as you start to deploy email-marketing campaigns and begin developing your social media presence.

Step nine: repeat customers

Once you have built a solid customer database, you will want to put in place processes to harness repeat customers. Repeat sales and developing a loyal customer base is the basis of a successful business and continued profits. One of the ways that you can achieve repeat or return customer sales is by having good customer service and establishing ongoing dialogue and communication with your customers. You can accomplish this good communication by using the following techniques, all of which are low-cost options that lead to more sales and profits.

Establish an affiliate program

An affiliate program is an advertising program offering a monetary incentive for webmasters to drive traffic to your website. This eliminates the necessity for the advertiser to find websites with related content to list their banners. It also increases the response rate by giving the "affiliate" websites a stake in the response rate. Affiliate programs are a great plan for the websites offering them.

Coupons for repeat customers

These may be through targeted email campaigns designed exclusively for your repeat customer base or through traditional mailings, where you promote the use of your website through a discount coupon.

Contests in which your customers can participate

Everyone loves a good contest (examples: free dinner, free hotel stay, or gift certificates). Online contests are a great way to keep people interested in your products and services and will drive them back to your website to track contest results. Atlantic Publishing Company created the "Top 50 Restaurant websites" several years ago. The free contest was simply to promote great website designs for small, newly established restaurants across the world. At the peak of its popularity, Atlantic had a panel of judges who not only rated the sites on a variety of requirements but also reviewed the menu, history, imagery, and overall appeal of the site. The reviewers wrote a small summary of how the site and actual establishment appealed to them, and winners of the award were presented with a logo that they could display on their website. For Atlantic Publishing, the benefit was a popular contest that drew thousands of site visitors per day to their website and encompassed reviews of more than 2,500 restaurant websites.

Newsletters that provide useful information

The use of a well-designed and targeted newsletter (printed or online) is an extremely effective marketing campaign. Obviously, the benefit of online newsletters is that you can track open, click-through, and other response rates.

A program for discussion groups and forums

Depending on your website, a discussion group or forum is a great addition to your website (and is also free through **www.phpbb.com** or simply link to your Facebook site. Companies use discussion forums to discuss anything from current events to new products. Many restaurants are establishing discussion forums as a marketing tool to attract new clients, offer recipes, offer cooking techniques, or for patrons to discuss their dining experiences. Having an active discussion group also provides valuable feedback about your company and services.

A chat room option for customers

This may be a controversial addition to a website if you expect associates to interact with the public or each other (some employers do not allow employees to engage in chat sessions, use chat software, or get paid to "chat"). There are many free chat applications, and a "live" session between customers and the business is often productive as customers can get immediate support and answers to their questions or concerns about products or orders. You can find free chat rooms at **www.parachat.com**. Facebook is another free option to directly engage with your customers and for them to interact with each other. Social media has its drawbacks, as powerful as a positive review or compliment can be, a negative review or comment can go viral with devastating effects on your business.

Blogs and social media

Blogs are incredibly powerful and free as are social media platforms. There are two separate chapters in this book that are dedicated to fleshing out everything you need to know; to read more, visit Chapters 10 and 12.

Step ten: maintaining good business records

Although this seems like common sense, it is also the one area with which most business owners and managers fail to comply, as revealed by numerous state and federal audits. You need to have good records of all your business transactions to ensure that your financial accounts as well as your sales and incomes tax records are in order. If you need to seek any type of financing in the future, having good accounting books will give potential investors a good look into the way your business is operated and will help them determine profit potential.

The above steps are a good, simple plan if you are going to be starting an online business or expanding your current business onto the Internet. Make sure that you have all bases covered by taking your time and completing all the steps before your website goes live; this will ensure that both you and your customers will be satisfied with the online experience.

Chapter 3

Branding

Branding is something that is talked about frequently in the world of marketing and advertising, both on and off the Internet. In a nutshell, branding is when you give your business or product a unique identity by using a combination of the following:

- A design
- A name
- A sign or symbol
- A specific term

It is this "brand" that is going to make you stand out among the competition. Branding can be defined as the process by which a commodity in the marketplace is known primarily for the image it projects rather than any actual quality. Branding is a promise, a pledge of quality. It is the essence of a product, including why it is great and how it is better than all competing products. It is an image. It is a combination of words and letters, symbols, and colors.

There are many companies (online and offline) that successfully use branding so that you can easily identify them over their competitors. Some of these companies that successfully use branding are Walmart^{SM}, IBM®, Travelocity®, eBay®, Amazon.com®, and Microsoft®. These names have become trusted among consumers throughout the world. With the huge increase in business activity conducted on the Internet, more companies use branding to help customers find them and to remember what kind of company they are. When it comes to your own business, you may wish to use branding in such a way that your service or product stands out among the many Internet websites that are all vying for attention and customers.

Branding is a mixture of creativity and the type of relationship that you strive to establish with your customers. The creative part of branding is all about the logo and the way that you advertise using it. The relationship part of branding is all about the way you make your customer feel when they come to your website. You want your customers to feel that they can trust you and your products or services so that they generate sales for your business. In summary, branding is all about the following:

- How your product or service looks on the website or on a shelf
- How your customer feels when they access your website
- How you handle customer orders
- The credibility and trust that you earn with your customers using a combination of branding and successful Internet marketing.

Developing your own branding for your business is an important step when it comes to the success of your company. This means that you need to spend quality time coming up with the right branding for your products and services.

Developing a company image

When you are developing a company image, it means that you will be creating a "personality" for your company with which customers can identify and want to do business. The personality of your company will be a combination of many things such as the facts of your business, the goals of your business, the style of advertising that you choose to use, and the history of your business. All these elements will tie together to leave a lasting impression on your customers that can make the difference between the success of your business or its failure.

Many large and successful companies have worked hard to develop their company image. Part of this image is having a logo, or brand, with which customers can identify. McDonald's has had a successful logo for years with which people all over the world identify: Ronald McDonald and the Golden Arches. Some of the most effective logos are by the following companies: Coca-Cola®, Sony®, Google, Dell™ and Yahoo!®. These companies maintain a corporate image that appeals to customers and helps to generate huge sales figures each year. However, do not rely on your brand to carry your business. Success still requires customer service, quality products and services, and dedication to excellence.

Most of us remember the company that sold computers with the white and black cow themed packaging. They were everywhere — who would have thought that in just a few years, Gateway Computer would no longer exist.

Developing your company image means that you need to identify many aspects of your business, including the following:

- Knowing just who your target market is and how to reach them
- Developing a company image that is constant and revolves around your target market.

How to determine your target market

When you are developing your company image, you need to focus your time, energy, and money on the portion of the market that you know will be the most likely to buy your product or service. There are certain things that you need to identify about your customers so that you can attract the right kind of sales to your business. Some of the things that you need to know about your potential customers include

- Buying habits
- Lifestyle: age, sex, marital status
- Location
- Occupation
- Budget
- Preferences

Any information that you find out about your potential customers and your target market will be a huge factor in the success of your online or brick and mortar business.

Expanding your brand

Choose packaging that is creative. You want to create packaging for your products that can be easily identified by your customers and that they will remember when they see your product online or offline in your brick and mortar store.

Strategies that will help you expand your brand include:

- Having clear and precise goals, and knowing that for which your company stands
- Having a mission statement that is strong and definite so that you know exactly where your business is going and how you want to arrive at that destination
- Being determined and constant in the way you deal with your customers so that they know what they can expect each time that they do business with you
- Remembering that branding is all about reaching your customers and staying in touch with them.

The bottom line is that branding allows you to sell your products or services to customers in a way that makes you stand out from the crowd of competitors, each of whom are looking for their share of Internet business.

If you already have an established corporate name or identity, you should try to base your domain name on that corporate identity. This will allow customers to identify your company name with your domain name. For example, Atlantic Publishing Company's domain name is **www.atlantic-pub.com**.

We also highly recommend that you secure any similar domain names, the main reason being to protect your identity from others who may use a very similar sounding or identical domain name, with a different extension. Using the example above, you would also want to tab **www.atlanticpub.com**, **www.atlanticpub.net**, and **www.atlanticpublishing.com**. Your primary domain name should be the domain name that is "hosted," while others may be parked at no additional cost and pointed to the main domain name URL. This way, you only pay for one hosted domain name but utilize many domain names on the Internet, all directing site visitors to your main hosted site.

Naming Your Business

What you call your company can be very important in providing you with a business identity that is strong and will leave a lasting impact. You want to choose a business name that is going to be a reflection of what your product or service is all about.

If you choose a name for your business that is too unique and creative, you may find that customers have a harder time finding you on the Internet or associating your name with your products or services. The same theory applies to your domain name selection on the Web — keep it relevant to the business and make it easy to remember.

It is important that you name your website after your domain name. The primary reason for this is so that people know your website and business by name. CNN[SM] stands for Cable News Network, but no one calls it that. CNN is simply known as CNN, and the domain name is **www.cnn.com**. While this may be a simplistic explanation, your domain name should easily relate to your company name so your "brand" or company name can be easily recognized or memorized.

Many professional Web designers recommend using keywords in your domain name rather than your company name. For example, the **www. strugglingteens.com** domain name specifically targets the industry of private schools and programs by using the keywords "struggling teens." Therefore, when you type the keywords "struggling teens" into the Google and Yahoo! search engines, this website pops up in the number one spot under the paid ads.

Your domain name may have relevance in how some search engines rank your website, so embedding keywords into your domain name may help you achieve better search engine success. Another option you may consider is to purchase both domains names that identify your business, and those that use keywords. Put your website files on the domain name with the keywords and redirect the domain names with the company name to the keywords domain name; that way you can market the domain name with your company name which helps with branding and helps to get the benefits of having the actual website located under a domain name with keywords.

Keywords built into website content and meta tags are essential to obtaining and maintaining visibility with these major search engines. Keywords are not something you implement once and forget; the keywords must be constantly updated to ensure immediate success in gaining visibility and to keep your site listed on the first page of the search engine results. Few people look beyond the first page of search engine results, so if you are located on page 10, or even page two, you may never be found.

Domain names should not be extremely long; this is going to be your URL address for your website, and the last thing you need is a long address no one can remember. Although some people may bookmark your page in their Internet browser, just as many, if not more, will not. You could lose valuable traffic if your website address is too long. If you are determined to have a long URL address, hyphenating the words will make it easier to read.

There was a time when domain names were readily available, but today you will find that many domain names are already registered by someone else. Typically there are variations of your desired domain name available, or perhaps other domain name extensions such as .org, .net, or .us. You can check the availability of a domain name by going to **https://who. GoDaddy.com** or **http://www.networksolutions.com/domain-name-registration/index.jsp**.

Another thing that you need to keep in mind when you are choosing a name for your business is that this name will be your first contact with your customers. The first impression that you present to your customers can often be a lasting one. If you have a business that is selling scrapbook products, you will want to have a business name that lets customers know that your business is about scrapbooks. For example, "Creative Scrapbooks" lets customers find you easily on the Internet and describes the product that you are selling. A name such as "Creative Crafts" will not be as definitive when it comes to the core of what your business is all about. Some people choose to name a business after themselves, and although this may work for companies that already have an established presence; it normally will not work well if you are just starting your company, unless you include mention of the product that you are selling.

An example of a business that includes your name would be "Carter's Creative Scrapbooks." This not only uses your personal name, it also lets your customers know what your business is selling. There are some benefits that come from using your name in your business title such as the following:

- Customers will be able to associate your personal name, corporate name, and your product together.
- You will become better known in the business community, both online and offline.
- Your credit rating may be higher and stronger when your personal name is associated with your business. Keep in mind that if your business is not successful, your credit rating may also pay the price. This is why many people, when they are first establishing a

new business, choose to keep their personal finances separate from their business finances.

Choosing a name for your company is a task that you should research carefully before finalizing and selecting an identity. You need to make sure that you are not infringing on another company name, or you may find yourself faced with a future lawsuit. The Small Business Administration has a great site to help you through this process at **https://www.sba.gov/blogs/how-choose-claim-and-protect-your-business-name-online-and-offline**.

What's in a name?

Everyone has ideas about what makes a successful name. Some are more straightforward than others. Some people might say the best names for businesses are not even real words at all (Google, for example). These people believe that such names can be remembered much more easily than conventional names like "Sally's Website Design Business." Sometimes, developing a name that is new is not feasible.

There are businesses out there that work to create names for other businesses. These naming firms have a system that they follow to come up with an appropriate name. Also, naming firms are well-versed in copyright and trademark laws. This can take a burden off your mind and give you one less thing to worry about when starting your website design business.

The downside to hiring a naming firm for your business is cost — this can range from the upper hundreds to over $40,000. If you do not have the extra cash to spend, you can always use some of the same strategies these companies use.

Pronunciation is also a factor when choosing the right name for your business. Many customers will prefer words that they immediately know how to pronounce instead of having to guess. Professionals at naming firms will never use many initials in a name, because it is not relatable and does not have any meaning for people. Another area that needs to be avoided in naming your business is putting a geographical location to your business name;

for instance, "Santa Monica Fashions." Your business could branch out to other places, and people in other cities may identify your business as one that would not be able to meet their needs if they live in a different place.

Take time to brainstorm adjectives that you want to be associated with your business. These adjectives will be able to spark inspiration for you to come up with unique but identifiable names. An example of using this technique would be a store that offers handspun rugs and one-of-a-kind home furnishings. The generic name for such a place could be called "Rug and Home Shop." But an even better name that evokes the senses would be, "Handspun Home." It conveys the message that what is inside is unique and has a specialty shop atmosphere.

When you are ready to start brainstorming, try looking through dictionaries, magazines, and newspapers. Enlist the help of friends and family who will understand your vision and be able to help you come up with some key words and phrases. When naming firms start working on a business name, they start out with a list of anywhere from 500 to 1,000 names. Do not worry; you do not need to come up with that many. After all, you understand your business vision better than any strangers would. A list of 25 names would be a good start. Critique each name carefully, one at a time. You will probably lose half of the list after one sweep.

Since your business will be global from the beginning through the World Wide Web, you may want to make sure your name will not offend someone who speaks another language or lives in a different culture. Also, assuming your business name will be in the phone book, you might choose to have a name that is closer to the beginning of the alphabet. Even though it is not recommended, that is why some businesses are "AAA Refrigerator Company;" it will put them first in the phone book.

Whenever you are coming up with your perfect business name, you should also look at your immediate competition. You do not want a name that is very similar to other businesses in your area of expertise. Trademarking is another issue that will come into play when choosing your name. Even companies that do not exist anymore or those who have never existed may have a trademark on a name. When you have trimmed your list of prospective names down to five, you can start to explore the world of trademarks. Some small businesses never even register their names to be trademarked. Most states do not require you to register your name before going into business. If there is another business with your name, you could be infringing on their trademark.

Your business name should be screened in the trademark database at **http://tmsearch.uspto.gov** to see whether it is already taken. You can even go to a search engine and type in your prospective business name and see how many true matches are returned. This can eliminate the ones that should be screened from the ones that are obviously already taken. If you find a few matches for your name, do not assume that the name is already trademarked. Some people never register their business names, and you can go ahead and use the name that you have your heart set on. That should be a lesson as to why you should trademark your website design business name once it is chosen. Someone might come up with the name later and trademark it.

There are attorneys who specialize in trademarking that will be able to help you if you need legal guidance. The fees will be well worth it, saving you the hassle of having to deal with trademark infringement down the line when your business is booming. If you do not have the extra money to spend on a lawyer to guide you through the trademarking process step-by-step, there are many books and resources out there to help you along the way.

If you are going it alone in the trademarking process, you can conduct your own trademark search. You can find online databases through the Patent and Trademark Depository Libraries, as well as those trademarks that are in the process of becoming official. Also, you can search the Internet for any businesses that may not be trademarked, but are bearing the business name that you want to use. Checking through domain name registers like **www.godaddy.com** or **www.networksolutions.com** can help you to identify if your name is being used by another business. Keep in mind that if a name you want is being used by someone else's business, you can possibly still use it. If a cake bakery in Akron, Ohio, has the same name as your business, you can still use the name since you are not registered under the same class of services or goods as a bakery under trademark laws. The Small Business Administration will help you through this process and a great guide is located at **https://www.sba.gov/blogs/how-choose-claim-and-protect-your-business-name-online-and-offline**.

When you have a name that meets the legal requirements and still has a nice ring to it, you may have a winner. If you are stuck on a few names, you can try and do a little research within your city to see what people outside your family and friends think about your potential business names. If you have a design that fits in better with one name than the other, you may choose that one because it will incorporate well with the logo. Live with those few names you have for a while if you cannot make a decision immediately, and see which one sticks.

The last legal bit of naming bears mentioning. A DBA, also known as "doing business as," is something that you may or may not have to file. If you have a business that is a sole proprietorship or a partnership, you will need to file a DBA. This could be at various levels, including your county, city, or state. Each state is different when it comes to DBAs. It may be as simple as going in and paying a small fee. Other states can be more complex. Check with your local business association or government offices to get the most accurate information for your place of business.

Choosing Your Company Logo

Start brainstorming by thinking about how you would explain your website to a stranger. Write a few sentences or a paragraph about it. Then try to express that same idea on paper by sketching out a few pictures. Although there is no real right way to do this, ask others for their opinion when designing the logo. The logo is often what represents the site all over the Web in advertisements and other banners.

You may want to choose a logo that not only identifies your business but that also ties your product to a symbol or image. If your product is scrapbooks, you may want to include an image of a scrapbook in your logo. This symbolic identification can be a big advantage when it comes to establishing yourself in your target market as an emerging corporate entity. You may wish to draft a mission or purpose statement to help you design your corporate logo.

When it comes to creating your company logo, there are some things that you should keep in mind.

- Your logo should be functional and multi-purpose; it should work well in color, black and white, printed, on letterhead, or on vehicles.
- Make sure that your business logo is tasteful and not offensive in any way.
- Try to make your logo as original and creative as possible without copying some of the other logos that fall into your target market.
- Many times, simplicity is the best rule to follow. You want to leave a clear and precise image with your customers that allows you to stand out from the rest of the competition. Studies show that customers are more able to remember companies that have simple logos that they can identify.
- Make sure that the logo you choose for your business has a marketable value. This means that you need to have a logo that you can use for the sale of your product or service, for advertising purposes, and for any future public relations.
- Use vector graphics, which can be resized easily without distortion. Unlike JPEGs, GIFs, and PNG images, vector graphics are not made up of a grid of pixels and can be scaled to a larger size without any loss in image quality.
- Protect your logo. You may find details at the U.S. Patent and Trademark Office (**http://www.uspto.gov**).

Image

Your company logo should be able to adequately and correctly encompass all aspects of your business. Another thing that you should consider when choosing a company logo is how you want the public, and the business world, to view your business. Some images that you can create include the following:

- An energetic and lively company
- A conservative company
- A company that is full of luxury
- A hip company

All of these company images can be created with the use of the logo that you choose.

Color

The color scheme of the logo usually tends to become the color scheme of the entire website. This consistency is necessary in order to preserve the flow of the site. You should also consider other places the logo might appear — emails, business cards, and page-headers — when you are designing it.

Choose colors that send a clear message to your customers. As a general rule to follow, dark colors are usually associated with conservative companies that are selling serious and functional products, while companies that are selling unique and fun products tend to choose logo colors that are bright. If you are selling scrapbooks, you will want to use bright and fun colors to get your message of creativity across to your customers.

Shape

Although the shape of your company logo may seem to be a small thing, just look at the many logos out there and the shape to which they conform. Straight edge logos are often used by more conservative companies, while circular logos are seen more often for businesses that sell unique and creative products.

Font

Typeface follows the same rules of convention as the colors that you use for your company logo. You can use typeface that is conservative, modern, or classical. You may want to come up with your own typeface that is unique to your company and logo. If you consider this route for typeface, you will want to make sure that you trademark it for your exclusive use. No matter what method you choose to use for finding the right typeface for your logo, make sure that the letter characters match the logo that you have chosen. Your company logo is a cornerstone of corporate branding, and the investment spent carefully designing a logo will reap dividends with branding, corporate identification, and product familiarity.

The same principles apply to Web design when selecting font type. Fonts need to align with the overall style and intent of your logo or website, they need to be easily readable, and they need to help the reader focus on the content and purpose of your logo or website. Typically, I recommend Times New Roman, Arial, or San Serif fonts for most websites, however you have some creative freedoms on logos and Web pages. Keep in mind that the ultimate goal is rapid legibility and flexibility across platforms. Browsers may display images and fonts differently, so make sure you test out your logos and Web pages in multiple browsers and devices.

Executing Your Logo

There are plenty of options for creating and executing an outstanding logo. You can create it yourself or contract it out to a graphics design professional. There are also many software packages designed to help you create them yourself, such as AAA Logo.

AAA Logo, found at **www.aaa-logo.com**, is one of many companies that allow you to download the latest trial version of the software. Although this is not free software, AAA Logo is reasonably priced and provides the user with more than 8,000 unique logo objects and templates that can help you build your own logos, business cards, banners, headers, and icons for your site. This software allows you to create nearly any graphic you might need for your business or personal use. AAA Logo offers industry-specific logos in its pre-built templates, including technology, finance, healthcare, general business and retail, education and training, travel and tourism, organizations, sports and fitness, and food and beverage.

Creating and selling logos

Another revenue stream you may consider is building logos for others and charging them a reasonable fee. If you purchase AAA Logos 2008, you can build and design logos to sell to other clients, and there is no limit on how many you can sell or create. There are also links on the homepage of this site that explain how to print and export high-resolution 300- to 600-DPI logos for high-quality printing. There are many other such programs available on the Web — just search the keywords "free Web logos" or "logo design companies," and dozens of other websites will appear in the search engine results. Take your time to research at least three or four of them before choosing the one you want to use.

Moving with the Times

Keep an eye on the industry. New gadgets and techniques are constantly emerging, and you want to be on the cutting edge of your field. This will keep you abreast of new trends that are hot at the moment and give you some creative inspiration. What is your competition doing? Do they have a new service that you can also offer your clients? Start with trade magazines or by subscribing to a news feed that is centered and focused in the Web design industry.

Get visible in your particular business or industry. Attend trade shows or conferences that can also offer some courses and workshops to improve your resume and skills. Just as you need to get visible, you also need to start making contacts with others in the field. Befriend the competition. Having other people you know in your field will open doors for you that otherwise would have been unknown. Having someone who is more experienced and established in the business on your side will give you a mentor to go to with questions.

I have been doing Web design work since the late 1990's, but I no longer have the time to build websites for clients. Instead, I use my network of associates that I trust and know will do a great job to refer new clients to. You never know when this favor may be returned; keeping on good terms, even with your competitors, is important.

The bottom line is that name recognition and reputations are important, no matter what line of business you are in. Having a brand name, trademark or image that is recognizable by others gives your business a unique identity and shows that your name, trademark, and image stands for honesty, value and excellent customer service. This in itself is worth its weight in gold in an ever increasingly competitive marketplace.

Chapter 4

Generating Website Traffic

ebsite traffic is determined by the number of visitors and the number of pages they visit. Websites monitor incoming and outgoing traffic to see which pages of their site are popular and whether there are any apparent trends, such as one specific page being viewed mostly by people in a particular country. Web traffic is measured to see the popularity of websites and individual pages or sections within a site. Most quality Web hosting companies provide you with detailed Web statistical analysis and monitoring tools as part of a basic Web hosting package.

Your website traffic can be analyzed by viewing the statistics found in the Web server log file or using website traffic analysis programs. Any quality Web hosting company will provide free, detailed statistics for website traffic. If your Web hosting company does not provide you with free, detailed statistics, you need to shop around for a new Web hosting company. A hit is generated when any file is served. The page itself is considered a file, but images are also files; thus, a page with five images could generate six hits — the five images and the page itself. A page view is generated when a visitor requests any page within the website. A visitor will always generate at least one page view — the home or main page — but could generate many more as they travel through your website.

There are many ways to increase your website traffic, all leading to greater sales and profit potentials. In this chapter we will discuss the following: general techniques, publishing articles, gaining media exposure, using Web directories, optimizing your mobile platform, and using blogs and social media. Social media does not offer nearly as robust statistics, but there are options to track Facebook beyond "likes" or "comments" such as Facebook page manager, which is a free app available in the app store.

There are other ways to generate website traffic, such as search engine optimization (SEO) techniques and link exchanging, but these will be discussed in great detail in the next chapter.

General Techniques to Generate Website Traffic

Produce fresh content

As with any business, it is vital to update your site constantly with fresh content and information for your viewers. Depending on your website, "fresh content" can vary immensely. If your business is a restaurant, you have an opportunity to let consumers know about new menu options or special meal offers. If your business is selling a product, then you have an opportunity to showcase new developments or special promotions. If your business is providing a service, then you can showcase the effectiveness of your services.

Most companies make announcements and updates to alert the public about a new product or service they offer. Do not underestimate the power of social media — it is free to use, very simple to maintain and update on the fly, and can reach thousands of potential customers instantly.

The key to getting attention is an interesting visual or presentation. Try a multimedia approach. If you are giving a live announcement, you can incorporate the audio or video files onto your website highlighting the key components, either to complement a text announcement or replace it altogether. It is highly recommended that you have a media section on your website to serve reporters, columnists, producers, and editors with your latest information. You can create a video and upload it to YouTube for free and then distribute the link through your website, blog and social media.

Many people find listening to an audio clip or watching a video preferable to reading a written press release. Trying a medium other than text to get your message across could be just the boost your company needs. You should also think of other website owners as another form of a media channel, since everyone is looking for fresh content and expert advice.

Consider using an online press release service, such as **www.prweb.com**, to generate successful media exposure for your online business. This free service is another tool you can use to distribute your press release information to thousands of potential new customers or clients. Post your press releases on your blog and social media platforms as well, including Vine, Facebook, YouTube and others.

Keep in mind the value of using highly relevant keywords often within the content of your online press release. Including live links within your online press release is another way to ensure increased media coverage. Linking to relevant websites increases the credibility and functionality of your online business.

Make sure that you give your customers a reason to visit your site, spend time browsing it, interact with it, and most importantly, return to it. Offer incentives by showcasing featured products or promotions, and use creative Internet tools, such as video and audio, to create an interactive experience. You can also import video clips or create your own to add to your website.

Publish testimonials

Using customer testimonials is a good way to promote the quality and reliability of your website and, more importantly, promote your products or services. This is an amazingly effective tactic. The media coverage you get is a subtle, third-party referral to you. However, the strongest, most effective sales assistance comes from direct customer testimonials. It is highly recommended that you use audio and video testimonials as well as printed quotes on your website. You should include your customer's name, age, and Web address with each unsolicited testimonial to increase believability, but avoid releasing any personal information such as emails or addresses as that would constitute a breach of privacy. No matter how flashy or impressive your website may look, it is customer service, satisfaction, and reliability that keep customers coming back.

Create a following

Have a presence on all forms of relevant social media, and make use of popular hashtags or events in order to garner a large following. Post often about your services and link back to your website with special offers.

Gain client trust

Gaining the trust of your customers is extremely critical in developing a continuing relationship that rewards your online business with repeat customer sales. The one-time sale may boost your immediate sales numbers, but it is returning customers that take your business from mediocre to fantastic profits. Your goal is to build quality customer relationships and then maintain them.

Also, try to take the occasional risk. Taking a stand, or opinion, in a respectful debate will win you attention and respect for your leadership in the marketplace. Establishing yourself as an expert and taking a position builds tremendous credibility and respect, even from those with opposing views or opinions.

Gaining media exposure, both online and offline, opens the doors to a potentially long-term relationships with customers by using implied third-party credibility, thus legitimizing you as the expert in your field. Once you attract the prospects, you still have to deliver your goods/services and ensure that the customer is completely satisfied. There are several rules that you should remember when it comes to building a relationship with your customers and gaining their trust: be honest, be up-front, and always do what you say you are going to do. By following these three simple guiding principles, you will have satisfied customers.

Improve your public profile

The more positive your public profile, the more success you will have both online and offline. This, of course, ties back in with gaining credibility with the public and with your customers. Your public profile is your trademark for success and profits. Your local and state Better Business Bureaus are great organizations to join and obtain positive ratings. Other online business profile ratings services worth considering are **www.reseller ratings.com**, **www.epinions.com**, and **www.consumerreports.org**.

Take some time to determine just what type of public profile you want to project to the public. Most likely, you will want a successful, upbeat profile that is based on your confidence and credibility supported by your products, services, and superior customer service and satisfaction. You can increase your public profile by taking advantage of opportunities that allow you to use your services and knowledge in a variety of venues, thereby gaining public awareness and online marketing exposure without spending your own funds on relatively expensive advertising. Think outside the box. Positioning yourself, and actually becoming an expert in your market takes time, patience, and personal confidence. Just knowing the advantages of effective marketing is half the battle in getting there. Remember, it is the combination of media and marketing that really communicates the benefits and unique aspects of your business, which in turn drive customers to your website.

Your goal when it comes to sharing your expertise is to publish for free, thereby allowing many other organizations, news services, and other publications or magazines to distribute your article throughout their distribution network in return for website links back to your website and direct product promotions to thousands of potential new customers. There are ways that you can publish a full-page ad promoting yourself and your business without spending a dime. Contact editors of publications and offer them your press release to add content to their next publication. Many editors are looking for useful and relevant content so that they can meet deadlines. You need to take advantage of this opportunity and create the perfect article for publication.

Use press releases to generate exposure

An online press release is part of the online medium of communication, which is all about timing. Your press release is one method of communicating with your customers and your industry. It is up to you to make the most of a press release so that it has as much impact as possible.

Most companies use press releases to alert the public about a new product or a new service they offer. These press releases, while informative, tend to be somewhat dry, and consumers typically skim over them, sometimes even missing the key points. The bottom line is, "If it's not newsworthy, then you won't be selected by the media for coverage." That being said, a press release promoting specific events, specials, or newsworthy items can be very effective.

As an alternative to a written press release, you could try a multimedia approach. If you are giving a live press release, you can incorporate the audio or video files onto your website, either to complement a written press release or to replace it altogether. It is highly recommended that you have a media section on your website to serve reporters, columnists, producers, and editors with your latest press release information. Many people find listening to an audio clip or, better yet, watching a video clip preferential to reading a written press release. This can be done free by simply uploading your video to be hosted on **www.youtube.com** and embedding the links from your website, blog, or social media platform. You should also think of other website owners as another form of media channel since everyone is looking for fresh content and expert advice.

Online public relations are easily marketable for several reasons. Let's take a look at some of them.

Accessibility

Using SEO and search engines can give you the visibility to drive traffic to your website or Facebook site.

Affordability

By using free online press release services, you can work within the tightest of budgets. You can also select small, tightly targeted press releases within a niche or specific industry. Even if you choose to use paid press release services, they are cost effective, and you will not be blowing your budget by sending the release to non-qualified markets or media platforms.

Internet speed

The speed of the Internet lets you seize business opportunities immediately. Millions can be made by tying your media events and campaigns to current events such as the World Series or the Super Bowl. It is up to you to follow up on all customer sales and communication.

Internet leverage

The Internet deals with facts and information without focusing on the size or prestige of your company. Potential customers are using the Internet for research and are obtaining helpful knowledge. Make yourself easy to find. If you build it, and they can find you, they will come!

Your focus when doing your own PR should not circulate around a press release. Although useful to use, the press release should not be your only technique when it comes to media exposure; rather, it should be treated as another tool in a well-stocked arsenal.

Free media coverage is a great way to get your name out to the public and build your credibility. It is "free" if you do it yourself without hiring a media agency, but it does require an investment of your time, focus, and effort. There are several tactics you can employ to generate free media coverage. Paid advertising should still be considered as a feasible and desirable component of your overall online marketing portfolio if you can afford it, if you choose to implement it, and if it typically has the potential to be highly effective. It is vital to use your advertising dollars wisely, as you want to ensure that you get the most bang for your buck.

You want to drive as many potential customers to your site as possible, even if each visitor does not result in a "sale." Depending on the type of business you operate, your goal may only be to increase website traffic or provide information for the visitor. For example, if you are operating a restaurant, acquiring an increase in the number of site visitors or page hits is considered a success as your goal is simply to drive visitors to your site, which will, in turn, inspire them to dine at your establishment. Likewise, if you use Facebook and Twitter, you can promote your menus, specials events, and dinner specials; you can also use Instagram and Facebook to post pictures of your meals, menus, and more. If you are selling products, you can expect many comparison shoppers who are shopping for features, product reviews, or other product information as they consider making a purchase.

Generate interest

You can generate interest through a variety of tactics. Here is a list of things you can do to create some hype for your business:

- Create a "What's New" or "New Products" page. Site visitors like to see what is new, trendy, or just released. Make it easy for them.
- Establish a promotion program. You can offer free products, trial samples, or discount coupons. Everyone loves a bargain, so give it to them.
- Establish a contest. Be creative; you do not have to market your products in a contest. Contests such as the "Top 50 Restaurant Websites" created by Atlantic Publishing cost nothing to create, are simple to manage, and draw visitors.
- Add content-relevant professional articles, news events, press releases, or other topics of interest on a daily basis to draw visitors back to your site.
- Establish a viral marketing campaign or embed viral marketing techniques into your current advertising programs or e-zines.

Viral marketing is when you incorporate such things as a "forward to a friend" link within the advertisement. In theory, if many people forward to many more friends, it will spread like a virus and eventually go to many potential customers.

- Use signature files with all email accounts. Signature files are basically business cards through email, so send your business card to all your email recipients. Signature files are included with every email you send out and can contain all contact information, including business name and website URL.

- Start an affiliate program and market it. Include your affiliate information in emails, newsletters, e-zines, and on websites to promote your program. A successful affiliate program will generate a significant increase in website traffic.

- Include your website URL on everything, such as business cards, letterheads, promotional items, and emails.

- Put a search engine on your website. Simply visit Google to add a free search feature to your website. This is a tool that site visitors will love, and you can customize it to only search within your site's parameters; instructions can be found through Google's Support page.

- Implement Google AdSense on your website to increase revenue and traffic.

- Implement Google AdWords^{SM} to increase website traffic and generate sales revenue.

- Register your site with online directories relevant to your content.

- Write free articles and submit them to other newsletters or websites in order to demonstrate your expertise.

- Post often on content-related forums and message boards, and post your website URL with each entry.

- Submit often to content-relevant email discussion groups, and post your website URL with each entry.

- Create a "Links" page on your website, and offer your visitors a reciprocal link to your site for adding a link to your site on theirs.

- Create a blog to complement your website and keep it updated often with fresh content.
- Use multiple forms of social media to attract customers, publish information and grow your business. You do not need to use "every" form of social media, pick what works for you and only what you can easily maintain and update.

Publishing Articles

Writing articles is amazingly effective for generating website traffic and increasing your ranking in search engines. You embed links to your site into articles, which may be published and re-published on several websites. The viral effect of this generates quality inbound links, promotes awareness of your website, and increases your reputation as an expert in your specialty, since you are publishing articles on the subject.

Embed keywords into your article, as well as links to your website. Keep your articles fairly short — generally no more than 750 words. If you need to write longer, break the content up into a series of articles. Draw readers to your website by giving them enough information to at least instill an interest in visiting your website. Publish your articles on your blog and then place links to your articles with short intro captions on your social media sites.

For all articles, ensure that you include a biography that includes contact information and information about your experience, education, company, and products, as well as links to all of your sites. Establish yourself as an industry expert, and you will be recognized as one by your peers. Host these articles on your own website or blog, and if your content is good quality, then you will naturally attract a viewership. Writing articles that are unsubstantiated or unprofessional will only serve to hinder your efforts and ward off potential visitors. Be the expert that you are and have a good editor, and you will do fine. If your Web presence grows large enough it may even pay to eventually hire on more content producers and editors to oversee this section of your Web presence and allow you to focus on broader business concerns.

Using Web Directories

A Web directory is simply an organized cataloging of websites by subject. The best examples of this are www.dmoz.org. Most provide you with a simple "Add URL" link, such as **www.dmoz.org/add.html** or you can add directly to search engines such as Bing at **www.bing.com/toolbox/ submit-site-url**.

While Web directories are often free, some will charge you for the listing. The following website provides you with links to all of the top-ranked Web directories and also provides you with cost information and Google PageRank™ information. This should be your guide to adding yourself to Web directories: **www.seocompany.ca/directory/top-web-directories. html**. When adding your website to directories, embed key words or key phrases into your title and description. There are programs that can automate this process for you, such as SubmitEaze, located at www.submiteaze. com. It should be noted that while many Web directories are free, many charge submission fees.

Media Exposure

Media exposure, of all kinds, is one thing that you can boost your Web presence visibly and increase the amount of website traffic. Media exposure can also be defined as "promotion and publicity" for the online success of your company. If you have an online business or a traditional brick and mortar business that you want to advertise and promote online, you need to make sure that you get as much as you can out of media coverage without spending too much of your advertising budget. You need to make the media work for you, not against you, so that customers can easily find you, learn to trust you and your product, and keep coming back to your website.

Your potential and existing customers are only going to buy products and services from a business that they feel is trustworthy. To earn that trust and reliance, you have to make the most of media exposure so that you can build your credibility and find a secure position for your business as an expert in your target market. What is going to work best is a combination of effective online and offline publicity and public relations that is geared toward affirming your corporate trustworthiness, reliability, and credibility. You should think of the Internet as your own personal publicity and media tool.

You need to learn how to develop your own public relations and media campaigns so that you can build up the value, creditability, and trust that creates satisfied customers. When you gain that credibility and trust, you get more sales, increased confidence from your customers, and you gain the public profile that you want and need for your online or traditional business. Do not forget about the power of social media.

Businesses used to pay thousands upon thousands of dollars for media exposure, publicity, and advertising. However, in the age where everyone is connected, you can get publicity and PR for your business with more humble resources. By engaging in Internet media campaigns, or "non-traditional" media methods, for gaining media exposure, you can accomplish two things: (1) you can save a significant amount of money, and (2) you get to be in full control of your own media techniques.

Just how do you gain media exposure? What you cannot do is wait around for the media or customers to find your company website, or you may be waiting for a long time with very low sales results. Publicity concepts are very simple: you need to get out there and create your own media opportunities instead of waiting for the press to find you.

Your customers are going to form negative or positive opinions about your business based on what they see and hear on the radio, on the television, or in print. Mass media, such as radio, television, and print, are often difficult and certainly very costly methods to promote your business, so we will concentrate on less costly methods to grab the attention of customers in a big way. By using positive media relations, you will be taking the first step toward your successful positioning in the Internet marketplace. This will allow you to convert more of the traffic to your website into satisfied, paying customers.

What do you do when you have a new (or even successful) online business, and you want to attract more customers by positioning yourself as an expert in your marketplace? You will want to merge the proven success of positive media coverage and a successful online presence to give yourself the winning edge over your competitors. It is the combination of both successful online and offline publicity and promotion that will guarantee your credibility, trustworthiness, and dependability, which all lead to greater sales and/or interest in your products or services. Your success will lead to more sales, increased client confidence, increased exposure at speaking appearances, and the positive public profile that you want for your online business. People who look on the Internet for merchants will only buy from someone that they "feel" they know and trust.

Media exposure is key to your successful online marketing profile. Your customers will form their opinions (positive or negative) based on what they hear and see in print, on television, on the radio, or on the Web. These "media" channels are not to be confused with the common short-form referral to online "multimedia" as media, too. Recognizing the importance of media exposure can boost the sales of your products or services. That positive media exposure is also a major step toward maintaining credibility in your online marketplace and ensuring that you compel visitors to channel more traffic to your website.

Five Ways to Improve Your Online Marketing

Site Design

Make sure that your website is professional and has a great design. You want your website to have a clean, tight look so that customers are compelled to return. Professional site design means having a website that achieves all of the following:

- Is easy to navigate
- Has appropriate logos
- Has up-to-date information

- Answers customer questions
- Has a polished look

Use these techniques will ensure that you have a professional-looking, quality website.

Honesty

Never hide anything from your customers. Give them all the data that they need to make an informative decision about your product or services. Follow through to maintain credibility and trust. You do not want to be identified in the media as a poor company, a scam site, or a rip-off artist. Bad news travels fast, and it travels even faster on the Internet.

A great example of this is in a PowerPoint® presentation titled "Yours is a Very Bad Hotel," authored by two extremely dissatisfied businessmen after their bad experience with a hotel. The hotel's poor customer service and failure to hold a "guaranteed" room reservation was widely distributed on the Internet. As a result of the negative publicity, the nationwide hotel chain changed corporate policies and no doubt suffered from the unwanted attention. This is a superb example of very negative exposure that was spread virally and very quickly around the world—literally.

Customer incentive

Make sure that you give your customers a reason to visit your site, to spend time browsing it, to interact with it, and most importantly, to return to it. Offer incentives by showcasing featured products or promotions, coupons, discount codes and more. Promote your social media sites on your website and vice versa. Encourage them to "like" your Facebook site and follow you on Twitter.

Domain name

Try to obtain your own domain name for your website. As simple as this concept may be, it makes the difference between prospects remembering who you are or moving on to your competition.

Testimonials and reviews

Remember that no matter how flashy or impressive your website may look, it is customer service, satisfaction, and reliability that keeps them coming back. The success of your online strategy relies on combining all of the above tactics for maintaining successful online positioning and presence.

The simplest way to accomplish this is to provide a good service or product. It goes without saying that word-of-mouth reviews and appreciation can travel faster than any form of glitzy advertising, and a good third-party review from a trusted public source or website can go a long way toward convincing people to come back to your business in the future. However, there are ways to better optimize or advertise your business in order to make sure that you get the public attention to be recognized in the first place.

Your goal is to increase profits and expand your business without spending a significant portion of your budget in the process. Publicity can earn you a reputation as the expert in your specialty or target market, gain public trust, recognition, and respect, which ultimately lead to new customers and increased profits for your business. Your goal is to attain this without spending thousands of dollars on traditional, and often risky, methods of marketing and advertising.

One way you can help achieve this is by developing your own media kits. When you "make" your own media kit, you will develop techniques that work for you and your company at minimal cost. A media kit can comprise written text as well as online or office videos, CD-ROMs, DVDs, or other distributable media. It is common to convert large media files to Adobe® Acrobat .PDF format to distribute easily on the Web or to create video files that can be shared on YouTube and through social media websites, such as Facebook.

Many times, potential customers will only buy from a business that they trust or that has been recommended to them by a satisfied customer or friend. Building a media kit or press release kit can reveal significant amounts of information about your business and will satisfy potential customers, distributors, and even public media platforms. By developing your own media kits, you can implement advertising and publicity campaigns that will affirm your position in the marketplace.

Mass media attention

Mass media is another potential platform for you to consider, although this is often a costly venture. Mass media includes radio, TV, and print (magazines and newspapers). Mass media will allow you to quickly create your own advertising exposure so that you build up the credibility that wins new customers and keeps these customers coming back. When you gain that level of trust, you get increased customer confidence, more sales, and higher profits.

Here are some ideas for increasing publicity and promotion offline, which are typically no cost and may even generate revenue for your business.

Speak at a seminar or lecture

You can also lead workshops that have a direct correlation to the products and services that your business is selling. This is a great way to gain the public exposure that you need to appear positive and confident about your business. This exposure will add to your trust and credibility for potential customers. Make sure that you hand out business cards that include your website URL so that people can find your website on the Internet.

Write opinions and articles for online publications

Make sure that you upload any articles that you write to your website. These online publications will provide what are called "hotlinks" back to your own website, which is a great way to further promote your online business. Make sure that you include your email address and Twitter user-name in the byline of any articles and opinions that you write.

Promote your business on the radio

Radio (including streamed radio) is a valuable resource for what is called "re-used" media. Make sure that you always get the most leverage out of anything you write or develop for any type of media. Make sure that you are prepared for any media opportunity that comes your way. Try to have several articles or press releases ready ahead of time so that you can read your article on the radio and promote your business offline.

Brand recognition assists you as you establish and expand your online presence. It is easier when you use a media kit to help secure your positioning in the marketplace. By creating your own media, you have the control over all the aspects of marketing, and you will have achieved a major milestone in promoting your business. The aim of successful brand recognition is that your customers will recognize your name and will be willing to buy, and even pay more, for your products and services because of your commitment to value and quality. You need to remind your customers often that their decision to buy from you was the right decision. You let your customers know this by sending links or email newsletters that highlight the media exposure that you have developed. You can never stop promoting your company — it is a continuous circle of advertising, promotion, and publicity.

By building your business profile, along with your brand recognition, you greatly improve your trustworthiness and credibility within the offline and online marketplace. This stops the high exit-and-drop rates that are often experienced by many websites as Web visitors come and go when they are not familiar with your company or its products and/or services.

Knowing you are an expert in the marketplace is not going to be enough; you need to let the public know that you are an expert and promote and market that expertise. Be recognized as an industry expert, and you will gain significant credibility, trust, and name recognition.

Try building an advertising campaign not only around your product or services, but around current events, community support, and unique marketing campaigns.

Positioning yourself as an expert in your target market takes patience, time, and confidence. Just knowing the advantages of effective marketing is half the battle in getting there. Remember, the combination of advertising on- and offline really communicates the benefits and unique aspects of your business that will drive potential customers to your website.

Every website on the Internet has one goal: attain the number one position in search engines. For every key phrase, there is only one top spot and not everyone can make it there. Time and persistence will help you achieve the highest possible results, and this is where the search engine optimization (SEO) comes in.

Paying for Website Traffic

Paid website traffic is when you pay to have a certain amount of quality traffic driven to your website. Quality is defined by the use of advanced search engine marketing tools, such as Google Adwords, where you "pay" for clicks on advertisements that drive traffic to your website — do not worry, all things Google will be broken down in Chapter 7. There are many other sources besides Google AdWords such as Bing Ads, Yahoo Gemini, and Reddit. I do not cover these in depth in this book, but be aware that there are many sources, and you should do your own research to determine which works best for your needs.

Optimizing Your Website for Mobile Users

You should ensure your overall Web design strategy includes targeting mobile users. Many larger companies opt for custom-built Apple® or Android™ apps, which are typically free for download and are optimized for mobile users.

Modern-day digital marketing has made mobile optimization necessary for SEO. With the explosion of mobile browsing, search engines — especially Google — now consider mobile-friendliness as a ranking factor. Here are some tips to optimize your current website for mobile users to get more website traffic.

Invest

Invest in your site to optimize it for mobile searches. This does not mean "make your website smaller;" it means use technology such as Cascading

Style Sheets (CSS) to adapt your website's appearance based on the device as well as which browser is being used by the user. Many users offer a "mobile version" of their site that is customized exactly to mobile device requirements and optimizes both the user experience as well as search engine visibility for the mobile site.

Optimize nagivation

You have substantially less real estate (screen space) to work with. Navigating your main website can be very challenging on a mobile device. When you build a mobile optimized site, ensure the navigation is also optimized for mobility users. Users will not stay on a site that takes too much effort to navigate. You can test your site on a variety of devices and resolutions for free at **http://quirktools.com/screenfly**.

One problem you may face regarding SEO, which is largely covered in the next chapter, is that your website navigation menu, which is commonly on the top or on the left-hand side of each page, is indexed by the search engine and can hurt you in search engine rankings. You need to get the search engines to index your content, not your navigation menus.

Some advice is to put the navigation menu to the right of each page, which can be effective, although it is non-standard navigation and may turn site visitors off. Another option is to use CSS to place your navigation menu later in the code, or you can use Web accessibility settings to have the search engine skip over the navigation menu and go right to your Web content.

Simplify

Reduce the number of images, video, and other content that takes a long time to load or that takes up too much space. People want information and responses on the fly with easy to navigate pages; otherwise, they will not be on your site for long. Likewise, if you must have images, and most pages do, reduce the size and quality of them to speed up the loading process on mobile devices. You do not have to prove that you are the smartest or most technically knowledgeable by using overly complex and unnecessary terms, jargon, or technical language. If you are selling products or services, use straight-forward descriptions.

Creating Quality Website Content

The content of your website and individual Web pages is the most important factor in driving traffic to your website. Your website's content should address and answer all of these four questions:

- Will your visitors know what your business is about at first glance?
- Will they know what page they are on and what it is about?
- Will the content let them know what to do next?
- Why should they buy/download/subscribe from your website?

If you think your site is readily answering these questions, then you are on the right track, assuming you have engaged in proper SEO techniques. Here are some more helpful tips to deliver the right message to your visitors.

Add depth

Create several interesting headings and sub-heading on your homepage and landing pages. These pages are the most important ones and should give a clear and compelling message regarding what your website is all about and how it will help them.

Guide the visit

Add "next steps" where appropriate to guide the site visitor in how to proceed. Nothing is worse than having to guess your way through a website's navigation to reach your desired goal.

Sell your site

Sell your website to your visitor. What is in it for them? You must draw in their interest, or they will move on quickly. Capture their attention with promotions, sales, marketing offers, free items, contests and more.

Be personable

Be personable and relatable in terms of your website content. Personalize with "we" and "our" and make content that is easy to understand and relate to, regardless of experience level or familiarity with products or services. For example, a beauty site might have something on their homepage that displays new arrivals with the tagline: "Products we're loving."

Avoid making claims

Avoid over-inflated claims that cannot be supported such as "we're the best" or "guaranteed results." Compelling and straight-forward content works best. Do not come across as a door-to-door salesman. Do not attempt to trick your customers and do not be overly clever — be honest and upfront; integrity is priceless. If you can really back your claims, then that is fine, but honesty wins in the long term.

Be original

Ensure you offer content that is related to your products and services and that is unique to your brand. Do not be overly generic; offer details about you, your company, and your products and services that personalizes the visitor experience.

Give credit

Ensure you give full and proper credit for content that is not yours and not original. This promotes honesty and open communications and builds trust and loyalty in customers.

Build your reputation

Be the expert in your specialty. Know your content and know it well. Publish articles, blogs, and social media posts to build your reputation as an industry expert, regardless of what business you are in. If you do not know much about building model airplanes, you should not be giving out advice on that topic.

Add landing pages

Landing pages give your website more opportunities for sales conversions. They can also direct site visitors to the particular offers or products you want them to see without the distraction of everything else on your website or the problem of having to navigate to the right "page."

Add call-to-actions

Add effective call-to-actions on the landing pages. A call-to-action helps drive a site visitor to a specific, desired action (for example, buy something or provide contact information). A call-to-action should be big and bold, should stand out, and should be clear and convincing.

Add forms

Add forms to landing pages. Forms are great for having site visitors sign-up or subscribe to your site. They also provide you with contact information for future marketing. Keep forms down to as little a number of fields as possible. The more the user has to fill out, the less likely they are to fill out the form. Do not use the standard default "submit" button on forms. Instead, use relevant phrases, such as "Start my Free Trial" or "Download Free E-Book Now."

Add newsletters

Consider offering email newsletters to site visitors. This will help you grow your email marketing list. You can offer discounts, promotions, coupons, and other information to grab the attention of your reader.

The topics covered in this chapter should get you well on your way towards building a toolbox of proven, highly effective methods to help you generate website traffic, build your customer base, and promote and market your business, products, and services.

Chapter 5

Search Engine Optimization (SEO)

Search engine optimization (SEO) is one of the proven methods that you can use to push up the ranking of your website within your target market. SEO uses keywords that are relevant to the product or services you sell. It helps your customers find your site while they are doing a Web search.

The concepts and actions necessary for successful SEO can sometimes be confusing and hard to grasp when you are first starting out. Here are some steps we will cover that need to be followed so that you can get the most out of your SEO:

- Choose the right keywords that are going to bring the most hits to your website.
- Use the right title tags to identify you within search engines.
- Ensure appropriate content is written on your website.
- Use properly formatted meta tags on your website.
- Choose the right search engines to submit your website to.
- Understand the free and paid listing service options available.

- Have quality inbound links to your website.
- Ensure that every image on your site has an **<alt>** tag.

Once you know which areas to focus on, your ranking in search engines will increase dramatically.

The main problem with SEO, and the No. 1 reason most site builders fail to properly ensure that a site is optimized, is that it requires significant time investment and patience. SEO will not get you immediate visibility in search engines. You need to be realistic in your expectations — it will take months to see tangible results.

SEO should be an ongoing process that you consistently re-evaluate on a period basis. There are billions of Web pages on the Internet, meaning that there are many websites that are directly competing with yours for potential customers. You need to take realistic, time-proven measures to ensure that your online business gets noticed.

To get started, let's take a look at the two major kinds of SEO — white hat vs. black hat.

White hat vs. black hat SEO

I have had great success obtaining high search engine rankings through proven white hat SEO techniques. White hat SEO is optimization strategies and techniques that target your intended human audience versus optimization that targets specific search engine algorithms. It focuses on relevancy of your topic to your audience and organic search engine rankings based on the keywords entered into a search engine. The use of quality keywords in your website is critical, as are other techniques such as link building and backlinks (links to and from your site to other relevant sites).

Black hat SEO, on the other hand, refers to other SEO strategies that disregard the human audience and target search engines. These strategies include things like keyword stuffing, hidden or invisible text, and more.

I will guide you through white hat SEO and recommend you completely avoid black hat SEO, as this will get you excluded from major search engines. If you are business for the long haul, white hat SEO will achieve the results you desire, as long as you are patient and diligent.

Understanding How Search Engines Work

There are several different types of search engines: crawler-based, human-powered, and mixed. We will discuss how each one works so you can optimize your website in preparation for your PPC advertising campaign.

Crawler-based search engines

Crawler-based search engines, such as the Google search engine or Bing, create their listings automatically. They "crawl" or "spider" the Web and index the data, which is then searchable through Google. Crawler-based search engines will eventually revisit your website; therefore, as your content is changed, your search engine ranking may change.

A website is added to the search engine database when the search engine spider or crawler visits a Web page, reads it, and then follows links to other pages within the site. The spider returns to the site on a regular basis, typically once every month, to search for changes. Often, it may take several months for a page that has been spidered to be indexed. Until a website is indexed, the results of the spider are not available through the search engines. The search engine then sorts through the millions of indexed pages to find matches to a particular search and rank them in order based on the formula it uses to find the most relevant results.

Human-powered search directories

Human-powered directories, like the Open Directory, depend on humans for their listings. You must submit a short description to the directory for your entire site. The search directory then looks at your site for matches from your page content to the descriptions you submitted.

Hybrid or mixed search engines

A few years ago, search engines were either crawler-based or human-powered. Today, a mix of both types is common in search engine results.

Search Engine Registration

It is possible to submit your website for free to search engines. However, when you use paid search engine submission programs, the process of listing may be faster, and it will bring more Web traffic to your website more quickly.

Submitting to crawler-based search engines

Submitting to search engines that are crawlers—search engines that look throughout the Internet to seek out websites through links and meta tags—means that you will likely have several Web pages listed within the search engine. The more optimized your website is, as discussed previously in this chapter, the higher you will rank within the search engine listings.

One of the top Internet crawler search engines is Google. Google is extremely popular because it is not only a search engine, it also is the main source of power and information behind other search engines, such as AOL®. The best thing that you can do when getting your website listed at Google is to make sure that you have links within your website. When you have accurate links on your website, you ensure that crawler search engines are able to find you. One thing to keep in mind is that if you have good links AND you listed your website with a successful directory search engine, such as Yahoo!, you may find that crawlers are easily able to find you, thus eliminating your need to list with Google in the first place. However, do not let this stop you from building good links into your website and constantly updating them. You can manually submit your website to Google and other major search engines for free at **www.dmoz.org**.

As about 85 percent of Internet traffic is generated by search engines, submitting your website to all the major search engines and getting them to be seen on the search engine list is extremely important. Search engines are the most effective way of promoting your website on the Internet. In order to maintain a search engine placement near the top for your chosen "keywords," it is essential to regularly submit your website details to these Web directories and engines. Some search engines de-list you over time, while others automatically re-spider your site.

Submitting to human-powered search directories

If you have a limited budget, make sure that you have at least enough to cover the price of submitting to the directory at Yahoo! (called a "directory" search engine, because it uses a compiled directory), which is assembled by human hands and not a computer. For a one-time yearly fee of approximately $300, you will be able to ensure that search engines that are crawlers (a search engine that goes out onto the Internet looking for new websites by following links) will be able to find your website in the Yahoo! directory.

It may seem like a waste of money to be in a directory-based search engine, but the opposite is true. Crawlers consistently use directory search engines to add to their search listings. If you have a large budget put aside for search engine submissions, you might want to list with both directory search engines and crawler search engines, such as Google. When you first launch your website, you may want it to show up immediately in search engines. If this is the case, you might want to consider using what is called a "paid placement" program.

Paid placement programs

Paid placement programs, such as Google AdWords, will get you immediate exposure in search engines. You get prominent listings in the search engines and results based on how much you will be willing to pay to display your links or ads. You also pay when someone clicks on the displayed links in the search engine results.

Using search engine submission software

There are dozens of software applications that can automatically submit your website to search engines — one of these is Dynamic Submission.

You can find a trial edition at **www.dynamicsubmission.com**. Software programs like Dynamic Submission were developed to offer website owners the ability to promote their websites to the ever-increasing number of search engines on the Internet without any hassles or complications. These types of software help you submit your website to hundreds of major search engines with just a few clicks to drive traffic to your website.

Since nearly 85 percent of Internet traffic is generated by search engines, submitting your website to all the major search engines and getting them to be seen on the search engine list is extremely important, especially in concert with your PPC advertising campaign. Some search engines de-list you over time, while others automatically re-spider your site.

You should be aware that the success of these submission applications has decreased over time as search engines began to reject these "autobot" submissions in favor of human submissions or paid submissions. Google and most other search engines do not recommend the use of products such as WebPosition Gold or Dynamic Submission, which send automatic or programmatic queries to Google. It is in violation of their terms of use and quality guidelines.

DMOZ

Be sure to manually submit your site to the Open Directory at **www.dmoz. org**, which is free. DMOZ is the free Open Directory, which feeds many of the major search engines, including Google.

Keywords

One of the biggest challenges when establishing your website is developing your initial list of keywords and key phrases. Key phrases are simply keywords that are joined together. They refine the search and narrow down generalized searches into very specific result sets. Key phrases are often overlooked as people create keyword lists, but they are vitally important to SEO for your website. You must develop a list of potential keywords or key phrases before producing your content. Here are some tips to guide you:

- Brainstorm a list of any relevant keyword or key phrase you can think of. Take some time away from the list, then over the course of a week or so, keep making additions.

- Be sure to incorporate your company name, catch-phrases, slogans, or other recognizable marketing material into your keywords.

- Add both the singular and plural spellings for your keywords.

- Avoid trademark issues and disputes. Although there is some degree of latitude in regard to trademarks, it is recommended to avoid using other companies' trademarks unless you are an authorized distributor or reseller of their products.

- Embed your keywords or key phrases into your website content.

- Utilize your Web server logs to research what keywords or key phrases people are using to find your website; this will likely help you refine your keyword and key phrase lists.

- Keyword density is important in website design. You need to feature keywords in your website content, but you must also ensure that the page content still reads properly. The number of keywords embedded into page content in comparison to your other text determines the "density" of a keyword. The proper keyword density for a Web page is typically considered to be from 5 to10 percent.

Do not only think about keywords for search engine optimization — think about the right types of phrases that people will use in search engines. General phrases often get lost in the shuffle of search engines, and phrases that are too broad in meaning will get no results. You need to find a fine balance between phrases that push you to the top of the rankings and phrases that leave you at the bottom of the pile. Unfortunately, there is not a magic formula to developing search engine optimized and effective search phrases, however there are many tools to help you choose keywords, such as **https://adwords.google.com/KeywordPlanner**.

As mentioned, you will have to have a different list of keywords and key phrases for each Web page based on the content of that individual page. Keywords that work for some of your Web pages may not work for others. This is why you need to constantly assess how your search engine optimization campaign is progressing and be prepared to make changes along the way.

Do a small market survey

Make sure that you do a small market survey to find out what keywords people use when searching for your product on the Internet. Screen your employees, friends, and customer base for a list of all the possible keywords or key phrases you believe they might use to try to find your website. If you rely on your own list of keywords, you will be limiting yourself from using keywords that other people are likely to use. Try to come up with a list of as many keywords and key phrases as you can so that you optimize your Web pages as much as you can.

Learn from your competitors

A good way to keep on top of top keywords is to keep an eye on your competition. Use a search engine yourself and use some of the keywords and key phrases that you know target your type of product or service. Take a look at the top-ranking websites and view the source HTML code as well as the keywords that are used in their meta tags. The HTML code will show you the keywords that the site's creator used. You will not only be able to come up with more keyword ideas, but you will also be able to keep up with your competition so that you rank at the top of search engines, as well.

Placement of text

The placement of text content within a Web page can make a significant difference in your eventual search engine rankings. Some search engines will only analyze a limited number of text characters on each page, usually about 200 words, and will not read the rest of the page, regardless of length; therefore the keywords and phrases you may have loaded into your page may not be read at all by the search engines. Some search engines do index the entire content of Web pages; however, they typically give more value or "weight" to the content that appears closer to the top of the Web page.

Tips and tricks

If you want to get the best results from search engines, here are some tips that you should follow.

Readability

No matter how much content you have after incorporating keywords and key phrases, make sure that the content that you have is still understandable and readable in plain language. A common mistake is to stack a website full of so many keywords and key phrases that the page is no longer understandable or readable to the website visitor—a sure bet to lose potential customers quickly.

Add more web pages

Add extra pages to your website, even if they may not at first seem directly relevant. The more Web pages that you have, the more pages search engines will have to be able to find you and link to. Extra pages can include tips, tutorials, product information, resource information, and any other information or data that is pertinent to the product or service that you are selling.

Include tags

The keywords and key phrases that you use in the content of your website should also be included in the tags of your website, such as meta tags, ALT tags, head tags, and title tags. The next section of this chapter will explain what meta tags are and how to incorporate them into your website.

Meta Tags

There remains controversy surrounding the use of meta tags and whether their inclusion on websites truly impacts search engine rankings. However, they are still widely held as an integral part of a sound SEO plan, although some search engines do use these tags in their indexing process.

You need to be aware that you are competing against potentially thousands of other websites, often promoting similar products, using similar keywords, and employing other SEO techniques. Meta tags have never guaranteed top rankings on crawler-based search engines, but they may offer a degree of control and the ability for you to impact how your Web pages are indexed within the search engines.

When it comes to using keywords and key phrases in your meta keywords tags, use only those keywords and phrases that you have included within the Web content on each of your Web pages. It is also important that you use the plural forms of keywords so that both the singular and the plural will end up in any search that people do in search engines using specific keywords and key phrases. Other keywords that you should include in your meta keywords tags are any misspellings of your keywords and phrases, since many people commonly misspell certain words, and you want to make sure that search engines can still find you.

Do not repeat your most important keywords and key phrases more than four to five times in a meta-keyword tag. If your product or service is specific to a certain location geographically, you should mention this location in your meta-keyword tag.

Meta tags comprise formatted information that is inserted into the "head" section of each page on your website. To view the head of a Web page, you must view it in HTML mode, rather than in the browser view. In Internet Explorer®, you can click on the toolbar on the "View" menu and then click on "Source" to view the source of any individual Web page. You can also use Notepad to edit your HTML source code.

This is a simple basic layout of a standard HTML Web page:

<!DOCTYPE HTML PUBLIC "-//W3C//DTD HTML 4.01//EN"
<HTML>

```
<HEAD>
<TITLE>This is the Title of My Web Page</TITLE>
</HEAD>
<BODY>
<P>This is my Web page!
</BODY>
</HTML>
```

Every Web page conforms to this basic page layout, and all contain the opening **<head>** and closing **</head>** tags. Meta tags will be inserted between the opening and closing head tags. Other than the page title tag, which is shown above, no other information in the head section of your Web pages is viewed by website visitors as they browse your Web pages. The title tag is displayed across the top of the browser window and is used to provide a description of the contents of the Web page displayed. Meta tags provide a way for you to provide all search engines with information about your website.

Meta tags provide a wealth of information, but understand that not all search engines use all of them. As mentioned, Meta tags are added to the **<head>** section of your HTML page and generally look like this:

```
<!DOCTYPE html>
<html>
 <head>
  <meta charset="utf-8">
  <meta name="Description" CONTENT="Author: B.C. Brown,
Category: Books, Price: $14.95, Length: 345 pages">
   <meta name="google-site-verification" content="+nxGUDJ4QpAZ5
l9Bsjdi102tLVC21AIh5d1Nl23908vVuFHs34="/>
<meta name="verify-v1" content="Fz/UednychCtkopP69siBGLSyjE
qkS4HsKcPhwxD+xo=" >
<meta name="googlebot" content="1FF29D1C495C9FE079361A03
09BFC30B">
<link rel="P3Pv1" href="http://www.atlantic-pub.com/w3c/
p3p.xml">
```

<meta name="msvalidate.01" content="15E2EDACAB77E9692D A3EE80A834A0B1" > <title>The Ultimate Guide to Search Engine Marketing </title>
<meta name="robots" content="ALL">

Google understands the following meta tags (and related items). You will notice that **<meta name="description">** and **<meta name="keywords">** are not listed, although they are both used by other search engines:

<meta name="description" content="Short description of the Page"/>
- The description tag is a "summary" of your page in text form and is used by some search engines to index your Web page.

<title>The Title of the Page show in Search Engine Results</title>
- The title is displayed on the top of your browser window and is used by some search engines to index your Web page.

<meta name="robots" content="..., ..." />
- This instructs Web crawlers to not index the page.

<meta name="googlebot" content="..., ..." />
- This controls the behavior of search engine crawling and indexing.

<meta name="google-site-verification" content="..." />
- This is used to verify site ownership.

<meta http-equiv="Content-Type" content="...; charset=..."/>
- This is used to define content type and character set.

<meta http-equiv="refresh" content="...;url=..."/>
- This is used as a redirect to another Web page or website.

The title tag

This is the first tag a search engine spider will read, so it is critical that the content you put in the title tag accurately represents the content of the corresponding Web page. Whatever text you place in the title tag — between the **<title>** and **</title>** tags — will appear in the reverse bar of an individual's browser when they view your Web page. In the example above, the title of the Web page to the page visitor would read as "This is the Title of My Web Page." Titles should accurately describe the focus of that particular page and might also include your site or business name.

The title tag is also used as the words to describe your page when someone adds it to their "Favorites" list or "Bookmarks" list in popular browsers, such as Internet Explorer or Mozilla Firefox®. The title tag is the single most important tag in regard to search engine rankings. The title tag should be limited to under 55 characters of text between the opening and closing HTML tags.

All major Web crawlers will use the text of your title tag as the text for the title of your page in their result listings. Since the title and description tags typically appear in the search results page after completing a keyword search in the Web browser, it is critical that they be clearly and concisely written to attract the attention of site visitors. Not all search engines are alike; some will display the title and description tags in search results but use page content alone for ranking.

The description tag

The description tag enables you to control the description of your individual Web pages when the search engine crawlers index and spider the website. The description tag should be no more than 250 characters. This is an important meta tag, since many major search engines use it in some capacity for site indexing. A page's description meta tag gives Google and other search engines a summary of what the page is about. Google Webmaster Tools provides you with a content analysis section, which will notify you if your meta tags are too short, too long, or duplicated too many times.

It is important to understand that search engines are not all the same, and that they index, spider, and display different search results for the same website. For example, Google ignores the description tag and generates its own description based on the content of the Web page. Although some major engines may disregard your description tags, it is highly recommended that you include the tag on each Web page, since some search engines do rely on the tag to index your site.

The keywords tag

The keywords tag is not used much anymore, as it has been heavily abused in the past. Today, page content is critical, while keywords tags are limited or not used at all by spiders indexing your site. However, it is recommended that you at least use the keywords tag in moderation. Using the best keywords to describe your website helps Internet users to find your site in search engines. The keywords tag allows you to provide relevant text words or word combinations for crawler-based search engines to index.

The keywords tag is only supported by a few Web crawlers. Since most Web crawlers are content-based, meaning they index your site based on the actual page content instead of your meta tags, you need to incorporate as many keywords as possible into the actual content of your Web pages. For the engines that support the description tag, it is beneficial to repeat keywords within the description tag that appear on your actual Web pages — this increases the value of each keyword in relevance to your website page content.

The keywords you want to use in the tag **<meta name="keywords" content="** should go between the quotation marks after the **"content="** portion of the tag. It is suggested that you include up to 25 words or phrases, with each word or phrase separated by a comma.

To determine which keywords are the best to use on your site, visit **www.wordtracker.com**, a paid service that will walk you through this process. Wordtracker's suggestions are based on over 300 million keywords and phrases that people have used over the previous 130 days. A free alternative for determining which keywords are best is Google Rankings, which can be found at **http://googlerankings.com/dbkindex.php**.

The robots tag

The robots tag lets you specify whether a particular page within your site should or should not be indexed by a search engine, or whether links should or should not be followed by search engine spiders. To keep search engine spiders from indexing a page, add the following text between your tags:

<meta name="robots" content="noindex">

To keep search engine spiders from following links on your page, add the following text between your tags:

<meta name="robots" content="nofollow">

You do not need to use variations of the robots tag to get your pages indexed since your pages will be spidered and indexed by default; however, some Web designers include the following robots tag on all Web pages:

<meta name="robots" content="all">

ALT tags

The **<alt>** tag is an HTML tag that provides alternative text when non-textual elements, typically images, cannot be displayed. The **<alt>** tag is not part of the head of a Web page, but proper use of this tag is critically important in SEO. The **<alt>** tags are often left off of Web pages, but they can be extremely useful for a variety of reasons:

- They provide detail or text description for an image or the destination of a hyperlinked image.
- They enable and improve access for people with disabilities.
- They provide information for individuals who have graphics turned off when they surf the Internet.
- They improve navigation when a graphics-laden site is viewed over a slow connection, enabling visitors to make navigation choices before graphics are fully rendered in the browser.

Text-based Web content is not the only thing that increases your ranking in the search engines; images are just as important, because these images can also include keywords and key phrases that relate to your business. If any visitors to your website have the image option off, they will still be able to see the text associated with your images. The **<alt>** tags should be placed anywhere where there is an image on your website. It is key to avoid being too wordy when describing your images, but include accurate keywords within the tags. The keywords and key phrases that you use in **<alt>** tags should be the same keywords and phrases that you use in meta description tags, meta keyword tags, title tags, and in the Web content on your Web pages. A brief description of the image, along with one or two accurate keywords and key phrases, is all you need to optimize the images on your Web pages for search engines.

Most major Web design applications include tools to simplify the process of creating **<alt>** tags. For example, in Microsoft Visual Studio®, right-click on the image and choose "Properties" and the general tab; you can then enter **<alt>** tag text information. Most website development applications actually prompt you for **<alt>** tags as you add images. To enter **<alt>** tag information directly into a Web page, go to the HTML view and enter them after the **<img>** tags in the following format:

<img border="0" src="images/manatee.jpg" width="300" height="103" alt="Florida Manatees are a protected species that roam freely in our local waters"></b></font></p>

You may also use the comment tag, which is primarily used by Web designers as a place to list comments relative to the overall website design, primarily to assist other Web developers who may work on the site in the future. A comment tag looks like this:

<!-begin body section for Crystal River Florida Vacation House Rental>

SEO checklist

The following checklist can serve as a helpful reminder to ensure that you have not forgotten any important details along the way.

- **Title tag:** Make sure that your title tag includes keywords and key phrases that are relevant to your product or service.
- **Meta tags:** Make sure that your tags are optimized to ensure a high ranking in search engine lists. This includes meta description

tags and meta keyword tags. Your meta description tag should have an accurate description so that people browsing the Internet are interested enough to visit your website. Do not forget to use the misspelled and plural forms of words in your meta tags.

- **ALT tag:** Add <alt> tags to all the images that you use on your Web pages.
- **Web content:** Use accurate, rich keywords and key phrases throughout the content of all your Web pages.
- **Density of keywords:** Use a high ratio of keywords and key phrases throughout your Web pages.
- **Links and affiliates:** Make sure that you have used links, and affiliates if you are using them, effectively for your website.
- **Web design:** Make sure that your website is fast to load and easy to navigate for visitors. You want to encourage people to stay and read your website by making sure that it is clean and looks good.
- **Avoid spamming:** Double-check to make sure that you are not using any spamming offenses on your website. This includes cloaking, hidden text, doorway pages, obvious repeated keywords and key phrases, link farms, and mirror pages.

Always be prepared to update and change the look, feel, and design of your Web pages to make sure that you are using SEO techniques wherever and whenever possible.

Establishing Links with Reputable Websites

You should try to find quality sites that are compatible and relevant to your website's topic, and approach the of those sites for link exchanges. For example, if you were maintaining a website to sell hair care products, forming a relationship with another website which wrote hair care guides and gave tips would give you something to post on your own site's front page and also drive their site traffic toward your website. This will give you highly targeted traffic and will improve your score with search engines. Your goal is to identify relevant pages that will link to your site, effectively yielding you quality inbound links. However, be wary of developing or creating a "link farm" or "spam link website" that offers massive quantities of link exchanges, but with little or no relevant content for your site visitors or the search engines.

Do not link to your competitors.

How to establish a reciprocal link program (back-links)

Begin your link exchange program by developing a title or theme to use as part of your link request invitations. This should be directly relevant to your site's content. Since most sites use your provided title or theme in the link to your website, be sure you include relevant keywords that will improve your website optimization and search engine rankings. Keep track of your inbound and outbound link requests.

Begin your search for link exchange partners by searching a popular engine, such as Google, and entering key phrases, such as "link with us," "add site," "suggest a site," or "add your link." If these sites are relevant, they are ideal for your reciprocal link program, since they, too, are actively seeking link partners. Make sure that the of other sites actually link back to your site, as it is common that reciprocal links are not completed. If they do not link back to you in a reasonable amount of time, remove your link to them, as you are only helping them with their search engine rankings.

You may want to use **www.linkpopularity.com** as a free Web source for evaluating the total number of websites that link to your site.

Submitting your site to other search engines

Most websites have mechanisms for you to add your website to their database to be indexed and included in their search engine results — for free. For example, go to www.google.com and type in "Submit URL;" then start going down the list of links. You will find hundreds of excellent links to add your website to a variety of search engines. Here are a few to get you started:

- www.dmoz.org/add.html
- www.scrubtheweb.com/addurl.html
- http://search.msn.com.sg/docs/submit.aspx
- http://siteexplorer.search.yahoo.com/submit
- http://addurl.altavista.com/addurl/default
- www.homerweb.com/submit_site.html

Other ways to generate website traffic and inbound links

Become an expert in your specialty. Post entries into blogs, forums, and discussion groups. Establish yourself as an industry expert by writing and submitting articles to the dozens of free article distribution sites on the Web. You can get started at **www.articlealley.net**. Include your name, URL, and contact information; you will be amazed at the viral distribution of royalty-free articles throughout the Web.

Press releases are another way to publish information about your company while including links and other contact information to drive traffic to your site. Strive to get quality inbound links from ".edu," ".org," or other public, non-profit organization sites. These quality links tend to weigh heavier than commercial ones in Google.

SEO & Images

Naming your image properly will help optimize it for search engines, allowing users to easily find the image. The mouseover text description, or tooltip, of an image is another factor to consider for SEO. Properly tagging images drives search engine traffic to your website. Proper tagging will also aid users with images disabled to navigate the site without trouble. Try the following code without having **"SampleImage.png"** in the local directory:

```
<img src="SampleImage.png" alt="Sample Image"/>
```

The Web page will display a blank square with the "image not found" symbol and the text from the **<alt>** tag. The **<alt>** tag still shows up whether or not the image is there. This adds an extra layer of protection to your Web page since it is still usable even without the images. The **<alt>** tag will also make your website more accessible to users with disabilities, since it is compatible with most assistive software such as Microsoft Narrator.

You can further improve accessibility by using "D" links and **longdesc**.

<img src="SampleImage.png" alt="A sample image showing the use of HTML attributes" longdesc="sampleImageDescription.htm"><a href="sampleImageDescription.htm" title="Sample Image">D</a>

The page that the **longdesc** points to can contain a further description of the image, allowing you to describe the image in higher detail while squeezing in a few more keywords related to the image. A sample description could look something like this:

"The image shows a sample image used commonly to demonstrate sample features. The sample image is ambiguous in nature. The blank background blends in nicely with the blank foreground. It also uses the PNG format, referring to another part of the article. The image shows how simple tags can be decorated to make it more accessible while also optimizing it for search engines."

The **<alt>** tag can contain a basic description of the image with a few keywords, while the **longdesc** should either be a longer sentence or should link to a better description of the image. One of the main differences between **alt** and **longdesc** is that the description in the **<alt>** tag is visible when you mouse over the image, while the description in **longdesc** is not.

Do not, however, stuff either of the descriptions with keywords. Modern search engines use spam filters that look for the excessive use of catch phrases without any real content. The **alt** and the **longdesc** should be a textual replacement for the image without simply being a list of tags. Also note that decorative eye candy is usually not tagged. This is to help keep the HTML page simple and clean without any unnecessary information. Ask yourself if the speed and bandwidth costs are worth the extra tag.

Another factor that search engines consider is the file type. JPEGs are often associated with photographs, while GIFs are assumed to be site graphics. Make sure to choose the right file type so that your images are categorized correctly. Using just one copy of an image and then referencing it consistently throughout your website could help its page rank in search engines like Google.

SEO Companies

If you are not up to the challenge of tackling your website SEO needs, it may be to your benefit to hire a search engine optimization company so that the optimization techniques that you use are properly implemented and monitored.

There are many search engine optimization companies on the Internet that can ensure that your rankings in search engines will increase when you hire them. One word of caution is to be wary of claims of anyone who can "guarantee" you top 10 rankings in all major search engines — these claims are baseless. If you have the budget to hire an SEO company, it may be extremely beneficial for you since (a) you know the experts at SEO techniques are taking care of you and (b) you can focus your energies on other important marketing aspects of your business.

Choosing the right SEO company

Look at the business reputation of the SEO companies that you are thinking about hiring. Ask the company for customer references that you can check out on your own. You can also contact the Better Business Bureau® in their local city or state to confirm their reputation at **www.bbb.org**.

Do a search engine check on each company to see where they fall into the rankings of major search engines such as AOL, MSN[SM], and Google. If the company does not rank high in these search engines, how can you expect them to launch you and your business to the top of the ranks?

You want to choose a company that actually has people working for them and not just computers. While computers are great for generating the algorithms that are needed to use search engine programs, they cannot replace people when it comes to doing the market research that is needed to ensure that the company uses the right keywords for your business.

You need to make sure that the company uses ethical ranking procedures. There are some ranking procedures that are considered to be unethical, and some search engines will ban or penalize your business website from their engines if they find out that you, or the search engine optimization company that you have hired, are using these methods. Some of these unethical ranking procedures include doorway pages, cloaking, or hidden text, as we have discussed previously.

The search engine optimization company that you decide to hire should be available to you at all times by phone or by email. You want to be able to contact someone when you have a question or a problem to which you need a solution.

If you decide to hire a certain SEO company, it is important that you work with the company instead of just handing over all the responsibility to them. The next section contains suggestions for how you should interact with your SEO provider.

How to interact with your SEO company

Listen carefully to the advice of the account manager. They should have the expertise for which you hired them and typically can provide factual and supportable recommendations. SEO companies are expected to know what to do to increase your ranking in the search engines; if they fail to deliver, you need to choose another company.

If you are going to be making any changes to your website design, make sure that you let your account manager know. This is because many times any changes that you make can have an effect on the already optimized Web pages. Your rankings in search engines may start to plummet unless you work with your search engine optimization account manager to optimize any changes to your website design that you feel are necessary to make.

Keep in mind that SEO companies can only work with the data and information that you have on your Web pages. This means that if your website has little information, it will be difficult for any search engine optimization company to pull your business up in the search engine rankings. SEO relies on keywords and key phrases that are contained on Web pages that are filled with as much Web content as possible. This may mean adding two or three pages of Web content that contain tips, resources, or other useful information that is relevant to your product or service.

Never change any of your meta tags once they have been optimized without the knowledge or advice of your account manager. Your SEO company is the professional when it comes to making sure that your meta tags are optimized with the right keywords and key phrases needed to increase your search engine ranking. You will not want to change meta tags that have already been proven successful.

Be patient when it comes to seeing the results. It can take anywhere from 30 to 60 days before you start to see yourself pushed up into the upper ranks of search engines.

Keep a close eye on your ranking, even after you have reached the top. Information on the Internet changes at a moment's notice, and this includes your position within your target market.

General SEO Tips and Tricks

Here are some tips to get the best results from search engines.

Word count

Make sure you have at least 200 words of content on each page. Although you may have some Web pages where it may be difficult to put even close to 200 words, you should try to come as close as you can, since search engines will give better results to pages with more content.

Keywords

Make sure that the text content you have on your Web pages contains those important keywords and key phrases that you have researched. These are the most common phrases potential customers might use to search for your products or services, which will help you to obtain competitive rankings. The keywords and phrases that you use in the content of your website should also be included in the tags of your website, such as meta tags, **<alt>** tags, head tags, and title tags. Ensure that your title and **<alt>** tags are descriptive and accurate.

Many websites use a left-hand navigational bar. This is standard on many sites, but the algorithm that many spiders and Web crawlers use will have this read before the main content of your website. Make sure you use keywords within the navigation, and if using images for your navigational buttons, use **<alt>** tags loaded with the appropriate keywords.

Do not list keywords in order within the content of your Web page. It is fine to incorporate keywords into the content of your Web pages, but do not simply cut and paste keywords from your meta tags into the content of your Web pages. This will be viewed as spam by the search engine, and you will be penalized.

Readability

After incorporating keywords and phrases, make sure that your content is still understandable and readable in plain language. A common mistake is to stuff a website full of so many keywords and phrases that the page is no longer understandable or readable to the website visitor — a sure way to lose potential customers quickly.

Also, make sure you check for broken links and correct HTML.

Add more Web pages

Add extra pages to your website, even if they may not at first seem directly relevant. The more Web pages that you have, the more pages search engines will have to be able to find you and link to. Extra pages can include tips, tutorials, product information, resource information, and any other information or data that is pertinent to the product or service that you are selling.

Avoid frames and high-end design applications

Never use frames, a technology that I have not seen used in many years. Search engines have difficulty following them, as will your site visitors. Likewise, avoid old technology using tables and other basic HTML Web design. Limit the use of Flash® and other high-end design applications, as most search engines have trouble reading and following them, which will hurt in search engine listings.

Create a sitemap

Create a sitemap of all pages within your website. While not necessarily the most useful tool to site visitors, it does greatly improve the search engine's capacity to properly index all your website pages. Ensure that all Web pages have links back to the homepage and be sure that every Web page is reachable from at least one static text link.

Breadcrumbs

Breadcrumb navigation is good for user-friendly site navigation and SEO. Essentially, breadcrumbs are a form of text-based navigation that shows where the current Web page you are viewing is located in the site hierarchy. It contains shortcuts to the next level of a website and lets you jump multiple layers at one time. An example of breadcrumb navigation may be: "Home > Real Estate > Home Inspections > Books."

SEO don'ts

Avoid tricks intended to improve search engine rankings. A good rule of thumb is whether you would feel comfortable explaining what you have done to a website that competes with you. Another useful test is to ask, "Does this help my users? Would I do this if search engines did not exist?"

Do not create multiple pages, sub-domains, or domains with substantially similar content and do not use "doorway" pages created for search engines.

Do not try to trick the search engines with hidden or invisible text or other techniques. If you do, the search engine may penalize you. Avoid black hat SEO techniques, they ultimately do more damage than good in search engine results.

Meta tags

Do not replicate meta tags. In other words, you should only have one meta tag for each type of tag. Using multiple tags, such as more than one title tag, will cause search engines to penalize you.

Implement the use of the **robots.txt** file on your Web server. This file tells crawlers which directories can or cannot be crawled. You can find out more information on this file by visiting **www.robotstxt.org/wc/faq.html**.

Design

Design pages so they are easily navigated by search engine spiders and Web crawlers. Search engines prefer text over graphics and HTML over other page formats.

Use Cascading Style Sheets to design your website and be sure to include "Copyright and "About Us" pages. Search engines prefer CSS-based sites and typically score them higher in the search rankings.

Do not use text on your Web page as the page's background color. This is another way of keyword "stuffing," and all search engines will detect it and penalize you.

The next chapter will explain the fundamentals and details of web page design.

Chapter 6

Website Design

*I*n many cases, websites are built by the business owner to save money; generally, there is nothing wrong with that. By using templates and tools from major sites such as **www.godaddy.com**, you can create beautiful websites without any design knowledge or experience. Sometimes, business owners decide to design and build their own websites using commercial Web design software. This is great; however, as your own Webmaster, it is important that the site you design is as polished and professional as a larger business site would be, because an unprofessional-looking website is liable to drive away customers.

What qualifies someone to be a "Web designer?"

The answer depends on whom you are asking. I started designing websites in 1997 using basic HTML to code pages. Over the years, I increased my skills and started to use Web development applications to improve the quality of my websites, interact with databases, and automate processes.

Web design applications such as Microsoft® Office FrontPage®, NetObjects® Fusion™, and early versions of Adobe Dreamweaver® are amazing technological advances for Web designers. If you are a beginner working with basic HTML code or using the latest version of Dreamweaver CS, you can build a website. Over time, you will increase in proficiency and skill. You may not want to build your own website in every case, since there are many times that it may be too difficult to do or you may want that professional, polished look that only a real designer can deliver.

Websites can be expensive, but they do not have to be incredibly difficult or challenging to build. I built my first website with no experience, and while it was probably not the best looking site I have ever developed, it served its purpose well.

Website Basics

There are really only two basic components to a website. They are your Web pages (the compilation of HTML pages you have designed), the images, content, and other information that will be displayed on your pages. Your individual Web pages create your website.

Your website can be as small as one page, or it can be thousands of pages. All websites have a home page. The homepage is the page that site visitors are taken to when they type in your website domain name into a browser. From your home page, visitors can navigate your site and visit other Web pages on your site.

All websites consistently change as new content and other Web pages are added, so while you may complete your initial design and publish your Web page, your site will require further maintenance, updating, and revisions. The most challenging part of creating a website is developing a blueprint for how you want your site to be organized; this includes what pages it will contain, how content will be organized, and how your pages will be laid out in relation to others as you design your navigation and page relationships.

Design your pages individually, formulate what each page should include, and then you can flesh out the actual content and site design later. You can do this work on a piece of paper or even with sticky notes on the wall since this will help you visualize the layout.

One of the first things to recognize when building a website is that you will either need some type of software program or you will have to learn HTML coding and build your site from the ground up. For those determined to learn all of the coding necessary to build and maintain a website, we will explore these options later in the book, particularly in Chapters 4-6, as well as look at a variety of software options to help you with your design goals.

Most of those interviewed for this book said that starting out with the availability of adding interactive content and items to your website is the best route to take. Even if you do not plan to use them in the beginning, you will most likely use them down the road. When approaching your website design, it is usually best to keep colors and fonts at a basic level.

There are four main components of a website:

1) **Domain name:** This name is registered and corresponds with where your website is physically located on a Web server; it is also used for your email accounts.

2) **Web hosting:** This is the physical "storage" of your Web pages on a server that is connected to the Internet. This machine "serves" your Web pages as they are requested by a Web browser, and this machine has an IP address. The Domain Name System (DNS) translates your domain name into your Web account IP address and serves up the appropriate Web pages as requested. Your domain registry will store the IP address of your DNS. The concept may be difficult to understand; however, it is actually quite simple. Your website consists of a series of Web pages. These Web pages are files, which are stored on a Web server along with images and other content on a Web server. This Web server has an IP Address that is a unique machine name for that Web server. DNS servers translate your domain name (for example, **www.mywebsite.com**) into the IP address where your site is

actually hosted. Your Web server then serves your page to the Web browser of your site visitor. Therefore, it is critical that your Domain Name Registry account (the company where you bought your domain name) is updated with the physical IP address of your Domain Name Server (provided by your hosting company). This ensures that anyone who searches or types in your domain name into a browser window will be directed to the Domain Name Server, which then translates this to the IP address of your site, ensuring your Web pages are properly displayed at all times.

3) **Web pages:** These are the Web pages you created and published to your Web server. You can create Web pages with programs such as Microsoft Office®, Microsoft Visual Studio, Adobe Dreamweaver, and many other free design applications.

4) **Optional items:** These might include shopping carts, forms, or databases. While none of these are required for websites, you will find your needs may change over time, so keep that in mind during the planning process.

Web Design Hardware Requirements

You do not need to invest significant funds to be able to create your own website. You only need to have a reliable computer. Websites can be designed and tested on your personal or business computer, and you do not need to have your own Web server — in fact, you should avoid this cost and pay for a shared Web hosting account with a reputable provider. Many Web designers work exclusively from their laptop computers, which is a great way of having mobility so you can keep working on your Web pages no matter where you are. My minimum recommendation for a laptop is an Intel® Core™2 Duo Processor, although you do not need the fastest model on the market. In fact, any mid-range processor will more than meet your needs for a long time. On the desktop, Quad-Core models are highly suggested because of the ability to effortlessly multitask.

You do need to have a fast, reliable Internet connection. It really does not matter what you choose, as long as it is high-speed broadband that is reliable and cost-effective. Do not cut corners on your Internet speed, and do not use dial-up, because it is far too slow and you will become frustrated with its limitations very quickly. You may want to use an external hard drive for regular backups; programs like Carbonite™ are extremely useful for full backups of websites. You can get a free trial of Carbonite at **www.carbonite.com**.

For graphics editing, popular options include Corel® Paint Shop Pro® X8 and the latest version of Adobe Photoshop®. Some well-known examples of Web design software include Microsoft Expression® Web (while out of date it still has several features users are likely to come across), and Adobe Dreamweaver CS. Other design applications such as Serif™ WebPlus X8 offer great tools for the novice designer. That said, you do not need to invest significant funds into advanced Web design applications. There are also many freeware, or free software, offerings for both your Web design and graphics editing needs, which will be discussed later on. Also, it is important to recognize that most Web hosting companies also provide easy to use website templates as part of your hosting package, enabling you to create a great looking site quickly and easily.

In the Web design and development communities, there used to be two distinct groups: the Microsoft group and the Adobe group. The Adobe group used Adobe Dreamweaver CS. Most Web developers consider Dreamweaver to be the professional Web designer's product of choice. In comparison, many used to consider Microsoft Office products to be the beginner's tool. Microsoft changed that with the release of Microsoft Expression Web, which matched up favorably with Dreamweaver. The release of this product is no longer supported, and a free download of the software is available from Microsoft.

Microsoft's more recent software, Microsoft Visual Studio, is a good beginner's tool that can repair any common errors you make with its code editor. However, Visual Studio does not always function as effectively outside of other Microsoft software and servers, which can prove to be a hindrance or cause user difficulties depending on that user's personal settings. Adobe Dreamweaver is a much more popular and sophisticated program, but it also costs you much more money for its tools than Visual Studio, which is a free download for the most basic version.

Adobe products are generally considered more sophisticated, but a bit more expensive to get. As a business owner, it is up to you to decide whether you want to spend more time working on fixing and designing your site with Visual Studio, or if you wish to spend more money on Dreamweaver for an easier experience. I would personally suggest Dreamweaver, because the ease of access by the larger public makes it worth a little extra start-up capital.

Website Hosting

Web hosting is a bit more complex than simply buying storage space, though that is essentially what you are doing. You are paying a provider to "host" your website on their Web server. The Web server has special software, which lets the server operate as a Web server. As pages are requested from your website, it "serves" them to the website visitor.

A Web server can host hundreds of websites simultaneously, which is how you can buy Web hosting services relatively inexpensively. Web servers have a unique IP address to identify the machine your site is hosted on. DNS servers translate your domain name into that IP address and this is how your Web pages are served to your site visitors. If you type in **www.atlantic-pub. com** (Atlantic Publishing Company) into your browser, the DNS server which is specified in your domain name registry translates this URL into the corresponding IP address for the website, and the home page for Atlantic Publishing will appear.

In most cases, you will buy hosting from a commercial service provider, though you can host your own website on your own servers. Commercial web site hosting is cheap and reliable, and puts the burden of supporting the equipment and maintenance on the service provider. Let your hosting provider deal with all the costs and challenges associated with keeping your website available; it is not worth investing in your own Web server equipment.

A Web host is the foundation you will need to build your website; without it, you cannot begin to implement your design plans. The Web host provides you with disk space, email accounts, and secured shopping carts. Although this book is all about finding the least expensive or free way to build a website, there are times when going the free route might end up costing you more money and headaches in the long run.

One of the key factors of using a free Web host might include limiting your ability to create interactive pages or having enough space to build the site you have designed in your planning stage. In most cases, none will support e-commerce or other advanced Web development needs. While there are "free" Web hosting services available, most of them push advertising onto your website and limit your creativity by forcing you to select from a limited number of website templates. If you want to build a site that contains 25 pages, many of the free Web hosts will not support that many pages or offer the ability to increase to that number as your website needs growth. The last thing you want is to build a site and then have to move it because the host you chose does not offer the support or tools you need to maintain it. Moving a site is not only costly, but time-consuming as well.

You can use Google or any other search engine to find reputable hosting service providers; you will be able to choose from both free and costly providers. Here are a few examples: **www.doteasy.com**, **www.mister.net**, and **www.webs.com**. Each of these sites has specific limitations, so you should carefully review them before you decide if you want a free option or one that will cost you money.

As you will find, feature-rich Web hosting packages can be readily obtained for under $100 a year. An index of Web hosting companies is provided in the back of this book. Applied Innovations (**www.appliedi.net**) is one such company. Their ValuePlus™ hosting solution features multiple domain support so you can actually host two individual domains on the same account. When you own and host your own domain name, your hosting account comes with email accounts as well.

Virtual dedicated server vs. dedicated server

At **www.godaddy.com**, hosting plans are relatively cheap, and you can upgrade to a virtual dedicated server with full administrative access or sign up for a dedicated server with administrative access. A virtual dedicated server has several businesses using it, but all are separated from each other by allotments of space and security, whereas a dedicated server is all yours — no one else uses any portion of it.

A virtual dedicated server is suitable 99 percent of the time. There is a steep increase in price between the two, and unless you have a need for a massive e-commerce enabled website with thousands of site visitors simultaneously, there is no need for a dedicated server — save your money. All plans offer full customer support and include routers, servers, firewalls, and Google Webmaster tools. As with most hosting sites, the costs can rise exponentially if you pile on the extras. No matter what site you use, research and read the fine print to understand exactly what you will get with the different packages. One thing to look for is whether any site-building tools and templates are included in the package you choose if you want to create quick and easy websites on the fly.

When using a free Web hosting server, it appears that the Internet spiders find the advertising on the pages, but often not your site content, which is one reason many people say free hosting does not work as well as commercial hosting. Free hosting and software sound like great concepts, but using them is one of the first pitfalls Web builders recommend against, because, as the old adage goes, you get what you pay for. Free services might not be worth the headaches you will face as you begin building your site.

According to Lisa Irby, the disadvantages of using a free hosting service far outweigh the advantages. On her website, Lisa emphatically writes, "After my nightmare experiences with using free Web hosts, I vowed to never go the free route again, because it is definitely better to invest a small amount of money." The following list from Lisa's website at **www.2createawebsite. com/prebuild/create-free-website.html** illustrates the disadvantages of using a free Web hosting site to build your new website.

Using free hosting and software might sound like the route to take, but when doing so, remember that it usually means you are getting exactly what you paid for, which is nothing. Another thing to remember is that despite the claims that these free Web hosting sites offer, they are not cheap to run because someone has to pay for the space they are offering you for free. This could ultimately end up with the hosting site losing so much money that they fold or your website is overrun with advertising to pay for these "free" services. Typically, banners and pop-up ads are how these free Web hosts provide you with a free site. Most, if not all, free Web hosting sites do not offer any guarantees that protect you against your pages being shut down without notice or suddenly changing their terms and converting to a paid hosting system.

Another downfall to free Web hosting is that search engines have a more difficult time finding your site, and in many cases, simply do not index it and include it in their databases. When you are building a website to make money, those search engine results are critical. You will never gain any momentum without the major search engines like Google and Yahoo! finding your website.

Here are the main reasons why "free" hosted websites are normally not found in search engines:

Too small and "unimportant"

Most free sites are generally small and are not of significant value, because they do not contain a solid theme or concept. They usually have more links to external sites than to their own internal pages. Content is one of the specific types of information search engines look for, and this means content that has a particular focus and a large number of pages.

Minimal updating of site content

Many people build a website, publish it, and never update it. Search engines are getting smarter, and the formulas they use to determine page rankings might not recognize free Web hosting sites. When a site is shown as being hosted on a free Web host server, the search engines appear to have greater difficulty indexing them, or they just exclude them entirely.

No links pointing to the website

Many or Web directories will not link to a site built on a free host. One reason is these sites might not look professional, and few people want to link to a poorly developed site with pop-ups and banners all over the place; it creates a negative image for their site. Another issue is that most know that free sites generally have short life spans. These days, the kinds of websites linking to you are important for achieving a good search engine ranking as you will discover later in this book. The truth is that free websites get little respect on the Internet.

When choosing a hosting plan, remember to research the company and find out what types of customer service they offer, whether you can update your site when you want to, and what types of email accounts and support the host provides. On the website **www.top-10-web-hosting.com**, the ten best Web hosting sites according to their survey of 58,000 are ranked and updated daily.

Software Applications

There are dozens of software applications on the market to help you create websites quickly and easily. Some of these help automate the creation of HTML, while others let you create Web pages in a design environment where the HTML is written for you. This section will provide you with an extensive review of several of the most popular Web design applications on the market. Often, it simply comes down to personal preference or what you are most comfortable with.

Another available avenue is to use a content management system (CMS), such as Joomla!® or Mambo™. These programs offer tools to create, modify, and organize information on your website. As with any design project, you should compare your needs and wants with the features offered to help you choose the best product to deliver you with the results you need.

Other suggestions for simple website development may be through your Web hosting provider. Many offer custom templates and simple applications to expedite Web development and let you get a site created and hosted within hours. Hosting providers like Applied Innovations offer free page-building tools, a large amount of space for your website, and all of the interactive capabilities you may want to incorporate either now or later included with Web hosting fees. The only drawback of free applications such as these is that you are limited in creativity; it can be very difficult to "move" your site to another hosting platform if required at a future date.

This chapter will also give you an overview of some free HTML editors, such as Nvu and WYSIWYG, and whether you need these editors once you have built your site. Other topics will include learning what open-source software like WordPress™ and Joomla! offer, how they work, and how you can use them to create a platform for your website.

WordPress

WordPress, at **http://wordpress.com**, used to be just another free, open-source option for building a blog. Since the release of the 1st and 2nd editions of this book, the functionality of WordPress has greatly expanded into a full content management system (CMS), which is used by companies, news organizations and even local governments for their websites. Currently, the WordPress framework boasts 24% usage as a CMS system on the Internet — that is more than every other option on our list. It is also open source, meaning that the source code of WordPress is available for anyone to study, modify, and customize to their heart's content.

WordPress is especially friendly to new users due to an active support community; because the software is open source, most users are writing their own patches to the software and basically forming their own support group for new users to develop. The net wide proliferation allows for thousands of free plugins and themes to be accessible to the public, which helps you to uniquely customize your own site. This is an attractive option to some people, because its opening interface is free and easy to use, but you will need to pay to make your own domain name and use some of the greater customization features.

Joomla!

Joomla! is a CMS that helps users build websites. Not only is this software free to use, but the Joomla! site, **www.joomla.org**, also provides a forum where users can find additional support and answers to their questions. Joomla! allows users to download an easy-to-install package that provides website builders with the ability to add, edit, and update images. It utilizes a simple browser interface that allows users to upload new items, job postings, images, and staff pages. It also allows users to create a subscriptions feature, which is helpful in learning who visits your website.

This software offers multiple applications to allow website builders to create add-ons and extensions. Some of the examples listed on the website include form builders, business or organizational directories, document management, image and multimedia galleries, e-commerce and shopping cart engines, calendars, forums and chat software, blogging software, directory services, email newsletters, data collection and reporting tools, and banner advertising systems. To find additional options, go to **www.extensions.joomla.org**. Joomla! is a great free, open-source application you may wish to consider if you want a robust, flexible CMS.

Homestead®

Homestead, found at **www.homestead.com**, offers many options for making your site extremely simple, interactive, and user-friendly. Homestead is designed to work with small businesses and helps them reach out to find new customers, while also getting their sites noticed by some of the major search engines like Yahoo! and Google. This site provides more than 2,000 website templates, which you can either use individually or to create your own customized template. You can also start from scratch and build your own template.

A unique aspect of Homestead is that it offers you the capability to edit text right on the Web page or completely replace it with your own content by pasting it on the page. You can upload images from your computer's hard drive or use some of the more than 1.1 million royalty-free images available to you.

Homestead will also provide support in transferring your current domain name and even help you to create a link to redirect your traffic to your new site. You can add forms to collect information from your visitors so that you can send them email promotions and newsletters, or you can get a guest book and allow your visitors to post comments. The site includes a PayPal® shopping cart you can set up to make it easy for your customers to purchase items or services without having to use a credit card, and it has an e-commerce option if you want to set up a larger business site. Homestead is a great option if you do not want to learn a Web design application and want to create an attractive site quickly.

The SeaMonkey® Project

The SeaMonkey Project is an open-source project by Mozilla, the company who manages and distributes the popular Internet browser, FireFox. The SeaMonkey Project (**www.seamonkey-project.org**) includes: a Web browser, an email and newsgroup client, an HTML editor, an Internet relay chat (IRC), and Web development tools. The SeaMonkey Internet Suite is completely free and is a great way to learn HTML. The SeaMonkey Internet Suite is available for Windows, Mac, and Linux-based systems. It also supports CSS and other advanced languages.

The SeaMonkey Composer, its WYSIWYG Web design program and HTML editor, features four different views in its user interface: Normal (WYSIWYG), HTML tags, HTML code, and browser preview. Because the program is open-source, there is a large community of support and plenty of documentation to help people who are working with SeaMonkey.

Website Design Fundamentals

One website designer was approached by a small business owner who needed to generate a brand for five websites. The designer was awarded the project not because they were offering the best rate for the sites, although they were, but because they immediately had the idea that the sites would work best as part of a brand if they were all designed according to a template. For the Web designer, this meant that only one template needed to be created, and it could be applied to all five of the websites the client needed.

Set a series of goals for each of your website design projects. Even if you are designing a relatively small site, establish some sort of schedule for your work. Determine your goals for the project with clear priorities and an understanding of what needs to be done when. When making a website, have more than one goal. For example, your immediate goal might be to develop a good homepage for the website so that you can at post this key page and have it running live relatively quickly.

On one level, a website design is an art form. It is the presentation of a concept or idea through the use of HTML coding, just as a painting is the presentation of an idea rendered using paints of various colors and other such mediums. To determine what type of pages you need for a Web design project, begin by determining what you expect your site to look like. Below are some considerations to take into account.

Organizing information

Under no circumstances should the site visitor be overwhelmed by the content. On one hand, your client might not want to develop a site that only has a few pages, a couple of pictures, and some spattering of text. On the other hand, you want to make sure that visitors are going to be sufficiently engaged to stay on the site. If there is too much information, you will probably have to think about creating a database to manage it all. Ordinarily, however, you should just think about developing a reasonable amount of information per page.

Most websites allow the user to simply sit back and read information. Most people spend their time online reading emails, catching up on the latest news, or occasionally tracking the financial markets. Online banking is big, too. Most of these activities fall somewhere between being entirely passive and being moderately passive, but that does not mean that people do not enjoy interactive websites and online activities. One of the ways you may be able to help your client keep their visitors on the site for the maximum amount of time is by finding some way to establish interactive activities on the site, whether that involves taking part in quizzes and survey polls or posting opinions on message boards for all to see. Also consider whether there is going to be any need for visitors to download content, such as video or audio files. For example, does your client want to stream videos?

User expectations

It is important in your design process to have a fairly clear idea of what people are going to want from the site when they visit. Most designers develop a practice of visiting websites that are, one way or another, similar to what they have been asked to design to get an idea of the features and functions people are going to be expecting. Since most users have a pretty clear idea of what they expect when they go looking for a particular website, it pays to look closely at what features are common between sites that are relevant to your project.

For the layout and multimedia content of the site you design, think about the best way to organize the information you need and the best way to meet the expectations of site visitors. Most sites have a unique homepage layout and two or three subordinate page designs.

Uniformity is important as an aesthetic element, too; people do not want to be overwhelmed by too many different page layouts any more than they want to be overwhelmed by too much information or too many multimedia features. Select the best elements — the top three or four page layouts, the best three or four colors, a single font style — and stick with them, applying a single resolution to all the pages. Websites are always a work in progress. There will constantly be products or information to add as well as updates to liven up your page and garner more page views. Aim for a site that is content-rich with images that catch the eye but is still easy to load and navigate. Many buttons, icons, and frames are good if they serve a purpose and make the site better, but if they serve as a distraction or a nuisance, people will look for a site that is less complex.

How your website will be seen

Just as there are some sites with too much, there are sites that are full of "under construction" pages and black holes. A messy, incomplete site will also steer the average browser to a better place, even if you do offer a better product or service. You never want to put a site up that is not ready for potential clients to see. They may think your work on their site will be incomplete and messy. A small, comprehensive website is a good foundation for better, more complex features as you learn more and grow. You can add things after you have established your basic website with all the necessities.

No amount of advertising or quality content can make up for an unattractive or sloppy design. Many websites have amazing content, but rarely get seen, because they are not appealing to a user at first glance. Take some time and plot out what you want to do on paper. List all of the links you want to have on your homepage. Color is crucial and should be given plenty of thought. A dark or heavily patterned background with a light text is hard to read and can divert people's attention from your products.

Many of us have had this problem and have had to resort to highlighting the text in order to read it. Someone who has searched and found other websites with similar content or products will pass your site up for one that is easier to read. Backgrounds should be white or a light color that dark text can stand out on. A dull website with no personality is not going to win you regular visitors either, so go with a combination that is universally liked.

Brightly colored text should only be used for highlighting words. If you choose to use a color other than black for your main text, make sure it is dark. If black is too plain, opt for a chocolate brown or navy on a light background. Color is an area where you, as a website designer, must choose good combinations. If a potential client sees your website and it has a color scheme they hate, they will probably find a better option that fits their tastes. It is crucial to find something most people will like, combinations that appeal to the eye and are easy to read. Black text with a white background is not the only option. Some combinations that work well, for instance, are a light blue with a dark chocolate colored text or a light green background with a navy blue text.

Also, keep in mind that every computer will view a page differently. Your site should be designed to look good no matter what the resolution or page view settings are. Using a percentage setting on your website can make it look good on a wide range of screens, not just yours. With 80 to 90 percent, your page will fill 80 to 90 percent of the screen width of every computer. Keep in mind that most monitors sold today are high-resolution, wide-screen LCD's. Some images you add can pose a problem if they are too big to fit within the percentage view. You should still check your page in all possible resolutions whenever you are going live for the first time or after you have added new pages.

One of the great benefits of using programs such as Dreamweaver is that they come with an arsenal of powerful tools for creating very impressive websites fairly easily. With these programs, it is also easy to create advanced effects such as rollover buttons, forms, navigation menus, and database integration. With the click of your mouse in Expression Web, you can create HTML web pages and a variety of other commonly used formats. It should be noted that Microsoft has discontinued support for Expression Web, so Adobe Dreamweaver is likely your best bet for a design tool. Dreamweaver (and other applications) can create styles for you, and you can customize your style sheets as you work through them. By using CSS to lay out your website, you eliminate the need to use HTML tables. You can also create amazing rollover navigation menus in a matter of minutes.

Make sure you are consistent throughout your website. "Clickable" text should be a different color than standard text. Fonts should be standardized throughout your site; generally, your Web pages should be based on the same template so that they appear seamless as they are served up one after the other by the Web server. CSS Sheets gives you enormous control over the look and organization of your Web pages, but you can still achieve this without the use of CSS.

Design for a 1024 x 768 resolution, which is the "standard" today.

The layout

The layout of a page and its components will make or break your website. You have limitless options in the layout of your website, but there are some general rules to follow that will make your page standard enough for even the extreme novice to use and understand easily. Avoid making things so busy that no one can focus on a single piece of your website. Including plenty of space where there is no graphics, text, or links is key to making a website clear and easy to maneuver. If you make it easy for your visitors to completely explore your site without any problems, they will come back for more.

The top of a page should be reserved as a marker for the name of the website or business. Think of it as a small billboard or a calling card. You can include a logo or another identifying image of your client's brand. Keep it simple and concise. The best positioning is in the middle third of a page. It will be front and center and impossible not to notice when a homepage loads. Make sure this area is neat, but still has personality and flair to give your website an identity. Make sure it is not a template or plain text that is boring and seen all around the Web.

Links to other pages on a website, called navigation buttons, are typically positioned in one of three ways. You can place them across the top, down the left side, or down the right side of each page. If you choose, you can place two sets of links at the top and bottom, allowing the visitor to click on links whether they have scrolled all the way down or all the way up the page.

Give your visitors options to increase the likelihood that they will move on to other pages on your site. If you have many different links on your homepage, you may choose to place them vertically on the left or right side just because of how many there are. A list down either side of the page is much neater than having several that stretch across the screen and out of the main view. If you can limit yourself to one or two lines at the top without having this problem, that is all right. If you have several links and the top of the page looks like a large block of links clustered together, go with a listing on the side.

Wording

Labels for links should also be short. They should convey the message of what it connects them to without being too wordy. For instance, instead of "All about us and our history as a company" go with "Company Bio" or "About Us." Whenever you add a link that is extremely long, the entire page is skewed off of its streamlined look. Keep it short and sweet.

People constantly play a game of "word association," especially when scanning through a site. If they are looking for something in particular, there may be a few words in their head that they are searching for. If someone is looking for information about your company's history, they will probably be scanning the page for "Bio," "About Us," or "History." Look at other websites and see what phrases pop up. It is a good idea to go with the grain. If you want to be unique, you can come up with your own link words, but make sure that people can make the connection you intend.

Typography

There are many free fonts available online. Choosing the right fonts and using them in the right places can really add to the style of a page. Be creative with titles, but be sure to choose a simple and easily readable font for the main text of the page.

The choice of font size is another important aspect of typography. Size 24 is commonly accepted as a good size for headlines and size 12 is common for regular text. Keep your audience in mind when choosing the font size. Font sizes should be relative. If your main text is going to be in a bigger text, then the headline must be much larger. The standard ratio between the body text and the title text is two to three times larger. Titles that are too large will attract attention, but it will seem unprofessional in nature. This is similar to the difference between tabloid headlines and newspaper headlines.

Website Design Mistakes

Here are some common Web design mistakes to avoid.

A deficient home page

You should be able to visit the home page of any website and figure out what the site is about, what type of products it sells, or what it is advertising within about five seconds.

Popup windows

The poor use of popup windows, splashy advertising, splash pages (pages with neat animations and sound but which you have to watch for five to ten seconds before you are taken to the real website), and other Web design features which draw interest away from your website, products, and/or services should be avoided altogether.

Poor website navigation

This includes broken hyperlinks, hidden navigation, poor wording of navigational links, links which take you to pages with no links, and links from a page to the same Web page and no links back to the home page; always include a link back to the home page so that regardless of where a site visitor goes, they can find their way back home.

Marketing misconceptions

Just because you have a website does not mean that you have a marketing campaign or overall marketing and advertising strategy. We will discuss the marketing of a website in great detail later in this book; however, you need to understand that your website is not your marketing strategy. Your website is just a part of your overall marketing strategy, depending on your business goals.

For example, if you have a successful restaurant but want to advertise and promote your business on the Web, creating a website is great, but if it is not promoted and advertised, no one will ever find it. By passing out business cards with your website URL embossed on them, you are using a traditional marketing campaign to promote your website. If you offer a downloadable coupon from your website, you are successfully using your website as part of your marketing strategy to meet your goal of increased restaurant sales.

Outdated content

There is nothing more dissatisfying to a Web customer than visiting a website that is grossly out-of-date. Incorrect pricing, products that are no longer available, dated content, and ancient advertising all signify to the website visitor that your devotion to your website is suffering greatly. During an interview with Gizmo Graphics Web Design, they revealed that one client has not updated their website in more than three years, and the site contains dated information (schedule of events, an outdated email address). Although the client is proud of their website and it looks great, it does not take a visitor long to realize that this site has not been updated since before the last presidential election, and typically, interest fades fast.

Misusing text

Forget flashing text, reversing text, gymnastics text, or other eye-popping and dizzying effects, which do nothing more than annoy your site visitor. Do not create a "loud" website that contains so many blinking, flashing, twirling, and spinning icons, text, or graphics; visitors will be overwhelmed by the effects and underwhelmed by the site content. Here is a great example of a website that is out of control: **http://arngren.net/**.

Overusing capitalization

Most people today know and understand basic Web communication, which means that if you choose to use capitalized words in your emails and chats, your customers or clients might feel as if you are yelling at them. On the Web, you can easily offend people by using capital letters to make a point. So unless this is your intent, use capitalization carefully and sparingly in all communications with your visitors. There are numerous methods you can employ to draw visitors to specific areas of your content without resorting to capitalization.

Overusing graphics

Limit the number of graphics on your website so that you do not overwhelm your site visitors with "graphics overload." Do not use animated GIF images on your website. These were cool ten years ago, but in today's professional environment, they are just another distraction that site visitors do not need to see. Speaking of graphics, make sure you use the ALT = Attribute tag to display text descriptions of the images on your website.

Web Page Content

Content drives search engine visibility and is vitally important to achieving success on the Web. Content is critical not only in drawing visitors to your site, but also getting them to return time and time again. Writing solid, comprehensible content means two things: You have to know your topic, and you have to have a good grasp of how to build your content into something of value.

Search engines look for well-written, interesting, and unique content and information that is updated and relevant.

Writing the content

Content should be written so that it can be easily scanned because site visitors may not have time to read lengthy text. Include bold-faced headlines with text to make it easier for visitors to find what they are looking for without having to read everything. Four basic tips for writing good Web content are: include keywords, use clear titles, keep it short and sweet, and forego the sales pitch so your visitors can get to the real meat of the site.

The lede

Your first sentence and paragraph is going to determine whether your visitors will read the entire Web page. One of the first things you learn in journalism is how to write a lede, which is that first sentence you see in most newspaper stories. It must be something that grabs the reader's attention and is best served with a solid verb to describe what the article is about.

Relevance and spell-checking

Make sure your content is not only timely but relevant to your readers as well. Remember to spell-check everything. Do it as you write and again when you are finished. Also make sure to check your grammar closely. Using fancy fonts will not help you to retain visitors because they are just too difficult to read and often not Web-friendly.

Links

Only hyperlinks to other pages or websites should be underlined. There are many other ways to emphasis a specific area of your content, such as bolding or italicizing sub-headlines to divide your content into predetermined areas. You can also implement bullets or numerical lists. Within the text and in sub-headers, you may create links to different areas of your website, single pages on your site, different sections of a document on the same page, or to other websites.

The flow

Another factor to remember is to leave enough space between your content and graphics or images. Do not allow your content to flow under or over these items. If you have content that is buried or unreadable, you will irritate your readers, and you may lose current and future customers, because the site looks unprofessional.

How users read the content

People seldom read Web pages word for word; instead, they sweep the page, selecting various words and sentences. In researching on the way in which people read websites, it was discovered that only 16 percent read word-for-word. Consequently, Web pages must use analyzable text and employ accentuated key words. Additionally, Web pages must contain significant sub-headings, bulleted lists, and ideas organized by paragraph.

Using Images

The use of images and visual impact is necessary in order to seize the attention of site visitors. You must gain their attention immediately, and the creative use of images is one of the best ways to do that. Keep in mind that the content is what is most important. Unlike window shopping, visual appeal of a website will not garner attention; someone must be searching on keywords to find your website. But the images you use will complement your content and provide a balanced presentation of your website. Images should be used strictly to enhance your content.

Excessive use of images characterizes a page as a hobbyist or entertainment page, while reserved use of images is usually correlated with information and news-related sites. Images can be used for representations of data in forms such as graphs and charts without having to script the necessary code to parse and display such information dynamically. They can be used to set the tone of an article through pictures and photographs. They can also be used to enhance the style of a website through advanced graphics techniques to mimic a three-dimensional look or to create effects of reflection.

In order to learn how to incorporate images onto your website, it is important to have a firm understanding of several fundamental aspects of graphics and images. This section will cover the basics of using free graphics and editing programs to create images. It will provide an in-depth look at two commercial photo-editing applications and will also explore the similarities and differences between different image formats.

General advice

Using images on your website can be tricky — here are a few, general pieces of advice to ensure your images are successful.

Use three graphics per page

Most Web masters believe the rule of thumb is to use no more than three pictures or graphics on any given page, and resize them to no more than 72 DPI, or dots per inch, to ensure they load quickly. Space out images so that the written content is clearly visible on the page, which allows your visitors the opportunity to begin reading your content as the pictures load. Be cautious with the sizing of your fonts — too large a font is not professional and is distracting; too small, and it cannot be easily read.

Ditch clipart — opt for royalty-free stock photos

Clipart should be used with extreme caution because it tends to make your site look amateurish in nature. Most of the clipart and graphics available for free download are low-quality. One of the best website investments you can make is to obtain royalty-free stock photos. These can add a touch of class to your Web pages and are absolutely free. They provide a visual center of interest on an otherwise plain Web page.

Use CSS

Use CSS when possible to control font size, color, and layout. External style sheets are typically used for this purpose because they control the entire site. The style sheet is actually a file on your Web server that stores all your CSS preferences. You embed HTML code into each Web page, and your style sheet is applied when the page is loaded in the browser. You can also use internal style sheets, which control only the page they are on; this is useful if you need one page to function or appear differently than the others.

Placement

The eyes of visitors often tend to travel to four critical points that are all one third of the way from the edges of the page. Place advertisements or other important content in these regions to gain maximum visibility. This rule also applies to the composition of an image. Place the important subjects of the image at these points to make them more noticeable at first glance.

Simplicity

Simple and usable is always better than stylish and complex when it comes to websites. Take a look at the Google homepage. The clean user interface allows first-time users to navigate the site and access its features without any trouble. Simplicity also helps with loading time and bandwidth, since there is less data to be sent and received. It reduces the strain on the user as well as the Web developer or Web host. Users will always prefer sites that are easy to use over the more complex alternatives. Simplicity sells.

Image size

As a general rule of thumb, images should be as small as possible to allow for faster load time of Web pages. Images should be saved at a resolution of 72 DPI, and image file sizes should be no larger than 20KB. Pixels are used to measure the height and width of an image file, and they are sized in kilobytes (KB) or megabytes (MB). If you have large image files on your site, you are driving away website visitors.

Backup your site

Always have a backup copy of your website that you can revert to in case of an emergency. Make copies every month, week, or even every day based upon the frequency of change to your site. You can buy external hard drives or store files online for added security. Images tend to take up a lot of room, so always compress images into Zip files for storage purposes. Name the files by content or by date of backup. You can choose to configure your server to automatically back up based on a schedule if manual backup is too much of a hassle.

Think from the perspective of the website user. What would they want from your site? What information are they looking for? All of the images, graphics, and design elements of the site should be focused around the content.

Image file formats

The three main formats of images seen on the Web are JPEG, PNG, and GIF. TIFF and BMP are other familiar formats. Although they might all look the same at first glance, each has its own advantages and disadvantages.

JPEG

JPEG stands for Joint Photographic Experts Group, the committee that created the standard. Its most common file extensions are .JPG or .JPEG. This is one of the most popular graphic formats on the Web, because it is usually the default output format for most cameras and other imaging devices.

However, default and most popular does not always mean the best. Certain versions of JPEG use an interlaced, progressive loading style. The rough outline of the image is displayed first before the details slowly start filling in. The difference is almost unnoticeable for smaller images, but on larger JPEG images viewed through slow connections, you can see the image slowly being formed as it loads. The advantage of this is that the user can view a low-quality, but full, version of the image before the high-quality version of the image loads. This is contrary to the linear loading style used by PNGs and other formats, where the image is loaded line-by-line, pixel-by-pixel, in its full quality.

One disadvantage of JPEGs is that they do not support an alpha component, so this format can only be used for full-size images without any transparency. This is one of the main reasons why JPEGs are not often used in features like menus and navigation bars that use irregular shapes such as round edges or circles with transparent backgrounds.

JPEGs can be compressed to your bandwidth needs, though this is at the cost of quality. Quality also varies based upon the system, since some browsers take shortcuts to decompress the file faster. The lossy compression is one of the main problems with JPEG. It is infamous for leaving behind artifacts. You can notice the JPEG artifacts by comparing the original and the compressed version of the file and looking for blocks of color and loss of minor details.

Lossless and Lossy compression are terms that describe whether all original data can be recovered when a compressed image file is uncompressed. Lossless compression means all data in the original image file remains after the file is uncompressed; in other words, it is completely restored to its original state. The Graphics Interchange File (GIF) is an image format used on the Web that provides lossless compression. The main purpose for using lossy images is to reduce their size when used on web pages to ensure the pages load fast. Generally, the loss in appearance is not noticeable. However, the loss in file size is significant. JPEG image files, which is the most common format on the web, has lossy compression.

PNG

Portable Network Graphics, or PNGs, are a newer file type with support for many features. They stand apart from JPEGs in the fact that they have an alpha channel, allowing transparency in PNG images. They also support indexing options that allow you to reduce the file size of an image by narrowing down the number of colors used in the image palette.

PNGs also differ from JPEGs in that they have support for lossless compression, which preserves the original quality of the image. The advanced preprocessing techniques this format utilizes for compressing files come at the minor cost of speed. It also comes with a gamma channel to adjust the brightness of the image. The main highlight of this format is its efficient compression. If you are looking for a small file size that is light on the bandwidth without any loss of quality, then PNG is your format.

TIFF

The Tagged Image File Format (TIFF) is a universally accepted file format for images compatible with most Windows, Mac, and UNIX™ operating systems. TIFF images incorporate a lossless compression, giving you small file sizes without loss of any quality. This is an important factor to consider when storing any quality-sensitive images. Compression always comes at the cost of speed in opening and saving files. Although the difference is minute with modern processors, the speed might be a factor to consider for images and files that need to be repeatedly opened or saved. TIFF files are used mainly for the purposes of printing and archiving.

BMP

Bitmap, or BMP, is another common file format. Bitmaps are usually un-compressed, leaving their file sizes much larger than equivalent PNG or JPEG files. There are multiple versions of BMP available, including a 32-bit version supporting an alpha channel for transparency. BMP files can be manually compressed into a fraction of their original size using free compression programs such as 7-Zip.

GIF

GIF images are one of the original image formats of the Web. They are usu-ally used for animations. Their use is limited because GIF images limit your pallet to 256 colors. Because of this, gradients and other shades are often hard to achieve within the limits of GIF, unless it is used for small images such as logos. Programs such as GIMP, the GNU Image Manipulation Pro-gram, can allow you to draw your graphics in full color and then reduce the pallet down to the essential 256 colors. This often results in grainy pictures.

The main advantage of GIFs is that they offer a simple alternative to band-width-intensive video. GIF files also support JPEG-like interlacing options that allow a rough image to be downloaded before the full detail image. This is especially useful for users with a slow Internet connection. The format also uses a lossless compression technique to compress the images into a smaller file size. Animated GIFs appear to be video files in that they show motion or action of the animated images, but do not have the ability to produce sound. Audio files may be used in conjunction with them, or with any other images or web pages.

SVG

SVGs are Scalable Vector Graphics files. Unlike JPEG or PNG files, SVG files store information as vectors. This allows you to scale the image indefinitely without losing any of the quality of the image. This makes it an optimal file type for logos and other images that are repeatedly resized, since resizing often causes blocky pixelation with most other file types.

The features of SVGs are limited when it comes to more advanced enhancements, so consider saving a basic outline of your images as an SVG and then doing the final touch up on it and saving it as a high-resolution JPEG or PNG.

Images and HTML

The way an image is incorporated into a page is very important when it comes to SEO, usability, and accessibility.

The following is an example of how to embed an image into an HTML document. Open Notepad or another HTML editor and create the following Web page. When you save the file in HTML or HTM format, you can open the file in any Web browser, and it will interpret the HTML code and display your web page:

```
<head>
<body>
<img src = "Images\SampleImage.png"></img>
</body>
</head>
```

Save it to your desktop or local folder. In the same location, create an "Images" folder and place a sample image in the folder from your system. You can edit the **src** attribute of the image to point to your particular image. It is also possible to add in an image without the end tag **</img>** by using this format:

```
<head>
<body>
<img src="Images\SampleImage.png"/>
</body>
</head>
```

Run the sample Web page file in a Web browser to see the output. The code displays the image **SampleImage.png** from the Images folder in the local directory. The default position of the image is at the top left corner. You can move the image around the screen by doing this:

```
<head>
<body>
<div style = "position:absolute;left:40px;top:20px;">
<img src = "Images\3.png"></img></div>
</body>
</head>
```

The line **<div style = "position:absolute;left:40px;top:20px;">** moves the image 40 pixels right and 20 pixels down. You can also align text as top, bottom, middle, left, or right by doing this:

<div style = "allign:center;position:absolute;left:20px;top:350px;">

It is possible to add borders to images by using the border attribute with the number of pixels as the parameter:

<img src = "Images\3.png" border = 10>

If you want to set an image as the background of a page, just add the background attribute linking to the background image to the **<body>** tag:

```
<html>
<body background="Images\background.jpg">
</body>
</html>
```

Although it is recommended that you do the formatting for images beforehand, it is sometimes necessary to do basic adjustments to the image while it is being displayed. You can adjust various properties of an image such as its source, width, height, and border through these lines.

```
<img src = "Images/sampleImage.png" width=1024 height=
768 hspace = 0 vspace = 0></div>
```

The **"width = 1024"** and **"height = 768"** attributes resize the image to 1024 × 768 pixels. Keep in mind that it can sometimes reduce the quality of the image if the original ratio is different from the new one. The **hspace** and **vspace** options adjust the vertical and horizontal spaces around the image. Setting these to 0 will align it to top corner of the page. Adjusting this value is also a way to move the image around the page without relying on the **<div>...</div>** tag.

Free graphics editing software

GIMP

GIMP is a widely used graphics-editing program. It is a free, open-source graphics program released under the GNU General Public License (GPL). Its functionality is similar to Photoshop in the sense that its main focus is to edit and enhance photos and other pictures. It supports all of the basic features such as cropping, color filtering, brightness and contrast, hue and saturation, and color modes.

It also comes with many filters and plug-ins for the more advanced editing requirements. These include blur, sharpen, oilify, edge detect, lens flare, fractal rendering, solid noise, plasma, ripples, and waves. Additional plug-ins can be created or downloaded from the official GIMP website.

GIMP allows you to open and save your files in a variety of file formats. Note that you can work with Photoshop files in GIMP, since it supports .PSD, the Photoshop file format. One disadvantage is that, like Photoshop, GIMP can sometimes be resource heavy. If you plan to add more plug-ins and external features to do more advanced editing, make sure you have a system that can support the RAM and processing needs of GIMP.

The support for brushes, patterns, and add-ons combined with a myriad of built-in features make GIMP a serious alternative for Photoshop. You can download the latest version of GIMP for free from **www.gimp.org**. It is also possible to download past versions of GIMP if the current version is not working for you. If you are a programmer, the source code is also available at the website.

Microsoft Paint

Microsoft Paint, also known as MS® Paint, is the built-in graphics program for Windows. Although it comes with the bare minimum in features, it is an easy to use, always at-hand option for simple tasks. The main focus of Paint is pixel-based drawing. It will take a lot more work to get the same effects as Photoshop or GIMP, because almost all of the work is done manually in Paint.

Paint does allow you to switch between three modes of painting: pencil, brush, and airbrush. You can zoom in and work on individual regions of the picture in detail and then zoom out for a higher-quality finished product. There are tools to create ovals, rectangles, polygons, straight lines, and curvy lines. If you are running a Windows system, MS Paint should already be on your system. Go to **Start > Run >** and type in "MS Paint." It should launch the Paint program.

Inkscape®

Inkscape is a vector graphics editor. It is used to create SVG files. It is the prefect tool for creating buttons, logos, and other simple graphics in a snap. You can also create a custom character set to use as a font for your site in Inkscape. The Calligraphy Tool is perfect for such tasks. If your mouse handling is not so great, draw rough outlines in Inkscape, then use the Node Tool to edit it to your liking.

Since SVG files are actually just XML files, it is actually possible to edit SVG files with any text editor. That, however, can be very tedious. Inkscape is an easy-to-use program that allows you create amazing artwork using simple shapes and tools. Inkscape can be downloaded for free from **www.inkscape. org**. You can take a look at the screen shots and the documentation available on the website to learn more about all of the details of the program.

Paint.NET

Paint.NET is another graphics program offering features similar to GIMP and Inkscape. It comes with the simplicity of MS Paint, the usability of Inkscape, and some of the advanced features of GIMP. Its main use, like GIMP, is photo manipulation, and it supports all of the popular file formats. The two programs are almost exactly the same in many aspects, but the interface of Paint.NET is different than GIMP in the sense that it only displays the basic tools and features. It offers features similar to, but better than, regular MS Paint, without the high-tech features of GIMP. You can download Paint.NET at **www.getpaint.net**.

The decision between these four free programs is the simple matter of time, place, occasion, and personal taste. Each offers unique features and capabilities that, when combined, can allow you to create eye-catching graphics without the cost of expensive software. All of these programs are being actively developed at their corresponding sites, so expect bigger and better features to be added to the bundles in the future.

Commercial graphics editing software

Adobe Photoshop CC

Adobe Photoshop CC is the most popular graphics editing software on the market. It is geared toward professionals and is incredibly complex and very expensive. However, it stands out among the competition for its incredible depth of features, functionality, and power. You can review the features of Adobe Photoshop CC at **www.adobe.com/products/photoshop/features.html**. Adobe CC is cloud-based, and you pay a monthly fee, tiered based on usage, needs, or your status (student, teacher, or business).

Corel® PaintShop® Pro Photo X8

Corel PaintShop Pro Photo X8 is a much more cost effective, yet still feature-rich alternative to Adobe Photoshop. The bottom line is that it is an excellent program that will meet the needs of most graphics challenges and is not overly complicated to learn. Corel Paint Shop Pro Photo X8 balances user-friendly design with powerful features at a reasonable cost.

It can be purchased on Amazon.com for less than $50. Corel states that Paint Shop Pro X8 makes any image better. Design for Web or print, business or fun. Instantly correct and enhance photos. Create impressive scrapbook pages, posters, and graphics with new Text Wrapping that quickly fills a selection or shape with text. Easily move elements of your photo and watch as the background is replaced automatically with new Magic Move. Smart enhancements like the new Batch Mode accelerate common photo tasks. Save time with more precise selection tools, faster brushes, and file saving. Bring ideas to life with the most versatile photo-editing software you will ever buy. See more at **www.paintshoppro.com**.

Color Schemes

When choosing a color scheme, keep the feeling you want to create for the website in mind. The choice of colors is usually a personal one, as everyone has his or her own individual preferences regarding color. However, different colors have different connotations; let's take a look at the meaning behind different color schemes.

Warm colors

Warm colors such as red, orange, and yellow can represent passion, energy, excitement, and happiness. Red backgrounds are used to emphasize white text on a page, and red is favored for advertisements and drawing attention to a particular section of a Web site. Orange is a great color to use as it is warm, yet draws the eye's attention to it and offers a bold contrast to other colors. Yellows are warm, cheerful, and soft and offer softer tones to other bolder colors; it is great for contrast.

Cool colors

Cool colors like blue, green, purple, and violet are used to create a sense of peace and serenity. They represent water, nature, and night and offer soothing and relaxing properties. These are ideal colors to give balance and stability to a website's overall appearance.

Neutral colors

Softer, neutral colors are created when the colors are closer together (Ex: 255, 200, 150). These should be used mainly for backgrounds and other large, solid-colored spaces. Shades of gray are created when the red, green, and blue values are all the same (Ex: 127, 127, 127). Neutral colors are pleasing to the eye and give a natural, balanced appearance. Other colors such as brights and neons tend to cause eye fatigue and drive customers away due to sensory overload.

Neon

Bright neon colors are created when one value is a lot higher than the two others (Ex: Neon Green: 0, 255, 0). Excessive use of neon colors is often considered an eye sore. I do not recommend using excessively bright or neon colors, nor do I recommend animation on Web pages, as it causes fatigue and confusion and will drive customers away.

Primary colors

Primary colors like red, yellow, and blue tend to be emphasize simplicity as well as speed.

Secondary colors

Secondary colors are created by mixing two primary colors together. These include green, orange, and purple.

Tertiary colors

Tertiary colors can be created by mixing secondary and primary colors together.

Integrating color

Use colors that are adjacent to each other to create a sense of consistency to your website. Use colors that are opposite of each other in the color wheel to highlight content by making it stand out. Over-contrasting everything could become an eye sore, so be picky in choosing what to emphasize.

The colors on the foreground of the page should be at the opposite end of the color wheel so they are easily visible against the background. Red text on a red colored background is unreadable, while green or blue text can be easily read on the same page. Look around at other websites to find complimentary images and colors.

Accessibility for vision-impaired users is another factor to consider when choosing a color scheme. While red text on a green background (or vice versa) stands out easily, it can sometimes be hard to read due to excessive contrast. To fix this problem, simply adjust the lightness of the colors so that the foreground is darker and the background is lighter. Easy readability is especially a concern if your website is for an elderly audience.

There are lots of resources available to help you with color palettes and Web design including **www.color-wheel-pro.com/color-meaning.html and vanseodesign.com/web-design/color-meaning**.

Website Navigation

The most common navigation "styles" are explained below with image examples.

HTML links: Simple, efficient and great for search engines. Not as appealing as fancy buttons or other methods.

Breadcrumb trail: This system uses a single line of text to show a page's location in the site hierarchy. This should only be used as a secondary navigation system, however it is very useful to the site visitor to show where they are in a website's hierarchy.

Back to: Technology / Calculators & Office Machines

Navigation bars/buttons: By far the most common type of navigation. Typically found on the left hand side of a Web page or across the top of a Web page.

Tab navigation: First made popular by Amazon, this can be considered a secondary navigation system; however, it provides a direct link to specific sections of a website.

Site map: A single Web page which shows the complete navigation structure for your website. This is critical for SEO.

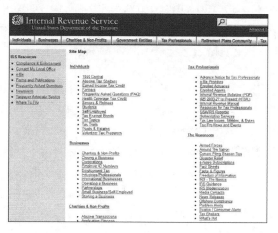

Drop-down menu: A menu, typically across the top or left hand side of a Web page that drops down or expands sub-menus as the mouse is moved over them. This lets you put many links into the navigation, but they stay collapsed except when used. These are typically made from Javascript, DHTML, or CSS.

The bottom line is that simple, effective, user-friendly navigation is one of the most important elements of Web design. I recommend you spend some time visiting other sites to get an idea of how different navigation methods are employed. This will not only give you great ideas for what to do, but it also helps you determine what to avoid. As discussed, the most common navigation system is based on buttons or dynamically generated button sets, placed on the left-hand side of a Web page. Navigation across the top of the Web page is the second most common placement location.

Your navigation should be consistent throughout your site. If you use buttons and drop down menus, they should appear on every page and in the same location. You should embed hyperlinks into your Web pages as an alternative method; site visitors are familiar with hyperlinks and can easily recognize them when embedded into Web pages.

Ensure your navigation system is "above the fold." Above the fold is a term taken from the newspaper industry, which means the "important" stories are placed above the fold in a newspaper and less important stories are placed below the fold where they are not seen when viewing the "front page." The concept translates to Web pages. You only have so much real estate in a monitor, and you cannot always fit your entire page into the browser window. Ensure your navigation systems are "above the fold" on a Web page – they should never have to scroll to find your navigation system.

Ensure you have a "Home" navigation link on every page. Give your site visitors an easy way to get back to the home page.

Large sites are challenging because of the number of pages. Organize your site by category, section, and products to simplify navigation. Users should be able to get to any page with no more than two mouse clicks.

Make your navigation systems attractive through the use of graphics, images, and advanced features such as a rollover button that changes color when a mouse is moved over the item.

There are many free options for website navigation. Dreamweaver and Visual Studio both offer fairly robust integrated solutions that create accessible and functional site navigation.

Necessary Website Attributes

Websites can be simple or complex. However, there are some basic attributes every website should have.

A home page

This is typically the first page a site visitor will see, and it is the anchor of your website. The focus of your design efforts should concentrate on your home page, and it should serve as the launch pad to other parts of your website. Some websites may use a splash or entry page before you hit the home page; typically these are done in flash as an "intro" page, and they can be quickly bypassed to get the visitor to the main site content.

This page must have defined navigation which is easy to find and easy to use. You should have navigation links or navigation buttons, as well as excellent Web content that is keyword-rich and is easily read and understood by the site visitor. Other common pages in a navigation structure would include pages such as contact, about us, photographs, product information, company information, terms and conditions, feedback, and a variety of other pages depending on your website content.

Search options

You must integrate some form of search capability into your website. This can be done with a site map as well as through additional applets from Google and other companies, which will index your Web pages and give you free search capabilities.

I recommend using the Google Custom Search Engine, which can be obtained here: **https://cse.google.com/cse**; however, there are many others you can find with a quick Web search.

A privacy policy

Internet users are becoming increasingly concerned with their privacy. You should establish a "Privacy" Web page and let your visitors know exactly how you will be using the information you collect from them.

You may also wish to develop a P3P privacy policy. This may be necessary to solve the common problem of blocked cookies on websites, as well as with shopping carts and affiliate programs. Details may be found at **www. w3.org/P3P/usep3p.html**.

This page should address the following for your potential customers:

- For what purpose do you plan on using their information?
- Will their information be sold or shared with a third party?
- Why do you collect their email addresses?
- Do you track their IP addresses?
- Notify site visitors that you are not responsible for the privacy issues of any websites you may be linked to.
- Notify site visitors of your security measures in place to protect the misuse of their private or personal information.
- Provide site visitors with contact information in the event that they have any questions about your privacy statement.

An "About Us" page

An "About Us" page is an essential part of a professional website for a variety of reasons. Your potential customers may want to know exactly who you are, and it is a great opportunity to create a text-laden page for search engine visibility. An "About Us" page should include:

- A personal or professional biography of you or your business
- A photograph of yourself or your business
- A description of you or your company
- Company objectives
- A mission statement

- Contact information, including an email address or social media link

A money-back guarantee policy

Depending on the type of website you are operating, you may wish to consider implementing a money-back guarantee to completely eliminate any potential risk to customers in purchasing your products. By providing them with a solid, no-risk guarantee, you build confidence in your company and products with potential clients. Of course, it goes without saying that should you make such a promise it is your duty to fulfill it lest you face possible legal ramifications and a major loss of customer trust.

A "feedback" page

There are many reasons to incorporate a feedback page into your website. There are times when potential customers will have questions about your products and services or may encounter problems with your website, and the feedback page is an easy way for them to contact you. A timely response to feedback is critical in assuring customers that there is a real person on the other end of the website, and this personal service helps increase the likelihood they will continue to do business with you.

A "copyright" page

You should always display your copyright information at the bottom of each page. You should include both the word "Copyright" and the © symbol. Your copyright should look similar to this: **Copyright © 2016 Bruce C. Brown, LLC.**

Copyrighted material

In addition to your own copyright page, you need to give credit to any and all material on your website that is not your own. A simple link with credit to the photographer and a short note about the license is usually enough, but check with the original author to see if they have any special preferences. Proper citation in accepted formats such as MLA is another one of the factors that search engines consider. This is one reason why Wikipedia® pages often get a high page rank.

Image leeching is considered bad manners in the world of Web development. Never use an image from another website without the expressed written permission of the website owner to make sure you are not violating any copyright laws. There have been instances where the original image owner replaced the images with "Don't Leech" signs. The signs can appear on the leecher's website without their knowledge, because the file link is still the same. This could create a tarnished reputation of the website in question, since hundreds of users might notice the signs before the site developer does.

Hosting images on your own server will take the element of risk and surprise away from all important content crucial to your website. You can find many free images online that are released under free and open licenses. Look for images marked "copyleft" or those released under the Creative Commons License. Be sure to read the license carefully to make sure you comply with the requirements listed before using the image for your website.

A "404" page

Even the best Web designers inevitably leave a link to a page that no longer exists. This is known as a 404 Error. Make sure you have a custom 404 page to redirect users back to a page from which they can navigate your site. Often, 404 pages will redirect you to the homepage. You may also wish to have links to your most popular pages. An auto-redirect will give site visitors a few seconds to click on a link, and if they take no action, it will bring them to the website homepage.

Google simplifies the processing of creating 404 pages by providing a Google 404 Widget in Google Webmaster Tools. You can also use the widget to identify which page has the links to the nonexistent page so you can take corrective action.

Section 508

In 1998, Congress amended the Rehabilitation Act to require federal agencies to make their electronic and information technology accessible to people with disabilities. Inaccessible technology interferes with an individual's ability to obtain and use information quickly and easily.

Section 508 was enacted to eliminate barriers in information technology, to make available new opportunities for people with disabilities, and to encourage development of technologies that will help achieve these goals. The law applies to all federal agencies when they develop, procure, maintain, or use electronic and information technology.

Under Section 508 (29 U.S.C. 794d), agencies must give disabled employees and members of the public access to information that is comparable to the access available to others. You should design Web pages with accessibility in mind, as there are benefits for everyone. While the Section 508 rules are quite involved and apply to much more than Web pages, here are the essential requirements for website design:

- A text equivalent for every non-text element shall be provided.
- Equivalent alternatives for any multimedia presentation shall be synchronized with the presentation.
- Web pages shall be designed so that all information conveyed with color is also available without color.
- Documents shall be organized so they are readable without requiring an associated style sheet.
- Redundant text links shall be provided for each active region of a server-side image map.
- Client-side image maps shall be provided instead of server-side image maps except where the regions cannot be defined with an available geometric shape.
- Row and column headers shall be identified for data tables.

- Markup shall be used to associate data cells and header cells for data tables that have two or more logical levels of row or column headers.
- Frames shall be titled with text that facilitates frame identification and navigation.
- Pages shall be designed to avoid causing the screen to flicker with a frequency greater than 2 Hz and lower than 55 Hz.
- A text-only page, with equivalent information or functionality, shall be provided to make a website comply with the provisions of this part, when compliance cannot be accomplished in any other way; the content of the text-only page shall be updated whenever the primary page changes.
- When pages use scripting languages to display content, or to create interface elements, the information provided by the script shall be identified with functional text that can be read by assistive technology.
- When a Web page requires that an applet, plug-in, or other application be present on the client system to interpret page content, the page must provide a link to a plug-in or applet that complies with Section 508 §1194.21(a) through (l).
- When electronic forms are designed to be completed online, the form shall allow people using assistive technology to access the information, field elements, and functionality required for completion and submission of the form, including all directions and cues.
- A method shall be provided that permits users to skip repetitive navigation links.
- When a timed response is required, the user shall be alerted and given sufficient time to indicate more time is required.

To check out your site for Section 508 compliance, visit: **www.power mapper.com/products/sortsite/ads/acc-section-508**.

Free Web Site Optimization Tools

- **www.wordtracker.com:** The leading keyword research tool. It is not free, but there is a limited free trial.
- **www.websiteoptimization.com/services/analyze:** Contains a free website speed test to improve your website's performance. This site will calculate page size, composition, and download time. The script calculates the size of individual elements and sums up each type of Web page component. On the basis of these page characteristics, the site then offers advice on how to improve page load time. Slow load time is the No. 1 reason potential customers do not access websites.
- **www.seocentro.com/tools/search-engines/metatag-analyzer. html:** A free website that analyzes your page content to determine whether you are effectively using meta tags.
- **www.mikes-marketing-tools.com/ranking-reports:** Offers instant online reports of website rankings in seven top search engines and the top three Web directories for free.
- **tools.seobook.com/general/keyword-density:** Free, fast, and accurate keyword density analyzer.
- **adwords.google.co.uk/select/KeywordToolExternal:** Gives ideas for new keywords associated with your target phrase, but does not indicate relevance or include details on number or frequency of searches.
- **www.google.com/webmasters:** Offers a large variety of tools, guides, and other services for Web design and optimization.
- **www.htmlbasix.com/meta.shtml:** Free site that automatically creates properly formatted HTML meta tags for insertion into your Web pages.

Free Web Site Search Engine Submission Sites

- http://dmoz.org
- http://tools.addme.com/servlet/s0new
- www.submitcorner.com/Tools/Submit
- www.quickregister.net
- www.scrubtheweb.com
- www.submitawebsite.com/free_submission_top_engines.htm
- www.nexcomp.com/weblaunch/urlsubmission.html
- www.submitshop.com/freesubmit/freesubmit.html
- www.buildtraffic.com/submit_url.shtml
- www.addpro.com/submit30.htm
- www.website-submission.com/select.htm

There are many other free services available on the Internet, and there is no guarantee as to the quality of any of these free services. It is recommended that you create and use a new email account just for search engine submissions, such as **search@yourwebsite.com**, to avoid spam, which is prevalent when doing bulk submissions.

Chapter 7

Google

oogle is the largest search engine in the United States of America with a market share of over 60 percent. When it comes to starting up your business, there are a lot of tools that Google can provide for you to make things not only easier, but also more effective.

In this chapter, we will take an in-depth look at everything that Google has to offer you, including the following: Webmaster tools, snippets, sitemaps, Google TrustRank, Google PageRank, Google's quality guidelines, Google AdSense, Google AdWords, the Google Merchant Center, and Google Shopping.

Let's get started.

Webmaster Tools

Google's own Webmaster Tools include powerful applications that help you achieve better and higher rankings in the Google search engine. These tools show your site from the perspective of Google and let you identify problems, increase visibility, and optimize your site.

To increase your website's visibility on Google, you need to learn how their robots crawl and index your site. Webmaster Tools shows you exactly how to do this. Everything you need is available at **www.google.com/ webmasters/tools**.

You can see when your site was last crawled and indexed, view the URLs that Google had problems crawling, and then take corrective action to ensure all of your pages are indexed. You can also see what keywords Google validates and which sites link to yours.

You can see what queries have been performed that are driving traffic to your site and where your site lands in the search engine result for those queries. You can review how your site is indexed and whether you have any violations that Google is penalizing you for.

To take a closer look at each of these amazing Google tools, first you must sign up with Google and log into your account. You will navigate to the Search Engine Console where you can view the sites that you have added into the tool. To add another website, simply click on "Add A Property" on the upper right hand side of the page.

You will be given a piece of code which you must upload to your website via File Transfer Protocol (FTP) or HTTP through a Web design application, such as Dreamweaver CS. Google requires proof that you are the site owner to prevent you from using the same tools on your competition's site. You can do this by adding a meta tag to your website, which Google provides, or by uploading an HTML file. In the example, the meta tag is added to the HTML code in the **index.asp** Web page. Once you add the code, simply click on the "Verify" button to continue.

Once the site is verified, you can review the status of indexing and Web crawls. You can look at the index statistics, and you can also submit a sitemap. By examining the Web crawl errors, you can see that the site has

25 URL's (Pages) not found. This is because the sitemap file is old and pages have been removed, so we will update this. On the left side, you can click on Messages, Search Appearance, Search Traffic, Google Index, and Crawl and Security Issues for greater detail into each of these categories. You can review your top search queries and the relative position in which your results were ranked on the Google search engine.

Spend some quality time with Google Webmaster Tools. They are all simple enough to use and understand as you analyze your site. You can even set up Google Webmaster Tools to monitor your site from your desktop, providing you with constant information about the performance of your site in relation to the Google search engine.

We will cover much of the Google Webmaster Tools as we continue. There are other similar tools offered, such as Bing Webmaster Tool; I recommend you spend time learning each and optimizing your site using the free tool available.

Google Webmaster Tools — Search Appearance

Under the Search Appearance tab, you will find links for "Structured Data," "Data Highlighter," "HTML Improvements," "Sitelinks," and "Accelerated Mobile Pages."

- *Structured Data:* If your page uses structured data such as "rich snippets," this link will help you to analyze them. Structured data helps Google understand the content on your site, which can be used to display rich snippets in search results.

- *Data Highlighter:* You can use Data Highlighter to further enhance Web page content in search engine results. If you use structured data like event listings or reviews and ratings, you can use Data Highlighter as a markup for helping Google to better understand your site. You simply use the provided tool to tag data. In our case, we will tag Medi Spa of Ocala (www. medispaofocala.com) as the Local Business.

You simply highlight data and "tag" it appropriately. As you can see, we have tagged the name, address, operating hours, phone number and corporate image. Click done and your data/tags are saved.

Google screenshots © Google Inc. Used with permission.

- **HTML Improvements:** This is where Google makes specific recommendations based on the scan of your website in regards to HTML and meta tags. By taking action on the recommendations, you may improve search engine rankings, overall site performance, and ultimately improve the user experience on your website. In the example below, Google tells us that our description tags are identical on all the pages. We should have unique descriptions for each page on a website. Google states that meta description information can give users a clear idea of your site's content and encourages users to click on your site in the search results pages.

- **Sitelinks:** These are different than "sitemaps," which will be covered in this chapter. Sitelinks are automatically generated links that may appear under your site's search results. If you do not want a page to appear as a sitelink, you can demote it.

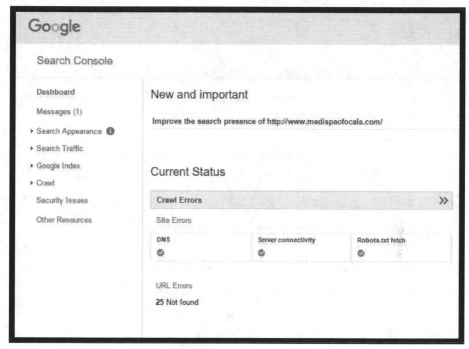

Google screenshots © Google Inc. Used with permission.

Google Webmaster Tools – Search Traffic

Under the Search Traffic tab, you will find links for "Search Analytics," "Links to your Site," "Internal Links," "Manual Actions," "International Targeting" and "Mobile Usability."

- **Search Analytics:** Tools for analyzing your performance on Google's Search Engine. This shows you clicks, click through rates, impression and average ranking.
- **Links to Your Site:** Shows you what websites (and how many) are linked to yours.
- **Internal Links:** Shows you all of your internal website links.
- **Manual Actions:** Detects any webspam actions on your website.
- **International Targeting:** If your site uses hreflang tags, Google will use this tag to match the user's language preference to the right variation of your pages.

- *Mobile Usability:* Detects and helps you to fix mobile usability issues on your website.

Google Webmaster Tools — Index

Under the Index tab, you will find links for "Index Status," "Content Keywords," "Blocked Resources" and "Remove URLs."

- *Index Status:* Shows you how many pages were indexed by the Google search engine, and if there were any errors.
- *Content Keywords:* Shows you content keyword density and significance ratings.
- *Blocked Resources:* Shows you if you have any blocked resources that impair indexing of your website by Google.
- *Remove URLs:* Lets you temporarily remove URLs that you own from search results. To remove content permanently, you must remove the pages from your website.

Google Webmaster Tools — Crawl

Under the Crawl tab, you will find links for "Crawl Errors," "Crawl Stats," "Fetch as Google," "robots.txt Tester," "Sitemaps" and "URL Parameters."

- *Crawl Errors:* Shows you server, DNS, or URL errors when indexing your website with the Google search engine.
- *Crawl Stats:* Shows you pages crawled per day, crawl time, and other statistics.
- *Fetch as Google:* Shows you how Google renders pages from your website. You can also initiate page and site crawls by the Google search engine and view errors.
- *robots.txt Tester:* Detects presence of and lets you edit your robots.txt and check for errors. Robots.txt files inform search engine spiders how to interact with indexing your content.
- *Sitemaps:* Lets you check performance of your sitemaps. Sitemaps are important; we will cover this in this chapter.

- *URL Parameters:* Generally, this link is not needed unless you need to provide additional data to help Google crawl your site more efficiently.

Google Webmaster — Security Issues

This is used to detect any security issues with your site's content. Google provides enormous resources for hacked sites and other security or malware issues at **www.google.com/intl/en/webmasters/hacked** and **https://support.google.com/webmasters/answer/2913382**.

Snippets

A snippet is the text excerpt that appears below a page's title in the Google search engine results and describes the content of the page. Words contained in the snippet are bolded when they appear in the query results. The premise is that these snippets will give the user an idea of whether the content of the page matches what they may be looking for. The description snippet is taken directly from the description meta tag. If no description meta tag is provided, Google may extract a description from the page content. One source Google uses for snippets is the Open Directory Project (ODP). It is possible to tell Google to not use the ODP for generating snippets by using a piece of meta tag code. To do this, use the following code on any Web page you want this rule to apply to:

<meta name="googlebot" content="noodp">

Sitemaps

Submitting a sitemap to Google is a critical step toward achieving top rankings in the Google search engine. If you do nothing else with Google Webmaster Tools, submit a sitemap. To do so, log back into Google Webmaster Tools, select the URL you want to work with that you have already verified, and click on the link "Sitemaps." A sitemap is an HTML page listing of all the pages in your site — it tends to be designed to help users navigate your site, and it is especially beneficial if your site is large. In the case of Google, you should create an XML sitemap, which provides Google with information about your site and improves your rankings with Google.

Essentially, a sitemap is an organized list of every page on your website. It helps Google know which pages are on your site and ensures that all your pages are discovered and indexed. According to Google, sitemaps are particularly helpful if:

- Your site has dynamic content.
- Your site has pages that are not easily discovered by Googlebot, Google's crawler, during the crawl process.
- Your site is new and has few links to it.
- Your site has a large archive of content pages that are not well-linked to each other or are not linked at all.

Your sitemap can include additional information about your site, such as how often it is updated, when each page was last modified, and the relative importance of each page. You must create your sitemap and either submit it or a URL to the sitemap to Google. You can create a sitemap in the following three ways:

1) Manually creating it based on the sitemap protocol.
2) Using the Google Webmaster Tools Sitemap Generator. If you have access to your Web server, and it has Python® installed, you can use a Google-provided script to create a sitemap that uses the sitemap protocol.
3) Using a third-party tool.

The easiest way to create an XML sitemap is to use the free tool at **www.xml-sitemaps.com**. This is an incredibly easy site to use; simply type in the URL, and it does the rest for you. You upload the XML file to your website, and in the Google Sitemap tool, add the URL for the new file you placed on your Web server.

Simply add your Sitemap URL into the form, which is in Google Webmaster Tools under "Crawl," then go to "Sitemaps" on the right hand side of the page, and click "Submit" after you have created and uploaded your sitemap file; then, refresh the browser.

Google confirms that your sitemap has been added and will update it. It is important that you check back to ensure that your sitemap has completed processing with no errors. The tool at this site creates an HTML sitemap that you can place on your website. It also creates the feed format to submit to Yahoo! as well as a generic XML format for other major search engines.

Creating a sitemap with Google is a must for every website, and it is one of the most important things you can do to improve your site rankings with Google. You will not find a more useful set of applications than you will with Google Webmaster Tools to ensure your site is optimized, error-free, and properly indexed by the Google search engine. You can view your sitemap results at any time.

Google PageRank

PageRank is Google's technique for determining the relative value of a page or a file based upon the number of inbound and outbound links. It is often referred to as the probability of a user randomly clicking links reaching a particular Web page. PageRank, like most modern search algorithms, is based on the quality as well as the quantity of links. This is one reason why you should always license your images correctly so as to protect them from being leeched to other sites. External sites can, however, link to them. This improves your page rank while protecting your Web property.

Google using PageRank has led to a huge increase in the emphasis on links to and from websites in efforts to increase PageRank scores. Google has since changed its algorithm to eliminate links it deems low in quality, lacking Web content, or being irrelevant topically.

You can check out the ranking for any website, page, or domain name at **www.prchecker.info/check_page_rank.php**.

How Google finds you

All search engines use "spiders" or "crawlers" to index your website. They find a page, follow the links to your Web pages, follow links to other pages, and "crawl" the Web in search of all Web pages, indexing each one as they go. This is how your site may be found by Google. You can also submit your URL to Google yourself by visiting **www.google.com/webmasters/tools/submit-url**, or sign up for Google AdWords, which triggers an indexing of your site. Because higher PageRank equates to better search engine placement in the Google search engine, quality inbound links are critical.

Google TrustRank

Google uses a concept known as TrustRank to give higher search engine rankings to trusted sites and lower rankings to sites that are not trusted. Exactly how this works remains a bit of a mystery, so use the advice provided here as you strive to optimize your site for Google.

Here are some factors that may affect your TrustRank ratings:

- **Updating your site:** Adding content shows your site is maintained and current.
- **Inbound links:** Ensure your site is stacked with quality links from websites that have relevant content to your site.
- **Domain name age:** Having an established domain name for several years shows credibility and should give you a benefit over newly established domain names
- **Use sitemaps:** Use XML sitemaps to ensure that search engine spiders can easily index your website
- **Avoid spam:** This means spam email as well as other techniques designed to trick search engines into giving you higher rankings, such as doorways, landing pages, hidden text, and stuffed keywords.

Google's Quality Guidelines

Google's quality guidelines address most of the common techniques employed to overcome and trick search engines in order to achieve higher rankings. This list is not all-inclusive. Use your time and energy to implement proven website design techniques and SEO standards to improve your site in Google's rankings. If you believe another website is abusing Google's quality guidelines, you may report it at **www.google.com/webmasters/ tools/spamreport**.

Here are Google's quality guidelines:

- Make pages primarily for users, not for search engines.
- Avoid tricks intended to improve search engine rankings.
- Do not participate in link schemes designed to increase your site's ranking or PageRank.
- Do not use unauthorized computer programs to submit pages, check rankings, or perform other functions.
- Avoid hidden text or hidden links.
- Do not use cloaking.
- Do not load pages with irrelevant keywords.
- Do not create multiple pages, sub-domains, or domains with duplicate content.
- Do not create pages with malicious behavior, such as phishing or installing viruses or trojans.
- Avoid "doorway" pages created just for search engines.
- If your site participates in an affiliate program, make sure that your site adds value and has content a person would visit based on the content, regardless of whether it has an affiliate program.

Google AdSense

Google AdSense is a program run by Google that allows publishers in the Google Network of content sites to advertise automatic text, image, video, or interactive media advertisements that target site content and audience.

These advertisements are administered, sorted, and maintained by Google. They can generate revenue on either a per-click or per-impression basis.

Google AdSense lets you place Google advertisements on your Web pages, earning money for each click by site visitors. While it is similar in concept to AdWords, you do not pay for it; instead, you give up some real estate on your website to "host" advertisements (relevant content to your website), which Google places onto this space. Instead of paying per click, you actually earn revenue per click, just for hosting the advertisements on your website. The bottom line is that AdSense is simple to use, costs nothing, and can generate significant amounts of residual monthly income for you. You simply sign up and place a small bit of code on your Web page.

Since Google puts relevant ads through the same auction and lets them compete against one another, the auction for the advertisement takes place instantaneously, and Google AdSense subsequently displays a text or image ad(s) that will generate the maximum amount of revenue for you.

The only reason to refrain from using Google AdSense on your site is if you absolutely do not wish to have any advertisements on your site. If you are willing to allow advertisements on your site, you open a new, very powerful potential revenue stream for your business. Do not forget that you should "drive" visitors to your site by promoting it through your blogs, articles, Twitter, Facebook and other social media platforms.

Let's take a look at some types of AdSense products.

AdSense for content

The content-based adverts can be targeted for interest or context. The targeting can be CPC (click) or CPM (impression) based. There is no significant difference between CPC and CPM earnings however CPC ads are more commonly utilized. There are various ad sizes available for content ads. The ads can be simple text, image, animated image, flash, video, or rich media ads. At most ad sizes, users can change whether to show either text and multimedia ads or just one of them. As of November 2012, a grey arrow appears beneath AdSense text ads for easier identification.

Publishers may place up to three AdSense for content units on one web-page. This includes a maximum of one 300×600 ad unit (or similar sized ad) per page.

AdSense for search

AdSense for search allows publishers to display ads relating to search terms on their site and receive 51% of the revenue generated from those ads. Ad-Sense custom search ads can be displayed either alongside the results from an AdSense Custom Search Engine or alongside internal search results through the use of Custom Search Ads. Custom Search Ads are only available to white-listed publishers. Although the revenue share from AdSense for Search (51%) is lower than from AdSense for Content (68%), higher returns can be achieved due to the potential for higher click-through rates.

A maximum of two Google AdSense for search boxes may be placed per page. Also, a single link unit or image ad only may be placed on pages with AdSense for search results. Queries must originate from users inputting data directly into the search box and cannot be modified. This includes pre-populating the search box with terms or hard-coding direct links to search results pages. AdSense for search code may not be integrated into any software application such as a toolbar. The online AdSense for search product is limited to five (5) billion queries per account from the period of July 1 to June 30 of the following year.

AdSense for video

AdSense for video allows publishers with video content to generate revenue using ad placements from Google's extensive advertising network. The publisher is able to decide what type of advertisements are shown against their video inventory. Formats available include linear video ads (pre-roll or post-roll), overlay ads that display AdSense text, and display ads over the video content. Publishers can also display companion ads, which are display ads that run alongside video content outside the player. AdSense for video is for publishers running video content within a player and not for YouTube publishers.

How do you use Google AdSense?

Becoming an AdSense publisher is simple. You must fill out a brief application form online at **www.google.com/adsense**, which requires your website to be reviewed before your application is approved. Once approved, Google will email you an HTML code for you to place on your Web pages. Once the HTML code is saved onto your Web page, it activates, and targeted ads will be displayed on your website.

You must choose an advertisement category to ensure only relevant, targeted advertisements are portrayed on your website. Google has ads for all categories of businesses and for practically all types of content, no matter how broad or specialized. The AdSense program represents advertisers ranging from large global brands to small, local companies. Ads are also targeted by geography, so global businesses can display local advertising with no additional effort. Google AdSense also supports multiple languages.

You can also earn revenue for your business by placing a Google Custom Search Engine box on your website — this pays you for search results. This service may help keep traffic on your site longer since site visitors can search directly from your site; it is also available to you at no cost and is simple to implement. For more details, visit **https://cse.google.com/cse**.

Google says about their ads, "[Our] ad review process ensures that the ads you serve are not only family-friendly, but also comply with our strict editorial guidelines. We combine sensitive language filters, your input, and a team of linguists with good hard common sense to automatically filter out ads that may be inappropriate for your content." Additionally, you can customize the appearance of your ads, choosing from a wide range of colors and templates. This is also the case with Google's search results page. To track your revenue, Google provides you with an arsenal of tools to track your advertising campaign and revenue.

Google AdSense program policies

All publishers are required to adhere to the following policies. If you fail to comply with these policies without permission from Google, they reserve the right to disable ad serving to your site and they can disable your AdSense account at any time. Once disabled, you will not be eligible to participate at all in the AdSense program.

Invalid clicks and impressions

Publishers may not click their own ads or use any means to inflate impressions and/or clicks artificially, including manual methods. This is committing fraud, and it is not tolerated. Clicks on Google ads must result from genuine user interest. Any method that artificially generates clicks or impressions on your Google ads is strictly prohibited. These prohibited methods include, but are not limited to, repeated manual clicks or impressions, automated click and impression generating tools and the use of robots or deceptive software.

Encouraging clicks

Publishers may not ask others to click their ads or use deceptive implementation methods to obtain clicks. This includes offering compensation to users for viewing ads or performing searches, promising to raise money for third parties for such behavior, or placing images next to individual ads. Participants in AdSense may not:

- Encourage users to click the Google ads using phrases such as "click the ads," "support us," "visit these links," or any other similar language
- Direct user attention to the ads using arrows or other graphical gimmicks
- Place misleading images alongside individual ads
- Place ads in a floating box script
- Format ads so that they become indistinguishable from other content on that page
- Place misleading labels above Google ad units. For instance, ads may be labeled "Sponsored Links" or "Advertisements," but not "Favorite Sites" or "Today's Top Offers."

Content guidelines

Publishers may not place AdSense code on pages with content that violates content guidelines. This includes pages that link to other pages that violate content guidelines. Examples may include adult content, violence, hate speech, profanity, pornography, malware, illegal drugs, human slavery and trafficking, products harvested from endangered species, beer and liquor sales, tobacco sales, sale of prescription drugs, weapons or ammunition, gambling, sale of student coursework and essays, racial intolerance, or any other illegal activity. Publishers are also not permitted to place AdSense code on pages with content primarily in an unsupported language.

Copyrighted materials

AdSense publishers may not display Google ads on webpages with content protected by copyright law unless they have the necessary legal rights to display that content.

Counterfeit products

AdSense publishers may not display Google ads on webpages that sell or promote the sale of counterfeit goods. Counterfeit goods contain a trademark or logo that is identical to or substantially indistinguishable from the trademark of another.

Webmaster guidelines for Google AdSense

In order to ensure a good experience for users and advertisers, publishers participating in the AdSense program are required to adhere to specified Webmaster quality guidelines. These guidelines provide many tips for creating sites that help Google search engines to find, index, and rank your site. In general, following these tips will help you to provide a positive experience for your users. The guidelines are quite extensive, so here is just some of the important information:

- Make sure your site adds value. Publishers are not allowed to create multiple pages, sub-domains, or domains with substantially duplicate content.

- Publishers must provide unique and relevant content that gives users a reason to visit their site first.
- Avoid "doorway" pages created just for search engines, or other "cookie cutter" approaches such as affiliate programs with little or no original content.

Below are a variety of guidelines to adhere to to ensure that you are correctly following the rules of the program.

Traffic sources

Google ads may not be placed on pages receiving traffic from certain sources. For example, publishers may not participate in paid-to-click programs, send unwanted emails, or display ads as the result of the action of any software application. Also, publishers using online advertising must ensure that their pages comply with Google's Landing Page Quality Guidelines. To ensure a positive experience for Internet users and Google advertisers, sites displaying Google ads may not:

- Use third-party services that generate clicks or impressions such as paid-to-click, paid-to-surf, autosurf, or click-exchange programs
- Be promoted through unsolicited mass emails or unwanted advertisements on third-party websites.
- Display Google ads, search boxes or search results as a result of the actions of software applications such as toolbars.
- Be loaded by any software that can trigger pop-ups, redirect users to unwanted websites, modify browser settings or otherwise interfere with site navigation. It is your responsibility to ensure that no ad network or affiliate uses such methods to direct traffic to pages that contain your AdSense code.
- Receive traffic from online advertising unless the site complies with the spirit of Google's Landing Page Quality Guidelines. For instance, users should easily be able to find what your ad promises.

Ad behavior

Publishers are permitted to make modifications to the AdSense ad code as long as those modifications do not artificially inflate ad performance or harm advertisers.

Ad placement

Publishers are encouraged to experiment with a variety of placements and ad formats. However, AdSense code may not be placed in inappropriate places such as pop-ups, emails, or software.

Google ads, search boxes, or search results may not be:

- Integrated into a software application of any kind.
- Displayed in pop-ups.
- Placed in emails, email programs, or chat programs.
- Obscured by elements on a page.
- Placed on any non-content-based page.
- Placed on pages published specifically for the purpose of showing ads.
- Placed on pages whose content or URL could confuse users into thinking it is associated with Google due to the misuse of logos, trademarks or other brand features.
- Placed on, within or alongside other Google products or services in a manner that violates the policies of that product or service.

Site Behavior

Sites showing Google ads should be easy for users to navigate. Sites may not change user preferences, redirect users to unwanted websites, initiate downloads, include malware, or contain pop-ups or pop-unders that interfere with site navigation.

Google advertising cookies

AdSense publishers must have and abide by a privacy policy that discloses that third parties may be placing and reading cookies on your user's browsers or are using Web beacons to collect information as a result of ad serving on your website. Google uses the DoubleClick cookie on publisher websites displaying AdSense for content ads.

Identifying users and privacy

You must not pass any information to Google that contains personally identifiable information (PII). You must disclose clearly any data collection, sharing and usage that takes place on any site, app or other property associated with your use of Google AdSense.

Landing page loading time

If it takes too long for your website to load when someone clicks on your ad, they are more likely to give up and leave your website. This unwelcome behavior can signal to Google that your landing page experience is poor, which could negatively impact your Ad Rank. That is why you want to make sure your landing page load time is up to speed.

Here are a few tips to help improve your load time:

- Make sure your landing page loads quickly once someone clicks on your ad, whether on a desktop or mobile device. A great resource to test speed and get specific recommendations is **https://developers.google.com/speed/pagespeed/insights**.
- Help customers quickly find what they are looking for by prioritizing the content that is visible above-the-fold.
- Learn how you or your Webmaster can use PageSpeed Insights to measure the performance of your landing page.

How to setup a Google AdSense account

Setting up a Google AdSense a ccount requires you to go through a four-step process.

1) Submitting your application
2) Placing ads on the site

3) Reviewing your account for approval

4) Having an approved account

The most important thing for success with AdSense is having a website with great content that delights your users — before you apply to AdSense, check that your site has interesting and original content. Make sure that people know about your site before you place ads on it.

First, you need to have a free Google account. Then, login on Google AdSense. Once you have logged in, you will be prompted to fill out information about your website. It involves two pieces of information only:

1) URL of your website

2) Language of the content on your website

Once you have entered the appropriate information, click on continue. You will be taken to the final step of the application submission process. Now, this final form can be almost divided into two halves. The first half asks information that would be used for the payment purposes. It includes your country or territory, time zone, account type (which can be business or individual), and finally the name of the payee.

The second half of the step asks you to fill out specifics related to your address and choices. The information includes your street address, city/town, phone, and email preferences. Once you have filled out the information, check the information you have entered and click "Submit my application" button at the bottom of the form.

How to setup Google AdSense on your website

Once your account has been approved by Google, it is time to integrate Google AdSense with your website. First, you must login to your AdSense panel. At the top, click on the option that says **My Ads**. Click the button named **New Ad Unit**. You will see a setup area where you can name your ad. Then, choose the way you want to show your ad. The options include horizontal banner, vertical banner, rectangular, responsive, custom size, and link ads. You can, for example, choose responsive if you want your ad to be displayed perfectly on a mobile or a tablet. You can leave all the other fields set as default. Click the save button, and a code will be generated for you in a pop-up window. Select and copy this code.

In the Google AdSense panel, you can check the reports regarding the Google AdSense activity on your websites. From there, you can generate code for advertisement blocks with different shapes and formatting and tune your AdSense setup. Once you have the Google AdSense unit code, you should embed the source code into your website.

Using Google AdSense ads effectively

While your goal is to maximize your ad performance with AdSense, it is also important to consider the user experience and the AdSense program policies when placing ads on your site. Here are some tips to keep in mind:

1) Consider your users

Organize your site's content logically and make your site easy to navigate. Here are a few questions to ask yourself when considering where to position your ads:

- What is the user trying to accomplish by visiting my site?
- What do they do when viewing a particular page?
- Where is their attention likely to be focused?
- How can I integrate ads into this area without getting in the user's way?
- How can I keep the page looking clean, uncluttered and inviting?

Think like a user, and you may see your page (and your ad placement) in a whole new way. If users can easily find what they are looking for, they will come back to your site. Also, choose an ad style that is easy for your users to read.

2) Show off your content

Here is an example of how your layout should be:

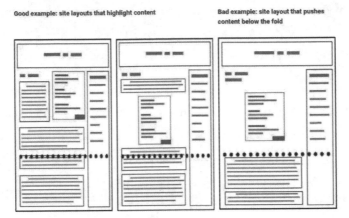

Google screenshots © Google Inc. Used with permission.

Place your ads close to the content that your users are interested in, also make sure that users can easily find the content they are looking for. For example, if your site offers downloads, make sure the download links are above the fold and are easy to find.

3) Keep your ads looking like ads

Choosing ad colors that complement your site is great, but avoid aligning images with your ads or making nearby content mimic their formatting. Displaying ads in these ways is not permitted by Google's program policies.

4) Call them what they are

While it may be tempting to call them "resources" or to place them immediately below your site's headings, take care to avoid labels and headings that may mislead users. Ad units may only be labeled as "Advertisements" or "Sponsored links." Also, avoid placing ads in locations where they might be confused with menu, navigation, or download links.

5) Less can be more

While you are allowed to place three ad units, three link units, and two search boxes on each page of your site, placing the maximum number of ads on your page may make it look cluttered. If users cannot find what they are looking for on your site, they may turn elsewhere for information.

5) Use wider ad sizes

As a rule of thumb, wider ad sizes tend to outperform their taller counterparts, due to their reader-friendly format. Readers absorb information in "thought units," several words at a time. Wider sizes let them comfortably read more text at a glance without having to skip a line and return to the left margin every few words.

If positioned well, wide ad sizes can increase your earnings significantly. The sizes Google has found to be the most effective are the 336x280 large rectangle, the 300x250 medium rectangle, the 728x90 leaderboard, the 300x600 half page, and on mobile, the 320x100 large mobile banner.

6) Use multiple ads the right way

Multiple ad units can help optimize your performance by leveraging Google's large inventory of ads. You can put up to three standard content ad units, three link units and two search boxes on each page of your site. The best way to measure the effect of multiple ad units is to examine the impact on your overall earnings. Multiple ad units may prove particularly successful for the following pages:

- Pages with lots of text, requiring users to scroll down the page.
- Forum or message board pages, particularly within threads.
- Pages where only smaller ad formats (such as the 125 x125 button) will fit.

Setting up Google AdSense payments

Here are the steps to follow to set up your AdSense payments:

1) Provide your tax information (not required in all locations)

To provide tax information, visit the Payee profile page in your AdSense account. Click the edit link next to "Tax information." The interface will guide you to the appropriate forms and requirements for your account.

2) Confirm payee name and address

Since Personal Identification Numbers (PINs) are sent to the mailing address in your account, it is important to confirm the accuracy of your payment address and payee name.

3) Select your form of payment

When your earnings reach the payment method selection threshold, select a form of payment and enter the form of payment details. Depending on your payment address, there may be several forms of payment available to you, including Electronic Funds Transfer (EFT), EFT via Single Euro Payments Area (SEPA), wire transfer, checks, and Western Union Quick Cash. To select a form of payment, visit your Payment settings page.

4) Verify your address

When your earnings reach the address verification threshold, you will be mailed a Personal Identification Number to the payee address in your AdSense account. You must enter this PIN into your AdSense account before you receive any payments. Your PIN will be sent by standard post and may take up to 2-3 weeks to arrive.

5) Meet the payment threshold

If your current balance reaches the payment threshold by the end of the month, a 21-day payment processing period begins. After the processing period ends, Google will issue a payment.

If your current balance has not yet reached the payment threshold, your finalized earnings will roll over to the next month and your balance will accrue until the threshold is met.

Google AdSense tips and tricks

Google AdSense is an outstanding way to generate website traffic, attract advertisers, and create a revenue stream for your business. Use these hints and tips to maximize your earning potential:

- Always follow the Google AdSense Guidelines.
- Do not modify or change the Google AdSense HTML code you place on your website.
- Do not use colored backgrounds on the Google AdSense ads. If you have a website with a colored background, modify the advertisement to match your background.
- Place your ads so they are visible. If someone needs to scroll down to see your ads, you will likely not get any clicks on them. Play with the placement to maximize visibility.
- Do not place ads in pop-up windows.
- Do not buy an "AdSense Template website," which is readily available on Ebay and other online marketplaces. These get-rich type "click" campaigns are against Google's policies and do not make money.
- Text ads tend to do better than Image ads. If you insist on image ads, keep them reasonable in size.
- You can modify the URL link color in the ad through the Google AdSense account panel to make it stand out among your ads and attract the eye of the site visitor.
- If you have a blog, use it to have others place ads in it. You will need to get Google approval for your blog.
- If your website has articles on it that you wish to embed ads in, use these guidelines:
  - o   For short articles, place the ad above the article.
  - o   For long articles, embed the ad within the content of the article.
- Wider-format ads are more successful. The best paying ad format is the "large rectangle."
- Distribute ads on each Web page. Combine ads with referrals and search boxes so your website does not look like a giant billboard.
- Put the Google search box near the top right-hand corner of your Web page.

- If your ads are based on content, the first lines of the Web page determine your site content for ad serving purposes.

- Set the Google AdSense search box results window so that it opens in a new window, as this will keep your browser open and users will not navigate away from your website.

- Google AdSense allows webmasters to customize their Google AdSense ads. Because of this, you can actually customize the links, borders, and color themes of your ads. Borderless AdSense Web banners tend to produce more clicks.

Here are also some top tips from AdSense specialists who work with publishers of all sizes:

1) Show both text and display ads

Display ads compete in the same auction for your ad space that text ads do. So, choosing to show both text and display ads increases the competition for ads to appear on your site, and may help you earn more.

2) Ensure your site has a positive user experience

User experience can make or break your site's success. With many other sites offering similar services, it is important to differentiate your site in the eyes of your users by providing a better experience.

3) Develop a multi-screen strategy

Ensure that you have a mobile strategy for your site (iPad, iPhone, tablet).

4) Experiment with A/B tests

Running an experiment allows you to compare one of your ad settings against a variation of that setting to see which performs better. Experiments help you to make informed decisions about how to configure your ad settings, and can help you to increase your earnings.

5) Integrate your AdSense account with Google Analytics

Google Analytics is a powerful tool that helps you better understand your site visitors and define the right strategy for your site. By integrating Ad-Sense with Analytics, you can improve your ad performance and your user's experience.

You can expand your AdSense account well beyond traditional Web pages. They can be implemented successfully into blogs and feeds. Last year, Google even implemented "Adsense for Feeds," which lets you place ads into RSS feeds, allowing you to increase the reach of your content while earning revenue.

How to set up referrals

The Google AdSense program policies allow you to place one referral per product, for a total of up to four referrals, on any page. You simply click on the referral link to choose your referrals.

Google AdSense will generate the HTML code for your website. Once the code is placed on your Web pages, your referral will be activated and displayed on your website, as shown in the following screenshot. You have a variety of options in size, color, and wording to choose from and are free to change your referral ads at any time.

Google AdSense is simple to implement, non-intrusive to your website, and allows you to open channels to earning potential revenue for your business.

Pay-Per-Click Advertising with Google AdWords

Pay-per-click advertising began in 1998 by a company called Goto.com, which eventually become Overture and was then purchased by Yahoo!. The original concept was that anyone with a business could manage and determine their own search engine ranking based on pre-selected keywords and how much money they were willing to pay for the resultant "click" on their advertisement. Pay-per-click advertising is the fastest growing form of online marketing today. Google is the industry leader in terms of market share and offers advertisers a feature-rich application called Google AdWords.

The difference between Adwords and Adsense is that AdWords allows you to advertise on Google search results, whereas Google Adsense is the tool you would use to display Google Ads on your website, as a potential source of revenue.

The key concept to understand regarding pay-per-click advertising is that unlike other paid advertising campaigns where you pay for the campaign in hopes of generating customers and revenues, you are not paying for any guarantees or promises of sales, website traffic, or increased revenues. You are no longer paying out money in print advertising or other online marketing techniques hoping for a return on your significant investment. Google, the #1 leader in pay-per-click advertising, makes pay-per-click advertising easy, effective, and profitable with Google AdWords; however, there are several other major search engines that offer pay-per-click advertising programs.

Banner advertising was once the largest type of advertising on the Internet, and it still holds a small market share, but its main disadvantage is that the ads are embedded within pages and can be intrusive on the website visitor. You had to rely on a Web designer to put your banner ad on a page that has similar or complementary content and, of course, it is useless unless someone clicks on it. With pay-per-click advertising, you do not pay to have your advertisement loaded on a Web page or to have your advertisement listed at the top of search engines. You only pay for results.

Your ads are only displayed in response to sophisticated formulas based on keywords, relevance, and other facts, which will be fully explained in this section. In other words, pay-per-click advertising is entirely no cost (minus potential setup costs), even if your advertisement is viewed by millions of website visitors. You only pay when your ad is clicked, thus the term pay-per-click.

When someone clicks on your pay-per-click advertisement, Google charges your account, based on a formula price. Bear in mind that the "click" in no way guarantees sales; it merely means that someone has clicked on your advertisement and will be routed in the Web browser to the pre-determined Web page you specified when you created your advertisement. Do not underestimate the importance of having a user-friendly, information-rich website to capture the attention of the site visitor and close the deal. Not all pay-per-click campaigns must result in a purchase — many advertisers use pay-per-click advertising to sell products, but many more use them to sell services, promotional material, news releases, and other media, all intended to build business or disseminate information.

You will likely admire the simplicity and functionality of pay-per-click advertising, which allows you to have significant control over your campaign. Before you forge the path toward implementing a Google AdWords pay-per-click marketing plan, it is critical to understand pay-per-click advertising and develop strategies to design an effective campaign, optimize and monitor overall ad performance, and employ sound business principles in the overall management and financial investment of your campaign. One of the success factors in creating and managing a Google AdWords pay-per-click campaign is the effective selection and use of keywords and key phrases in the creation of your advertisements. Google AdWords offers a variety of tools to help you test out the effectiveness of your advertisements.

To ensure the potential for success of a Google AdWords pay-per-click campaign, you must choose the most effective keywords, design an effective and captivating advertisement, and, as we mentioned earlier, have a well-designed, information-rich website with easy navigation.

What is Google AdWords?

Google AdWords is a user-friendly, quick, and simple way to purchase highly targeted cost-per-click (CPC) or cost-per-impression (CPM) advertising. AdWords ads are displayed along with search results on Google, as well as on search and content sites in the growing Google Network, including

AOL, Ask.com, and Blogger. When you create an AdWords keyword-targeted ad (pay-per-click advertisement), you choose keywords for which your ad will appear and specify the maximum amount you are willing to pay for each click. You only pay when someone clicks on your ad.

When you create an AdWords site-targeted ad, you choose the exact Google Network content sites where your ad will run and specify the maximum amount you are willing to pay for your ad to appear on those sites. In other words, if your ad is displayed in the search engine results with a site-targeted ad, you pay a fee each time for that displayed ad. In traditional AdWords PPC campaigns, you only pay when someone clicks on the advertisement, regardless of how often it is displayed.

We recommend you start out with a Google Adwords keyword targeted ad, and do not allow content matching. There is no minimum monthly charge with Google Adwords, but there is a one-time activation fee for your account. Although your campaign can start in minutes, we highly recommend you invest the time to identify the best keywords possible, and follow our guidance on creating your ad.

Google has hundreds of thousands of high-quality websites, news pages, and blogs that partner with them to display AdWords ads. The Google content network reaches across the entire web, and you can use text, image, and video formats for your ads.

Using the keywords you specify when you create your ad, Google's contextual targeting technology automatically matches your ads to websites that are most relevant in content to your business — this means your ads are displayed only on relevant content sites in relevant content searches. For example, an ad for a laptop hard drive may show up next to an article reviewing the latest notebook computers.

By using the Google Placement Performance Report, you can monitor where all your ads appear, as well as their performance based on impression, click, cost, and conversion data. You can use this in-depth analysis tool to adjust your campaigns, change content, and remove under-performing ads from your campaign. There is no minimum spending threshold, and you can set your maximum monthly budget for each ad. Google provides you with a wealth of tools and information, which will help you choose keywords and stretch your budget to its fullest potential.

Google lets you specify country, state, city, or regions as you create your ads, so they are only served in the markets you choose. This will save your budget from clicks in markets where you have no presence. Thanks to Google Maps, your business location will show up on Google Maps along with contact information. We will discuss Google Maps in detail later.

Creating an AdWords Account

Go to **adwords.google.com** and access the sign-up/sign-in page. Once you are there, enter your email address, select your country, and choose a time zone and currency you would want to operate in.

Then, enter your basic information, create a password, and enter you mobile number to continue. Click **Next** and you will be logged in. Finally, you are prompted to set up billing information.

With AdWords, you have two payment options. Automatic payments allow you to pay after accruing clicks. You will be charged upon reaching your billing threshold or 30 days after your last payment, whichever comes first. If you opt for manual payments, you will prepay AdWords and charges will be deducted from the prepaid amount. When your prepaid balance is diminished, all advertising will be suspended until you make another payment.

You can elect to have payments drafted from either a credit card or a bank account. Keep in mind that Google must verify the bank account, which can take a little while. If you are eager to get your ads up and running, your credit card may be a better option.

Once you have chosen a payment method, you can create your first AdWords campaign.

Creating a Google AdWords campaign

Step 1: Start your campaign

From your Campaign Summary screen, click on **Create your first campaign**.

Step 2: Name campaign and choose campaign type

You will then be greeted with a long form to create the campaign. Create a campaign name and choose the type of campaign you want to create. **Your campaign type determines where your ad shows and the settings and options that are available to you.**

The campaign type you pick determines the places where your ads can appear through Google's advertising networks (Search Network, Display Network), and the different settings and options available to you, such as bidding, location targeting, ad scheduling, or the types of ads you can create.

Choosing the right campaign type can help you tailor your campaign to what is appropriate for your goals, so you can spend time focusing only on the features most relevant to you.

Step 3: Choose location and language

Choose locations where you want to show your ad. It can be a country, city, region, or even a postal code.

Next, choose the language of the sites that your ads can appear on. To decide where to show your ads, AdWords looks at a user's Google language setting or the language of the user's search query, currently viewed page, or recently viewed pages on the Google Display Network (GDN).

Step 4: Choose bid strategy and budget

Bidding is how you pay for users to interact with your ads, which we will look at in further detail soon. Your bid type lets us know if you want to pay for ad clicks (CPC), viewable impressions (vCPM), or conversions (CPA). Your bid amount is the most you are willing to pay and influences how your ad is ranked (ranking will also be discussed in this section).

Your business goals should drive your bid amount, method (manual or automated), and bid type. For example, if you do not want to pay more than $5 for a conversion, you would set a $5 CPA.

Your daily spend varies, and may peak at 20% above your daily budget to help your campaign reach its potential.

If your daily budget is $10.00 throughout the entire month, you will not be charged more than $304.00 for the month ($10.00 daily budget × 30.4 average days per month).

Step 5: Choose ad extensions, if any, and finalize campaign settings

Location extensions display your address and phone number with your ad. If you have a physical storefront, location extensions can show your business address and phone number in your ad. This can help attract customers who are looking for businesses in your area.

Sitelinks expand your ad with extra links to specific pages of your website. The sitelink ad extension lets you show several links beneath your ad. It is free to add these links to your ad, and clicks on a sitelink are priced in the same way as normal ad clicks. Customers get quick access to pages of your site and can choose the specific page they are most interested in.

Call extensions let you add a phone number to your ads. With call extensions, you can connect your customers directly to your business by showing your phone number on ads that run on high-end mobile devices, such as the iPhone or Android phones. If you enable call extensions, your business phone number will show with your ads. You can also use call extensions with forwarding phone numbers to get detailed reporting on calls originating from ads shown on all devices, including computers and mobile phones.

Once you have chosen the extensions you want, verify all the settings you have chosen, and click **Save and continue.**

Step 6: Create an ad group

The next step is to create an ad group. Create an ad group name and start creating an ad.

Creating an ad is a trickier part and needs some explanation at this stage. A Google ad has 5 major parts: headline, description line 1, description line 2, display URL, and final URL.

When it comes to creating your ad, there is essentially a formula for it, since Google limits the number of characters you can use. The four numbers you need to remember are: 25, 35, 35, and 35.

	Example ad	Limit for most languages	Limit for double-width* languages
Headline:	Example website	25 characters	12 characters
Description line 1:	Summer sale	35 characters	17 characters
Description line 2:	Save 15%	35 characters	17 characters
Display URL:	www.example.com	255 characters (35 shown)	255 characters (17 shown)

Image Source: Google

Google screenshots © Google Inc. Used with permission.

You have 25 characters for the title or headline, which is displayed in blue text as the first line of the ad. Then you have 255 characters (35 shown) for the display URL (also called the "vanity URL"), which is not the actual URL to which your ad directs viewers, but is simply for display purposes.

The URL to which you actually direct clicks to your ad is called the "destination URL." These will often be longer and may contain tracking codes, which makes them messier — so, of course, you would not want these displayed in your ads anyway.

Then, you have two description lines of 35 characters each. You will notice in the sample ad above that there are actually a few incentives there. The first line informs viewers that they can shop the summer sale, a more general piece of information, whereas the second line is a call to action for a special offer — save 15 percent.

This is the typical format of a paid search ad, but Google has been doing a lot of testing, so if your ad is displayed at the top of the search results, it may look more like the one below. Here, Google consolidates the title, URL, and the first description line into a banner format. Whichever ads structure you are working with, make sure you maximize use of the limited number of characters you are given, and make your ad as effective as possible.

Step 7: Create an ad group (Select keywords)

The next part of creating an ad group is extremely important; it will determine how your ads will actually perform. A good keyword strategy is to use broad match and phrase match to drive traffic; then, use the Search Terms report to find the keywords that convert well and make sense for your business, and set those to exact match, because they have been proven to work. The best thing to do to figure out your match type strategy is to just keep testing.

Use your performance metrics to optimize your keywords, which could include adding and deleting keywords or changing their match types. It is an ongoing process; keyword performance will change over time, and your campaign strategy should change with it.

Once you have created the ad, enter the keywords in the left text box, one in a line. Click **Save and continue to billing** to proceed.

Step 8: Enter billing details

To activate your AdWords account and run your campaign, you need to enter your billing information. This process is just as important as the previous steps.

Choose a country that will determine the mode of payments you can avail. Enter your tax information. If you are a business, entering your Tax Deduction and Collection Account Number (TAN) will be mandatory. Then, enter your name and billing address.

Here, you choose between automatic payments or manual payments.

The availability in payments will depend on the country from which you are operating. Enter the payment details corresponding to the mode of payment you chose. Choose your billing communication language and click **Complete sign up**.

You have successfully created your first Google AdWords campaign.

Google Adwords Tools

Google provides you with a variety of tools to manage and optimize your campaigns with; they include:

- **Campaign Optimizer:** Automatically creates a customized proposal for your campaign.
- **Keyword Tool:** Builds a list of new keywords for your ad groups and reviews detailed keyword performance statistics, like advertiser competition and search volume.
- **Edit Campaign Negative Keywords:** Manages your negative keywords and reduces wasted clicks.
- **Site and Category Exclusion:** Prevents individual websites or categories of Web pages from showing your ads.
- **IP Exclusion:** Prevents specific Internet Protocol (IP) addresses from seeing your ads.
- **Traffic Estimator:** Estimates how well a keyword might perform.
- **Ad Creation Marketplace:** Finds specialists to help you create multi-media ads.
- **Ads Diagnostic Tool:** Shows how and if your ads are showing up as a result of a search.
- **Ads Preview Tool:** Allows you to see your ad on Google without accruing impressions.
- **Disapproved Ads:** Lets you review ads that have been disapproved.
- **Conversion Tracking:** Lets you see which ads are your best performers.
- **Website Optimizer:** Helps you to discover the best content for boosting your business.

- **Download AdWords Editor:** Enables you to make changes offline, then upload your revised campaigns.

Editing Campaign Settings

To edit your campaign, go to the campaign page. Then, select the campaign you have already created.

Once you click on the ad, you will be directed to the ad groups related to the campaign. You can choose any of the ad group that you feel needs editing; start making the relevant changes.

Moreover, you have a top bar inside the campaign window, which you can use to make other changes in the campaign related to campaign settings, ads, keywords, ad extensions, and other dimension changes.

There are also other tabs in the ad groups window like **Edit, Details, Bid Strategy, and Automate,** which you can use to make other significant changes in the overall campaign.

Using the **Edit** tab, you can pause and remove the campaign altogether or you can change your bids for each of the keywords you have in the ad group.

Pay-per-click advertising benefits

The rules for most pay-per-click search engine applications operate on the same principles: the advertiser with the highest bidder gets top billing in the search engine return. It is a combination of experience, knowledge of the market, and some trial and error, which lets you balance keywords and phrases to deliver optimal results; the tools provided by Google AdWords help you achieve that goal.

One of the benefits of Google AdWords is that your advertisement will be placed right up there with the top-ranked websites in your search category. This is certainly not the only benefit. Here is a list of all of the things that Google AdWords has to offer:

- It is easy to implement.
- The results are clearly measurable.
- It is cost-effective in comparison to other types of traditional and online advertising programs.
- It is for both large and small businesses.
- It is ideal for testing out market response to new products or services.
- It gives you full control over your budget — you can set systematic budgetary limits to minimize your overall financial risk and investment.
- It is more effective than banner advertising.
- It delivers a higher click-through rate than banner advertising.
- Ads are ideally placed with top search engine results on the world's most popular search engine.
- It is only delivered to your potential customers when they are searching on keywords related to your products or services contained in your pay-per-click ad.
- Ads are delivered based on keyword searches and are delivered immediately — meaning the chances of turning one of those potential customers into an actual customer is dramatically increased.
- It allows you to design your ad, which is strategically placed in a prominent location on the website.
- Ads can be delivered in search engine results or within the content of a Web page.

The ads are located at the top of the search results, known as "sponsored links," as well as in the column along the right side of the page:

In the "Sponsored Links" section on the top and on the right-hand side of the page, you will see the pay-per-click results based on the query "laptop computer." As you can see, Sony is top shelf, with Toshiba in second. There is no cost to any of these advertisers to have their sponsored links shown in your search engine results. If I were to click on one of those links, say, the link for Sony, I would be taken to their site, and they would be charged a pre-determined amount for that click.

Another primary benefit of a Google AdWords pay-per-click campaign is that you have fully customizable advertising solutions in your toolbox. You can create dozens of separate pay-per-click ads, with different wording, based on different keywords, all within a single advertising campaign. This gives you tremendous flexibility to target a wide array of potential customer segments. Having a wide variety of advertisements available is a critical component of Google AdWords.

Google screenshots © Google Inc. Used with permission.

Paid vs. organic search

Search Engine Marketing (SEM) is a term used to describe the various means of marketing a website via search engines, and entails both organic search engine optimization and paid search strategies.

Organic search is based on unpaid, natural rankings determined by search engine algorithms, and can be optimized with various search engine optimization practices.

In contrast, **paid search** allows you to pay a fee to have your website displayed on the search engine results page (SERP) when someone types in specific keywords or phrases to the search engine. The SERP will display the ads that you create to direct viewers to your site. The fee you pay is usually based on either clicks on or views of these ads. In other words, you can pay to rank on sponsored search listings.

Google screenshots © Google Inc. Used with permission.

In the image above, the area marked with a dark grey box shows the organic results while the area marked with light grey shows paid results.

On the next page, you will see a diagram of a search engine results page that highlights the positioning of the paid links vs. the organic search results. According to HubSpot data, most searchers click on the organic results — in fact, over 70% of people click on the organic search results, while only 30% are likely to click on the paid links.

This does that mean you should disregard paid search. Paid search is a great option if you are not ranking well in the search engines with organic search alone. It is an extremely powerful tool and a valuable asset for enhancing your company's online presence.

Now that you have a fundamental understanding of what paid search is, let's talk about how you should use it. Note the emphasis on how you *should* use it, not how you *can* use it. The reason for this important distinction is that all too often, companies (especially small businesses) think that if they just pay to be on a search engine, they do not have to invest time and resources in search engine optimization to rank higher organically.

It is important to make clear that paid search is not a replacement for other advertising and marketing efforts nor is it a replacement for SEO and the many other techniques covered in this book. Instead, it should be used to complement other inbound marketing strategies. Paid online advertising can take a lot of time and effort, a lot of resources, as well as a lot of management.

How paid search works

There are three main elements of a paid search campaign:

1. Keywords
2. Ads
3. Landing pages.

You start out by giving Google a list of keywords, which tells Google to display your ads on the results page when people search for those keywords. You then design your ads to be shown for these keywords. Your goal is to make them both relevant enough to the search query and attractive enough to get the searchers to click on them. Then, when viewers click on your ads, the ads direct them to your landing pages. The goal of your landing pages is to get the visitor to convert in some way — for example, by buying your product or downloading an offer. Effective paid searches really come down to managing, matching, and optimizing those three main elements.

The cost of Google AdWords

Google AdWords or any other pay-per-click advertising is, of course, limited by the size of your advertising budget. There are two versions: the Starter Edition and the Standard Edition. Starter Edition is for those who want to advertise a single product or service and for those who are new to Internet advertising. You can upgrade from the Starter Edition to the Standard Edition at any time. You may pay a small set-up fee (currently $5) to set up your Google AdWords account.

Essentially, you "bid" with your competitors with the amount you are willing to pay for each click on your advertisement based on the keywords you choose. It may be cost-prohibitive to be the top bidder, as your advertising budget will be consumed much quicker than if you were a #2 or #3 bidder, but there are also times when it is more critical to be the #1 bidder, regardless of the financial impact. Your bid is the maximum amount you are willing to pay for the website visitor to click on your advertisement, so be careful what amount you are willing to bid per click, as you may have to pay it.

You will know in advance how much each click will cost, and most start out with a minimum price per click, such as 10 cents, and can quickly escalate to significantly more money, even as much as $100 per click, depending on the keyword.

Pay-per-click bidding

What determines how much you pay per click? Google uses an auction-style bid to set their prices. For any given keyword, you have the top bidder – let's say they bid $5 for someone to click on their ad. Then, you have the next highest bidder who values a click at $4.50, another at $3.75, another at $3.00, and so on, all the way down to the last person who says that they value a click on their ad for that keyword at, let's say, $2.25.

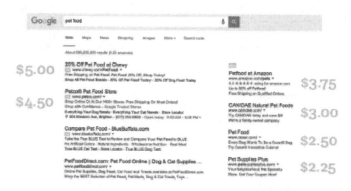

Google screenshots © Google Inc. Used with permission.

These are not the prices you actually pay for each click. Instead, the lowest of these bids is used as the price for the least valuable (least visible) spot on the results page, and then each spot going up in value (more visible placements) is priced at an incremental dollar value higher (we will use a $.05 incremental bid for this example). So in this case, the top bidder ends up paying only $2.50 per click, even though they bid at $5.00.

Google also offers a variety of bidding strategies to help you maximize your budget and maintain flexibility in how your ads are placed. The options you may choose are:

- **Manual bidding:** This option sets the highest price you are willing to pay for each click. Use this option if you need maximum control of each bid.

- **Conversion optimizer:** This option sets the highest price you are willing to pay for each conversion. Google will optimize your performance to aim for the best possible return on investment. To use this feature, you must use Google Conversion Tracking.

- **Budget optimizer:** No bids needed; your budget is set on a 30-day budget, and Google will manage your bids, trying to earn you the most possible clicks within that budget. This is the best option for simplified bidding and is the best choice for new users.

- **Preferred cost bidding:** This option sets the average price you want to pay for each click and lets Google manage your bids to give you a predictable average cost per click.

Establishing a budget

You need to give some considerable thought and planning in determining a manageable budget before starting your pay-per-click campaign. Establishing a monthly budget for a Google AdWords campaign is difficult, because pricing is based on keyword bids, which change in value and fluctuate over time. Most businesses tend to shift advertising funding from traditional marketing programs, such as print media and radio, toward pay-per-click advertising.

An alternative method is to estimate your increased revenue based on your pay-per-click campaign and to establish a percentage-based budget (percent of anticipated or realized increased revenue due to the pay-per-click campaign). The advantage of this type of budget is that you can scale the percentage up or down based on your actual sales derived from the pay-per-click campaign. Google provides you with a Budget Optimizer for AdWords, which helps you to receive the highest number of clicks possible within your specified budget.

The Google Keyword Tool generates potential keywords for your pay-per-click campaign and tells you their statistics, including search performance and seasonal trends. Your CPC will drive your total cost for AdWords, so knowing how much a keyword "costs," is critical to estimating your total monthly costs. Google provides a wide variety of tools to help you establish your account, choose keywords, and manage your budget and your account.

When you pay Google for your PPC campaign, you set a daily budget on the campaign level. So, for each campaign, you can dictate how much money Google can spend on those ad placements per day. I can say, "I want to spend $300/day on my shoe campaign and $200/day on my shirt campaign," and Google will not exceed those limits.

What if all that money is spent in only an hour or two? After all, if you have highly relevant or very popular keywords, you do run the risk of blowing through your budget quickly. Google also offers a feature that allows you to request that your budget be spread out throughout the entire day. This works well for brands that want to establish a presence all day long.

The daily budget cap is certainly a reassuring feature, especially for those who are just starting out with paid search. You can set a low budget when you get started and slowly begin measuring success and lead quality. Try your hand at optimizing your campaign before you really invest a lot of money into it.

You can also measure the return on investment (ROI) for your Google AdWords campaign. Also, if you exceed your budget, a pay-per-click campaign can be cancelled at any time.

To determine what your starting budget should be, you will need to decide how much a pay-per-click conversion (this is when someone clicks on your advertisement and subsequently places an order) is worth in profit to your business, how many additional sales leads your company is ready to handle, your conversion rate (provided by your PPC company), and what your conversion goal is. The formulas below will help you to establish your pay-per-click budget:

- Number of conversions = sales leads per day × % of conversion × 20 work days in month
- PPC budget maximum = $ in profits per conversion × number of conversions
- PPC profit = total profit from pay-per-click campaign – total budget for PPC

Choosing the right keywords

In the use of Google AdWords, a keyword is a word or phrase that people (consumers or businesses) would employ to locate information on the products or services or topic that they are interested in. When choosing the right keywords you will eventually bid on and embed within your advertising campaign, you need to think like a potential customer, not as the seller or advertiser.

You must determine which search terms a potential customer might use to find you through Google. Success is directly related to how "competitive" your chosen keywords are in relation to the terms used by individuals searching in the Google search engine.

You do not own any keywords or have exclusive rights to them, and chances are, your competitors are targeting the exact same keywords. The cost to buy a keyword in a Google AdWords pay-per-click advertising campaign is primarily determined by how many other websites are competing for the same keyword or key phrases.

The Google Traffic Estimator tool provides a wealth of data relevant to your chosen keywords and assists you with determining expected traffic, daily budget, costs per keyword, and overall campaign success.

Keep your keywords focused and specific to your products or services. Extremely general keywords, such as "real estate" are typically more expensive, since many people search on them, but for these same reasons, are not as productive as specific keywords or phrases, such as "real estate foreclosure Miami." Using specific keywords to narrow the amount of times your ads are served will ensure that your advertisement is seen, and potentially clicked by those who are most interested, reducing your overall cost and avoiding paying for clicks that do not convert into sales.

Google's Exact Match is a good feature that serves your advertisement only when the search phrase is an "exact match," instead of a close match or matching on one or more keywords in the search parameters. If your advertisement is on "private mortgage financing," Exact Match will eliminate your ad being served when someone searches on "mortgage financing." If your keywords are not popular, generic terms, then Exact Match may not be the best option. For example, if you are selling ChefTec software, which is Recipe Costing Software, the searcher may not know the brand name

"ChefTec," and may be searching for "Recipe Costing Software" with Exact Match, in which case they would never see your ad.

Essentially, Google recommends that you choose your keywords carefully by including specific keywords that are directly related to your ad group or landing page. You should include relevant keyword variations, along with singular and plural versions. The goal is to have your ad served often (impressions), but drive your click rate up. Using keyword-matching options enables you to drill down to your specific audience by ensuring that your ad is served to the best audience. Using negative keywords will reduce your ad impressions and increase your quality score with Google, which will ultimately save you money by avoiding clicks.

If the user is searching for a specific product or information, take them directly to it so they have the information they are seeking instantly. Sending them to the home page to search for information will drive customers away from your website. Incorporate your keywords into your ad text, and especially into the title of the ad. Provide insightful, unique, or captivating information in your ad and landing pages that will draw in customers.

To use the Google Keyword Tool and Google Keyword Cost Calculator, enter keywords into the appropriate fields along with some optional entries, such as maximum CPC, daily budget limits, and targeted languages and locations; click continue to see the results. The results provide you with an average cost per click, volume, estimated ad position, estimated number of clicks per day, and estimated cost per day.

The primary factor in determining cost is the relationship of the keyword to top 10 rankings within a search engine. If your keywords are not competitive (meaning that not many companies are trying to use the same keywords in their campaign), then the cost of the keyword is relatively low, and they will yield high search engine rankings if used in a keyword search. If you are competing with hundreds or thousands of other companies for the same keywords, the cost of those keywords will escalate dramatically. Google AdWords' minimum cost-per-click base rates depend on your location and currency settings. Your minimum CPC rates can fluctuate for each keyword based on its relevance (or quality score). The quality is the most important factor in determining the cost you will pay when someone clicks on your ad. Your quality score sets the minimum bid you will need to pay in order for your keyword to trigger ads. If your maximum CPC is less than the minimum bid assigned to your keyword, you will need to either raise the CPC to the minimum bid listed or optimize your campaign for quality.

A key principle in selecting keywords is in the determination of how often someone will search the Web using that keyword or phrase. Logically, keywords that are less competitive will typically bring you less traffic, simply because the keyword is not used often during a search. Conversely, you can expect more traffic with highly competitive keywords, but this may not always be the case, as the field of competitors often grows directly in proportion to the keyword competitiveness.

When you begin your PPC campaign, you should be provided with an in-depth analysis on a regular basis to help you monitor, adjust, and evaluate the performance of your marketing campaign. These reports should tell you exactly what keywords are being used by people who are using search engines with your campaign, which helps you determine whether your chosen keywords are effective.

Keyword Research Tools

Another method to determine what keywords you should use is to use one of many keyword research tools provided on the Internet (please note that not all these tools are free). Here are some of the keyword research tools you can use to display results.

WordTracker: Promises to find the best keywords for your website. You can enter any word or phrase, and a list of possibilities will appear.

You choose the keywords you want to use and the application returns "count" and "prediction" reports. Count is the number of times a particular keyword has appeared in the WordTracker database, while prediction is the maximum total predicted traffic for all of the major search engines/pay per bids and directories today.

Google Keyword Planner: The Google Keyword Tool generates potential keywords for your ad campaign and reports their Google statistics, including search performance and seasonal trends. The Google Keyword Tool can generate a variety of data, including keywords, key phrases, keyword popularity, cost and ad position estimates, global search, positive trends, and negative keywords.

Of the tools listed, Google is by far the most user-friendly and comprehensive. There are also dozens of other keyword generation tools available on the Internet. The Google Search-based Keyword Tool provides keyword ideas based on actual Google search queries, matched to specific pages of your website with your ad.

How to Develop Keywords

One of the biggest challenges when establishing your website and Google AdWords campaign is developing your initial list of keywords and key phrases. You must develop a list of "potential" keywords or key phrases. Here are some tips:

- Brainstorm. Develop a list of all the possible keywords or key phrases you believe people might try to find your website with.
- Screen your employees, friends, and customer base for a list of all the possible keywords or key phrases you believe they might try to find your website with.
- Screen your competitor's websites for a list of all the possible keywords or key phrases on their website.
- Incorporate your company name, catch phrases, slogans, or other recognizable marketing material into keywords.
- Add both the singular and the plural spellings of your keywords.
- Add your domain names to your list of keywords — you will be surprised how many people search for a company by the URL

instead of the company name (i.e., **atlantic-pub.com** instead of Atlantic Publishing Company).

- Take a peek at the meta tags on competitors' websites, in particular, the "keywords" tag; review this list and add them to your keywords list.

- Avoid trademark issues and disputes. Although there is some degree of latitude in regard to trademarks, it is best to avoid using other companies' trademarks unless you are an authorized distributor or reseller of their products.

- Put keywords in the *title* of your pay-per-click advertisement to generate a much higher click-through rate.

- Use bold face font in the *title* of your pay-per-click advertisement.

- Incorporate words that add to your pay-per-click advertisement, such as amazing, authentic, fascinating, powerful, revolutionary, or unconditional.

- End your ads with words that promote an action on the part of the reader, such as Be the First, Click Here for all the Details, Limited Time Offer, or Free Today.

Take your entire list of keywords and key phrases and use the tools we have provided to refine your list and identify the most competitive, cost-effective keywords.

Quality score

While your bid does play a large role in determining whether or not your ad is served for a given keyword, Google also uses something called "quality score" in making these decisions. Quality score is an algorithm that scores each of your ads for relevancy — it looks at how closely your keyword relates to your ad and how closely your ad relates to your landing page content. In other words, Google actually scans your landing pages to ensure that you are not just buying keywords and directing them to totally irrelevant pages.

Google's motivation for including quality score in the evaluation of each keyword is to provide an optimal user experience for their searchers. It used to be that ad placement was determined solely by bids, but then some-one could easily bid on "toothbrushes" when they were really selling lawn mowers. Google introduced quality score to make sure that the ads they were displaying were always relevant to the search terms, and to keep their advertisers in check.

How quality score works

Quality score is on a scale of 1 to 10, with 1 being the lowest rating and 10 being the highest. What this means is that if your competitor bids on a keyword at $5 and has a quality score of 4, and you bid on that same keyword at only $3 but you have a quality score of 7, Google may give you the top position for the price you bid because your ad is more relevant. It makes more sense to serve your ad because its higher relevancy makes it more likely that viewers will click on it.

Quality score can also help you determine what keywords are cost-efficient for you to use. Let's say, for example, that you have a site about fitness tips, and you bid on the keyword "nutrition." If you find that you have a low quality score, it may indicate that the content on your site is not relevant enough to compete in that space, and it is not a cost-efficient channel for you. You can use this information to optimize your choice of keywords, Great tools to help you with keywords are located at **https://serps.com/tools/rank_checker**, in Google AdWords, and at **https://adwords.google.com/KeywordPlanner**.

If you want to set yourself up for a successful PPC campaign, show Google how tight you can make the relationships between the keywords you are bidding on, and the ad copy that you are displaying, and the landing pages you are directing to. If you can do this, Google will see that you really know what you are doing, and they will be far more likely to put your ad in that top position for the least amount of money possible.

Now that we know what the terms "bidding" and "quality score" mean, we can take a look at how they interact to affect your Ad Rank.

Google Ad Rank

Ads are positioned in both search and content pages based on their Ad Rank. Simply put, the ad with the highest ranking appears in the first position, and so on down the page.

Here is where it starts to get confusing. While the Ad Rank determines where an ad is placed, the criteria Google uses to determine Ad Rank differs for keyword-targeted ads, depending on whether they appear on Google and the search network or just on the content network.

Google's search network

Ad Rank determines the order in which competing ads should be ranked on a SERP, which has a huge impact on the visibility of your ads to potential customers.

$$Ad\ Rank = CPC\ bid \times Quality\ Score$$

A keyword-based ad is ranked on a corresponding search engine result page based on the matched keyword's cost-per-click (CPC) bid and quality score.

The quality score for Ad Rank on Google and the search network is determined by a number of factors, including the following:

- Historical click-through rate (CTR) of the keyword and the matched ad on Google
- Account history, measured by the CTR of all the ads and keywords in your Google Adwords account
- Historical CTR of the display URLs in the ad group
- Relevance of the keyword to the ads in its ad group
- Relevance of the keyword and the matched ad to the search query
- Your account's performance in the geographic region where the ad will be shown
- Other relevance factors, as determined by Google

Google allows up to three AdWords ads to appear above the search results, as opposed to on the side. It is important to note that only ads that exceed a certain quality score and CPC bid threshold may appear in these positions. If the three highest-ranked ads all surpass these thresholds, then they will appear in order above the search results.

The CPC bid threshold is determined by the matched keyword's quality score; the higher quality score, the lower the CPC threshold.

Content network

Your keyword-based ad is positioned on a content page based on the ad group's content bid and quality score.

$$Ad\ Rank = Content\ Bid \times Quality\ Score$$

The quality score related to Ad Rank is determined by:

- The ad's past performance
- Relevance of the ads and keywords
- Landing page quality
- Other relevance factors, as determined by Google

If a placement-targeted ad wins a position on a content page, it uses up all of the ad space so no other ads can show on that page. To determine whether your placement-targeted ad will show, Google considers the bid you have made for that ad group or for the individual placement, along with the ad group's quality score.

$$Ad\ Rank = Bid \times Quality\ Score$$

Google states that the quality score for determining whether a placement-targeted ad will appear on a particular site depends on the campaign's bidding option.

If the campaign uses cost-per-thousand-impressions (CPM) bidding, quality score is based on the quality of your landing page.

If the campaign uses cost-per-click (CPC) bidding, quality score is based on the historical CTR of the ad on this and similar sites as well as the quality of your landing page.

How to improve your ranking

The following factors all result in a higher position for your ad:

- Relevant keywords
- Relevant text within your ads
- A good click-through rate on Google
- A high keyword cost-per-click bid

The theory is that this system, which is not based entirely on the price you are willing to pay per click, uses well-targeted, relevant ads to ensure that the quality of your ads is factored into the placement. It also helps ensure that your ads can get placed, despite not being the top keyword bidder.

The AdWords Discounter monitors other ads and will automatically reduce the CPC for your ads, so that you pay the lowest possible price for your ad's position on the search engine results page. One of the main advantages of this system is that you cannot be locked out of the top position, as you would be in a ranking system, based solely on price.

When you have completed the account setup process, you will be required to activate your account through an opt-in email, which is sent to your specified email account. Once this is confirmed, your account is activated and you can log into your new Google AdWords account.

At this point, you will be required to enter your billing information. Upon completion of your billing information, your ad often appears within minutes. Google AdWords is set up to operate with three distinct levels — Account, Campaign, and Ad Group.

In summary:

- Your account is associated with a unique email address, password, and billing information.

- At the Campaign level, you choose your daily budget, geographic and language targeting, distribution preferences, and end dates.
- At the Ad Group level, you create ads and choose keywords. You can also select a maximum CPC for the Ad Group or for individual keywords.
- Within each Ad Group, you create one or more ads and select a set of keywords to trigger those ads. Each Ad Group runs on one set of keywords. If you create multiple ads in an Ad Group, the ads will rotate for those keywords.
- When you log in to your account, you can see your ad's click-through rates (CTRs) listed below each of the ads. If a particular ad is not performing as well as the others, you can delete or refine it to improve the overall performance of your Ad Group.

Ad options

Google features multiple advertisement options, which include text ads, image ads, local business ads, mobile business text ads, video ads, and display ad builders.

Text Ads

Text ads are advertisements on the Web that are text or character based and do not contain any images, photos, or videos. See the example below:

Luxury Cruise to Mars
Visit the Red Planet in style.
Low-gravity fun for everyone!
www.example.com

Google screenshots © Google Inc. Used with permission.

Image Ads

Image ads are advertisements on the Web that contain images, photos, or videos Text is integrated into the images. See the example below:

Google screenshots © Google Inc. Used with permission.

Local Business Ad

Local business ads are AdWords ads associated with a specific Google Maps business listing. They show on Google Maps with an enhanced location marker. They also show in a text-only format on Google and other sites in our search network.

Mobile Business Text Ad

Your ads will appear when someone uses Google Mobile Search on a mobile device.

Video Ad

Video ads are an ad format that will appear on the Google content network. Your video ad will appear as a static image until a user clicks on it and your video is played.

Display Ad Builder

This new feature lets you create your own display ad as easily as building text ads. When you are done creating your new ad, it will run on Google partner sites based on the target settings you choose.

I recommend you start out your campaigns with the text ad. Google AdWords provides you with a simple form to create it. As you enter data into the form, the example is updated with your data. You will need to give some extra time and attention to the wording of your ad. Wording can be tricky because of the limited space you are given on each line of the ad, as well as the restrictions imposed by Google.

It is critical to load the title (first line of your Google AdWord ad) with keywords. Your goal is to capture the attention and interest of a potential customer. If you can do that, your ad will be successful. Test multiple versions of an ad to see which works best, and change keywords to help you analyze which is most effective. Review the ads of competitors; you may find they are outperforming you simply because their ad is better written, more captivating, or has more customer appeal. The use of words like free, rebate, bonus, and cash are perfect for attracting the attention of website surfers. Other words that may encourage website visitors to click through your ad should be used, as long as your ad message is concise and clear.

You should also consider the domain name listed in your advertisement, as it may have an effect on your ability to draw in potential customers. Your domain name should be directly related to your products or services and should be professional in nature.

Copywriting

You will find an abundance of companies that offer search engine copywriting services, which is a good option if you are having problems developing successful ad campaigns.

Some recommended sources for copywriting include:

- **www.searchenginewriting.com**
- **www.roncastle.com/web_copywriting.htm**
- **www.futurenettechnologies.com/creative-copywriting.htm**
- **www.tinawrites.com**

Search engine copywriting is critical to a successful pay-per-click advertising campaign. While we have recommended professional services for this task, it is not overly difficult to achieve if you apply some basic discipline and rules.

I have stressed the insertion of keywords into an advertisement, but simply cramming keyword after keyword into your pay-per-click advertisements may be counter-productive, and is not search engine copywriting. Successful SEO copywriting takes planning, discipline, analysis and a degree of trial and error.

Below are some guidelines for successful SEO copywriting:

- Use no more than four keywords per ad. Four keywords provide a wide keyword variety without saturating the ad with keywords and losing the meaning of the ad.
- Use all your allowed characters in each line of the advertisement. There is no incentive for white space.
- Write in natural language. "Natural language" is a popular term used extensively with copywriting. It simply means that the reader should not be able to — or should barely be able to — detect what keywords the ad is targeting. The best ads are written for an individual to read and understand, embedded with subtle keywords, and project a clear message; thus, they read "naturally." The opposite of this is a keyword-crammed ad that is nothing more than a collection of keywords, and is therefore entirely "unnatural" to read.
- Use keywords in the title and description lines, but use common sense so that you do not overload them with keywords.
- Test your ad and analyze your reports and results. Your ad may need tweaking or improvements, or it may be entirely ineffective and may need to be replaced.

You may discover that the costs can escalate quickly if you do not set daily and monthly budget limitations. Keep in mind that limits on your budget will also affect your ad performance, since your ad will not be displayed once you hit your budget limits. Google recognizes when your advertisement is bumping against its budget constraints and may suggest you increase your budget amount to increase visibility of your advertisement.

PPC fraud

Google AdWords PPC advertising can be extraordinarily profitable and, if managed correctly, will dramatically increase your customer base and potential revenue by driving targeted visitors to your site. Once you master the techniques of PPC advertising, in addition to managing and optimizing your campaigns, one of your biggest challenges will be recognizing and combating fraud.

PPC fraud refers to a well-thought-out, targeted, technologically advanced, and highly destructive automated process of creating applications, scripts, robots, or even sometimes humans, which will continue to generate thousands upon thousands of clicks using ingenious techniques to disguise their identity with IP spoofing (and many others), all designed to cost you thousands of dollars in fraudulent clicks.

You need to recognize and understand that you will not sell a product with every click on your advertisement. If you have ten clicks today on your advertisement and sell two products as a direct result of those clicks, your conversion rate is 20 percent. Most PPC providers provide you with free tools to automate the tracking of your conversion rates. Not everyone who clicks on your pay-per-click ad will buy your products, some of these reasons may include:

- Lack of interest in your products
- Being turned off by your Web page or website
- Inability to find enough information about your product on your site
- Price
- Brand
- Availability
- Competition
- Technical problems, such as a malfunctioning shopping cart

As much as 70 percent of annual online advertising spending is wasted because of click fraud. Corrupt affiliates of ad networks, such as Google and Yahoo!, account for 85 percent of all click fraud. The website **www. clickfraud.com** is one of the growing number of companies that can assist you in combating PPC fraud. Clickrisk offers "Click Verification Service," a full-service 12-month engagement that helps detect click fraud, guard against it in the future, and obtain refunds on your PPC ad spending.

You should know the following facts about PPC fraud:

- Search engine companies, PPC providers, and advertisers agree that click fraud exists.
- Search engine companies and PPC providers agree that PPC advertisers should not be billed for fraudulent click activity.
- Search engine companies have stated that they have effective "click fraud" protection built into major search engines.

Here are some tips and suggestions on how you can combat click fraud without breaking your budget:

- Keep current with published anti-click fraud tips and suggestions.
- Do your research when selecting a pay-per-click provider. While there are many reputable providers, review their policies and tools for combating fraud before you sign up.
- Do not sign up with PPC companies that allow "incentive sites." An incentive site is one that offers free products, free competitions, or "junk" promotions (this applies to AdSense-type campaigns where you are allowing advertisement on your website).
- Monitor click-through rates.
- Review your website traffic reports.
- Place daily click limits in your campaign.
- Establish a daily budget to limit your total costs per day.
- Limit your ad to your target geographic audience.
- Review your IP referral logs (usually provided by your website hosting company or the PPC provider). If you have multiple clicks from the same IP address, you are likely the victim of fraud.
- Report potential fraud to your PPC provider.

This list of recommended fraud protection providers will help you in your fight to combat fraud and protect your financial investment in your pay-per-click marketing campaign. All major pay-per-click providers have active fraud protection measures in place, but their degree of effectiveness is difficult for you to determine. If you want to provide an additional layer of protection for your investment, you may want to consider AdWatcher:

- **AdWatcher™ (www.adwatcher.com):** AdWatcher is an all-in-one ad management, tracking, and fraud prevention tool focused on helping businesses automate and improve their online marketing efforts. It was developed by the team of advertising experts at MordComm, Inc. — a New York-based online marketing firm. Founded in 2003, the company has gained early success providing practical tools to help business owners get more out of search marketing. It currently also operates AdScientist — PPC bid management and optimization software that helps you manage your keyword bids in all the major PPC search engines.

Tips, Tricks, & Secrets for Google AdWords PPC Advertising

This is a compilation of some tips and hints that will help you to develop and manage a highly effective Google Adwords Campaign, which will generate higher click-through rates, lower your cost per click, and get conversions:

- Ensure your Google AdWords ad is specific in nature.
- Target one product for each Google AdWords ad instead of using a generic ad that targets a large market segment.
- Make your ad link directly to the product page with a link to buy the product on that page, instead of to a generic page or the website home page.
- If your Google AdWords ad targets a specific product, you may see a reduction in clicks because your advertising segment is narrow, but those clicks are most likely extremely profitable since you are only getting clicks from individuals seeking information

on your specific product — this means your advertising cost may actually be reduced, while your sales go up.

- Be willing to bid for a good position. If you do not want to spend much money or are willing to settle for the bottom of the bids, no one is going to see your ad.

- Bid enough to gain the exposure you need, but balance exposure to stretch your advertising budget. It rarely is worth the cost to have the No. 1 bid, and it is often significantly less costly if you are in positions 2 through 10.

- Being the No. 1 listing on search engines may not be all it is cracked up to be. The top listing is the one that is clicked the most often, but is also has the worst percentage of converting clicks into actual sales. Many "click happy" people click on the top listing without ever making a purchase. Those "clicks" will quickly eat up your advertising budget. You may have better luck by being below the No. 1 listing, since you have the potential for better-qualified clicks.

- Use the provided tracking tools to monitor performance and adjust keywords/bidding as necessary.

- Use capital letters for each word in the title and in the description fields of your ad.

- Use demographic and geographic targeting.

- Use the Google Keyword Suggestion Tool to help you determine which keywords are most effective for your campaign.

- Keep an eye out for fraud.

- Check the spelling in your ad to ensure it is correct.

- Develop multiple advertisements for each campaign, and run them at the same time. You will quickly determine which is effective, and which is not. Do not be afraid to tweak advertisements or replace poorly performing advertisements.

- Monitor and use Google Reports by tracking your costs, return on investment, and the click-through ratios for each ad.

- Include words that stand out and grab the attention of potential customers, such as "New" and "Limited Offer."
- Free may not be good for you. If your advertisement says "free," then you can expect considerable traffic from folks who just want the "free" stuff and will never actually buy anything, which will just increase your costs. Consider limiting the use of "free" to cut back on traffic that will never result in a sale.

Google Merchant Center

Google Merchant Center allows you to upload your product data, which potentially allows millions of shoppers to see your online and in-store inventory. You create shopping campaigns with your product images, item prices, and business information into an online database which allows your products to be displayed in Google Searches. Google Merchant Center uses a familiar pay-per-click formula where you only pay when people click through to visit your website or view your inventory — the advantage is that your items show up in Google searches at no cost to you.

Google Shopping ads are displayed along with Google search results when people are searching for similar types of products. Ads will show in a variety of platforms. You have full control over the products, inventory, formatting, promotions, and sales. You can become a "Google Trusted Store" which displays the words "Google Trusted Store" on the ads returned on search engine queries, giving buyers peace of mind in knowing that your business has earned the seal of approval from Google.

Google Merchant Center also displays product ratings, very similar to "product reviews" you would see on Amazon. Your ads can tie your ad directly into Google Maps showing your business location and other pertinent information directly in the application. Google Merchant Center works with Google AdWords; Google AdWords lets you set up your shopping campaign, establish your advertising budget, and set how much you are willing to pay per click.

Google Merchant Center is a great choice if you wish to sell products on the Web harnessing the power of Google, but do not want to set up a website, shopping cart, Secure Socket Layer (SSL) Certificates, and so on. Some businesses have chosen to use Google Merchant Center to complement their existing retail business or their existing website, while others use it simply as a low cost option for selling products without much work and with the help of Google AdWords.

Once you set up your Google Merchant Account, you create and upload your product data, which is done in a preformatted data feed through the Google API for Shopping. If you have an existing e-commerce shopping cart, many will produce and export the properly formatted data file which is ready for input into Google Merchant Center, or you may even link directly from your e-commerce platform directly to your Google Merchant Account, which provides you with a live and continuous update. You can find out much more about Google Merchant Center at **https://www. google.com/retail/merchant-center**.

Google Shopping

Google Shopping is the online Google store that is populated by participants in Google Merchant Center. While most results are returned as a result of Google searches, you can also shop at www.google.com/shopping.

You can type anything you wish into the search box. In our case, we will type in my name, Bruce C Brown, and see what results we get:

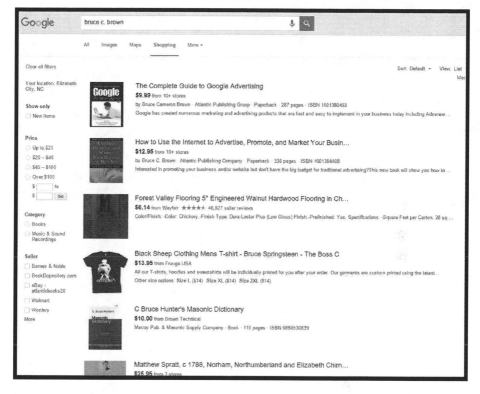

Google screenshots © Google Inc. Used with permission.

As you see above you will get a variety of returns. In our search, it brought up several of my books including "The Complete Guide to Google Advertising." You can see that it is available for sale from 10+ stores. If you click on the product link, you get a detailed breakdown of purchasing options. You can compare pricing and shipping costs between all of the sellers including their seller ratings; this lets you make your most informed buying decision as a shopper, and it lets you see how your Google Merchant Account compares to your competitors.

You will notice a link to Google Play in the image, which is the official app store for the Android operating system as well as a digital media store with music, books, movies, games and television shows; it is very similar to Apple's iTunes®.

Google Shopping is an outstanding price comparison program. You can use it to drive business to your website and to promote your products. You can easily submit your products to Google Shopping, thereby allowing shoppers worldwide to find your products, as well as your website, blog, or social media platform quickly and easily.

Uploading products to Google Product Search is very simple, and Google guides you through the step-by-step process. You can access Google Product Search through your Google account. To access the user interface, go to **http://www.google.com/products**.

Chapter 8

Various Types of Internet Advertising

*W*hile Google provides you with many ways to successfully advertise and market your business, there are some other tactics you can use to achieve the same result. In this chapter, we will take a look at banner advertising, Groupon, Living Social, Pandora, and Spotify.

Banner Advertising

A Web banner or banner ad is simply a form of advertising on the World Wide Web. Banner advertising involves embedding an advertisement into a Web page. Banner ads are designed to draw traffic to a website by linking them back to the website of the advertiser. The advertisement is typically comprised of an image (GIF, JPEG) but can come in Flash or other technologies. Banner ads are typically placed on pages with relevant content.

The Web banner is displayed when a Web page that references the banner through its source code is loaded into the browser. When the banner is loaded into a site visitor's browser, this is what is known as an "impression."

When the site visitor then clicks on the banner, the visitor is directed through a hyperlink embedded in the banner ad to the website advertised in the banner. This is what is commonly known as a "click-through." Banner ads are commonly "served" through a centralized ad server; however, they may also be embedded directly into the Web pages. Even if they are embedded, they can be rotated by using scripting to rotate multiple image files, or by creating an animated GIF file, which automatically changes the displayed images on a preset timer.

Most banner ads operate under a "pay-per-click" system or under an affiliate system. With pay-per-click, such as Google AdWords, you create your banner ads on the fly within the AdWords application. With affiliate software, you typically either create an array of banner ads (if you are hosting the affiliate program), or simply have an array of banners to choose from if you are joining an affiliate network or becoming an affiliate of someone else.

Software tracks the number of "clicks," and each click will generate revenue to the content provider of the banner ad (not the advertiser). The advertiser typically does not make any commission on the click-throughs; instead, they get the direct sales if a customer buys from them.

Banner ads are very similar to traditional roadside banner or billboard advertisements. They notify potential consumers of the product or service and strive to create enough interest to get that customer to click the banner and travel to their website to buy their products or services. Banner ads also allow you to be much more dynamic when it comes to your advertising techniques, because you can change the way the image looks at any time and you can add unique forms of animation to the banner ad. Banner ads are typically annoying, and many Internet users consider them as spam or a nuisance. All modern Web browsers have the ability to block most pop-up banner ads.

Why should I use banner ads?

There are several reasons why online or traditional storefront businesses may choose to use banner ads to promote their products and services. Some of the reasons include:

- To increase the amount of Web traffic to their website
- To increase the sales of their products and services
- To let their customers know about any special deals that they are offering or any new products or services that they are selling
- To get their name out onto the Internet so that potential customers know who they are

How do they work?

Banner ads are essentially an image with embedded HTML code, which launches a hyperlink when clicked. The HTML code tells the Web browser, or server, to pull up a certain Web page when someone clicks on that particular hypertext which is displayed in the banner as text, graphics, or a combination of both.

Typically, a third-tier server is utilized to track the impression and click-throughs. Overall, traditional banner advertising success continues on a downhill trend, while pay-per-click advertising grows. The models for both are different, and the dynamically generated pay-per-click ads are much less obtrusive than larger, traditional banner ads. That said, particularly when used as part of a PPC or affiliate marketing campaign, they are still an effective, low-cost form of advertising (usually under ten cents per click) and the banner provider or hosting company then bills the advertiser on a pre-determined basis.

Over the past five years, Shockwave® and Adobe Flash technology have become increasingly popular by incorporating animation, sound, and action into banner advertisements. Banner ads are created in a variety of shapes and sizes depending on the site content and design and are designed to be placed unobtrusively in the "white" space available in a traditionally designed Web page.

When a page is loaded into a Web browser, the banner is loaded onto the page, creating what is called an "impression." An impression simply means that the Web page containing the advertisement was loaded and potentially viewed by someone who is browsing that website.

Impressions are important to advertisers to track how many visitors loaded that particular page (and banner ad) in a set period of time. If the impression count is low, it is logical that the click-through rate and subsequent sales will also be extremely low.

Click-through's are important to advertisers, because they track how many visitors actually clicked on a particular banner ad and how many resultant sales were generated by the banner ad in a set period of time. Unfortunately, a high click-through rate does not necessarily guarantee high sales. Banner ads can be static (embedded within the actual HTML page) by the webmaster or may be "served" through a central server, which enables advertisers to display a wide variety of banner ads on thousands of websites with minimal effort.

Types of banner ads

Using banner ads does not mean that you are limited to one kind of ad to use to advertise your product or service. In fact, there are many different types of banner ads from which you can choose, including altering the shape and size of the banner ad to suit your purposes. There are eight different unique sizes of banner ads from which you can choose, as indicated by the Internet Advertising Bureau (IAB). Each of these banner ad sizes is based on a pixel, which is the unit, or section, of color that creates the images that you see on your computer or television. The standard specific sizes for banners, as dictated by the IAB, are as follows:

- A full banner: 486 by 60 pixels
- A vertical navigation bar on a full banner: 392 by 72 pixels
- A half banner: 234 by 60 pixels
- A vertical banner: 120 by 240 pixels
- A square button banner: 125 by 125 pixels
- Button size, number 1: 120 by 90 pixels
- Button size, number 2: 120 by 60 pixels
- A small, or micro-size, button: 88 by 31 pixels

The most commonly used banner size is the full banner, at 486 by 60 pixels. However, you will find all sizes of banner ads in all areas of the Internet, with many variations of the standard sizes.

The above banner sizes of pixels are not the only banner sizes that you need to stick to, but they are by far the most common, and you should stick to the standards whenever possible. Keep in mind that banner size is also dictated by the amount of memory size that can be given to the banner.

When you look at already existing banner ads on the Internet, you will notice that there are many different varieties of graphic and other animated creativity to be found among banner ads. Some of the most simplistic banner ads will have only one JPEG or GIF image on them that link the banner ad to the main website of the company doing the advertising. By far, the most popular of all the banner ads is an animated ad that uses a GIF animation tool. GIF animation allows the banner ad to change over a few minutes, showing various GIF images one after the other, and many times in a flowing sequence. These ads instantly grab the attention of visitors. There are many programs available that help you create animated GIF images, and many are free and can be found with a quick Web search.

How to make banner ads

Even if you have minimal knowledge about computers, you will be able to make a simple banner ad for your website. Making a banner ad is simply a matter of coding and imaging with HTML hyperlink tags that are going to link back to your website. You will be able to develop the graphics for your banner ad with the use of software such as Paint Shop Pro or most other graphics programs such as Microsoft Digital Image Suite. The following is the simple coding that is used for a banner ad:

<a href="http://www.YourWebSiteHere.com"> <img src="http://static.YourWebSiteHere.com/gif/banner-ad-static.gif"> </a>

You can make simple banner ads on your own without too much computer knowledge, and keep in mind that GIF-animated banner ads are not that much more difficult to make yourself than any other banner ads. If you want to use banner ads that are filled with media, such as Shockwave programming, Java programming, audio techniques, or video techniques, you might want to hire someone to do the banner coding for you; however, this is typically not cost effective for emerging online businesses. You want your banner ads to look as professional as possible so that you keep up with your competition.

The price that you pay for your professionally designed banner ad will vary from as low as $75 to as much as $1200, depending on what type of banner ad you want and how much you are willing to spend. If you use services such as Google AdWords, you can create your ads on the fly in the Google AdWords system, greatly simplifying the process for you.

You can also pay certain websites to be a host for your banner ads, you can do an exchange program, where you post the banner ads for another advertiser and they post your banner ads on their website, or you can pay a fee to what is called a "banner network," where you then can post your banner ads on a certain number of host sites according to the amount of money that you have paid. An example of a successful "banner network" is DoubleClick by Google (**www.doubleclick.com/us**).

Successful banner ads

One definite formula for success is to place your ads on Web pages that have some type of content that has a relationship to the product or service that you are selling. If you are selling chocolate, your banner ads might not be too successful if they appear on websites that are focused on diet-related information.

Internet advertising studies show that the more relationship there is between banner ads and the websites on which they appear, the greater the number of clicks that take place. When you are creating your banner ads, you may want to make sure that the ad promotes your product or services and not your website, as the appeal is in the products.

When Web visitors see a banner ad on a website, they are less likely to click and find out more than if the banner ad advertises a certain product that they are interested in. Banner ads should be a reflection of the things that you are selling and not about your website alone. Banner ads should take Web visitors directly to the portion of your website where that product or service is sold or promoted. You do not just want banner ads to link to your home page, since this means that visitors will have to read your site to find the product that they just clicked. Banner ads are designed to get you the sale, not to find potential customers who have time to browse your website.

Aim to put your banner ads at the top of a Web page and not at the bottom. The farther down on a Web page your banner ad is displayed, the less likely it is to be noticed.

Studies show that the more complicated your banner ad is, the less likely Web visitors are to read it long enough to want to click. You want the statement on your banner ad to be catchy, simple, and accurate. Internet advertising studies also show that animated banner ads do better than those ads that are stationary. Also, Web visitors are less likely to click on banner ads if they have no idea what the graphic is trying to tell them — be sure you have a clear correlation between the graphic and what you are selling.

The smaller your banner ad is, the faster the Web page it is on will load. Large banner ads are not only slow to load, they are also too big and intimidating and often deter Web visitors from clicking on them.

One of the key elements of using banner ads is to make sure that you target the right Web visitors. "Targeting" is a technique that focuses on the type of Internet browsing that a person does when they're on the computer. Web visitors that are searching for a specific item that they type into a search engine are then presented with website results that match their keyword search. If your banner advertisements match these keywords, your ad is more likely to be found by people, and you increase your page views and click-through totals.

The future of banner ads

As we discussed at the beginning of this chapter, there is some speculation that banner ads will soon be a thing of the past, since more and more Web visitors are avoiding clicking on these ads. While banner ads have been refined and have a viable use when used in conjunction with a larger banner exchange network, the reality is that other programs are beating them out. These programs include Affiliate Marketing, Google AdWords, and Google AdSense, which have changed the model of online advertising forever.

Here is the real truth: if I wanted to generate additional income from my website by selling advertising space, I would use Google AdSense. If I wanted to create a network of advertisements to place on other websites and in search engine results, I would use Google AdWords. Google AdSense and Google AdWords are both incredibly easy and cost effective. You have complete control over your campaigns without intrusive banner advertisements.

Groupon

Another great Web marketing tool is Groupon (**www.groupon.com**). Groupon is "a deal-of-the-day" site that offers discounts on products and services. The goal is to introduce consumers to these new businesses and companies by hooking them with a great discount. About 950,000 businesses have marketed on Groupon, and there have been 850+ million deals made so far. About 78 percent of customers said they would not have purchased an item or service if they had not purchased it off of Groupon.

The downside of Groupon is that you must offer your product or service for between 50 and 90 percent off the original price and then pay Groupon half of the amount you received. You do not make much, but it does successfully advertise your business. Some people are "bargain hunters" and do not come back a second time, but sometimes you can attract many customers and have successful results.

Groupon is ideal for small businesses, because there is a feature on the app called "Groupon Local." This allows the user to browse through special deals in their city. On a national scale, it is going to be tough to get your name out there; however, on a local scale, this is a great first step.

Becoming a merchant

If you are interested in becoming a merchant on Groupon, you have to interact with a Groupon Account Specialist.

To begin, visit **www.grouponworks.com/get-featured**. From here, you can choose what you are looking to advertise. You can choose from local deals (local businesses), getaways (traveling), and live (selling tickets to events).

From here, you will be taken to a form where you fill out information about your business.

Once you fill out the information, your form will be sent to an Account Executive, and they will be in touch with you.

Disadvantages of using Groupon

If you are an optimist, look ahead for the benefits. However, knowing the pros and cons is important when it comes to the success of your business.

One disadvantage is that your brand might be connected with the idea of discounts. Potential customers might wonder why your brand is associated with the cheaper prices — is there a deficiency with the service or product?

Another question to ask is if using Groupon is worth it. They take half of your discounted price; take a look at your social media following. If you have a strong following, try offering a deal on your Facebook fan page. This way, you will not be forfeiting a lot of your profit to a middleman.

You will also get customers who only go to your business to use the Groupon discount. The key to making sure this does not harm your business is knowing how to price the offer. Your goal is to have the customer spend more than what the value of the coupon is. For example, if you are a restaurant, try to offer a Groupon deal for a free dessert or a free appetizer. The customer is more likely to go for an entire meal, which will offset the cost of the coupon.

If this model is not easily applicable to your service, there really is no good way to ensure you do not get irrelevant customers, which is a disadvantage to using the service.

A study done by Rice University's School of Business found that more than 40 percent of businesses would not run a Groupon promotion again. The study also found that spas and salons had the most success, while restaurants fared the worst (**www.inc.com**).

The key to using Groupon successfully is making sure you offer a particular dollar amount off, not a service. This discourages people from coming in, claiming the free service, and leaving.

Benefits of using Groupon

While offering your products or services for a huge discount is not ideal, there are a lot of benefits that Groupon has to offer.

If you get your deal to go through, and you become a merchant on Groupon, everything else is done for you. You can sit back, relax, and enjoy the free advertising. You do not have to pay for anything, including the promotions and the purchasing done by the customers.

If you do decide to offer a deal, be sure that you are prepared. Businesses experience an intense surge in customers once a deal is offered, so make sure you have a full staff and a large inventory. The last thing you want is to be overwhelmed and to offer an unsatisfactory service because you were not prepared.

That being said, if you own a restaurant, this is a great way for you to get your name out there. Carey Friedman, owner of Grandpa Eddie's BBQ, said that about 70 percent of his Groupon customers returned to his restaurant (figure taken from the small business open forum on **www.american express.com**).

Lastly, if you have a product or service that is not doing as well as others, offer a Groupon discount. This is a great way to advertise a specific item while also introducing new customers to your business, and you do not have to spend a dime to do it.

Living Social

Living Social is a competitor of Groupon that offers advertising services on the Web for your business. If you compare the Groupon and Living Social sites side-by-side, you will find that they are nearly identical. The main difference between the two sites is that Groupon is pickier about which merchants they let in, while Living Social is more accepting of "indie" brands.

In general, Living Social is a more start-up friendly option. Living Social makes their money by negotiating a split with the merchant. This number is not set in stone like Groupon's is — it ranges based on the initial popularity of your business, your social media presence, and your online reviews. Once you set up your account, you will be able to negotiate this split with your account assistant.

On the Living Social website, you can see some specifics on the kinds of people that are using the site, which is helpful for you when deciding if their audience matches up with yours. Here are their customer demographics: 70 percent are female, 56 percent make more than $75,000, 70 percent are between 25 and 54, and 76 percent have a college degree.

Becoming a merchant

To begin, visit **https://merchant.livingsocial.com/welcome**. From here, you can choose the category that best defines your business. You can choose from food & drink, health & beauty, fitness & active, events & activities, travel, seller & suppliers, and services. Once you choose your category, you will see some information that gives averages on first-time customers, average amount spent, and returning visitors.

There are three steps to having a successful campaign: creating your promotion, launching it, and engaging with your customers.

To create your promotion, you need to get engaged with a Sales Specialist. To do that, scroll to the bottom of the page, and click "Get Started." From here, you will fill out a form about your business, and once you submit it, Living Social will be in contact with you.

Disadvantages of using Living Social

These are identical to those of Groupon. When you offer a discount on, say, a service, your pervious customers will get angry: "Why did I have to pay $100 for a massage, while this newcomer is paying $50?"

You need to be aware of how you are treating your existing customers as well as how you are pricing your deals.

Advantages of using Living Social

The concept here is the same as Groupon, but the Living Social site has some specific numbers that might peak your interest.

If you are a new company and want to get your name out there, this is a great way to do it — 68 percent of the purchasers on the site are first-time visitors to the business, and 70 percent plan on returning to that business.

This site also encourages word of mouth advertising, with about 55 percent of the users claiming that they refer others to the local business they tried.

Another great thing about this site is that customers are not known for only using the coupon and then never returning again. In fact, most customers are said to spend about $26 more than the amount of the voucher.

Beyond these facts, the advantages are identical to that of Groupon. You get free advertising and a great customer support team when you use this site.

Pandora

Pandora is a popular music app with over 80 million users (about one-quarter of the U.S. population). Listeners enjoy Pandora wherever and whenever they like — on over 1,700 connected devices and over 190 car models — for effortless connectivity. The concept of the app is that you choose an artist or a song that you love, and the app quickly scans its entire database to create a personalized playlist of music that it thinks you will love.

There are two versions of Pandora: paid and free. The free version is supported by ads, which randomly play throughout the song sets, and are about 15 to 30 seconds in length. The paid version is called Pandora One, which costs $4.99/month.

Becoming an advertiser

To get started, you have to submit some information to Pandora. Visit **http://advertising.pandora.com/advertise**, fill out the form, and Pandora will be in contact with you.

Advantages of using Pandora

If you decide to partner with Pandora, there are some great benefits. First of all, all ads are served one at a time, which means that your ad is getting 100 percent of the consumer's attention. Unlike a radio commercial segment, your ad is standing out in that it is not part of an ad stream.

Pandora has a lot of success stories, from Taco Bell generating more in-store traffic to BioPharmX seeing a 30 percent increase in website traffic.

Pandora also boasts a huge, diverse audience, which means that this is a great place for any company to advertise. You can target demographics pretty specifically, down to age, type of music, zip code, and county.

If you are wondering about the cost, Pandora is shockingly inexpensive. A Pandora user explains that you are essentially paying "pennies per ad" (**http://whatadvertising.blogspot.com**), and on a CPM basis (this rate is negotiable).

There really are not any negatives to using Pandora unless you cannot fit it into your budget. The fact that you can target your demographic so specifically is a huge help to any up-and-coming businesses.

Spotify

Spotify is also a music streaming service somewhat similar to Pandora in that it is free and also offers a premium service. Spotify is generally considered to have a large music library and has better social networking tools built into the application.

The paid version is Spotify is more expensive than Pandora at $9.99/month with a discounted price of $4.99/month for students and family members.

The main difference between Pandora and Spotify is that with Spotify, you can choose exactly what song you want to hear. With Pandora, you are subject to the playlist that is created for you. Spotify also offers a music library that is 30 times larger than Pandora's. Users are also allowed to skip songs they dislike, while with Pandora, there is a limit to how many times you can skip a song. Spotify's song quality is also much better than Pandora's.

As far as advertising goes, the user will only see the ads on the free version.

Becoming an advertiser

To get started, you have to contact the company by — you guessed it — filling out a form. Visit www.spotify.com/us/brands, and scroll to the bottom to fill out the form. When you submit it, Spotify will get in touch with you.

Advantages to using Spotify

Using Spotify is sure to reach a lot of new customers. The average listener uses Spotify for 148 minutes each day and is engaged at all hours (there is no real "peak" listening time). Spotify users also participate with the app on social media, with two-thirds of the users sharing material to Facebook, Twitter, and other popular platforms. Their mobile presence is also huge, meaning that you are able to reach your consumers wherever they go.

You can also target your consumer, reach them on different formats (mobile and desktop, for example), and across the world.

Like Pandora, the costs of ads are based on a CPM rate. These rates are negotiated, so there is no set price. To find out exactly what you would be paying, you would need to get in contact with the company. Spotify's site does not give any sample figures, but various sources have quoted numbers in the $10-30 CPM range.

Chapter 9

E-Commerce
& Shopping Carts

*A*s your website or company grows, you may find yourself looking for ways to streamline your business activities and increase profits — one of the logical choices is to sell products online. At some point, the expansion of both your online and traditional retail storefront will depend on how well you automate your various processes.

One of the first steps you should consider involves selling merchandise over the Internet and automated invoicing through an online Point of Sale process. The concept is simple, and most of us have purchased items online. You browse a website for the products you want, add them to an electronic shopping cart, apply applicable discount codes (if any), and check out by entering your name, address, and other information as well as credit card information into a secure and encrypted website which completes your transaction.

The merchant Point of Sale system processes your credit card authorization and generates an online receipt as well as an email copy of your transaction, and the company processes your orders and ships your merchandise. The best example of a highly refined website with a highly advanced shopping cart is, of course, Amazon. This company has truly optimized the online shopping experience, and in addition to getting virtually any product you want online, they offer a very simple, yet highly advanced shopping experience. While you may not need to build the next Amazon, with a little planning, your website can be turned into a vehicle for the facilitation of swift, hassle-free payments for your goods and services.

What is E-Commerce?

E-commerce (Electronic Commerce) is a subset of e-business (Electronic Business), through which transactions are processed for purchasing, selling, and exchanging of goods and services over computer networks with the help of the Internet. E-commerce is easily explained as the buying and selling of goods and services without the use of paperwork, as everything is handled through the Internet. It is achieved through different mediums such as Web services, email, file transfer protocol and shopping carts. The most common for the average small business is through a hosted website with a shopping cart or using a third party seller. There are four main categories of e-commerce:

- **Business-to-Business (B2B):** Businesses such as manufacturers selling to distributors and wholesalers, who in turn, sell to retailers.

- **Business-to-Consumer (B2C):** Businesses selling to the general public through catalogs and online retailers through an online payment system.

- **Consumer-to-Consumer (C2C):** Businesses or individuals buying and selling products through an online payment system to each other. EBay's auction service is a great example of where person-to-person transactions take place daily.

- **Consumer-to-Business (C2B):** A model in which consumers create a value for a business, and, in turn, the business uses that consumed generated value for their own purposes, usually to promote or grow their business. The best example is when you create product reviews or provide product recommendations to a company and those ideas are adopted and/or incorporated into the design. Reverse auctions are also examples of the C2B model in which the consumer names prices they are willing to pay and the sellers may accept or rejects the bids, a good way to think of this is the "name your price" sales concept.

To e-commerce enable your website, you must install and configure your products in a shopping cart. It is important to recognize the elements of a credit card transaction: your website contains the product pricing, description, products weights, product sizes, color, and product images. The shopping cart is embedded into your website and stores the dynamic data regarding your product typically through a SQL-based database provided with your Web hosting package, although this varies depending on the shopping cart you choose.

All credit card merchant services companies charge a percentage of the sale as an overhead fee for using their credit processing services. The added service layer between your credit card processor and your website is known as a payment transaction service or gateway service. This layer recognizes an e-commerce transaction, performs immediate credit card authorization, and processes the transaction.

There are two distinct possibilities that account for how your order may be processed. As discussed previously, after the order has been placed, all of the necessary information travels through a private gateway toward the "transaction/gateway processing network." This processing network is where the transaction is approved or denied, depending on the credit history of the consumer and the funds available. Although this may seem like a long process, it only takes seconds to complete.

For the business owner, offering an e-commerce enabled website means an added service and an added fee to operate the website. Payment gateway services, such as QuickBooks™ Payment Gateway, are highly reliable and help to ensure a smooth payment processing transaction and give you instant approval or denial to help eliminate errors and combat credit card fraud or misuse. We will discuss the other shopping cart and authorization systems in detail throughout this chapter.

What is a Shopping Cart?

A shopping cart is a software application that runs on the server where your website is hosted. It allows customers to browse the products in your store and make purchases on the Internet. Typically, a shopping cart functions similarly to retail shopping: you browse the store, place items into your shopping cart or basket, and then check out, paying with a credit card or another electronic payment system.

A shopping cart is integrated into your website so that from any page, a customer can easily find products, view their cart, and proceed to the checkout portion of your store. Shopping carts are written in a variety of programming languages, run on a variety of Web server platforms, and can be either basic in functionality or very advanced. Many are free, but some are not. In all cases, you will need an SSL certificate to encrypt your website and protect customer data as well as a merchant account to process credit card payments unless you utilize another payment processing method. A shopping cart normally includes product details, pricing, and customer data all stored in a database hosted on the Web server in a very secure location.

There are two components to a shopping cart: the storefront and the administration module. The storefront is what your customers see, and the administration module is what you use to add new products or change pricing, shipping costs, and inventory. Shopping carts perform a variety of functions, including shipping and tax calculations, processing secure transactions, and providing email order confirmation. Some websites using cookies to track you may even recognize you upon return and make recommendations for you based on prior purchases. Often, they are configured for softgoods downloads, such as purchasing software and downloading it instantly after checking out of the Web store. You can use shopping carts to promote sales, discounts, and coupons.

Shopping carts have a wide variety of functionality and features. These can include:

- The ability to accept credit cards
- The ability to accept third party payments such as PayPal and Bill Me Later
- The ability to accept E-Checks
- The ability to add and remove items from the shopping cart and adjust quantities
- The ability to calculate shipping and sales tax automatically
- The ability to generate shipping tracking numbers
- The ability to generate a customer email with the receipt as well as tracking numbers
- The ability to handle returns and return label generation
- The ability to have bulletproof security against hackers

The features you need and desire will drive the price of the shopping cart. Advanced carts that integrate deeply into inventory management are more complex and thus more costly. However, if you manage thousands of products, having this level of integration is very appealing. Again, for the average small business, you do not need the most advanced or robust shopping cart solution and may find that PayPal or other options meet your needs at no cost.

Some great websites to visit for shopping cart reviews include **http://shopping-cart-review.toptenreviews.com**, **www.seoshoppingcarts.com**, and **www.bestshoppingcartreviews.com**.

Choosing the Right Shopping Cart

There will be many questions you will want to ask yourself when compiling a shopping cart requirements list. Go through the series of questions below and compare your answers to the features desired, as outlined previously.

Compatibility

Shopping cart scripts are written in many different coding formats—Perl, PHP, and ASP just to name a few. Be sure to check with your host before purchasing a program to ensure it is compatible with your website. You may also inquire about support, since many installations and customizations require Web server administration support actions on the host end. Most Web hosting companies will tell you exactly what shopping carts they support and/or recommend, so most of the work is done for you.

Also, you will want to make sure the cart is compatible with your credit card/merchant payment gateway. Most major payment gateways easily integrate with most shopping cart applications. Know which payment gateway you will use and ensure that it is 100 percent compatible with your shopping cart before you select your shopping cart application.

Budget

Web hosting, SSL certification, website development, and the cost of procuring and implementing a shopping cart can add up quickly. Make sure you consider all the costs involved, and buy the shopping cart that fits your needs and budget. If you only need a basic cart for less than 100 products, PayPal is free, simple to set up, and definitely fits into any budget. Likewise, if you are selling a variety of products, you may consider using eBay or Amazon Seller as an alternative. While you will pay a percentage of sales for each item sold, you do not need a website, and you harness the massive market reach of eBay and Amazon to reach millions of potential customers.

Delivery method

All shopping carts are designed for products that need to be packaged and mailed by a carrier such as FEDEX, UPS or USPS. However, if you want to offer electronic softgood downloads (electronic documents, video files, software), you need to make sure that your cart has that capability. If you are considering softgoods for a delivery method, you should only consider carts that limit downloads or provide a temporary download URL (to prevent fraud, abuse, and distributing your product for free). Softgoods are instant downloadable items that the customer can access immediately after purchase, such as software, electronic books, or images. Another softgoods delivery method may be to send the customer an email confirmation with a hyperlink to download the product. You should also limit the user to a specific number of downloads to minimize fraud and abuse.

The future of your business

You need to ensure that the shopping cart has the features you may "eventually" implement so that you do not quickly outgrow your cart as your business grows and expands to offer more comprehensive options. Make sure you check the fine print as many shopping carts are modular in design, and many advanced features are not included in the basic package.

Payments

All shopping carts allow you to accept credit card transactions. You may consider other options for payment such as e-checks. PayPal is incredibly popular, and I have found it can meet or exceed most online shopping cart needs for many businesses, while being very cost effective. Most quality shopping carts integrate with the PayPal system to allow customers to pay via their PayPal account as an alternative to paying with a credit card. A good shopping cart should also give you the ability to offer discounts and other promotions easily.

Back-ups

All quality shopping carts provide support for backing up files and allow for export into a variety of formats. Equally important is the ability to quickly restore data in the case of a catastrophic Web server failure.

Support

Most shopping carts are difficult to install and configure. Many companies do include free installation and setup, and we highly recommend this option. Make sure that you are prepared to invest in technical support as most offer limited or per-fee support only. Many shopping cart software companies also offer free user forums as part of their service. This is unequivocally the best free support system available, as technical experts and users post similar problems or challenges with actionable solutions for others in similar situations.

You need to carefully analyze your company's needs and weigh the costs and features of shopping cart applications. Be cautious in your decision to purchase based on promotional features, exaggerated claims, and features you will never utilize. Most reputable shopping cart companies feature trial versions of their software. Do not hesitate to try out several to see which works best for your business. It is worth investing the time and energy in testing trial applications out to pick the one that best meets your needs.

Secure Sockets Layer (SSL) Certificates

During secure payment transaction processes, information is safely transmitted between the customer's bank account and your website, and between your website and the customer and merchant accounts. One thing you will need to obtain is a secure sockets layer, SSL for short, certificate for your website. SSL certificates indicate that good security measures are in place on a particular website. They operate through a combination of programs and browser programs like Internet Explorer, Microsoft Edge, Google Chrome and Mozilla Firefox.

Among the best-known SSL certificate providers are:

- VeriSignL®
- ThawteL®
- InstantSSLL®
- EntrustL®
- GeoTrustL®
- GoDaddyL®
- ComodoL®
- SSL.COML®
- DigiCertL®
- TrustWaveL®
- RapidSSLL®
- Network SolutionsL®
- Alpha SSL®

Many Web hosting providers supply free shopping cart software with their hosting packages. In most cases, installation is free, and the software itself is not usually difficult to use. Most hosting companies also offer SSL certificates as an add-on service, usually at very competitive rates. You can usually expect to spend about $100 per year for an SSL certificate, however you will find a wide range in pricing and many offer discounts for multi-year purchases.

Shopping Cart Options

As I mentioned previously, many major Web hosting companies offer free shopping carts with a hosting package including installation and support.

GoDaddy

GoDaddy offers a complete Web Hosting solution which includes the e-commerce website builder, which allows you to build and customize the look of your online store with built-in payment processing.

Applied Innovations

Applied Innovations does not include a shopping cart, but fully supports most shopping cart software on its shared hosting plan with built in support for Microsoft SQL Server 2008 / 2005, Microsoft Reporting Services 2005, MY SQL 5, PHP Driver for SQL and Database Manager.

Shopping carts do not actually process a payment for you, they integrate into the website to allow you to sell multiple items, which allows the customer to browse, select, add items, change quantities, and check out with automated shipping and tax calculations.

PayPal and shopping carts

There are many major shopping carts which have PayPal built in, which make it very easy to setup. These include: **www.miva.com, www.3dcart. com**, and **http://smallbusiness.magento.com**.

If you simply need to add a PayPal enabled cart to your existing website, these may be of interest to you: **www.godaddy.com**, **www.wix.com**, and **www.ecwid.com**. Most of these offer a free trial or a discount.

PDG Commerce

I have used PDG Commerce (**www.pdgsoft.com**) for years with great success. PDG Commerce claims to be the #1 rated e-commerce shopping cart system for QuickBooks and QuickBooks Point of Sale with in-house support. PDG Commerce is both a feature rich shopping cart and the built-in tool for QuickBooks and QuickBooks Point of Sale synchronization, offering complete and flexible QuickBooks integration. It features a flexible template system, which allows you to implement your own design, build from scratch, or use popular CMS tools such as WordPress or Joomla!. Atlantic Publishing Company (**www.atlantic-pub.com**) is an example of a website with a PDG Commerce solution integrated with QuickBooks, as shown below:

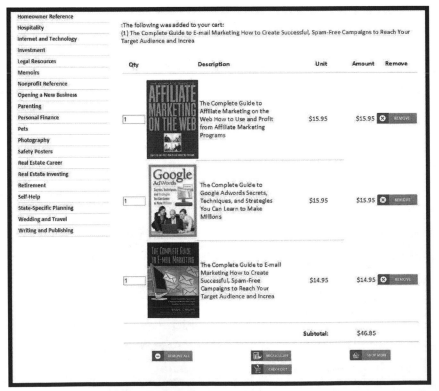

ShopSite Manager

ShopSite Manager (**www.shopsite.com**) is a full-featured shopping cart comparable to high-end e-commerce packages, which claims to cost a fraction of the price. ShopSite says you can have a successful online store with no limit on the number of products you can sell, configured within 15 minutes, which has the following features and abilities:

- Generates store pages
- Allows you to add order buttons to an existing website
- Edits text using a built-in HTML Editor
- Accepts PayPal, Google, and credit card payments
- Calculates real-time UPS, FedEx, and USPS shipping rates
- Uses ZIP or postal codes to calculate sales tax
- Runs sales and promotions
- Tracks customers using Google Analytics
- Generates a Google-style XML sitemap
- Submits product information to Google Product Search

You can even configure your store to accept payments using an online payment service such as PayPal or Checkout with Amazon. Other programs such as ReadyHosting's ReadyCommerce Plan include features from Shop-Site — it is a staple in the industry. To see ReadyHosting's plan details, visit **http://www.readyhosting.com/readyhosting/hosting.bml**.

Merchant Account vs. Third Party Payment Processors

Establishing a merchant account is relatively easy, but this may not always suit the purpose of the business. You will have to determine whether a merchant account is right for you. Depending on the size and type of your business, it may be too expensive to set up a website and purchase an SSL certificate. You should weigh the pros and cons of having a merchant account versus processing your transactions via a third party payment processor like PayPal, which has its own merchant account and payment gateway.

Third party payment processors allow individuals and companies to process transactions without having to sign up for their own merchant accounts, and virtually anyone can sign up to use these processors. These are the definite advantages of third party processes. The major disadvantage is that the third party processor company makes its money by taking a slice of each transaction processed by your company, which eats into your profits. As your sales increase, a merchant account will likely become more cost-effective.

To have a true merchant account, yours must be a business entity; you cannot obtain a true merchant account as an individual. As the business owner, you would only be personally responsible for monitoring the account. A major advantage of having your own merchant account directly with processors like Visa® and MasterCard® is that you are in total control of how your sales are processed. You can process large volumes of sales and add your own personal touch to your online checkout pages with an application program interface (API). You can also build a professional yet personalized look and image on your customers' statements of purchase. Done properly, having a merchant account can be a good way to market your business.

When a company has a true merchant account, they can also use a separate processing gateway. You are in control of negotiating your own rates for purchases and establishing a unique protocol for each of your sales. One major drawback of getting your own merchant account, particularly for individuals and many small business owners, is the credit check. All true merchant accounts require applicants to undergo a credit check. Since the credit check is likely to be run against the business entity, any business with either low volume business or bad credit, both of which are more common among small businesses, may not be eligible for the account.

A high-risk business, generally identified as such by the credit check, is charged a higher rate. Depending on the background and financial standing of the business, some are also required to sign on to multi-year contracts before their account is approved. Because of the contract element, a true merchant account is one of those business decisions that you have to live with if you decide to go for it. While many businesses benefit from having true merchant accounts, and many businesses need true merchant accounts to make the most of online sales, make sure it is right for your situation before acquiring one. Many businesses start off using a third-party processor, which is quite appropriate. When sales reach a certain point, however, it makes sense to move to a merchant account.

A true merchant account is perfect for businesses with large volumes of sales that need to process many transactions. These accounts do have some additional fees compared to third-party providers. On balance, however, large volume merchants pay less with true merchant accounts. With a large volume to process, merchants receive good discount rates when they maintain their own accounts. The discount rate with third-party providers can be as high as 6 percent per transaction, with an additional transaction fee of $1 applying in most cases. A true merchant account offers rates less than half of what most third-party providers offer.

When you look into automating a business process, focus on defining the process, coordinating the activities required, and facilitating the necessary transactions. If you bring every aspect of your business together properly, it should be clear which parts of your business can be automated and which parts you have to handle yourself. All online payments establish merchant accounts and payment gateways as central elements. It does not matter whether third-party providers like PayPal are being employed or whether merchant facilities are being used; gateways must be used to accept payments over the Internet.

PayPal

PayPal is a special type of account from which money can be taken to pay for goods and services. Although few companies tend to pay via this method, do not rule it out as an important payment option to offer your customers. PayPal is convenient, quick, and easy to implement. One attractive feature of using PayPal is that your customer does not have to be a PayPal member to pay you with their credit card to your PayPal account.

PayPal is simple to implement — there is nothing to install, no scripting required, and like other carts, it keeps detailed records of all transactions and generates email notifications. PayPal offers Website Payments Standard and Website Payments Pro, which are integrated into most shopping carts and lets you use PayPal within your existing shopping cart. Website Payments Standard is free except for transaction fees per sale, while Website Payments Pro includes a monthly charge along with the transaction fees. There is no need to purchase an SSL certificate as this is provided through PayPal.

To use PayPal to make a payment, a person must already have a PayPal account. For security reasons, PayPal establishes limits on how much a person can spend online without verifying the details of their account (bank account ownership, credit card ownership, or social security number for U.S. citizens and residents).

In most cases, a person will have deposited funds into his or her account prior to making a purchase. This means that they are then able to pay for goods and services using the PayPal account. When a seller allows PayPal payments, the payee is able to make a payment by simply disclosing his or her PayPal information. In most cases, this is simply an email address and password that are entered as log-in information. PayPal is both a method of payment for customers that have a PayPal account and a third-party payment processor. It can be used for accepting payments made using credit cards, debit cards, e-checks, and PayPal customer accounts. Although many people prefer to have a personalized payment gateway, one that provides a company specific interface, PayPal is an extremely versatile, suitable option.

The history of PayPal has a role in determining the way it is used. EBay users made the system popular as a payment medium. Buyers could deposit and then spend funds. For a long time, PayPal was the only option for individuals without credit cards, and it currently stands as a payment method in its own right and is widely supported as such. It is a measure of the program's success. Even novice Web designers can easily integrate PayPal into their websites to accept credit card payments.

Details on PayPal's shopping cart can be found here: **www.paypal.com/ Shopping-Cart**.

Static & Dynamic Websites

A **static website** is one that has Web pages stored on the server, and when the user types the URL in their Web browsers, the pages appear in the browser. These types of sites are primarily coded in Hyper Text Markup Language (HTML). CSS is used for the presentation of the information.

JavaScript may be used for client side scripting, when required. This type of website displays the same information to all visitors. The main objective of a static website is to present and provide consistent, as well as standard information for an extended period of time. To update the new information, the owner has to edit the information manually, which includes modifying text, adding or removing photos, and various other features.

With the use of software tools such as Dreamweaver CS or Microsoft Expression Web and with some basic Web designing knowledge, a website owner can easily create and modify a static website. In fact, many hosting companies provide free templates that can be easily customized with a few mouse clicks requiring no Web design software and Web design experience. These are limited to the templates provided and may not give you the true "personalization" you would get from a professional Web designer.

A **dynamic website** is one that changes and customizes the content of the Web page automatically and frequently based on certain criteria. Suppose a person from New York and a person from Sydney each have an account on Yahoo!. The data of these two persons, such as their contacts and mail, are different, but they are sharing the same Yahoo! platform. When they are signing in to their account, depending on the login information, data is shown tailored to their account and region of the world. This is an example of dynamic websites.

The main purpose of a dynamic website is that it is much simpler to maintain the site with just controlling a few template pages and a database.

Otherwise, the site owner, or the developer, has to build and update hundreds or thousands of different Web pages and links for different purposes.

A dynamic website takes information from users, imports all the necessary information from databases, and shows it to the user. It interacts with users in a variety of ways including reading cookies, recognizing a user's previous history, session variables, server side variables, or by using direct interaction.

Creating a Security Plan

Providing your customers with safe and secure methods of shopping or purchasing services from your site is critical. Making purchases is often the scariest part of the Internet for people because they will have to share credit card numbers or banking information. According to the Federal Trade Commission (FTC) website, **www.ftc.gov/infosecurity**, you need to "take stock of the personal information and files on your business computers or websites, scale down the amount of information you store, properly dispose of the information you no longer need, protect what information you have, and design a plan to address any security breaches."

Any good security plan has to begin with identifying who in your company has access to customer data and developing a clear understanding of how this information is transmitted to your company or website. The FTC suggests inventorying all computers, laptops, flash drives, disks, home computers, and filing cabinets to learn where all of your company's sensitive data is stored. In the case of running an e-commerce website, you also need to be sure that your host server is secure because that is where your data actually lives when transactions occur via an Internet connection. It is not just your website that has to be secure; it is every aspect of your site, including your host server. This is another reason to read all the fine print and make sure your server will offer the quality security protection you want for your clients.

Investigate the history of any company you plan to use to host your e-commerce site. Find out if there have been any data breaches to their system and, if so, what additional security measures they have taken to protect your site. The FTC also suggests that, depending on your internal operations, you might want to have a website technician run "off-the-shelf security software, or hire an independent professional to conduct a full-scale security audit."

The above image represents a typical shopping cart checkout page. Make sure the site is encrypted and protects your personal information. Another important factor when using the Internet to sell products or services is to use encryption on your site when sending a customer's personal information to a third party, when storing any information on your computer network, and even when sending emails that contain any personally identifiable information (PII). Set up your anti-virus and anti-spyware software to run daily on in-house computers, and make sure that these are also running on your host server along with good, secure firewalls. When you visit an e-commerce site and decide to buy something, you might see a VeriSign Secured® Seal or similar logo, usually at the bottom of the page. Check the URL you are at for the **https://,** which means the page is encrypted; you can click on

the "lock" icon in the address/URL bar to view information about the company from the Secure Socket Layer Certificates.

You also may see other validation on websites that offer buyer confidence that the site is secure and well-protected, such as:

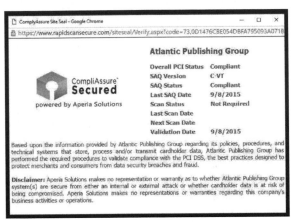

After you click the "Select" or "Purchase" button on a website to buy the product or service, a dialog box will open that says you are entering a secured area of the site. Sometimes, it will say you are entering both a secured and unsecured area, and you have to click the "OK" button to acknowledge that you know this before entering the area where you will provide your credit card number or banking information. Often times in modern browsers, this is completely seamless. You should be looking for the "LOCK" icon in your browser to validate that you have entered a secure session, and the URL should change from **http://** to **https://**.

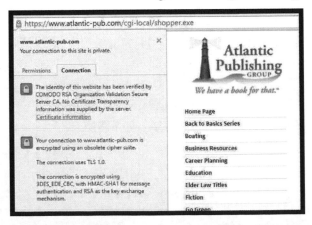

The FTC says that it is extremely important to "pay particular attention to the security of your Web applications." They add, "Web applications may be particularly vulnerable to a variety of hacking attacks, and one variation is called an injections attack, where a hacker inserts malicious commands into what looks like a legitimate request for information. Once in your system, the hacker transfers the sensitive data to his or her computer and can then use it for identity theft or fraudulent transactions."

Another aspect to securing information is to also know where the money or credit card information is coming from, because in some instances, the information could already be stolen property. According to the FTC, there are legal statutes in place like the "Gramm-Leach-Bliley Act, the Fair Credit Reporting Act, and the FTC Act that may require you to provide reasonable security measures for all sensitive information." You should not request any more information from your customers than is absolutely necessary, and destroy it as soon as possible; once the purchase is finalized and the customer has the product or service completed, you do not need it any longer.

Firewalls are designed to prevent hackers from connecting to your network or computer while it is connected to the Internet. In many instances, businesses and individuals leave their computer systems and networks running 24/7. In the event that your system is breached, the FTC says it is important to have a system in place to catch that breach immediately, because if it goes on for any amount of time, the odds are that every sensitive file on your system will be accessed.

Design a system where you are alerted if an outside attempt to enter your network occurs, and make sure it is updated on a regular basis to stay on top of new types of hacking. Another suggestion from the FTC is to monitor all incoming traffic, which you can do by accessing your data logs. Visit the FTC site or OnGuard Online at **www.onguardonline.gov** for additional tips and information regarding the safety of your website and the customers you serve.

The Microsoft Safety and Security Center, at **www.microsoft.com/ security**, has some great information on protecting yourself and your business against credit card fraud, phishing, and other scams. For example, they discuss how some website owners and builders might use phishing scams to create a mirror image of a legitimate site. They try to trick you into thinking you are visiting the real site so you will submit your personal information and/or a credit card number.

Over the past several years, people have received emails telling them their accounts on eBay were suspended for various reasons, and these looked like real eBay emails, complete with the logo and official-looking information. These emails were immediately recognized as fraudulent for those who did not have eBay accounts, but some of those who did followed the instructions. These emails were not from eBay; they were from outside sources who were attempting to obtain the account information of the eBay customers. Microsoft terms these sites as "spoofing" sites, because they are normally used in "conjunction with phishing scams, and the sites are designed to look like the legitimate site." In many instances, they might even have the same URL in the address bar because "there are several ways to get the address bar to display something other than the site you are on," Microsoft explains.

The best way to verify that you are not on a spoofed site is to use the SSL certificate. If you enter the secure portion of a site that uses an SSL connection, you can double-click on the padlock icon to display the security certificate that proves the real identity of the website. The name on the certificate should match the site you believe you are visiting. Microsoft explains that if the name is different from the one you think it should be, you might be on a spoofed site, so do not leave any personal information. Most popular Internet browses have phishing filters.

Chapter 10

Harnessing the
Power of Social Media

he global population as of 2015 is 7.357 billion people. According to the global agency We Are Social, over two billion of those people use social media — that is about 30 percent of the world. Facebook alone adds ½ million users every day (**http://wearesocial.com/uk**). These numbers are growing at astonishing rates, and many companies have caught on to the power of social media as a tool to grow their businesses.

In this chapter, we will take a look at the following social media platforms: Facebook, Twitter, LinkedIn, Google+, YouTube, Instagram, Pinterest, Tumblr, Snapchat, and Vine. Social media has dynamically changed how we communicate, how we share information, images, and videos, and how we interact through games and messages.

You can grow your business, expand your reach, connect with existing customers, find new customers, and create a highly searchable social media outlet that is current, fresh, and relevant for absolutely no money. Your investment is your time, creativity, and talent.

You have the option of using paid advertising with social media, and we will discuss the options, but concentrate on what you can do for free. There are some very exciting social media outlets that bring enormous marketing resources to you and your business.

According to estimates, more than 75% of adults have (or had) a Facebook account. That number continues to grow, as does the number of individuals using Twitter, LinkedIn, and Pinterest. The numbers are staggering, the use is expanding, and you do not want to miss out on exploiting social media as a benefit for your business. Social media lets you reach customers that you simply could not reach previously.

You do not need to hire someone to manage your social media for you, and you do not have to use every social media outlet — pick one or two you are comfortable with and try them out. You can always expand into others or stop using those that you feel are not growing your business. Social media lets you target your audience by using demographic data that you control including country, region, age, gender, interests, and more.

As popular as social media has become for business, both big and small, not every social media outlet is the best fit for you. Facebook is clearly the most popular social network in the United States, and it seems to have a very solid foothold in the social media market, but the same was said about MySpace a few years ago.

Nothing is permanent; social media continues to evolve and today's popular apps may be replaced with something newer and better in the near future. Businesses, especially corporate America, use LinkedIn. While I encourage you to set up a LinkedIn account, you are likely better off to invest in Facebook, Twitter, YouTube, and Pinterest.

Social media is all about making connections and building relationships. It is not about selling products, although that may be the net result of your efforts. You must know your customer base and build your social media strategy around your core customers. Compare social media networks and make a list in priority order of where you want to start and where you want to end up. You do not need to start with, say, four social media platforms on your first day. If you want to start with a business Facebook site, start there, spend some time on it, grow it, advertise, and market it, and then move on to your next social media network while you continue to maintain your Facebook site.

Next, crystallize your message. Based on your defined target audience, what are the key problems or concerns you can address or solve? Expand on and define those main points for each character and write it under each profile. Take a look at the pros, cons, and capabilities of each social media network. (We will do this in this chapter.)

While social media has enormous reach, you need to start with a basic building block and grow from there. In my opinion, your website is your solid foundation. Build and establish that first, then continue to grow with social media from there.

Use each to complement (and promote) the other in a harmonious relationship; together they will help you to achieve the success and growth that you desire. Chapter 12 is dedicated to helping you learn how to establish a blog for your business, and I encourage you to do this. Display icons for your various social media platforms on your website, blog, social media outlets, and email.

You can integrate live "feeds" from Twitter, Facebook and others into your website. This essentially provides "live" data feeds to your site powered from your social media networks and is a great way to draw attention to your message, products, or brand.

Encourage readers to share your content with readily accessible "share" buttons for various social media networks.

You will need to dedicate some time and energy to grow you social media presence. Dedicate some time each and every day, if nothing more than 15 minutes, to add photos, make a few posts, reply to comments, and most importantly, engage with your customers. If you are a restaurant owner and someone posts that they enjoyed the Ribeye special last night, acknowledge them and thank them for the positive review. Encourage them to post a positive review on other social media networks or on other relevant websites that are critical to your business such as Yelp or TripAdvisor. Offer advice, opinions, and positive thoughts; these can go a long way towards building brand loyalty and word of mouth advertising.

If you wish to take social media to the next level in terms of marketing and promotion, you can explore options that include paid advertising, which we will discuss later in this chapter. Again, I am convinced the average business does not need to spend money on paid advertising with social media, nor do you need to hire a social media "specialist" to manage your social media outlets. If you wish to invest funds in paid advertising, it may speed up the process to growing your social media networks, but this can be very easily achieved through some time, patience, and diligence for free.

Facebook

Brief History: Launched in 2004, Mark Zuckerberg and his college roommates at Harvard University created the early beginnings of what was then called "The Facebook" right in their dorm room. Facebook started out as a website that was only available to Harvard students and then expanded to everyone who had an email address and was at least 13 years old by 2006.

Quick Facts: Facebook is the most popular social media platform on the Internet, and more than a billion people use it on a daily basis; it is also the best social network for marking to a specific audience. Apart from connecting with friends and sharing pictures, Facebook is one of the most effective marketing platforms for businesses. Although it does not give businesses the most traffic to their website, Facebook marketing receives the most customer sales and sign-ups. About 70 percent of marketers who used Facebook gained new customers, and around 47 percent of Americans said that Facebook influences their purchases more than any other social media platform. Studies have shown that the best time to update your status, post photos and interact with customers is between 1 p.m. to 4 p.m. daily.

Best Qualities and Benefits: Setting up your business page is free. To "boost" your page (which means promoting content to gain more likes and views), you can set your own budget (for as little as $5) and create advertisements to reach a specific audience. Most online advertising only reaches 38 percent of its intended audience; Facebook reaches 89 percent. Facebook advertisements are also best for reaching more people, raising awareness, and generating sales.

Advertising on Facebook is very discreet. The more "likes" and interests a Facebook user clicks on, the more money Facebook makes. If your business sells makeup and other beauty products, Facebook will find users who have liked makeup companies such as Sephora, MAC, or Revlon and directly advertise your business to them. Every "like" creates more opportunities to advertise products to consumers.

Facebook Terminology:

- **Friend(s):** a person or people you connect with on Facebook; generally, only friends have direct access to personal information, photos, and status updates on a person's profile.
- **Like:** When you enjoy someone's content, you can "like" the post. The more likes your content receives, the more potential customers you will have.
- **Share:** If there is a photo, status, or video that shows up on your newsfeed, you have the ability to share it with your other friends. Encouraging your friends or followers to share your business page's content is key to promoting your business.
- **Pages:** what a business creates to list its information and to share content with potential and current customers.

- **Timeline:** where all your shared content and information is located. Customers can visit your timeline to see what you have posted in the past.

Step-By-Step Guide: You have two options to market your business on Facebook; you can either create a business page for free or create an ad for a small fee.

To create a page, there are a few easy steps to follow. First, upload a photo and insert all your business' information. Then, add friends on Facebook or upload an appropriate email list to invite people to "like" the page. After that, keep your page updated. Write status updates about events, contests, giveaways, and new products. Offer sales — anything that will grab your audience's attention. You can have personal Facebook pages and business Facebook pages; there is no limit to how many pages you can manage within one account.

In regards to creating a Facebook ad, you can specify what you want out of ads, such as commenting on posts, clicks to your website, page likes, website conversions, and event responses. If you are looking for a specific customer engagement, then creating a Facebook ad will help market your business. Note: Facebook ads are not free. The cost will highly depend on your budget and how much you are willing to spend, but the minimum ranges between one and five dollars per day.

How Advertising Works: Facebook incorporates these top specific-targeting options: location, behavior, demographics, connections, interests, and custom/lookalike audiences. Below are their descriptions:

- **Location:** If you just opened a local sushi restaurant, then a Facebook ad can reach out to Facebook users who live in the area and who may be interested in checking out your restaurant.
- **Behavior:** Facebook can take a user's "behavior" and activities on Facebook into account and advertise relevant ads toward them.

- **Demographics:** If you own a pedicure spa and want to advertise to women from ages 18-60, then Facebook will promote your business to that targeted audience.
- **Connections:** You can advertise to people who are connected (friends of your friends) on Facebook.
- **Interests:** If Facebook users like or follow interests, such as TV shows, food, sports teams, or beauty products, then Facebook can advertise to potential customers who may have an interest in your business' products.
- **Custom/lookalike audiences:** If your business offers a product that might interest a Facebook user, then Facebook will advertise that product and your company to them.

Measure Analytics/Readjust: Measuring and tracking your marketing success is vital and will take time to properly adjust to have a high success rate of business improvement. There are four ways to track your results on Facebook: page insights, ads manager, audience insights, and conversion tracking.

1) **Page Insights:** According to Facebook, "page insights are the analytics behind your Page that will give you information about who is connected to you and an overview of how they are responding to the content you share." After reviewing this information and seeing which posts received the most activity and which that received the least attention, you can plan better, more effective posts for the future.

2) **Ads Manager:** After you set up an ad campaign, you can use the ads manager to see if you are hitting your specific goals. You can also manage your ad accounts, billing information, and reports.

3) **Audience Insights:** This tracking tool allows you to understand your audience better, see where they live, and understand what they are interested in.

4) **Conversion Tracking:** This is where you set up and manage conversion tracking pixels on your website. If you want your

audience to do a specific action, such as attend an event or sign up for something, then you can track it here.

Facebook makes advertising fairly easy to use and cheap for your limited budget. Start out with a business page, and keep it updated. After a few months of running your business page, create an ad if you want to increase your presence. If you do not see immediate results, do not worry. Having a Facebook page will put your business on the map and give you great exposure for new customers.

Nothing prohibits you from linking both your personal Facebook and your business Facebook to your primary Facebook account so that you can manage one or more Facebook profiles easily.

Facebook allows you to easily share information such as your business location, operating hours, website, contact information, photos, videos, events and much more. It is very simple to set up and maintain and requires no advanced skills at all.

There are guides and tutorials on Facebook as well as all over the Internet on how to set up and optimize your Facebook profile and settings. In a few minutes, you will have a Facebook site that you can customize, and you can instantly start reaching customers. Facebook pages are very search engine friendly, meaning they rank high in search engine results, so you should promote and share your Facebook URL on your website, blog, emails and more.

Twitter

Brief History: Created in 2006 during a "daylong brainstorming session," Jack Dorsey, Evan Williams, Biz Stone, and Noah Glass started a timely, news-oriented revolution. In just 140 characters, tweets can send out fast, relevant information to reach anyone across the world. What started out as a news source soon turned into a fantastic marketing platform for businesses whose customers crave rapid and relevant information.

Quick Facts: Most companies think the 140-character social media platform should not be taken too seriously, but 34 percent of marketers who use Twitter saw great results for their companies. There are about 500 million tweets and 271 million users active on Twitter every day. Twitter was also the fastest growing social media platform from 2012 to 2014, with a follower growth of 44 percent. Getting information out fast on the Web is Twitter's specialty. If your company provides content-based, relevant information, then Twitter is the best social media platform for you. The best time to tweet for the most effective results is between 1 p.m. to 3 p.m. every day.

Best Qualities/Benefits: Twitter is the best social network for timely, relevant news. Their marketing motto, "Connect your business to what people are talking about right now," keeps your business updated and relevant for customers. Users want to hear from businesses, and according to Compete (a social media analytic company), Twitter users follow six or more brands on average. In today's society, customers want to engage with businesses on a personal level and stay up-to-date about their favorite products and services. Tweeting allows you to reach out to customers and share valuable information instantaneously.

Twitter Terminology:

- **Tweet, Tweeting:** A message or act of posting a message on Twitter containing 140 characters or less.
- **Re-tweet (RT):** the middle button below a tweet that allows you to re-post that specific tweet on your timeline and newsfeed.
- **Mention:** include a person's @username in a tweet so you can grab their attention
- **Direct Message (DM):** is a private message that only you and the recipient can see.
- **Reply:** the first button below a tweet. You can reply back to a tweeter who tweeted to you.

- **Hashtag (#):** this symbol can be used before a word or phrase. This organizes conversations around a specific theme. (Example: "I can't wait for Monday Night Football to start again on #ESPN.)
- **Trends:** a series of hashtags that many tweeters are tweeting at the moment. These tend to change on a daily basis as new news occurs.
- **Follow, Follower, and Unfollow:** subscribing to someone's tweets; a Twitter user follows your tweets; the act of unsubscribing to a user's tweets.
- **Timeline:** where all your tweets show up.

Step-By-Step Guide: There are a couple of ways to market on Twitter. You can use Twitter ads, specific web-marketing tools, or a tweet activity board.

First, make a Twitter account for your business. Then, engage followers with great tweets, trends, and relevant information. You can also use promotional tactics to launch a product, drive sales, or increase brand awareness, such as getting followers to retweet a specific tweet in order to receive a gift or to tweet exclusive offers and deals that customers can only learn about through Twitter.

There are different options when it comes to advertising on Twitter. If you use an objective-based campaign, you can focus on receiving more followers, website clicks/conversions, tweet engagement, or your business' app installs or engagements. You can specify what you want out of marketing, and you can always switch it up whenever you want.

How Advertising Works: If you pay for a Twitter ad, then you can promote and recommend your Twitter account to a surplus of users for a certain amount of time. Twitter will incorporate user information, interests, and followed accounts, and will refer them to follow you if they may have a potential interest in your business.

Measure Analytics/Readjust: In your Twitter dashboard, you can look at the number of follows, mentions, trend impressions, tweets displayed, tweet-level metrics, tweet impressions, and engagement rate you get on a monthly basis. Whether it is re-tweets or a promoted account, marketing on Twitter will benefit your business in one (targeted) way or another.

Many businesses have adopted Twitter for customer service; instead of calling a live person, you can send their Twitter address a question or complaint, and they respond via Twitter. You can use Twitter to send information, engage with your followers, promote your business, and drive your customers to your website as well as your other social media platforms.

Keep in mind that your posting abilities are limited — your messages have to be concise and to the point. For this reason, many businesses have not fully embraced Twitter.

LinkedIn

Brief History: Launched in 2003, a combined group of SocialNet and PayPal workers thought of a business-networking idea and made it happen. While the growth was very slow at first (as little as 20 new visitors per day, at times), within a decade, this social networking website reached 225 million members. LinkedIn became an avenue for businesses to grow together and have easy access to resumes. Although it does not compete with social media platforms, LinkedIn connects businesses together better than any other social networking site.

Quick Facts: LinkedIn has become one of the best business-to-business networking sites on the Internet and is considered the world's largest audience of influential, affluent professionals in one place. Marketing your company on LinkedIn also brings in new customers and potential business connections. Although marketing on Facebook, Twitter and Pinterest should take precedence over this social media platform, LinkedIn is still a great way to get your name out there. The best time to post updates and reach new customers is between 7 a.m. to 9 a.m. and 5 p.m. to 6 p.m.

Best Qualities/Benefits: If your business focuses on business-to-business (B2B) connections and interaction, then LinkedIn is your best site to use.

You can find and connect with businesses easily; it also provides an excellent platform to get your company's name out there.

LinkedIn Terminology:

- **Connection:** LinkedIn members who have accepted invitations to connect are connections. Connections can view profiles and networks of one another.

- **1st Degree Connection:** Users you have personally chosen to connect with.

- **2nd Degree Connection:** A contact of a 1st degree connection (a friend of a friend). You must request an introduction from the 1st connection.

- **3rd Degree Connection:** A contact of a 2nd degree connection. You must request an introduction but requires an intermediary step.

- **Intermediary:** The process whereby a 1st degree connection must request an introduction from the secondary connection in order to connect to the 3rd.

- **Activity Feed:** Displays network activity such as joining/starting groups, comments, profile changes, and application downloads.

- **Activity Broadcasts:** What is sent to the Activity Feed and is visible to others.

- **Groups:** These often serve as discussion forums on LinkedIn between group members.

- **Mention:** Similar to other social networks, LinkedIn allows you to mention other members in your updates.

- **Recommendation:** Allows users to share recommendations of one another, which are visible to anyone who views your profile. You can ask your connections for recommendations.

- *Skill Endorsements:* Lets you recognize your connections for skills you have seen them demonstrate. Your connections can also endorse skills you have listed on your profile. Endorsements can strengthen a profile and help to keep connections strong within your network.

Step-By-Step Guide: Start by making a company page. Your page raises your business' awareness, promotes career opportunities, and reaches out to potential customers. When you interact with people on your page, you educate them about what you do, which builds trust and a potential set of new clientele. You can also target people by job function and industry, which can grow your professional network, attract followers and build relationships. Customize your LinkedIn page as much as possible. Your professional contacts and customers want to know you, your company, and that they can trust and value you; this is just one way to establish and enhance your professional reputation.

How Advertising Works: LinkedIn advertises your business based off of demographics, interests, job descriptions and other categories. If you are looking for a very specific audience, then your LinkedIn company page will get the job done.

Measure Analytics/Readjust: LinkedIn provides measurement and analytics to see if you are reaching out to the right people and doing it the most effectively. Take some time to review what works and what does not work for your page so that you can expand your potential customer base.

LinkedIn is much more about you than your business; however, connecting with other similar types of businesses may help with collaboration, information sharing, and more.

Once you set up your profile, you will get "connection" requests from friends and other professionals. You can link your LinkedIn to other social media accounts, but only do so if you are maintaining this for your business or professional relationships. Keep your professional reputation separate from your personal life.

For the photo, use one that best represents you as a professional. Your dog is cute but that is not you, and a family photo is not ideal either for purposes of establishing professional connections.

LinkedIn promises to help you establish a professional profile, build and maintain a professional network, find and reconnect with colleagues and classmates, learn about other companies, get industry insights, find other professionals in your industry, and find new career opportunities.

Google+

Brief History: Founded in 1998 by two Ph.D. students at Stanford University, Larry Page and Sergey Brin, Google was created "to organize the world's information and make it universally accessible and useful." Apart from being the world's most used search engine, Google created a social-networking service called Google+ in 2011 to help out local businesses. Google+ serves as a free business-marketing tool, as well as a social networking site for individuals.

Quick Facts: Once again, Google has taken over the Internet by storm. With a little over 100 million active Google+ accounts, the platform grows at a steady rate of 33 percent every year. Marketing with this platform would be a very smart move if you want to boost your local business' awareness. This is the best social network for visibility and reviews. The best time to reach out to customers is between 9 a.m. to 11 a.m. every day.

Best Qualities and Benefits: Google+ makes it easy to access everything you need to promote your business. Your Google+ page helps build a loyal fan base and raise awareness. Customers can rate and review content to endorse your business by clicking on the "+1" button and re-sharing posts to their friends across the Web. The more +1's you receive, the more your page and content will pop up on searches related to your business, such as Google Maps and other Google searches.

Activities include starting conversations, finding people to connect with, responding to customer feedback, connecting face-to-face through video chats, following organizations and interests, and receiving quick updates on any type of information.

Google+ Terminology:

- **Hangouts:** video chat services that you can host to connect with customers, conduct business meetings, or use to talk with an employee. You can group video chat up to 10 people and share photos, as well.
- **+1:** The +1 button allows you to appreciate and rate which updates, videos and photos grab your attention. For every +1 you earn on shared content, the more that content will spread on the Web.
- **Circles/Communities:** These serve as individualized communities of friends, connections, and family. You can choose to send updates, photos and videos to specific circles or to the public.

Step-by-Step Guide: Setting up your Google+ page is quite simple. You will be asked to create a Google account (if you do not already have one), and then answer a few questions about your business.

After your page is set up, continuously update your content with event announcements, statuses, shared photos and videos, and whatever else you think your audience and customers may enjoy.

How Advertising Works: All the +1 content you share with customers, friends, and family will boost your unpaid search results on the Web and improve your local visibility search for small businesses. Google does not take demographics or any personal information; you and your content advertise what your business has to offer: great products, great service, and a passion for what you do.

Measure Analytics/Readjust: Google+ makes it very easy for you to manage your page in one place. The Google+ dashboard allows you to update your information, track how much of your page is complete, monitor notifications/updates, share content with customers, video chat via Hangout, view top searches for your business on Google, see where your customers live, view social insights to track your posts' successes, and manage ads on your page. This all-in-one section makes it very easy for Internet-marketing beginners to advertise their business successfully.

After viewing the most and least popular content on your page, you should adjust status updates, photos, videos, and events to cater to your customers' wants and needs. If you are diligent and pay attention to what is working for your page, then your business will receive more customers and will continue to grow.

With a recent overhaul in late 2015, Google+ seems to be growing in terms of acceptance and popularity. You must have a free Google account and, of course, it interlinks all of Google's applications, such as Google Maps, Search, YouTube, GmailSM, Picasa®, Blogger, and more. If you are a huge fan of Google products and use Gmail accounts, you may find Google+ to be great.

The question is: why should you use it for your business? First, anything "Google" is going to be very SEO friendly to the Google search engine, so there are advantages for search ability on the Web. Like Facebook, it recommends "friends" to you based on your settings and associations. You can join various communities where you can share information, comments, and photos.

Google+ for Small Business (**https://plus.google.com/+GoogleBusiness**) is set up specifically for businesses on the Google+ platform. This free service will help you get your business to connect with customers through the Google search engine, Google Maps, and more. It lets you ensure that your customers have the right information including directions, hours, contact information, and more. This is also the service where customers post reviews and ratings of your business, products and/or services.

YouTube

Brief History: YouTube was launched in May 2005, and is a Google company. Three PayPal employees, Chad Hurley, Steve Chen, and Jawed Karim started YouTube and then sold it to Google in 2006 for over $1 billion.

YouTube's website explains that this a place where people can create original videos that work to inspire and connect with people across the world; not only is this a great avenue for individuals to connect, but it is also a great place for advertisers, both large and small, to be heard.

Quick Facts: YouTube boasts over one billion unique visitors. YouTube remarked in a blog post: "If YouTube were a country, we would be the third largest in the world after China and India." YouTube is the third most visited website on the Internet, behind only Google and Facebook.

Content of virtually every kind is available on YouTube, but music videos have soared in popularity. Here is a list of the top ten most watched videos on YouTube as of 2015, according to Billboard (note that all are music videos except one). Also, I have looked up all of these videos and adjusted the views to reflect the total views as of 2016.

1. "Gangnam Style" by Psy: 2.5 billion views
2. "Baby" by Justin Bieber: 1.3 billion views
3. "Dark Horse" by Katy Perry: 1.2 billion views
4. "Roar" by Katy Perry: 1.2 billion views
5. "Party Rock Anthem" by LMFAO: 1 billion views
6. "Love the Way You Lie" by Eminem: 1 billion views
7. "Waka Waka" by Shakira: 1 billion views
8. "Gentlemen" by Psy: 930 million views
9. "On the Floor" by Jennifer Lopez: 905 million views
10. "Charlie bit my finger — again!" by Harry and Charlie Davies-Carr: 835 million views

These numbers make it clear that YouTube has immense power when it comes to gaining visibility. You may be thinking — so what? I am not in the music business — and that is fine. Being in the number one spot on YouTube is not our goal; our goal is to access and target the most relevant consumer and maybe even create an ad in the process.

Best Qualities and Benefits: Now that we have a basic understanding of what YouTube is, let's step back and take a look at YouTube as a business opportunity. This platform has a lot to offer you in terms of growing your brand. Keep in mind that YouTube is owned by Google, so these two entities are closely related; many of the opportunities that Google presented are easily transferred to YouTube (for example, advertising abilities and search engine rankings).

Because of YouTube's reach, you are bound to find a group of people that are interested in what you have to offer. Also, Google picks up on YouTube videos just as much as text-heavy pages — if you create YouTube videos, you are more likely to be searched and found through Google.

Another great benefit of YouTube is that you can take material you already have — say a blog post, or a page on your website — and you can turn it into a video, creating yet another avenue that may be able to reach a new consumer.

YouTube also lets you bring people to your other platforms. When you upload a video, there is a description box, and in that box you can add text. This is the perfect place to link your website, your blog, and your other social media outlets.

Remember Google AdWords and Google AdSense? These apply to YouTube, as well — you can advertise through videos, and the best part is that you only pay for engaged views and clicks.

Finally, the best thing that YouTube has to offer you and your business is its ability to emotionally and personally connect you with your audience. According to Grow, the small business marketing experts, research shows that if a consumer sees "a video of a person in the company speaking about [a] product or service, it can dramatically increase your list of leads and sales" (**www.wearegrow.com**).

YouTube Terminology:

- **Channel:** When you sign up to YouTube, you are creating your own "channel." This is similar to a Facebook page or a Twitter username — it is the avenue through which you use YouTube and display your videos.

- **Subscribe:** This feature allows you to follow a particular YouTube channel, giving you an easy way to see their new videos without having to search through YouTube to find that particular channel. This feature is accessible right from your personal homepage, which is completely customizable.

- **Playlist:** This is a collection of videos; in other words, it is a folder of videos that anyone can create.

- **Trending:** These are videos on YouTube that have recently gained a lot of popularity. They are not necessarily the most watched videos of all time; rather, they are videos that have gained a lot of views in a short period of time.

Step-By-Step Guide: YouTube itself has a fantastic tutorial to help new users create an account. This page is called "Getting started on YouTube," and you can find it through Google's support page at **https://support. google.com/youtube/answer/3309389**.

This tutorial will show you how to sign in, how to subscribe to channels you love, and how to build playlists. That is all you really need to know — the rest is a matter of exploration.

To learn how to upload your own video, visit **https://support.google. com/youtube/answer/57407?hl=en**. This will ask you what device you are working with and will explain the process, step-by-step.

How Advertising Works: Advertising on YouTube is much more simple than it may seem. Once you have the basics of Google AdWords and Google AdSense under your belt, the rest is very simple.

If you plan on using Google AdWords in YouTube, this means that you are trying to promote one of your videos, which means that you need a video to be uploaded on YouTube. You will also need to have a video ad created. Once you have these two things done, then you can get started.

First, you select your video. Then, customize your ad settings. This will include setting your budget and targeting the consumers (age, gender, interest, and location). Then, all you have to do is finalize your billing method and launch your ad. More details are available at **www.youtube. com/yt/advertise/launch-ad.html**.

If you plan on using Google AdSense in YouTube, this means that you are allowing other people to promote their interests on your videos, which will earn you money. You can see that AdWords and AdSense work together on YouTube — one advertises and costs money; the other accepts those advertisements and gets paid.

To set up Google AdSense on your YouTube page, go to your homepage. From there, navigate to the monetization page (click your icon at top right, click creator studio, go to left menu and click channel, then monetization). Go to the "How will I be paid?" section. From here you will be directed to your AdSense account where you can connect that account to your YouTube channel. To see these steps in more detail, visit **https://support. google.com/youtube/answer/72866?hl=en**.

Measure Analytics/Readjust: Once you have set up your advertising campaign on YouTube, you can view the Analytics by visiting www.youtube. com/analytics. From here, you can choose which report you want to see, including total views, your estimated revenue, and your subscriber count.

YouTube is a great place to watch videos on nearly any topic imaginable and is also free to use. You can rate content, post comments and reviews, and like or dislike videos. If you post regularly, you can establish yourself as an expert in your specialty or niche. I subscribe and follow a few experts on home repair and other topics. The videos are professional and informative, and new content is published often. I can access YouTube on my iPhone, iPad and every other mobile device, so content is available on the fly. You can connect with "friends" through YouTube, and you can bookmark your favorites as well.

As a YouTube user, you can add comments, respond to comments, and engage with your audience, making YouTube a great place to interact with your consumers.

Instagram

Brief History: Instagram was founded by Kevin Systrom and Mike Krieger in October 2010. Facebook bought the company in April 2012 for about $1 billion. Systrom, CEO, previously worked for both Twitter and Google, and Krieger, the technical lead, previously worked for Meebo. Instagram has a community of over 400 million users who "capture and share the world's moments" through this social media outlet (**www.instagram.com/about/us**).

Quick Facts: According to Daily Pastime, when teenagers were asked the question "What's your favorite social media network?" about 23 percent of them responded with "Instagram" (**www.dailypastime.net**). Instagram gained about one million users in its first month — it took Facebook ten months and Twitter two years to gain that kind of following.

The majority of users are women (about 68 percent), and almost all of the users are under 35 years of age (**www.dailypastime.net**). Keep this in mind if you are deciding what social media platform is best for your company. If you are targeting older, male consumers, this may not be the best time investment to grow your business.

The most popular hashtags are #love and #selfie, which says a lot about the kind of content you will find on this platform (largely positive, self-centered photos).

Best Qualities and Benefits: Compared to sites like Facebook and Twitter, Instagram has a more active user following. This means that while there may be less total users, these users are more active on the site, to the tune of 120 times more engagement (**http://blogs.constantcontact.com/use-instagram-for-business**).

If you are selling a product that is easily photographed, such as food, people love to share it. This provides a great opportunity for you to expand your business. For example, say someone visits your restaurant and shares a photo of their favorite dish with a tag to your restaurant's location. This gives your restaurant free advertisement while also reaching new consumers through a trusted, credible source.

Hashtags are a huge way to find new customers. Hashtags are searchable on Instagram, so if you want to find posts with a certain hashtag, all you have to do is search the phrase and all the photos with that particular tag will appear. This helps you find consumers that are already interested in your genre. From here, you can like their photos, comment on them, and follow them, giving that user the option to view your page and interact with you. This can quickly generate into future business.

Like other social media platforms, Instagram lets you access all your other accounts. When you share a photo, you have the option to share it on Facebook and Twitter as well, which helps you reach all of your consumers.

Finally, the best thing about Instagram is the fact that it is photo-driven. If you are selling products, Instagram is a great way to showcase that product in the best light possible. There are many ways to edit the photo, such as cropping, lighting, and filters. Fine-tuning your photo and sharing it for all your customers to see is a great way to market your brand. A report from Shopify states that Instagram is the best place to sell products: "the average price tag for a sale referred from Instagram is $65, compared to $55 for Facebook and $46 for Twitter."

Instagram Terminology: Many terms in Instagram are identical to terms on other social media platforms (post, like, comment, follower, hashtag, newsfeed, and username). However, there are a lot of terms that you will want to know if you decide to use this social media platform to market your business.

- **Bio:** This is the area on your home page where you can briefly describe you and your brand. Here, you can link to your website, blog, and other social media outlets.

- **Filters:** These are editing tools that add certain effects to your photos. There are 20 total, and they are known for adding a "vintage" feel. They are different combinations of the following elements: exposure, color balance, and contrast.
- **Caption:** This is your description of the photo you are posting. This is where you can include hashtags, which link your photo to relevant subject matters.
- **Feed, Gallery, and Album:** These are all synonymous for your collection of photos.
- **Personal Activity Feed:** This is where you can see the interactions others are having with you. This will show you which of your photos people have liked and commented on and whether or not another user has tagged your photo.
- **Following Activity Feed:** This is where you see the activity of the users you are following (who they are following, what photos they are liking, and what photos they are commenting on).
- **Explore:** This is where you can search and discover new users and posts.
- **Direct:** This is where you can send a photo to a single person. It is private, much like a Facebook message.
- **Geotag:** This is when a location is attached to an image.

Step-by-Step Guide: Instagram is based on using the mobile app. You can access the site through a desktop computer, but to receive all the benefits of the platform, using the mobile app is necessary. To get started, you need to download the app and sign up. You can either create an account, or you can "Log In with Facebook," which connects your Instagram account with Facebook. To see more details on how to get started, visit **https://help. instagram.com**.

How Advertising Works: Ads are marked with the term "Sponsored." When creating an ad, you have three options: photo ads, video ads, and carousel ads. Photo and video ads are pretty self-explanatory, but carousel ads allow a user to swipe to see more than one image.

Instagram says that they support ads that have the following objectives:

- Clicks to website
- Website conversions
- Mobile app installs
- Mobile app engagement
- Video views
- Reach and frequency
- Page post engagement
- Mass awareness

Instagram's close relationship to Facebook is no surprise (Facebook owns Instagram), so much of the advertising is done through Facebook's Ad Manager and Power Editor.

To get started, visit **www.facebook.com/business/help/9762408324 26180**. This is the home page for beginning to advertise on Instagram. From here, you can explore the options. We will begin by clicking on "Where can I create Instagram ads?" and clicking the big blue button that says, "Create an Ad."

From here, you choose your own objective. For the purposes of this explanation, we will choose "Send people to your website." From here, you simply input your website URL and "Create a Pixel." Then, you either install the Pixel yourself, or you can email it to your website developer, if you have one.

If you choose to install it yourself, a code is provided, which you add to your website.

This is just one example of a way to promote your business through Instagram. Many companies have had success with this. Instagram has a list of case studies to prove how powerful their app is in promoting businesses: Poshmark, an app where users buy and sell clothing, had an 85 percent increase in their campaign objective, Birchbox, a makeup subscription box service, experienced a 26 point lift in ad recall through 15 second video ads, and Maybelline, a drugstore cosmetics brand, boasts a 2.4x sales increase on brow products.

To explore the advertising options, visit **https://business.instagram. com/advertising**.

Measure Analytics/Readjust: To track how well your advertising is doing on Instagram, you will need to use a program that can provide you with a report, because Instagram itself does not offer this feature.

One of the most popular sites that offer this tool is Simply Measured (**www. simplymeasured.com**). They do offer a free demo, but once that trial is up, it is a very costly service with the cheapest plan topping off at $500/month.

Another option is Mintor.io (**https://minter.io**). This company also offers a free trial, but once that expires, the cheapest plan is $100/month. The cost of the plan is entirely dependent on how many followers you have.

These services are costly, and unless you rely heavily on Instagram to generate business, they may not be the best way to spend your money.

All-in-all, Instagram is a great place to publish high quality, business related imagery. Keep in mind the kind of audience this platform has, and make sure it aligns with your audience before investing your time, and possible your money, into it.

Pinterest

Brief History: Started in 2010 by founder Ben Silbermann, Pinterest became a social image bookmarking system that surprisingly revolutionized Internet marketing. Silbernmann previously worked for Google, moved on to create a program called "Tote," and then finally created Pinterest. Pinterest is "a visual bookmarking tool that helps you discover and save creative ideas" (**www.pinterest.com**).

Quick Facts: According to recent surveys, Pinterest users are 79 percent more likely to purchase items they saw "pinned" on Pinterest boards versus products Facebook users saw on their newsfeed. Consumers are more responsive to image-based ads, and Pinterest makes it easier to connect a customer to a buyer's page — it is just a click away. The best times to post pictures and share content on Pinterest are between 2 p.m. to 4 p.m. and 8 p.m. to 1 a.m. daily.

Like Instagram, Pinterest is full of mostly female users (about 79 percent) and users between 18 and 34 years of age; these users are interested in arts and crafts (**www.jeffbullas.com**). Shopify reports that users are likely to spend about $80 from a Pinterest referral — that is even higher than Instagram's referral rate.

Pinterest boasts billions of pins, and unlike any other social media platform, these pins are very likely to go viral — over 80 percent of pins are re-pins, compared to Twitter's 1.4 percent rate on re-tweets.

Best Qualities and Benefits: Pinterest is the best social network for image-related content. Click-through and conversion rates are better on Pinterest than Twitter or Facebook.

The beauty of Pinterest is that ads are not necessarily seen as ads. The platform has an artsy look to it, so even when a post is a sponsored ad, it does not have that standard "ad" look to it. The pins take away the retail setting, and instead create images that illustrate real-life usage.

Also, Pinterest users are 10 percent more likely to make a purchase based off a referral than on other social media sites such as Facebook. Around 25 percent of Fortune Global 100 companies have a Pinterest account.

Pinterest Terminology:

- **Board:** where your pins are saved and available for other users to view.
- **Pin, Pinning:** an image that you can share to followers, a visual bookmark; the act of putting an image on a board.
- **Re-pin:** when you like someone else's pin, this feature lets you place the pin on a board of your own.

Step-By-Step Guide: To create a Pinterest page, visit the site and sign up (**www.pinterest.com**). When you do this, you have the option to connect your Pinterest to your Facebook and Twitter account. From here, you will create your profile, including your username.

To learn more about how to use the site, such as creating a pin and managing your boards, visit **https://help.pinterest.com/en/guide/all-about-pinterest**.

How Advertising Works: Pinterest uses something called "Promoted Pins." These are just like regular pins, but more people see them and they cost money. Pinterest says these pins can help you with the following goals:

- Awareness
- Engagement
- Traffic

There are essentially four steps to using this advertising feature. First, you pick a pin. Then, you decide you views it through targeting your specific demographic. Unfortunately, you have to pay for it. Finally, you track how well your promoted pin is working.

The total cost is hard to calculate, because like Google AdWords, it ranges depending on your bid. Pinterest explains this process on their website: "For traffic campaigns: Maximum CPC means Maximum Cost Per Click. This bid is the maximum you are willing to pay when a Pinner clicks through on a Promoted Pin to visit your website. For example, if you set a $2.00 CPC, this means that you are willing to pay as much as $2.00 per click through on your Promoted Pin to your website" (**https://help.pinterest.com/en/articles/creating-and-editing-promoted-pins**).

Pinterest has many success stories — Walgreens has tripled their referral traffic, Bank of America reached six million unique pinners in less than five months, and Adore Me increased Pinterest-referred revenue by 4000 percent.

Measure Analytics/Readjust: In regards to Pinterest analytics, you can track how many people are pinning from your website, viewing your pins, and clicking on your content. To do this, you must have a business account. From there, you can visit **https://analytics.pinterest.com** for all the details.

Pinterest is a great tool to use, but like Instagram, be sure that your audience is one of the demographics that is most likely to be using the app.

Tumblr

Brief History: Founded in February 2007 by David Karp, Tumblr is a microblogging social media platform. Tumblr was started and continues to live in New York City, is home to almost 400 employees, and, as of 2016, hosts almost 130 billion blog posts.

Quick Facts: While Tumblr's headquarters are in NYC, there are two other office locations — Richmond, VA, and Los Angeles.

Every single day, over 50 million blog posts are made. About 40% of these blog posts originate in the US, but Tumblr has a presence all over the globe (**www.tumblr.com/about**).

Like many other social media platforms, a big company bought Tumblr out. In 2013, Yahoo! obtained Tumblr for just over $1 billion.

Young people are particularly attracted to this site with about half of the users being under the age of 25.

Tumblr explains what makes their site different from all of the other social media sites out there: "We made it really, really simple for people to make a blog and put whatever they want on it. Stories, photos, GIFs, TV shows, links, quips, dumb jokes, smart jokes, Spotify tracks, mp3s, videos, fashion, art, deep stuff" (**www.tumblr.com**).

Best Qualities and Benefits: More than 260 of the world's top brands have a Tumblr presence, and there is a reason why. A lot of their potential customers are already looking at the site. Tumblr even says on their business home page: "Hello, brands. Welcome to Tumblr. Your biggest fans are already here."

Also, the users of Tumblr are generally more interested in sharing content than creating it. There are about 300 million unique visitors every month, but only about 279 million blogs. This means that there are many more users than there are creators of content, which is a great environment for you to grow your business.

Tumblr also offers promoted posts, which is a great way for you to reach a lot of consumers. Promoted posts are targetable by demographic, and since Tumblr is owned by Yahoo! — you guessed it — your Tumblr post is highly likely to appear in a Yahoo! search. The only drawback is that Tumblr users are interested in unique content. If your ad does not offer something different to see, no one will pay much attention to it.

Terminology: Tumblr has similar terms as other social media platforms, but there are a few that are unique.

- **Dashboard:** Your home page; the page that displays all of your content; similar to the term "newsfeed."
- **Reblog:** If you like someone's post, you can "reblog," meaning that that post will then appear on your own personal dashboard.
- **Ask box:** This is where other Tumblr users can submit questions to you. Your response will show up publicly on your dashboard.
- **Queuing:** If you want to publish posts while you are offline, you can add those posts to your queue. You can set at what time these posts are posted, which is helpful if you know you will be busy doing something else at a certain time.

Step-by-Step Guide: To create a Tumblr, all you have to do is go to Tumblr's home page (**www.tumblr.com**). From there, you will be prompted to sign up.

To make a post, you just click on the blue compose button. For more detailed information on how to use and navigate the site, visit **www.tumblr.com/docs/en/posting**.

How Advertising Works: With Tumblr, you have three options to advertise: you can promote a pin, promote a video, or you can sponsor an entire day. A sponsored day means that basically own Tumblr's dashboard for an entire day, which is the most trafficked page on the entire site. You can use this space and time to do whatever you want, which includes using your own posts, reblogging posts that help tell your story, or a mixture of both.

To get started, you have to actually contact Tumblr. To do this, you are required to fill out the form at **www.tumblr.com/business#strategist-form**.

Once that is complete, you will be in contact with a Tumblr sales rep. From here, you have two options. You can either advertise through cost per impression (CPM) or cost per engagement (CPE).

Your other option is to go through the AdWords Display Network. This leaves a lot of the decisions out of your control — the program decides when and where to place your ads. However, you can always check your AdWords account to see how things are going. If you are unimpressed, stick with the Tumblr sales rep.

With all of this being said, Tumblr is an expensive place to advertise because of its enormous reach. According to Business Insider, Tumblr said in an email that the entry-level ad price is $25,000. If you are a small, start-up business, this is not going to make financial sense. However, if you have the ability to do this, you will see a huge return on your investment. Twitter has a variety of case studies on their business home page that will tell the story of companies seeing huge amounts of growth. To browse through these, visit **http://marketr.tumblr.com/tagged/case-study**.

Measure Analytics/Readjust: If you do decide to use Tumblr to advertise, the platform has something called "Tumblr Advertiser Analytics," which lets you get a complete look at how your content is working. If you are running a paid campaign, this is available to you at the right side of your dashboard.

With billions of blog posts and specialized sub-communities, it is not hard to find a niche within Tumblr to begin social engagement and business marketing. As with the other social media outlets, there is no cost to sign up, and if you find that you and your brand do not fit in, simply dump it from your portfolio.

Snapchat

Brief History: Snapchat's history begins at Stanford University with Evan Spiegel, Reggie Brown, and Bobby Murphy. One day, Brown said, "I wish these photos I am sending this girl would disappear" (**http://techcrunch.com/gallery/a-brief-history-of-snapchat**). The boys started working on the idea, originally calling the idea "Pictaboo." The app was moving at a very slow rate, only gaining 127 users in the first few months. Then, things went downhill, the founders started arguing and Brown was kicked out of the company.

In the fall of 2011, just a few months after the initial launch, Spiegel and Murphy changed the name to Snapchat. By April of 2012, perhaps due to the fact that school was starting again and the news of the app was travelling at light speed, the app had reached 100,000 users.

From here, the app took off. As you can probably guess, Brown came back and filed a lawsuit against Spiegel and Murphy, which was settled in late 2014. Nonetheless, Snapchat is a powerhouse for sharing images.

Quick Facts: There are over 100 million daily active users on Snapchat. About 400 million photos are sent every day.

The age group for this application is around college age. About 50% of male college students and 77% of female college students use the app. Almost three quarters of the users on Snapchat are under 34 years of age.

Many companies have tried to buy out Snapchat, but the company is holding firm, holding out for huge returns on the almost $700 million in investments that have been put up.

Facebook tried to buy out Snapchat for $3 billion in November of 2013, but Spiegel declined. Many were shocked, as Snapchat had yet to even produce any revenue. However, as of July 2014, Snapchat was valued at $10 billion and just one year later, the company was evaluated at $19 billion. The app has yet to turn a profit, but it is clear that investors are seeing the huge opportunity that Snapchat has.

Best Qualities and Benefits: If you are marketing to an audience that is between 13 and 34 years of age, Snapchat is going to be your best friend.

Unlike other photo and video sharing apps, Snapchat's main feature is that the content disappears. If you send content to a single user, they only have access to the content for a few seconds. If you add the content to your story, which will be defined below, all of your followers have access to material for 24 hours.

This may seem like a drawback, but it provides something new for your users — it provides content that is always current. "Snaps" are a reflection of the moment; they define what is happening now. On Snapchat's website, it is said that you do not have to worry about creating "an everlasting persona" (**www.snapchat.com/ads**).

The other great thing that Snapchat provides is perspective. They let your users see something personal, a window into the way you see the world. A lot of advertisements and social media platforms can seem distant and corporate — Snapchat allows someone to get behind the lens and offer a personal experience, which makes your consumers feel more connected to you and your brand.

As far as advertising goes, Snapchat has just launched the concept, and it has taken off with incredible results. The movie Furious 7 was advertised on Snapchat, and it turns out that there is a "3× likelihood that a Snapchatter who watched the ad saw the movie" (**www.snapchat.com/ads**).

This is also a great place to advertise videos, because of the fact that the video is vertical and not horizontal; since users do not have to bother with turning their phone, they are actually 9× more likely to finish the video.

Terminology:

- **Snaps:** The photo you send another user, which disappears after a certain amount of time has passed; the Snapchat medium of exchange.
- **Stories:** This is where snaps can be strung together to create a sideshow that is viewable by all of your followers; it is viewable for 24 hours.
- **Snapchatter:** A user of Snapchat.
- **Snapback:** A reply to a snap.
- **Score:** Total number of snaps sent and received.

Step-by-Step Guide: To create a Snapchat, you must download the app through your mobile device. Once it is installed, you can create an account. After that, you are all ready to go and can start navigating the app.

To learn how to send snaps and add friends, visit Snapchat's support at **https://support.snapchat.com/ca/howto**.

How Advertising Works: As mentioned before, advertising on Snapchat is fairly new; however, the company is not shying away from asking for top dollar, to the tune of $750,000, according to Adweek.

Because of this price tag, which is unattainable for a huge amount of business owners, let's focus more on how to use the app to reach customers in a free way.

For starters, there is no search box on Snapchat. For your customers to find you, you essentially must have other social media platforms. Through those platforms, you can mention your Snapchat username, and those customers can then add you. This can be done in the YouTube description box, your Instagram bio, or your Facebook About Me, for instance.

The best way for you to use Snapchat to advertise is to use the "story" function. Add pictures of you doing business-related activities: working in the office, creating the product, creating the labels, showcasing your products and services, and perhaps even introducing you and your employees. Snapchat is a great way to personalize your brand — let your consumers get to know who you are and what you stand for. This new perspective will add a layer of dimension to your business and can help you bring in new sales.

If you have already established your brand and have a solid following, Snapchat is a great way to advertise and educate your customers on new products or new services.

Keep in mind that you should not be trying to sell something in every photo — you want your customers to see you as a person, not a corporate entity.

Measure Analytics/Readjust: There is really no way to measure how well this is working unless you ask your customers. For instance, the beauty expert, Dyls Makeup, uses Snapchat and Instagram together. He posts images and videos to his story and asks users to go to his Instagram and comment a certain emoji so that he can see who is supporting him through Snapchat. This is a great way to engage your customers and make them feel as if they are more connected to you.

Do not shy away from Snapchat, even though it is fairly new. It is quickly gaining popularity, and if you connect it with your other social media sites, you can add a layer of personality to your business.

Vine

Brief History: Vine was founded in 2012 by Dom Hofmann, Rus Yusupov, and Colin Kroll. Right before its launch, Twitter bought the company for $30 million. Now, Vine is the most popular video-sharing app on the market. While there is no exact number to say how much Vine is worth, it is estimated that it ranged between $500 million and $1 billion.

Quick Facts: The thing that makes Vine differ from other video sharing apps is that the time limit is six seconds. This requires the user to be creative; the message they are sending must be short and to the point.

If you visit the website, you will notice that the address is **www.vine.co**. Vine wanted to have **www.vine.com**, but Amazon owns that domain name and asked for $500,000 of which Vine politely declined.

The name "Vine" is short for "Vignette," which is a short, impressionistic scene.

Best Qualities and Benefits: Branded vine videos are 4× more likely to be seen than a branded video.

There are over 200 million users, which is a huge audience for you and your business. 1.5 billion Vines are played every day.

Weekends are the best time to reach consumers, which is interesting considering most brands have difficulty reaching consumers at this time. Like many other relatively new social media platforms, most of the users are young (under 34 years old).

In a world where our attention spans are growing shorter and shorter, Vine is a great way to get your message out in a quick — six seconds to be exact — way.

Terminology: Vine is a fairly straightforward app as far as coined terminology goes. You can explore, like, comment, post, and so on. The only unique term is "loop," which refers to the automatic, continuous replay of a Vine (the "vine" being the video post).

The only phrase that is directly attached to Vine is the sentiment, "Do it for the Vine!"

This is what people say when they are encouraging someone to do something they would not normally do, just so that they can record it and have it on Vine. Examples of popular videos that showcase someone "Doing it for the Vine" include dancing, jumping in front of cars, and interacting with strangers.

Step-by-Step Guide: To create a Vine account, you need to download the app; at that point, you will be asked to either create an account or sign in with Twitter. Once that is done, the app will guide you through a series of steps that will help you decide who to follow. Once that is done, you are free to make posts or explore the app.

How Advertising Works: The way to reach consumers is not through creating your own video; it is through getting a popular viner to create one for you. Joel Lunenfeld, Twitter's VP-global brand strategist explains, "A brand or an ad agency comes to us and says, 'I'm launching a new product; it's targeted to this audience. We'll say, 'Okay, here's 15 people [and] five of them, alone, have a combined audience bigger than BuzzFeed.'"

The thing about Vine is that the users are not too hyped up about ads being incorporated into their streams, but if the ads are given by the viners they follow and love, it is not as much of a hassle, and in many cases, it can be received in a positive way.

For example, HP reached out to Vine users to create short, six-second videos promoting their launch of the convertible laptop. The Vines were so great that the company mashed them together and turned them into a TV commercial. All of their numbers, including brand awareness and purchase intent, went up as a result. To view the HP ad, visit **www.youtube.com/ watch?v=B9Tx6olI3l8**.

There is no flat fee on how much these Vine stars charge, but according to The New York Times®, one Vine star says he is paid several thousand dollars to do a video.

Measure Analytics/Readjust: Because the concept of advertising on Vine is so new, there is not really a way to measure the analytics at this time. The only way to do this would be to simply look at how many followers you have and to calculate the overall growth of your business; however, if you are employing multiple types of advertising, there is no way to isolate Vine as being the sole cause of your success.

Social Media Advice

First, leverage social media to promote, advertise and market your business. Use the free services and promote your business to grow your customer base. If there is no return on your time investment, you may consider using other social media networks.

Attract customers with promotional offers and informative information. A dormant social media site is not good, nor is a new post, photo, or entry every few minutes. Find the right balance that works with your schedule so you stay relevant and fresh but not overly intrusive, obnoxious, and unnecessary.

Use built in statistics and analytics to help you determine success or failure, and adjust it if you are not finding success. Use your time and energy wisely, and keep your personal accounts separate from your business accounts. Try to show creativity and ingenuity; have fun with social media. If you are bored, your posts may also be boring, and your audience will be bored and stop paying attention.

Your employees and friends may be your best assets when starting out social media. Get them to like, share, follow, and comment often. They will draw in their own circle of friends helping your social network grow. Take criticism with stride. Not everyone will agree with what you post or will like what you have to say, just as every customer may not be 100% satisfied every time.

Respond to negative comments with professionalism (do not simply delete them); you gain more credibility by publicly working toward customer satisfaction and resolution than "hiding" the issue. Be engaged and respond when you can to as much as you can. A personal "thank you" or response to a question or comment means a lot to individuals. Do not post "contact us on Facebook if you have a question or comment" and then not respond to the questions or comments. This means you simply do not care, and if you do not care, then your customers will not, either.

Now that you have a good idea of what social media platforms will work best for your business, let's move on to another important aspect of growth: email marketing.

Chapter 11

Email Marketing

A round 85 percent of the world uses email to communicate (**www.huffingtonpost.com**). While social media is a great way to reach your customers, emailing is even better, as it reaches an even wider audience. A 2013 study from a predictive analytics firm states that customer sales have quadrupled within the last five years from email marketing.

Email marketing continues to be highly effective when done in a compliant opt-in program, although the volume of spam has also grown exponentially, clogging most of our email inboxes with dozens of useless emails on a daily basis. Although there are challenges to developing successful email campaigns, they have carved out a significant portion from Direct Mail business lines and are significantly more cost-effective than creating, printing, and mailing flyers, promotions, and other material.

Email marketing, when designed and implemented correctly, can be one of your most effective advertising, marketing, and sales tools. It can also be one of your most cost-efficient means of disseminating large amounts of information, promotional materials, advertisement, special offers, coupons, new product announcements, and relevant news to a large audience for absurdly low costs when compared to traditional print media advertising and marketing campaigns.

In this chapter, we will discuss the often misunderstood world of email marketing. Email marketing is not spam when it is done properly and legally. A properly designed email marketing campaign is targeted, relevant, and useful to the recipient.

Email marketing is simply a tool in your overall online and offline marketing portfolio. Email marketing allows you to instantly disseminate information about your company, products, or services to thousands (or hundreds of thousands) of recipients with the click of a button. To be fair, if you want a successful and spam-free campaign, it does take some planning, design, and organization to ensure your email marketing campaign is optimized for success. If you have a personal computer and check email, then you are already familiar with email marketing, since you most likely get it multiple times per day, often unsolicited and unwanted.

Email marketing is simply defined as the promotion of products or services via email. Email is a very versatile and widely used form of communication. Thanks to advancements in technology with email clients such as Microsoft's Outlook® and Mozilla's Thunderbird™ and the offer of free email accounts from industry giants such as Google and Yahoo!, email is affordable, readily available, and used by nearly everyone both at and away from their work environment. Email formats can be very simple text-based or more complex HTML with embedded graphics and advanced website design techniques. The content of an email can be customized based on size or target audience and you can have scheduled deliveries, nearly automating the entire process. Of course, one the biggest benefit is that overall costs for implementing an email marketing campaign are very low, especially when compared to other traditional advertising means.

Email marketing is ideal for:

- Businesses with products to sell

- Businesses wishing to distribute news
- Businesses who wish to maintain contact with customers
- Businesses wishing to promote new business lines, products, and services
- Businesses seeking to increase revenue
- Businesses who seek to announce special events
- Businesses who seek to offer coupons or discounts to customers
- Businesses who strive to save money on advertising costs or have a limited advertising budget
- Small, independent businesses competing with industry leaders
- Businesses seeking to expand their customer base or reach into new market areas

Email marketing is **not** ideal for:

- Businesses who wish to harvest email names from the Web using a "harvesting" program to build their email lists (harvesting programs scan websites collecting any email addresses listed on their site, enabling them to add these harvested emails to their list. This is illegal, unethical, and will not be successful. Harvesting is big business — there are companies who are profitable because they harvest email addresses and sell them to others. Harvesting can be targeted by keywords, allowing you to "harvest" email from websites that have specific terms on them, thus "targeting" the audience
- Businesses that engage in the creation of spam
- Businesses that promote illegal activity or pornography
- Businesses that promote marketing schemes, financial scams, and other fraudulent hoaxes (such as helping out the son of the deposed king of some country you have never heard of before by giving him your bank account so he can transfer his billions of dollars and escape his impoverished country, letting you keep a few million for your assistance). This is a scam; do not fall for it.

- Businesses who buy CDs containing hundreds of thousands of email addresses (from the email harvesters) hoping to quickly establish an email list of "new" customers

Email Marketing Walkthrough

As you move forward with plans to implement an email marketing campaign, you will follow these basic steps, each of which will be explained in detail in this chapter:

- Plan your email marketing campaign
- Target your audience and content
- Write and design your email
- Setup your online mail distribution method
- Review your email list
- Test your email
- Schedule your email blast
- Send your email blast
- Analyze results

Below is an example of a typical e-mail e-blast:

Plan your email marketing campaign

The biggest challenge you will face is the actual design of your email marketing campaign. You must determine what your desired results are and how best to capture that in a single email. It is important that you identify what your goals and objective are with your email campaign.

For example, your goal may be to distribute industry relevant news, articles, or information or it may be to promote specific new products that you can provide. Your goal may be to promote a discount for your business or offer your products and services to others. The best advice when designing an email marketing campaign is to start small and think clearly. In other words, do not try to reach all of your business objectives in one email, because this will overwhelm and turn off any potential customers.

Compile a list of the many objectives you would like to achieve, then start with the simplest and go from there — it may be as simple as an introduction to your company, a short summary of information, and a discount coupon for placing their first order. Sending an email with an introduction, news articles, product information, discounts, subscription offers, and a variety of other potentially useful information will saturate your customers with information overload.

Introduce them to your company, give them an incentive to go to your website, and then let your business win them over. As you build successive email campaigns, you can target products, provide industry relevant information, give advice, provide news, and build your email client list.

Target your audience

You may be able to (depending on your email list) target a wide variety of demographical information, such as age, gender, interests, or geographical information such as country, state, region, or even limit your campaign to your specific local area.

Write and design your email

Writing an effective email can be a challenge. You will need to decide if you want to use text-based email or HTML (or both). In addition, you will need to ensure your email is balanced, error-free, and is properly formatted to be displayed in the recipients' email client.

How you deliver your message is critical to the success of your campaign. If your recipient will not open your email, it is a failure; therefore, you must at least capture the interest of the recipient to open your email and hopefully click-through to your website. Obviously, if your goal is to sell products through your email marketing campaign, its success hinges on the ability to actually close the deal and ultimately sell products on your site as a result of your email marketing campaign.

Setup your online mail distribution method

There are many companies that offer all-in-one solutions for managing your email lists, creating and sending your email campaigns, tracking statistics, and even offering exceptionally well-designed templates to simplify the process of designing your email campaigns.

I highly recommend you use either an all-in-one solution provider or one of the industry experts to manage your email campaigns. Do not attempt to send out email marketing campaigns through your local email client or you likely will find yourself suspended for "spamming" through your Internet Service Provider; you should also avoid using one of the many "bulk" email providers who offer to send your email to hundreds of thousands of recipients for one low fee.

Know your service provider and have confidence in the quality of your list. Do not use overseas providers to send your email to recipients who did not ask to receive it. Topica (**www.topica.com**) and Constant Contact (**www.constantcontact.com**) are the two providers I recommend for dependability, ease of use, and cost effectiveness.

Review your email list

Your email list is important. A quality email list of opt-in recipients is a valuable asset to your company. Chapter 11 will teach you how to expand and grow your email list and gain quality leads, while avoiding bulk email providers who often send your email as unsolicited spam. Protect your email list — it is valuable. Most all-in-one service providers also provide you with HTML code for "subscriptions," simplifying the process of allowing website visitors to join your mailing list.

Test your email

One of the most important (and often overlooked) steps in the development of an email marketing campaign is to test emails before you actually send them. You need to test your emails, open them in a variety of email clients so that the format and appearance is exactly as intended.

In addition, you should test each part of the document to ensure that it works properly. If you send an email with mistakes, errors, or broken lists, you will lose potential customers fast. Be sure to pay special attention to the embedded graphics in your emails by viewing your email on a computer other than the one you used to create your email campaign. Many times I have seen emails sent out using relative links instead of absolute links, which can be critical if you are pulling images into your email from other Web servers.

An absolute link defines a specific location of the Web file or document, including the protocol to use to get the document, the server to get it from, the directory it is located in, and the name of the document or file, such as:

<a href="http://www.mywebsite.com/graphic.png"></a>

A relative link will not work in an email because, unlike a Web page on a Web server, it does not already know the domain URL and where the document or image is located. An example of a relative link is:

<a href="graphic.png"></a>

Since the domain name and **http://** is not included with this, the recipient email client does not know where to pull the graphic file from and it will not be displayed in your email.

Bottom line — use absolute links when developing email marketing campaigns. When you are satisfied with the quality, quantity, and functionality of your email, it is time to schedule it.

Schedule and send your email blast

The act of sending your email is actually the simplest. By utilizing an all-in-one solution provider or email campaign manager, this will be scheduled far in advance. You will not have to do anything except wait for results once your email campaign is developed, tested, scheduled, and actually launched.

Analyze the results

Similar to testing your email before actually sending it, analyzing the results is often overlooked. You must analyze the results if you want to understand what is effective and what is not effective for your business.

Essentially, you need to know how many emails were sent and delivered to your recipients, what percentage of your subscribers opened each email, who opened and clicked through any of the embedded links in each email, which links generated the most click-throughs (and which did not generate any), and how many individuals removed themselves from your list (or who joined your list).

Understanding what works and what does not work is critical to refining the process and increasing the effectiveness of your email marketing campaigns. Do not be afraid to tweak your emails and re-evaluate the results. Your emails should have a clearly stated purpose and should have an expected action.

Email marketing is, of course, limited by the size of your advertising budget, but it is one of the most cost-effective methods of advertising you will find.

How to Design an Effective Email Campaign

Writing an email masterpiece is not as difficult as you may believe. While there are certain challenges you may have to overcome, the actual creation of the email blast is probably easier and less time-consuming than developing and growing your actual email list. Be sure to decide your overall goal for designing an email campaign; this can cover everything from increasing sales, growing customer base, and raising product awareness to distributing newsworthy industry related information, distributing discount coupons or promotional offers, or hundreds of other possibilities.

What is the most commonly asked question of an email marketing specialist? It is simple and has been the number one question for years. The question is a variation of this theme: Can I buy a list of email addresses that I can use to start my email campaigns? The answer to this is typically no, unless you follow some of the methods covered on how to grow your email list. You will quickly discover that renting or buying email lists typically fails to return the results you expect and will get you in hot water fast with anti-spam laws. You need to build a quality email list and it can take some time, even years to do. Having a quality opt-in list ensures that you have clearly established a relationship with your customers and they eagerly accept your email communications with them.

Opt-in and opt-out emailing

To maintain spam compliance and ensure your email list is both legal and contains those subscribers who actually want to receive your emails, you need to understand opt-in and opt-out emailing. The underlying principle behind opt-in is very simple: If I have expressly given you permission to add my email address to your email list, then I have "opted-in" to your list. On the other hand, opt-out refers to the process where the email recipient requests that a list owner take his name off of the list and ensures that he is not sent any future emails.

Let's take a look at some definitions which may help you understand the concepts we will discuss:

- **Single opt-in:** Email addresses are added to your email list through a subscription, such as completing a "join our mailing list" form, sending an email to a subscription email address, checking a box on an order to add your email address, or providing your email address to customer lists through business reply cards, at conferences, or other online or offline methods. Your email address may also be added to multiple lists simultaneously by submitting your email address through one of many free offer and other promotional based websites. This is a simple process and is not validated or confirmed. In other words, your email address is added to one or more email lists and you do not have to perform any specific actions to confirm that it has been added. Often, the subscriber is sent a welcoming email and instructions on how to unsubscribe if he did not intend to join the email list — however, this is often not the case.

While an opt-in list is effective and simple to manage, there are some potential drawbacks to maintaining such a list:

- **Subscription errors:** It is not uncommon for subscribers to mistype their email address, making the email address unusable. An invalid email address will bounce back when sent, or worse, may actually be delivered to someone who did not join your list. Mistyping a single character in an email address can cause email to be undeliverable or sent to someone else. When an email bounces back, it means you may be sending the email to the wrong recipient or you may have the incorrect email, which means that the subscriber never receives their email to opt-in to your list.

- **Invalid submissions:** Because of the prominence of spam in today's environment, many individuals may fill out Web forms and other subscription vehicles and enter a false or invalid email address to avoid being added to potential spam lists. As with the subscription errors, an invalid email address will bounce back when sent, or worse, may actually be delivered to someone who did not join your list.

- **False subscriptions:** Submitting someone else's email address to one or more lists. This really accomplishes nothing other than causing the recipient the frustration of receiving emails they did not subscribe to and also forces them to remove themselves.

- **List poisoning:** This is when invalid email addresses are intentionally added to your email list. In most cases, these will simply bounce back and should be removed from your list, but it does cause you extra administrative work. If your list is excessively poisoned, it may be rendered useless for its intended purpose. Another way lists are poisoned is by intentionally adding anti-spam email addresses to your list, so that when your email is sent to your list, these "anti-spam" email addresses trigger "spam-traps" which can automatically put your IP address on a "blocklist" that keeps the sender's messages from getting through any mail servers.

- **Notification opt-in:** Email addresses are added to your email list through a subscription. A welcoming email is immediately sent to the subscriber with instructions on how to unsubscribe if they did not intend to join the email list. This is very similar to single opt-in with the exception that the welcoming and opt-out email is always sent. The main advantage of this over single opt-in is that you are notified of the list subscription and are given the opportunity to remove yourself from any email lists to which you have been subscribed.

- **Double opt-in (closed loop opt-in):** Email addresses are added to your email list through a subscription. A welcoming confirmation email is immediately sent to the subscriber with instructions on how to unsubscribe if he did not intend to join the email list. The recipient must then confirm their subscription to be activated and are added to the email list. This is typically done through a hyperlink embedded within the confirmation email. When the subscriber enters their email into the "join our email list" form, for example, he is immediately sent an email confirmation. He must click on the embedded hyperlink to "confirm" his subscription or he is not added to the list. This means the person who wishes to join your list must complete two steps to activate a subscription (initially joining the list and then confirming that subscription).

While a double opt-in list is the most spam compliant, it is not without its problems. Most of the problems are for you, not the recipient:

- **Complexity:** Double opt-in is more complex and requires a more advanced system to manage the double opt-in process; thus, most small businesses or those with limited budgets often find this system is not affordable or readily available. You will discover in later chapters that many all-in-one service providers include double opt-in.

- **Negative impact:** As you now know, a person who wishes to join your list must complete two steps to activate a subscription (initially joining the list and then confirming that subscription). While this seems pretty simple, the fact is that the percentage of individuals who actually complete the double opt in is very low. In fact, you can expect to lose as much as 50 percent of your potential email customers through double opt-in when compared to single opt-in. Often, the confirmation email is captured by spam or junk filters and is never even delivered to the recipient so he can confirm the subscription.

When you craft and send your email campaigns, you must comply with the CAN-SPAM Act, which will be discussed at the end of this chapter, and always include a method for opt-out. Most all-in-one providers do this for you by automatically adding opt out features to each email blast that you send.

Email campaign basics

Here are some of the basics you need to review as you design your email marketing campaign.

Identify your audience

Identify your audience so you know whom you are targeting and why. You will often find your target audience varies depending on the type of email you may send and often you will have multiple email lists based on segmented target audiences.

Establish purpose

Establish the purpose and nature of your emails (i.e. newsletter, advertising, coupons, product announcements, press releases, articles, or a combination of any of these).

Choose format

Choose your format (HTML, text, or both). This is a subject of great debate. Ten years ago text was king. Five years ago you should have used both text and HTML. Today, I would recommend using HTML primarily, with text as an alternate.

Decide who is in charge

Who is responsible for your email development efforts? Are you going to manage all aspects of your campaign or will you use an all-in-one service provider? Will you create, edit, format, and test your actual emails or will you contract this out to an email marketing specialist? Who will manage the administration of your program (opt ins, opt outs, scheduling, reports, etc).

Create a schedule

What are your short- and long-term plans? Do you intend to do email blasts on a regular schedule (i.e. weekly) or randomly?

Ensure your list is opt-in

Ensure whatever method you use to manage your lists is 100 percent opt-in to maintain compliance with anti-spam laws and always include a method for anyone to opt-out of your lists at anytime.

Choose your growing methods

What methods will you use to gather email addresses and grow your current email list? At a minimum, you should include a sign-up form on your website that is prominently featured on your home page, and you may consider additional "Join our Mailing List" forms on your shopping cart checkout pages, in your customer emails, order notifications, or any other media which you use to exchange information with current and potential customers. You may even want to include this information on print media such as brochures and business cards. Do not forget to ask customers to join your list during phone conversations, at trade shows, and at other industry events.

Use rented lists

Use co-registration and rented lists to grow your customer base. By this I do not mean "steal" the email addresses from rentals and co-registration lists. As you send your email blasts through co-registration and rental lists, be sure to include something to get them to sign up for your email list, thus adding quality email addresses to your list.

Discuss technical requirements

Discuss the technical requirements of your marketing plan. This covers a wide variety of items such as managing your email lists, sending the actual email blasts, bandwidth constraints, ISP policies, email software, HTML development expertise, automation of opt-in and opt-out techniques, and required hardware (such as email servers). Do not discount the expertise of the individuals who will be required to manage and administer your program, including the development of your actual email blasts.

HTML vs. text format

The first issue you need to address is whether to utilize HTML-based email or text-based emails. Several years ago, this was a fairly pertinent question, as many email programs were text-based and could not handle HTML-based content. Today, that is not the case, as every major email application effectively handles and interprets HTML code and presents it in the proper format to the reader.

Just because these email programs read HTML does not mean that they are configured to allow it; plus Microsoft Outlook 2002, Outlook 2010 and Outlook 2013, by default, do not allow the download of images in emails (although you can change this with a simple mouse click). The Department of Defense (DOD), the Department of Homeland Security (DHS), and several private corporations have enacted security restrictions on receiving HTML formatted email messages. They strip the HTML coding and convert the email to a text-based format. If you are only blasting with HTML formatted email messages, your message will be received at DOD + DHS facilities as scrambled HTML code, which is practically unreadable. This means there is some advantage to sending both HTML and text-based emails to recipients or sending HTML with an alternative link to text versions of the email. However, DOD and DHS do offer the ability to "view as HTML," but this feature is not guaranteed to last as the federal government combats spam and cyber attacks.

HTML formatted messages are simply Web pages that are sent through an email server that are re-assembled and presented to the recipient in his or her browser. The advantage to HTML is that you can use highly customized formatting, embedded graphics, and other dynamic features that require HTML coding. HTML allows you to use fonts, colors, graphics, and interactive rich media technology. Text-based emails are simple text with little formatting, no graphics, no colors, and no special font formatting, but these do allow you to embed absolute hyperlinks in the text.

So, which is better? I recommend both, if possible. Most all-in-one providers allow you to craft both text and HTML formatted messages.

The key to determining which format to send primarily depends on your email list. Typically, you allow those who subscribe to your list to choose which format to receive, either HTML or text. If you do not have a preference selected in your email list, I recommend using HTML-based messages since most email applications are HTML capable. You will not find many email applications that are not HTML friendly unless you are using a 1990s vintage email program.

That said, a text-based alternative is still readily accepted and may be preferred by some users. As I mentioned earlier, some companies and the government may actually force your HTML formatted messages back into a text-based format. In Outlook, the recipient may convert the message back to HTML format, which makes the subject line all the more important if you expect the recipient to identify your email when presented with the HTML code in a text representation.

Advantages of HTML-based email
- Professional appearance, visually pleasing
- You can embed graphics into your email
- You can use a variety of colors, fonts, styles
- Your email can-be interactive with Web forms
- Emails are statistically more effective

Disadvantages of HTML-based email
- Email client may not support HTML format
- Some companies/government may not allow HTML format
- Graphics intensive emails are slow to load
- Outlook 2003-13 blocks graphics by default (although most users change this to download by default after installation)
- More likely to contain viruses and Trojan horses
- Graphics are blocked by default in Microsoft Outlook and Others

How to Write an Effective Email

This is essentially the heart and soul of an email marketing campaign. The subject line is the first thing that a recipient will see, followed by your actual email. Your email blast is the direct communication from your company to each of your recipients and often serves as the initial contact from your company to a potential customer; therefore, you want to ensure it is professional, effective, and error-free. We all know what junk email and spam look like as we receive it daily and your email creative must be designed so it does not look like amateur spam. Likewise, a poorly designed email creative will not inspire confidence in the recipient and will typically not result in landing sales.

The subject line

The importance of the subject line cannot be stressed enough. This is the first thing your email recipient will see, and it can be the single determining factor in whether they will open your email or delete it. Additionally, it is one of the primary flags for spam filtering software; therefore, you need to avoid certain words that tend to trigger spam filters.

You should put as much thought and analysis into the subject line as you do for your actual email creative. Take a quick look through your "junk" folder or "trash" bin — chances are you will find a variety of subjects which immediately trigger you to add the sender to your spam list and send the email to the junk folder without giving it a second thought. I spent 60 seconds scanning the emails I have received today (including my junk folder) and found some of the typical suspect subject lines:

- Your $10,000 line of credit has been approved
- Get Slim For 100,000.00 & A New Car
- Need a Date? Find one now!
- Best prices for u
- Exclusive Site for Single Women and Men
- Thank you for your loan request

- This is your big opportunity to double your investment for short period
- This is not Spam!
- Participate and Receive $1,200 to Pay Credit Cards for One Year
- Add 1000++ global TV channels into your PC

The list is seemingly endless; I could write an entire book of bad subject lines. Luckily all of these emails found their way to my junk folder, and if they had actually gotten into my inbox, I would have happily sent them on their way. However, you do need to consider that the potential exists where many of your well-intended, spam-free emails may suffer the same fate. Even if they do make it into the inbox, most people simply scan the subject line and determine if it is spam or junk mail without ever opening or reading it. If they decide that there is a chance that this is a legitimate email, they may look at the sender name.

Basic rules for writing subject lines

The content of your email will drive the construction of your email subject line. There is a fairly simple formula to follow when creating an email subject line depending on your email content; however, no matter what your subject, it definitely needs to describe the subject of your email. If your email subject is entirely different than your email creative content, your email will be heading to the junk bin quickly, along with any chance of establishing a positive relationship with the recipient. Your email subject line should fall into one of the following categories:

- Be an announcement, newsletter, publication, or article — Typically the subject line is the title of the article, publication, newsletter, or the month/issue of a publication.
  - o   The Food Service Professional Issue #124
- Entice the recipient with an intriguing offer or something which would make them want to open and read your email.
  - o   Southwest Airlines: Special Two for One Flight Sale

- Entice the recipient with something that may benefit them by reading your email.
  - o Email Marketer Monthly News: "How to write an effective email"
  - o Jogging Daily: "How to choose the best running shoes"

What email subjects entice you, make you curious, sound like great deals, and have new information which may benefit you personally or professionally?

Subject lines which emphasize and promote cost-savings, opportunities for learning, new products or services which may improve their business or personal lives, or other benefits are the most likely to succeed. Keep your subject short and get your message delivered clearly.

Personalization of emails is a topic we have already discussed; doing this in the beginning of your email can be great, but consider staying away from personalizing the subject line. The theory is that a personalized email subject will make the recipient think it is from someone who knows them and they are more likely to open it. Statistics actually support this, but I believe this trend is reversing. In my experience, 90 percent of the emails I receive with my name included in the subject line are either spam or unsolicited emails. Again, there are contradictory opinions on this, and you need to decide if you want to personalize your subject lines.

If you are producing newsletters or other recurring email blasts, it is important that you maintain consistency in both your subject and your "From" email address. As I have already said, I recommend you stick to your company name, newsletter title, or other standardized "From" email address. If you publish a series of email newsletters, you should use a consistent format for the subject so your recipient recognizes it.

Do's and don'ts

Do not use subject lines that shout. You will have much better success with "Improve your Email Marketing Campaign," than with "IMPROVE YOUR EMAIL MARKETING CAMPAIGN." This is essentially the same message, but it is perceived entirely differently.

Do not overuse the word "Free." It is okay to use it if you are truly promoting something that is free, but do not make it the first word in the subject or spam filters will quickly file it away.

Do not mislead your recipients with false claims, offers, or misinformation. Make sure your email subject matches the content.

Do not get carried away with punctuation and avoid using exclamation marks in your subject lines.

Do not forget to spell check. Yes, it sounds very obvious, but there are plenty of poor spellers out there. Do not be one of them.

Do not use the cash symbol ($) in the subject line. This is associated with spammers.

Do emphasize urgency in an email. If you have a deadline or some other form of compelling action, you will achieve better results (for example, 50 percent off all orders placed by midnight).

Do keep the subject short, simple, and to the point.

Do incorporate your brand name or company name where possible. This increases brand recognition and builds trust and confidence with recipients. If they recognize your brand name, they are more likely to open the email.

How to design an HTML email

When designing an HTML email, you should follow the same principles of website design. You should also follow the rules for SEO when you design your emails and incorporate meta-tag data and keywords into the design. Many companies place their email newsletters, articles, and other email blasts on their websites. There are several reasons to do this, which may include:

- Allowing your articles and newsletters to be available to anyone visiting your website

- Allowing your HTML formatted email blasts to be picked up by search engines and indexed

Essentially you will be using your email campaigns (when properly designed with SEO techniques) to increase your overall website rankings with search engines.

I recommend designing HTML emails in a Web design application, such as Microsoft Expression Web or Adobe Dreamweaver CC. You can even use older Web design applications such as Microsoft Frontpage® for creating emails. You certainly do not need the latest version of a Web design application for creating your emails, and there are numerous other alternatives. I do not recommend attempting to use Notepad or any other non-graphical user interface application, nor should you use Microsoft Word. Also, keep in mind that many programs, including older Web design applications such as Microsoft Frontpage may insert additional code into your HTML emails; therefore, it is critical you test each email before you schedule an email blast.

The process of actually creating your email blast is exactly the same as designing a Web page. With Microsoft Expression Web, Dreamweaver CC or your favorite Web design application, the learning curve for non-Web designers is very small and most novice users can craft a professional looking email campaign. Microsoft Expression Web is more complicated (although far superior) to Frontpage and will work fine, but is truly designed for creating websites utilizing cascading style sheets and other advanced features you will not need in an email marketing campaign. Even if you have upgraded to Microsoft Expression Web, you may want to hang onto Frontpage or another familiar HTML editor for the creation of your email campaigns.

If you want to ensure you have a professional campaign, there are numerous email marketers and Web design companies who are cost-effective and highly reputable. Let's look at some HTML email design basics:

- Do not embed graphics into your actual email blast; instead place your graphics on a Web server and "call" the graphics by a URL embedded in your email. Embedded large graphics can cause significant download problems for recipients.

- When designing your HTML email, use absolute URLs for all of your graphics or hyperlinks. A common mistake when designing is to use the relative URL, which may work fine when designing and testing, but will not work when delivered. For example, a relative URL may be "/emailblast/images/radio1.jpg." As long as you are on your Web server, this relative location is understood, and the images will be served properly; however, if you are not on the server, the URL will fail and the image links will be broken.

- I recommend designing your email blast with a combination of HTML formatting (tables, text, and colors) and embedded graphics instead of in a graphics program and sending that graphic creative as your entire email campaign. However, if you choose to send a large graphic as your email campaign, you can still apply SEO principles and you should "slice" your email to facilitate download speed. All graphics software such as Macromedia® Fireworks® and JASC® Paint Shop ProTM allow you to take an image, slice it into pieces, and export it into an HTML document with absolute URLs.

- Where possible, minimize the use of graphics to improve download speed. Use HTML coding, tables, and background colors to design your email.

How to design a text-based email

It is advised to use text-based emails with your HTML email blasts. If you do not want to invest the time in converting graphic-rich HTML content into basic text formatting, you do not have to. The use of text emails is optional. The fact is that a majority of spam emails are text based.

The only reason for using text-based emails is so that you can provide a non-HTML, non-graphical email for those whose email clients cannot read HTML format or cannot display it properly. If you want to be 100 percent certain that your email will be received and displayed properly, text is the answer. All email clients can properly read text-based emails and you can use hyperlinks in your text emails as well.

Here are some general guidelines for creating text-based emails:

- Use Notepad. Do not use Microsoft Word or any other program. Notepad is perfect for text-based email creation and comes with all versions of Windows.
- Limit your line length to no more than 80 characters.
- Limit your email to two to three paragraphs and bullet critical points you need to get across to recipients.
- As with HTML email, the shorter the better.
- You can use hyperlinks, but you must use the absolute link in proper HTML formatting.
- Do not use ASCII graphics. ASCII graphics are graphics created by using ASCII key symbols, such as the caret symbol.

Do not be afraid to ask others to review your email content. You will find that how others perceive your email will help you to improve the content and ultimately improve your chance for email marketing success. The following are some great reference sources for learning how to write the content of your emails:

- A Beginner's Guide to Effective Email: **http://webfoot.com/ advice/email.top.html**
- Writing Sensible Email Messages: **www.43folders. com/2005/09/19/writing-sensible-email-messages/**
- Writing Competitive Email: **www.powerhomebiz.com/vol8/ Writing.htm**
- Six Steps to Selling by Email: How to Write Email Sales Messages that Gets Results **www.powerhomebiz.com/vol10/email.htm**
- Business Writing: **www.businesswritingblog.com/business_ writing/email/index.html**

Email examples

Basic HTML Email (HTML View)

In the email above, notice that the absolute URLs are used for each graphic. In this example, the image in the creative was sliced into 3 x 3 rows and columns; each "piece" of the image is placed in the appropriate cell in the HTML table to ensure exact positioning. Since each image is unique, each has its own hyperlink associated with it.

The HTML view below is what will be received by the user when the email blast is sent:

Sample HTML Based Email

Sample HTML-Based Email

Target Your Audience

Targeting your audience is a fairly simple concept. You want to send your emails to the recipients who will most likely respond. The more targeted your email message is, the higher the likelihood is that it will be successful. Since most email programs and all-in-one solution providers give you the capability of creating targeted emails, you can create highly customized and personalized messages targeting only those who are most likely to act on the email message, thus increasing return on investment and decreasing costs. Statistics support that personalized and targeted email campaigns realize improved results when compared to generic emails.

Personalization

Personalization is simply the process of customizing your email blasts with customer data, thus making them more personalized to the recipient. In other words, your email blast to me might start with Dear Bruce, instead of no greeting or a generic introductory greeting. There are several reasons to personalize, which include increased recognition by customers, the "friendly" factor, potential increased return on investment, and many recipients expect it and may be turned off when they do not receive personalized emails. In general, using personalized email softens the email and promotes a "friendly" exchange of information.

You need to decide how much personal data you wish to collect and how to use it. Be aware that there are risks in asking for too much information; you will lose potential list subscribers who do not want to spend five minutes filling out their life history on your website and even more who feel like you do not need to know. My recommendation is to require the email address and to try to collect first name, last name, and state at a minimum, where possible. You can certainly collect more data if you want, but make the fields optional so the list subscriber can choose what they want to reveal to you. Also, when using the personalization in an email, be careful of overuse. Using their name is fine in the introduction, but do not use it (or the recipient's name) in every paragraph. The overkill will drive away potential customers.

Collecting demographic data

The great thing about Web-based forms is you can capture any data that is entered and then use that data to target and personalize your emails. As I mentioned earlier, you can collect a wide variety of data elements, but you may lose potential subscribers if your subscription form is too lengthy and time consuming to fill out. Topica recently expanded the personalization feature in their all-in-one solution by providing up to 12 unique fields including both single-select and multiple-select category fields such as name, city, state, etc. and other behavioral or demographic data, such as product purchased or area of site visited. Most solution providers allow you to customize the degree of personalization and demographic data you wish to collect.

However, in light of the volume of potential demographic data you can collect, go with the minimum and ask for an email address and name and then only what other data you believe is critical for use in your email campaign. There is no point in soliciting or collecting data you do not intend to utilize in your campaigns. The golden rule is the less information you ask for, the better the chance that someone will fill out your subscription forms and join your email list. As you develop a relationship with your email subscribers, you can always try to solicit more information later. Build the relationship first, then expand your demographic to extra information such as address, gender, age, income, marital status, etc. No matter what, if your email subscriber list only contains email addresses, you are way behind the power curve.

Maintaining multiple lists

One of the best features of email marketing is the ability to perform list segmentation or sub-lists. If you have a variety of email lists for different product lines or for targeting different customer needs, you can use multiple lists within in a single account, allowing you to maintain one cost-effective account but still maintain lists separately. This is ideal for companies who have collected email addresses only and do not possess the demographic data to allow for automated segmentation or targeting within their lists. They can continue to develop email campaigns based on their targeted lists and maintain each list within one single account.

A common question is, "How can I personalize emails or send targeted emails if my list only contains email addresses?" The answer is you cannot. There is no magic program that will "know" the name of the recipient, nor can you determine demographics data based solely on an email address. Establish a rapport and trust with your existing subscribers, and if you want, you can ask them to provide demographic data (on an optional basis) at a later date.

Timing Your Email Blast

Now that you have created your email masterpiece, you must address the issue of when to send it, how often to send it, and what time of the day is best to send out your email blast. There is no cut and dry answer to any of these questions, so I will give you the best advice possible and you will have to determine what works best for you, based on the type of emails you are sending.

The day of the week

The answers may surprise you. Traditionally, Mondays and Fridays have been the worst days to email. The reasons are fairly obvious — Monday is the traditional first day back to work after the weekend and is typically a busy day for meetings, catching up from the previous week, planning the week ahead, and clearing out emails from the weekend. Your emails may fall victim to overload. Fridays have long been considered the worst day to email, simply because it is the end of the work week, people are looking forward to the weekend, cleaning out their emails, and may be less inclined to review new, incoming emails.

Tuesdays and Wednesdays are nearly evenly split for the title of busiest day for email marketing. More are sent and received on Tuesdays and Wednesdays than on any other day of the week and more than 95 percent of all email marketing campaigns are sent Tuesday through Friday. Research also reveals that emails sent out Wednesday through Friday will yield the highest open rates. Surprisingly, the highest click rates are obtained on emails delivered on weekends. The truth is the "best" day to send emails is a constantly moving target and you will have to test the waters to determine what works best for your type of business or email marketing campaign.

My advice is to start your email campaigns on a Tuesday or Thursday and then test the waters from there. Once your campaign is established, try a weekend and compare it to your other results. Try a Friday, check your open rates, and compare them to your averages on Thursdays. Depending on your target audience, you may have better luck on Mondays or weekends. Do not discount the weekends. I spend more time on email on the weekends than during the week and this is becoming common in the workplace as traditional working hours are replaced by flex schedules, telecommuting, and remote access. You should definitely avoid scheduling email blasts on holidays and holiday weekends unless they contain special holiday promotions or discount offers that target a specific holiday or time period.

The time of day

Research shows that the best time to send an email blast is between 7 a.m. and 10:30 a.m. Keep in mind that time zones may wreak havoc on an email campaign unless you segment the delivery schedule by time zones. A 7 a.m. delivery on the East Coast is a 4 a.m. delivery on the West Coast. Be aware that email may take seconds to hours to deliver to all of your recipients — they will not receive it at the exact same time. If you are delivering articles or newsletters, you may want to ask your subscribers what day of the week and time they prefer to receive your email blasts. By making the time convenient for them, you will increase the likelihood of achieving positive open rates.

Email frequency

Some of the issues regarding email frequency may be established by the type of email you are sending. For example, if you are generating newsletters, articles, and other items on a recurring basis, you need to establish the frequency up front and make it clear in your email creative so you can establish a positive relationship with your subscribers.

Timing is everything, and the best advice to follow is to not overload your subscribers with emails. Once per week is the general rule of thumb. If you exceed that, you will quickly annoy your subscribers and find that they remove themselves from your list. Use segmentation to avoid saturating your list with emails that are not relevant to the recipients.

The bottom line with frequency is to establish what works best for you and your customers. Creating email campaigns can be time-consuming. Do not commit to sending weekly emails if you do not have the time and resources to produce them. As with when to send your emails, you will have to experiment and test your email frequency to balance optimal results with workload to ensure that the return on investment is maximized. Depending on the type of email campaigns you are sending, different rules may apply.

Growing Your Email List

The biggest challenge you will face is creating and growing an effective mailing list. There are a wide variety of techniques for how to grow your email list and I will cover each of them, giving you candid advice and proven techniques for ensuring that your list will grow over time. There is no point in having a list with hundreds of thousands of email addresses which are not relevant to your email message or are invalid email addresses which will constantly bounce back as undeliverable. The most effective lists are those which contain only individuals who expressly wish to receive your email marketing message and may potentially act based on the message you send. Realistically, depending on the type of email marketing message you send, you can expect between a 1 percent to 10 percent return; however, the 2 to 4 percent range is fairly typical.

There have been pushes for changes in regulations of email marketing and the handling of spam, such as the creation of a "do not email" list, similar to the nationwide "do not call" list used for telemarketers. Obviously, this is a hotly contested issue and would require significant changes in the management of email lists. As of today, there is not such a thing as an official do not call list for email.

One of the questions you must answer is what demographics you wish to collect for your email list. While capturing an email address is the most basic, it may not be the most effective if you wish to target your email blasts by region or other demographic data. You can collect a wide-variety of demographic information, but keep in mind: if you try to collect too much data, you will turn off potential subscribers who do not wish to fill out a lengthy subscription form or provide too much personal data. At a minimum, if you are going to collect more than just an email address, you should collect the first name, last name, gender, and state of the subscriber so you can use this information for email targeting in your campaigns.

Proven methods to grow your email list

Let's discuss some of the ways you can grow your email list. Remember, this list is not inclusive of all methods and a little creativity can go a long way in creating an effective email list.

1) Collect email addresses on your website

This is the best method of growing your email list. If you have visitors on your site who have an interest in your products or services, it is an ideal time to capture their email address. You can simply place a subscription form on your home page (or other pages) that is clearly visible and readily accessible. Since this form is directly on your website, you know that subscribers have an express interest in your products and/or services; therefore, this is a highly effective means of acquiring quality email addresses.

2) Collect email addresses from customer orders

If you sell products through your website, you are most likely already collecting email addresses. However, you still need to ask permission to add this email address to your list. A simple method of doing this is placing a question directly on the website order form asking the customer, "Do you want to join our email list?" You can customize this to provide a brief description of what the list contains (such as special promotions) as an incentive to get people to sign up. Once individuals check the "yes" box, you should still run the email address through your double opt-in process to ensure that your list is completely anti-spam compliant.

3) Collect email addresses through offline methods

If you produce traditional media products or marketing campaigns such as print advertising, flyers, brochures, catalogs, business cards, paper order forms, and other means of disseminating and collecting information from potential customers, then you have an opportunity to ask them to join your email list. Since mailings, catalogs, and other print media are often sent to hundreds of thousands of recipients, you have an ideal target audience from which to collect email addresses. If a customer is returning something to your company, it is as simple as asking her to check a box and fill in her email address or you can put your website address or social media on the print media, telling her to visit the URL if she wishes to join your email list. Either way, there is no additional cost for asking for this information, and even if you only get a 10 percent return on a mailing of 100,000 individuals, you have just added 10,000 quality email addresses to your list.

4) Collect email addresses through surveys

Online surveys are a great way to attract interest and draw in potential customers. Since you have captured their interest in a survey, this is a great time to also ask them to join your email list and capture their email address. You can also do the same thing for print surveys.

5) Collect email addresses through e-newsletters

This simply means that you use your email list to distribute your email marketing campaigns, such as e-newsletters. One of the great things about e-newsletters is that you can include subscription forms right on the newsletters and also incorporate a "forward to a friend," which can exponentially increase your target base distribution and potential subscriber list. Also, you should take your e-zines or e-newsletters and publish them on your website. This does two things for you:

- Publishes your historical e-newsletters online so that customers can read back issues that may have relevant information. By including subscription information on them, you may draw in email subscribers who never actually received your e-newsletter via email.

- Lets you place a keyword rich HTML formatted e-newsletter on your website, which will be scanned and indexed by search engines and spiders, so your e-newsletter can work for you by increasing your overall visibility in search engines. It is important to include proper HTML formatting, including meta-tags in each HTML newsletter to maximize the effectiveness within search engines.

6) Collect email addresses through promotions and giveaways

Promotions, free offers, and giveaways are great ways to attract attention, draw in new customers, and acquire new email leads. Some caution needs to be taken when you offer free products, though. First, the use of the word "free" in email subjects is a standard target for spam filters. Your message may be flagged as spam before it ever gets to its intended target. Secondly, when you offer something for "free," you can expect a lot of interest by people who have no real interest in your product lines, and you may not be collecting quality email addresses. It is standard practice for many companies to collect email addresses and personal information in exchange for a free product or sample. From experience, free offers usually generate tremendous response.

7) Collect email addresses by purchasing email lists

This is the most controversial subject and there is no definitive answer on the subject of buying email names or lists, although I would recommend you avoid it. It is highly discouraged and may be illegal. A simple Internet search reveals hundreds (or more) of companies that sell targeted email lists, often for an extremely low cost. Some offer up to one million emails for as low as $199. They also claim to be completely CAN-SPAM Act compliant. Technically, it is a convoluted subject, one I would avoid as an email marketer, and I personally find it questionable how a company can have "spam compliant" email addresses and sell them to another company and still consider them "spam compliant." Most of these lists have some serious drawbacks, which may include:

- **Price:** They are typically very expensive. Unlike direct mail lists, which are both affordable and readily available, email lists come at a higher premium.

- **Quality:** Expect nearly 50 percent to bounce immediately. I have found most of these purchased lists to be low quality, often harvested email addresses, which will quickly land you in trouble with the CAN-SPAM Act.

If you are having trouble adding email addresses to your list and wish to pursue "buying" email addresses (which I do not recommend), you should pursue what is known as co-registration instead of the outright purchasing of email lists. Co-registration involves joining forces with another advertiser, marketing company, or website which collects permission-based name and email addresses to sell to other companies. Essentially, your company information, products, subscription information, or other type of data is placed on their website asking them to join your (and possibly many other) email lists. If someone chooses to join your list, you are then charged for this "lead," typically costing between 50 cents to upwards of $2 per lead. Again, be warned, most of the co-registration networks utilize contests and other promotional material to entice someone to give them their email address in exchange for free products, contest registrations, etc. You typically get very low quality (or invalid) email addresses.

Co-registration is not a low-cost solution; however, it can be used to quickly generate thousands of email names, which are opt in and spam compliant. There are hundreds of co-registration "networks" or "solution providers" which offer this service. Many will resell these names to you as bulk email addresses for a flat rate fee, but you will still have to deal with anti-spam issues, as well as the effect of utilizing potentially low quality leads in your email marketing campaign.

8) List Exchange and Rental

This differs from buying a list; instead of importing the email addresses into your email list, you "rent" a list and have someone else send your email message using their list. You will need to do your homework to ensure that you stay away from "junk lists," which are mostly harvested email addresses. You can verify the quality of rental lists by validating the opt-in source records for the list you plan to use. Keep in mind these must be obtained by traditional means including subscriptions, market research or surveys. Ensure that you receive tracking and other detailed delivery reports as part of the list rental agreement and ensure that the list brokers comply with the CAN-SPAM Act by honoring all opt-out requests. List exchange is very similar to list rental except instead of a monetary transaction for a list rental, you actually exchange list services. In other words, your actual lists never change hands, but you use your list to email their email marketing campaign and they use their list to email your email marketing campaign, thus significantly increasing both distributions at little to no cost (the only cost may be if the list sizes are significantly different in comparison).

9) Collect email addresses through viral email campaigns

A viral email campaign is a type of campaign that is typically used for petitions and requires you to complete a form, then forward it to a specific number of persons, in the hopes that each person then forwards it to ten more and so on, thus expanding across the Internet like a "virus" (although not necessarily the bad type of virus). These campaigns are not very successful, yet you can garner some email addresses if your viral campaign requires registrations or filling out a Web form to participate in a poll, campaign, or other similar technique. The quality of the leads is questionable at best and many people will immediately hit the delete key upon receiving a viral email. However, you may find that viral emails can spread quickly across the globe reaching a wide audience base.

10) Collect email addresses through banner advertising

The days of banner advertising are past us. Many sites use banner advertising as a method to generate income; however, it has been replaced by the more effective pay-per-click advertising market. Banner ads will typically cost you money to have them placed on websites hoping that they will attract the attention of the site visitor so that they click on them, travel to your website, and ultimately sign up for your subscription email list. If you can get free banner ads, it is not a bad option, but do not expect a significant return, as most website visitors have become trained to ignore banner advertising.

11) Collect email addresses through discount offers

This is one of the most effective ways to attract potential customers and hopefully convert them into return customers. If your goal is to both collect permission-based emails for your email list and to build your customer base, you need to specify the terms of the offer very clearly, such as offering a 25 percent discount on any product on your website. One of the terms of your offer may be that they join your email list, thus converting not only a sale, but also a quality addition to your website. You can then use the email list to solicit repeat business by sending your "preferred" customers another discount certificate, drawing them back to your site. If they are satisfied with your products and service provided to them, you may have just made a repeat customer for life.

12) Collect email addresses through associate and affiliate programs

For example, Atlantic Publishing Company (**www.atlantic-pub.com**) offered a free affiliate program for their wide-ranging products (those actually published by Atlantic Publishing Company only). You could become an affiliate for free and earn a flat 20 percent commission for every sale through your website. Since you now earn money for essentially doing nothing other than listing products on your website, the affiliate sponsor is hoping you will send out your affiliate links to all your friends, business associates, and others hoping they will buy the products. Obviously, the affiliate sponsor is looking for customers and also subscriptions if you wish to join their email list. If you host an affiliate program, you can even ask your affiliate to include a subscription form to your email list on their website as part of the affiliate terms.

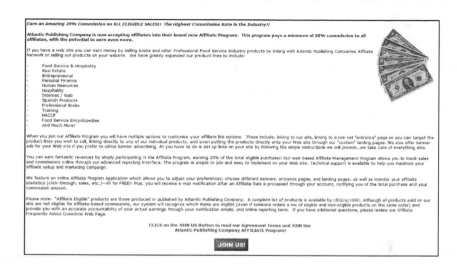

Make sure that if you host an affiliate program, you have a solid anti-spam policy to protect you in case one of your affiliates decides to promote your affiliate link through less than reputable email distribution lists, such as the one below:

> Spam: Atlantic Publishing Company has a zero tolerance policy for spam. Any Affiliate accused of spamming will be immediately removed from our affiliate program. The only recourse you will have to maintain your affiliate relationship is proof of "opt-in" that will undermine the validity of the spam complaint. Valid spam complaints will result in the immediate termination of your account and forfeiture of any commissions owed you.

Limiting opt-out customers

There is no secret formula you can use to keep people from unsubscribing to your list; however, a little common sense can go a long way to solve this problem. The main reason people unsubscribe from a mailing list is that they are not receiving the material they expect or desire. You have to give your subscribers what they signed up for. If that is news, information, new product releases, etc., then that is your primary focus. You can always add additional information which may be of interest, but you must provide them with what you told them they would be getting when they first signed up with your email list. Keep your list active, at least quarterly or more frequently or it will be forgotten quickly. Keep your information fresh, relevant, and interesting. If your email is of no value, does not benefit the reader in some way, or is completely off-target, your email subscriber will jump ship quickly.

It is commonplace to see companies selling email lists that they claim are "spam compliant," or 100 percent opt-in. Five years ago, most of these offers were simply scams containing thousands upon thousands of illegally harvested email addresses. However, in contrast, you will find that there are many highly respected and reputable companies that offer list rentals and even purchase lists from other companies seeking to start or expand email-marketing efforts.

You will find the scams continue; many list rentals and sellers that are still selling harvested emails typically operate off-shore servers which are shut down and restarted under another domain overnight, so you need to be cautious, check references, and do some research before you sign up with someone for list rentals or purchase. You do not want to be targeted as a spammer on your first attempt at email marketing. Here is some candid advice to ensure that you do not end up on a spam blacklist:

1) Check references
Ensure that the company you choose to use has been in business for a period of time, has established customers, and a good record with spam compliance.

2) Provide a clear opt-out
Ensure that each email contains an easy-to understand method for the recipient to remove themselves from your email list. Ensure this actually functions as advertised, and you may consider adding your email address for them to contact you directly if they have concerns or need you to manually remove their email address from your list. There is a large population out

there that believes that by clicking on the "remove" links, they are simply validating that their email address is valid.

3) Do not sell your email lists

Rentals and co-registration is fine, but do not lose the trust of your subscribers by selling them out.

4) Only add subscribers to your list

If you ask someone to join your list, then they only want to be on your list. Do not assume this is opt-in and add them to dozens of other junk lists. If you want to build and maintain trust, only add subscribers to the list they actually join.

Email Marketing Service Providers

Consider using an all-in-one service provider to transmit your emails, provide tracking, manage your lists, and perform maintenance such as managing bounces, importing new emails, and other tasks if you want to automate most aspects of the email campaign management. Keep in mind that this does not relieve you from creating your actual email campaign; you will still need to do this, although they will provide you with templates to simplify the process. These tasks can be daunting on your own, and it is not realistic (nor typically allowed by your ISP) to host your own email lists on your local PC or domain. You essentially have four choices.

1) Utilize an all-in-one service provider

The service provider will provide you with self-managed tutorials so you can perform all management tasks. You are provided with templates, help guides, and many of the tasks are automated such as sending the emails, tracking the results, providing detailed statistics, and managing email lists. This method can be less costly, but will require you to manage your accounts, create your email blasts, manage your lists, and schedule your own email blasts. The service provider actually sends out your scheduled email blasts using their service with your lists.

2) Utilize an email marketing specialist

This specialist will perform all tasks for you, including the management of lists, creation of all email blasts, sending of email blasts, and the tracking, reporting, and performing of all maintenance tasks associated with your account. This is essentially a full-service provider solution — you do nothing more than tell the specialist what you need and when to send it and they do all the work. While this is much simpler for you, it is more costly.

3) Purchase a commercial off-the-shelf program

This program can automate your email campaign management on your own email servers or POP3 mail servers. Arial Software (**www.arialsoftware.com**) features a suite of products designed to manage your entire email-marketing program. Arial Software's products certainly make this an appealing option if you want total control of your email campaigns and want to eliminate the recurring monthly costs associated with an all-in-one solution provider.

4) Do it all yourself

This includes the management of lists, creation of all email blasts, sending of email blasts, and the tracking, reporting, and performing of all maintenance tasks associated with your list. You can do this with Microsoft Outlook and a built in contact manager/address book; however, most ISPs do not allow you to perform email marketing or bulk emails as part of their terms of service. This is certainly the most cost-effective, but may not be efficient or even realistic. If you have a very small business with a limited customer base and have 500 names or less on your email list, you may be able to manage your entire campaign, but, again, you need to check your local ISP policies and terms of service regarding email use. This is also an option for new websites or businesses seeking to grow their lists. Once you grow it to a certain level, you may opt to use an all-in-one service provider to automate most of the processes involved in managing the email lists and creating campaigns, or you can upgrade to a product which can provide you with total control of your campaign.

All-in-one email marketing service providers

There are many all-in-one service providers and I have used several of them with superior results. All of the ones listed here are reputable, cost-effective, and easily manageable without hiring specialists.

Topica (www.topica.com)

Topica's Online Marketing and Sales Solution seamlessly integrates time-tested, performance-based advertising services (PBA) with a sophisticated yet easy-to-use hosted application (ASP), which combines data integration and analysis features, conversion optimization tools, and industry-leading email marketing capabilities. Together, they provide a reliable and extremely cost-effective way to create new leads, turn them into paying customers, and generate maximum value from them. Topica provides customized solutions for Internet retailers, online publishers, direct marketers, and interactive agencies.

I have used Topica for years and have found them to be a great fit for a small business who wants to use an all-in-one solution provider to manage their lists and email campaigns. Topica is very simple and flexible to manage. Since Topica is a full feature provider, there are recurring monthly fees for using their service, as with other service providers. Topica offers an abundance of services at a relatively low cost. They also offer a significant discount if you sign up for a yearly contract.

Pricing with Topica is based on the number of emails you send out each month, not the number of email addresses on your list. Additionally, Topica offers annual plans with 25 percent discounts on their pricing, making them very cost-effective for small business ventures. You can send out HTML, text, or multi-part emails; when subscribers join your list, they can select which type they prefer to receive. There are a wide variety of user-friendly templates, which simplify the process of creating your emails.

This means you do not have to be an HTML expert to create professional looking HTML email blasts. Topica automatically provides an opt-out option on each outgoing email message and even allows subscribers to update their account online.

The reporting and delivery tracking are excellent, providing you with real-time statistics, deliveries, bounces, and open rates. You can even track clicks to see how often each link within your email is clicked on. You can easily import lists, including demographic data. One of the best features is you can have multiple lists within a single account if you have lists which target different segments of your business (such as retailers vs. wholesalers).

You can also personalize emails and segment/target them based on demographic data. Topica offers a wide variety of targeting and segmentation options based on any field or combination of fields for which you have collected data including:

- Demographics or Interests
- Campaigns Opened or Clicked
- Campaigns Not Opened or Clicked
- Time Delta from Demographic Date (Renewals)
- Purchased Items
- Amount of Purchase
- Recency of Purchase
- Shopping Cart Abandonment

There are tiers at Topica, which determine not only the features and functionality, but the pricing structure. If you need the most feature-rich functionality, Topica can get very expensive quickly. If you only need the basic functionality for email marketing and can live with the entry level email marketing plans, Topica remains a good choice.

JangoMail (www.jangomail.com)

JangoMail is another industry leader in email marketing. They provide all the standard features of most email service companies, like open tracking, click tracking, HTML/plain text messaging, personalization, unsubscribe/ bounce management, data import/export capabilities, email list hygiene capabilities, and a double opt-in option. They also provide extra special unique features such as:

- 24 hour support
- 100 percent branding control: You will never see a "Powered by JangoMail" footer or tagline appended to the bottom of your emails. You are in full control of the look and feel of your emails. You can even control where CAN-SPAM requirements like an unsubscribe link and your postal address go, so that even these elements can be fully integrated into your email's design.
- Advanced HTML editor
- Advanced personalization
- Foreign language capabilities
- JangoMail claims to be the only email service provider that has built a distributed, rather than centralized, network of email senders across the world allowing for complete fault-tolerance and redundancy across SMTP email senders. Additionally, JangoMail personnel review SMTP log files on a daily basis to ensure optimal deliverability of customers' email messages and they develop and maintain relationships with ISPs and participate in a wide variety of white listing programs
- Connect to external databases in real time
- Tracking down to the recipient level: JangoMail's reporting module tells you who has unsubscribed, bounced, replied, forwarded, opened, and clicked through to your website on a per-email campaign basis. You can even track an email recipient's movement through your website after clicking a link in an email message.

Constant Contact (www.constantcontact.com)

Constant Contact is highly respected and provides a robust, yet simplified interface providing you with total control over your email marketing program. Similar to the other programs listed, Constant Contact is full featured, and has been very successful in meeting the needs of both small and large businesses for email marketing. Constant Contact enables you to create and send top-notch email newsletters and promotions with no technical expertise. They excel at making the process easy for you, including list management, reporting, and free live support. You have a wealth of features including an email campaign, pre-designed email templates, advanced HTML editing functionality, customizable visitor sign-up forms for websites, bounce and unsubscribe management, list segmentation functionality, email tracking and reporting, and email delivery management.

eLoop by Gold Lasso (www.goldlasso.com)

Another product which has realized tremendous success is eLoop™ from Gold Lasso, Inc. eLoop was designed specifically for the marketing professional to effectively integrate email as part of their promotional mix using a closed-loop concept.

eLoop™ is a Web-based email marketing system comprised of three distinct tools (modules): Out-Bound Messaging, Data Management, and Data Collection. These tools provide all the functionality needed for a professional marketer to develop a successful email-marketing program with very little technical knowledge.

- **Out-Bound Messaging:** From a simple text message to a dynamic HTML version, eLoop provides a message editor that is as easy to use as a word processor and gives you complete control of your message's design and layout. In addition, the Out-Bound Messaging tool provides a host of campaign scheduling features and campaign automation including Gold Lasso's proprietary Action Based Messaging™ (ABM) system, where campaign recipients receive follow-up messages based on links clicked and forms completed.

- **Data Management:** eLoop's Data Management tools provide you with the ability to build a customized database to import or collect any data necessary to personalize your messages or segment your lists appropriately. Extensive list management options enable you to build lists based on complex algorithms with multiple data variables. eLoop's Data Management tools come complete with automated list cleansing features such as email automated de-duping processes, merge/purge, and email validation.

- **Data Collection:** eLoop has extensive data collection features for building landing pages, surveys, and opt-in lists. All data from your Web forms can be fully customized, and the data collected is housed and linked within your eLoop database. Also, the data can be used for additional list building and message personalization.

Spam, Spoofing & Phishing

Email spam is the sending of unsolicited commercial messages to many recipients without the explicit permission of the recipients.

Another major concern with spamming is the "spoofing" of email addresses. Spoofing is a method of concealing the identity of the sender and making you believe the email is in fact from a reputable business. With spoofing, the spammer modifies the email message so it appears to come from another email account. Spoofing can occur with any email account or domain name. For example, you may get an email from Bruce Brown with the email address of bruce@email.com, which may be a legitimate email account, thus avoiding spam filters and giving you, the recipient, peace of mind. Spoofing can cause you a multitude of headaches. Dealing with spoofed emails is frustrating and time-consuming. As for the website or domain name owner, it is much worse; typically bounced emails are sent back to the spoofed domain email account — yours. You may find you are receiving replies, bounced emails, and nasty grams for an email that you never sent. The main goal behind spoofed emails is to release privacy information or passwords to third parties who will use them against your business. If you suspect spoofing of your email accounts or want more detailed information about spoofing, you should contact the Cert Coordination Center at **www.cert.org**.

Most spammers are after privacy and/or financial data, or they offer illicit activities such as pornography, get rich quick schemes, pirated software, or overseas business scams. The best combatant against spam is anti-spam filters, junk mail filters, and specialized software at the email server and the mail client to protect your email accounts.

Another major threat is phishing. Phishing is actually a variation on the word fishing, which means that "phishers" will throw out baited websites hoping someone will "bite. Phishing is always a scam, and it is used to convince the recipient to surrender private information for the use of identity theft. The email directs the user to visit a website where they are asked to update personal information, such as passwords credit card information, social security numbers, and bank account numbers that the legitimate organization already has. The website, however, is bogus and set up only to steal the user's information.

The key difference between operating legal permission-based email campaigns and spam is the use of permission-based or "opt-in" email lists. Spam or junk email is email that is sent to one or more recipient who did not request it. We will discuss the differences in detail between opt-in and opt-out lists in the next chapter, but it is important that you have a clear understanding on what spam is and how it can affect your business.

CAN-SPAM Act

The CAN-SPAM Act of 2003 (Controlling the Assault of Non-Solicited Pornography and Marketing Act) establishes requirements for those who send commercial emails. It spells out penalties for spammers and companies whose products are advertised in spam if they violate the law, and gives consumers the right to ask emailers to stop spamming them. The law, which became effective January 1, 2004, covers email whose primary purpose is advertising or promoting a commercial product or service, including content on a website. A "transactional or relationship message"

— email that facilitates an agreed-upon transaction or updates a customer in an existing business relationship — may not contain false or misleading routing information, but otherwise is exempt from most provisions of the CAN-SPAM Act according to the Federal Trade Commission.

The Federal Trade Commission (FTC), the nation's consumer protection agency, is authorized to enforce the CAN-SPAM Act. CAN-SPAM also gives the Department of Justice (DOJ) the authority to enforce its criminal sanctions. Other federal and state agencies can enforce the law against organizations under their jurisdiction and companies that provide Internet access may sue violators as well.

Several years ago, a former client chose to launch an ill-advised email campaign. They bought numerous email lists from mostly un-reputable list clearing houses and imported more than 100,000 email addresses into their email management program. They set off on their campaign and launched multiple emails with some very surprising and disturbing results. Instead of receiving their email campaign with open arms, they had an almost 40 percent bounce rate (not uncommon for harvested lists) and nearly another 30 percent had requested to be removed or had removed themselves. Many of these unsubscribed requests were extremely nasty and threatening. Within a week they found that the email marketing provider had shut down their account for suspected "spam" activity and a few days later their website hosting company had terminated their website under threat of legal action from the backbone provider. This meant that their entire online business was shut down within days, just for being accused of spam. Luckily, they had backups of their entire website and were able to move their domain name to another Web hosting company and re-establish their website; however, this process left them essentially out of business for nearly 72 hours and permanently out of the email marketing business.

CAN-SPAM Act requirements

- **Bans false or misleading header information.** Your email's "From," "To," and routing information — including the originating domain name and email address — must be accurate and identify the person who initiated the email.

- **Prohibits deceptive subject lines.** The subject line cannot mislead the recipient about the contents or subject matter of the message.

- **Requires that your email give recipients an opt-out method.** You must provide a return email address or another Internet-based response mechanism that allows a recipient to ask you not to send future email messages to that email address and you must honor the requests. You may create a "menu" of choices to allow a recipient to opt out of certain types of messages, but you must include the option to end any commercial messages from the sender. Any opt-out mechanism you offer must be able to process opt-out requests for at least 30 days after you send your commercial email. When you receive an opt-out request, the law gives you ten business days to stop sending email to the requestor's email address. You cannot help another entity send email to that address or have another entity send email on your behalf to that address. Finally, it is illegal for you to sell or transfer the email addresses of people who choose not to receive your email, even in the form of a mailing list, unless you transfer the addresses so another entity can comply with the law.

- **Requires that commercial email be identified as an advertisement and include the sender's valid physical postal address.** Your message must contain clear and conspicuous notice that the message is an advertisement or solicitation and that the recipient can opt out of receiving more commercial email from you. It also must include your valid physical postal address.

Penalties for each violation of the CAN-SPAM Act are subject to fines of up to $11,000. Deceptive commercial email also is subject to laws banning false or misleading advertising. Additional fines are provided for commercial emailers who not only violate the rules described above, but also:

- "Harvest" email addresses from websites or Web services that have published a notice prohibiting the transfer of email addresses for the purpose of sending email
- Generate email addresses using a "dictionary attack" — combining names, letters, or numbers into multiple permutations
- Use scripts or other automated ways to register for multiple email or user accounts to send commercial email
- Relay emails through a computer or network without permission — for example, by taking advantage of open relays or open proxies without authorization

The law allows the Department of Justice to seek criminal penalties, including imprisonment, for commercial emailers who do or conspire to:

- Use another computer without authorization and send commercial email from or through it
- Use a computer to relay or retransmit multiple commercial email messages to deceive or mislead recipients or an Internet access service about the origin of the message
- Falsify header information in multiple email messages and initiate the transmission of such messages
- Register for multiple email accounts or domain names using information that falsifies the identity of the actual registrant
- Falsely represent themselves as owners of multiple Internet Protocol addresses that are used to send commercial email messages

The FTC has issued additional rules under the CAN-SPAM Act involving the required labeling of sexually explicit commercial email and the criteria for determining "the primary purpose" of a commercial email. See the FTC website at **www.onguardonline.gov/articles/0038-spam** for updates on implementation of the CAN-SPAM Act.

Most recipients of bulk email, spam, or unsolicited advertisements view them as unwelcome, unpleasant, or offensive. However, there are many mailing lists that deliver solicited (opt-in), useful information to recipients based on a variety of subjects they have expressed an interest in and have given their permission to allow companies to add their email address to bulk mailing lists. The key to utilizing email as a tool for marketing or advertising is to build your customer lists using opt-in methods (or double-opt in) to ensure that your email lists comply with the requirements of the CAN-SPAM Act.

Spam tools

Luckily, there are numerous, reputable resources available to assist you with identifying and combating spam, spoofing, and phishing, and I have outlined the best of them for you:

- **http://spam.abuse.net:** This site contains an ongoing listing of spam related news, articles, and information.

- **www.ftc.gov/spam:** The official spam site for the Federal Trade Commission. It outlines the laws for consumers, businesses, and current penalties for violating anti-spam laws. This is the site where you can file spam complaints; just click on the "File a Complaint" link on the home page.

- **www.spamlaws.com:** This site has all the most recent legislation and laws from the United States, Europe, and other countries, as well as state laws and selected case histories.

- **www.cauce.org:** The Coalition Against Unsolicited Commercial Email; A group whose primary purpose is to advocate for a legislative solution to the problem of unsolicited commercial email.

- **www.spamcop.net:** SpamCop determines the origin of unwanted email and reports it to the relevant Internet service providers. Reporting unsolicited email also helps feed spam filtering systems, including, but not limited to, SpamCop's own service.

As an email marketer, it is critical that you understand what is and what is not spam, spoofing, and phishing. You do not want to be associated with spamming. With spam being in the spotlight, there have been ongoing debates about the true cost and effectiveness of email campaigns and the effect of spam regulations on the success of your email campaigns.

Tools and Advice

Let's walk through the basic tools and advice for creating an effective email:

Software tools for creating HTML email

- Microsoft Expression
- Microsoft Frontpage
- Adobe Dreamweaver CC
- Do not use Microsoft Word or any other Word Processor
- Do not use Notepad — it will work fine, but significantly increases the complexity

Software for creating graphics
- Corel Paint Shop Pro X8
- Adobe Photoshop CS

Design an effective and creative layout

You need to place special emphasis on the overall design and layout of your creative. Use SEO techniques and Web design fundamentals. Your goal is to captivate the reader, get them to your actual email blast, and then follow your desired action. There are dozens of websites dedicated to how to properly format the text of an email, news article, or newsletter that can guide you through the process of writing an email masterpiece. For now, we will concentrate on the actual format and layout of the email, not the content. You will find the layout may be the easier task, while designing the content is a much bigger challenge. Here are some examples for how to lay out a great e-mail campaign: **blog.hubspot.com/blog/tabid/6307/bid/32984/ Feast-Your-Eyes-on-These-9-Examples-of-Beautiful-Email-Marketing. aspx**, **www.dtelepathy.com/blog/design/28-tips-for-designing-effective-html-emails**, and **www.pardot.com/blog/7-examples-successful-email-templates-case-study**.

Use HTML tag for proper formatting

I have read many opinions that tell you to remove all or most HTML tags from your email. Remember, an HTML email is essentially a Web page, so you should use the basic HTML tags to properly format your email. An HTML capable email application will know how to read, interpret, and properly display your emails. Browser-based email clients, such as Gmail and Yahoo! will also read and properly display HTML emails. Additionally, this simplifies the process of taking your HTML email and turning it into a page on your website for references, news articles, and newsletter archives. (Remember, you want these to be indexed by search engines, so the use of keywords and proper HTML formatting is important.). Keep in mind, if you use a commercial product for your emails, which states which HTML tags are allowed, you should follow that guidance. In absence of any restrictions, include the following HTML tags:

- **DOCTYPE**
- **<HTML></HTML>**
- **<Body></Body>**
- **<HEAD></HEAD>**
- **<LINK>**
- **<TITLE></TITLE>**

Do not include Scripts (javascript, VB scripts), Java, Java Applets, other Applets, Frames, or Comments in your email creative.

Host images on a Web server

Do not embed images directly into an HTML email creative. Many email programs strip out an embedded image and your email will not display properly. Additionally, embedded images affect the download and display times, negatively impacting your potential success rate. Many spam filters will block the embedded images or cause your email to be sent directly to a junk mailbox. When you are sending an image file that is large and hosted on a Web server, slice the image into smaller parts to facilitate the download process.

Use a smart auto-responder

A smart auto-responder is a bit more intelligent than the standard auto-responder. The smart auto-responder directs a new lead, or potential customer email, into what is called the "hot lead" part of the responder. If you send out five or six auto-responder messages to that possible customer, and they come back to your website and make a purchase, you would not want to continue sending them your prospect message now that they have become a paying customer. The smart auto-responder takes them off the prospect list and puts them on the customer list. This way, you continue communicating with your customer in a way that makes sense.

Use absolute URLs for all of your graphics or hyperlinks

A common mistake when designing is to use the relative URL, which may work fine when designing and testing, but will not work when delivered. For example, a relative URL may be "/emailblast/images/radio1.jpg." As long as you are on your Web server, this relative location is understood and the images will be served properly. If you are not on the server (if you are reading the email in your email client), the URL will fail, and the image links will be broken.

Using color

Use a white background on all table cells and fill in with graphics and text. Colored backgrounds tend to cause problems with some email clients and can conflict with font colors. If you want to use a background image to fill the empty space outside of your HTML table, it may work; however, it is not recommended. Be sure to stick to a white background for your table.

Some email clients may not display background images, so ensure your email creative is satisfactory with a white background as well as in the event the image does not display properly.

You should explicitly state the colors, font styles, font sizes, etc. in your HTML coding because some Web-based email programs may apply their own style sheets to your email if you do not specify them. This may cause them to appear significantly different than you intended.

Don'ts

Do not use Cascading Style Sheets in your email. They tend to cause multiple problems with a variety of email clients. You should ensure that your final HTML creative will appear as you intend based solely on the HTML coding you used, not on external style sheets.

Do not embed forms in your email creative; instead direct them to a form on your Web server. There are some Web-based email clients that do not properly support forms. Hyperlinks work great in all Web-based email clients (and all other email applications), plus they provide you with a great way to track how your recipients are responding to your email blast by tracking activity on each hyperlink.

Do not be intimidated. Creating an HTML email is not difficult, but takes some patience and skill. Track results; if they are not what you anticipated, tweak your campaigns and try again at a future date. If you do not get any significant responses, do not continue to send the same emails.

Tags

Use the <BR> tag instead of the <P> tag in your HTML.

Spam compliance

Follow the basic rules of spam compliance. Include an unsubscribe link and a link to your Web administrator in the event that there is a problem with the auto-unsubscribe so that they can contact you for a manual removal.

Test your email blast

Ensure you test each email blast with a variety of email clients to ensure it is displayed properly. Also, it may be a good idea to include a link at the top of your email that states, "If this email is not displayed properly, click here."

Simplicity

Keep the emails concise, short, and to the point. If you want someone to read your emails, you need to get to the point quickly and grab their attention. If your message is long, you may opt to provide a captivating, brief intro and provide a link back to your website with full detailed information. Your communications should be inspiring or compelling. Use strong action words that communicate your message quickly and clearly. The rule of thumb is two to three paragraphs maximum. Use keywords, and if your message is primarily text-based, bullet the information to make it easy to read.

Content

Use a strong subject and introduction. You need to use a strong introduction to grab the attention of your recipients. You need to quickly convey a message that will make the recipient want to read on instead of hitting delete. Personalize your email blasts where possible.

Include contact information and be clear on what you want the recipient to do. If you want them to call you, make sure you have full contact information and it is clear. If you want them to buy products or fill out a form, be sure that the forms and other contact methods function properly. If you are providing or seeking specific information, create a Web page on your site with the information they will want to read. Do not direct them to your home page and expect them to hunt through your site to navigate to the right page. Give them the right page and lead them to it.

Interject your business name into your email. You want them to learn your company name, so put it in the email early.

Give some thought to the "From" address you will be using. I recommend using a "From" email address which is first and foremost a valid email address and one that represents your company. Using personal emails is not advised. Be straightforward and use your full company name. You want them to recognize your company as a legitimate one. Do not use ridiculous sounding email addresses such as freestuff@, bestdeals@, or nospam@.

Ask for help

If you need professional assistance, ask. Many all-in-one service providers walk you through the process and even provide you with pre-built templates. They dramatically reduce the learning curve and simplify the process. Topica's basic package pricing, for example, is based on email volume. If you sign up for a year of service, you get a good discount and have a monthly allotment of emails you can send. When you exceed that limit, you will pay overage charges, which can add up quickly. However, the support, free templates, and other features are all included with your subscription, so you might as well take advantage of them unless you want to create your own custom HTML email blasts.

In Sum

Email is the fastest form of communication to a wide audience, with nearly instantaneous results and at practically no cost. Harnessing the power of email through targeted email marketing campaigns and newsletters is one of the most effective methods to advertise and market your e-commerce site, products, and/or services. With email marketing, you get direct and immediate communication with thousands of current and potential customers.

Chapter 12

Blogging

A blog is an ideal alternative to a website or an ideal way to complement a website and gain instant search engine visibility. You can set up a blog for free in just a few minutes. Blogs offer a wide variety of pre-designed templates, the ability to customize to suit your needs, and are excellent for search engine visibility. You need to know and understand what a blog is, how it functions, what it does and does not do, and how it can help you to achieve your personal or business goals.

What is a Blog?

The word "blog" is a combination of the words "Web" and "log." A blog is a website in which short entries or "postings" are made in an abbreviated style format, and they are displayed in reverse chronological order. Blogs can consist of numerous items, from a personal standpoint to a political or business collaborative that discusses specific topics, products, or services. Blogs can also be used as a news-style of publication; this is something that a lot of journalists are beginning to utilize to publish their thoughts and perspectives on a variety of issues, or to get the word out instantly about a breaking news item of concern to a local community.

Blogs can be about any subject, including politics, news, world events, public opinion, and cooking. There are also many personal blogs from celebrities, world leaders, and aspiring political candidates, for example. If you can think of a topic, there is most likely a blog related to it. Personal blogs are often considered online versions of a diary or journal. Although this is a pretty good comparison, they are far different from paper-based diaries or journals since they offer interactivity you cannot get with these more traditional forms, or even with a static HTML-based Web page diary or journal.

A blog uses a combination of text, graphics, images, and hyperlinks to other blogs, websites, Web pages, and multimedia content such as movie or audio clips. One of the features associated with blogging is that blog visitors can leave comments on the blog, thus creating a collaborative dialogue between you and potential customers, donors, or others you may wish to interact with. A blog opens the door to two-way communications between yourself and millions of people on the Internet. A blog can be used as a website or in place of a website.

Everything on a blog, especially if it is a news-oriented project, must be consistently and routinely updated, including the answers to your visitor's comments and questions. Unlike a website where visitors can post a comment on a news article and you respond if you choose, blogs require a more in-depth commitment because your visitors expect you to answer their comments and questions, which can be time-consuming if you are trying to update your site several times a day to keep it active. Think of a blog as more of an online conversation.

If you are going to build a blog, you also have to remember that blogs become outdated much faster than a regular website. The need to update is continuous because if you do not, visitors will disappear much quicker than if you were hosting a normal static website. People navigate to a blog for information, news, or other relevant topics, and they may go to a website for the same information, but more typically it is for shopping or less engagement than you might otherwise get with a blog. People visiting a website expect it to be updated regularly, but if you miss a day (or a week), you do not necessarily lose all of your visitors. In contrast, if you miss a day or two updating your blog, your visitors will move on to someone new who updates his or her blog more consistently and publishes "fresh and relevant" information.

A blog is an ongoing journal of events, news, or opinions offered for others to interact and respond to, creating an ongoing dialogue between the "blogger" and the reader. The key difference between a Web page and a blog is that the Web page is static content — you can read the page, but not interact with it — while a blog is interactive. Another major difference between static Web pages and blogs is that blogs can be syndicated using RSS or Atom feeds. Syndicated blogs allow subscribers to "join" the blog and receive updates automatically.

If you write a blog, you are a "blogger." There are millions of blogs, and thus millions of bloggers, and the numbers grow every day as blogging continues to gain popularity. The majority of blogs are personal blogs, but there is a growing trend for businesses and organizations to produce blogs for their company, products, and services. The exception is in news media and politics, where blogging is a part of the culture and an integral form of accepted communications.

Blogging is all about linking. As with websites, links can help raise visibility with search engines. Links to and from blogs to other blogs and websites are directly relevant to the popularity and overall visibility and ranking of blogs. A blog is an invitation for customers to look into your company and allows you to develop trust, two-way communication, and, ultimately, increased sales.

The Construction of a Blog

There are many tools available to help you write and publish blogs. Many are retail software, but there is also a wealth of free products to simplify the process. Before delving into a discussion about writing blogs, however, you first need to understand how a blog is constructed.

Every blog essentially consists of the following:

- **Title:** The title of the blog provides the blog reader an overall idea of what the blog is about.
- **Date:** The date of the blog's most recent update or post. Blogs are displayed in reverse chronological order, so the most recent post is at the top of the blog.
- **Post Title:** The title of each blog post.
- **Blog Text:** This is the actual text of each blog post.
- **Blog Post Information:** This is information about the individual or business who actually wrote the blog. Sometimes this contains contact information as well.
- **Blogger Comments:** This is an area for the readers of a blog to place comments, responses, opinions, or reactions to a blog post. This is not a mandatory field; if your intent is only to push information via your blog, you do not have to accept comments.
- **Previous Blog Posts:** This is the reverse chronological listing of previous blog posts from most recent to oldest.
- **Archived Posts:** Even the best blogs get unwieldy; it is not uncommon to archive old posts after a preset period of time.
- **Blogroll:** A list of links to other related sites.
- **Advertising:** This is a common sight in the world of blogging. Many advertisements are prominently featured, typically in free blogging applications. In some cases, you can generate revenue through the use of advertising, but often these are third-party advertisements you allow for the use of blogging software.
- **Feeds:** Feeds to push blogs posts automatically to subscribers, either in RSS or Atom form.

To begin creating your own blog, you need blogging software and a Web host.

Blog Software & Blog Hosting Options

Essentially, you have four choices when deciding how to publish your blog. They are all variations of paid versus free versions of blog software and blog hosting.

Free blog software with free blog hosting

This option is of no cost to you. However, you must often allow paid advertisements to be placed within or on your blog pages. These paid advertisements may be obtrusive and will not generate any residual income for you as you might through Google AdSense.

One of the main advantages of having your own website is that you own the domain name, so you can choose a domain name that is directly related to your company or corporate image. With free hosting, you have no control over your domain name. In fact, you will most likely be hosted under another domain name and utilize a subdomain name. A subdomain is a domain name that is part of another domain name, such as **www. yourfreeblog.yourbusinessname.com**. This might not be bad if your blog is hosted on your corporate website; however, if it is hosted by another free hosting provider, your blog domain name may be very lengthy and not at all related to your company name or profile.

Also, free blogging software typically has some reduced functionality compared to paid software. But there are two outstanding, advertisement-free options available to you. Both Blogger and WordPress produce professional blogs and are customizable through templates. Blogger lets you switch between a hosted application and publishing directly to your Web server via FTP. My recommendation is always to do what is cheapest and easiest but delivers the quality results you seek.

Free blog software with paid blog hosting

You pay for the domain name and/or hosting space with the hosting company, and the blog software is provided at no cost to you. This is very common with many Web hosting companies; as part of the hosting package, you get "free" blog software. If your current Web hosting provider allows you to install third-party blog software on their servers, this is also a possible option, especially if you already have a website and domain name. Be sure to check with your current Web hosting provider; they most likely already offer free blog software to you as part of the hosting package.

While you do not have advertising on your blog, the software may have reduced functionality compared to commercial software. In most instances, this is an attractive option, since your blog is usually hosted under your own domain name; however, some providers charge you an extra monthly fee for the blogging service. If this is the case, you will most likely do better to use Blogger or WordPress for free. However, if you wish to use your own domain name and want to use the blog software your hosting company provides, this may be an option to consider. Since your hosting company is providing the blog software, you are stuck with the brand they use. They take care of the installation and maintenance, which is one major plus.

Paid blog software with paid blog hosting

This means you buy the full-featured software and also pay for the hosting service through a service provider. This is a great option if you need a very powerful blog or CMS software and a very large hosting account under your own domain name.

One advantage of a dedicated blog hosting account is that the rates are typically flat, meaning they do not change based on the volume of blog traffic. From the technical support perspective, multiple accounts and multiple hosting providers typically equal multiple headaches when it comes to support and troubleshooting. Although the software and hosting is supported by the commercial provider, it does not mean you will not have a degree of tech support and troubleshooting headaches of your own if the service is unreliable.

Paid blog software hosted on your own web servers

This means you buy the full-featured software and install and host it on your own servers — you must physically own or lease the servers; this is not just a shared hosting space. This is a good option if you do not want to use open-source or free software but already have Web servers, meaning you do not need to pay for hosting commercially.

One of the main advantages with this option is that you have full control over the look of your blog and can mimic your main website branding, and since you own the servers, the cost for hosting is non-existent. Additionally, you have full control over your hardware and server maintenance. With leased servers, although you are leasing a dedicated machine, you will still rely on the service provider to perform installations and hardware maintenance, so you will need to check to be sure that your provider will support the blog software installation and other requirements.

Another thing to keep in mind is that blogs and CMS software are distinctly different, although related. Blog software simply provides you with the features and functionality to create, maintain, and manage your blog. A CMS typically has a built-in blogging module, but it provides significantly more features and functionality across all spectrums of content management than blog publishing software.

The free options may not offer all the functionality you desire, but both Blogger and WordPress will meet the needs of most small businesses and individuals, making this the perfect option for a small budget. Even with free blog hosting, do not forget the power of hyperlinks. You can easily establish a blog on a commercial hosting provider, and link or integrate that blog into your own website, even though it is not physically hosted on your own Web servers and does not use the same URL as your company's website. This practice is very common. Blogger allows you to host under your domain name as part of their built-in functionality, and WordPress allows you to export your blog if you wish to move it to a new domain. The only real factor in deciding whether you want to host your blog under your own name may appear years down the road if you outgrow the free products and want to move to a new domain name. Your audience will already know the old domain name, so it may be hard to move your blog without losing them.

Who Blogs?

Obviously, a critical component to the success of any blog is who will participate. A blog is nothing without participation from subscribers, readers, and customers. Your target blog audience will be determined by what you are trying to promote — whether it be your business, your organization, or your cause.

Bloggers come from every walk of life, including professionals, executives, blue-collar workers, housewives, and tech-geeks. The beauty of blogging is that it is very simple to do. Not only is it easy to establish a blog site, it is very easy to become an active blogger. You do not need any technical knowledge, special skills, or training to establish a highly effective blog site or to become an expert blogger.

It is often difficult to convey a message through social media's own limitations. Either they are flooded with information and comments or are restricted to character limits. In such a crowded environment, it may be difficult to carve a space for yourself or your business. Here are a couple of questions to ponder:

- What is the best platform to share and interact with other people or businesses?
- Where can I promote myself, my business, or my viewpoints without limitations?

A blog may very well be your best solution. A blog is your own personal space, where your words speak for you and your business. There is no censorship or restrictions on your content. Only those people follow you who are interested in your business, products, or services, so you target a select audience as large or as small as you desire. A blog is interactive; you engage your audience through regular comments on your posts.

Blogging is modern means of journalism. It is not only restricted to spreading words but it has developed a market for itself. Blogging in last decade has transformed into a powerful tool to disseminate information and earn money as well as promote and grow your business. You can blog from home, your office, your smart phone, iPad and literally any connected device. Blog marketing requires you to be patient and deliberate in your approach to attract, grow and retain readers. Here are some facts regarding readership and income potential through sales of advertisements:

- A top blogging network, Weblogs, Inc., is believed to earn about $30 million a month from 13 million unique visitors.
- 22-year-old Johns Wu sold his blog for $15 million.
- Arianne Huffington of The Huffington Post makes an estimated $2.33 million per month through her blog (**www.incomediary.com**).

You want bloggers to talk to you and with each other, discussing your company and products and/or services. Ultimately, if you can engage current and potential customers through conversation, you will successfully promote your products and services through blogs. Anyone on the Internet can read your blogs and they are searchable and indexed through most major search engines. You will quickly discover that your blogs are a primary source for promotion, marketing, and building brand-name reputation and recognition.

Pings and Trackbacks

The most unique feature of blogging is comments. Comments create the two-way communication between you and your blog readers. Bloggers read your blog and post comments, questions, opinions, and concerns. This dialogue is what makes blogging unique. Your readers can also link directly to your blog posts and recommend your blog to others. This is known as trackbacks and pingbacks.

Trackbacks are simply a notification method between blogs. It allows a blog reader to send a notice to someone else that the blog might be something they would have an interest in reading. Here is an example:

- You publish something in your blog.
- One of your blog readers sees this blog post and decides to leave a comment. In addition to having other blog readers see what they have posted, the commenter also wants to allow any fellow readers to comment on his or her blog.
- The blog reader posts something on his or her own blog and sends a trackback to your blog.
- You receive the trackback and display it in the form of a comment on your blog along with the link back to the blog reader's post.
- Anyone who reads this blog can follow the trackback to your blog, and vice versa.

This illustrates how blogging is unique from websites and discussion forums. The theory is that blog readers from both your blog and the commenting reader's blog can read the blog posts, and ultimately more people will join in the blog discussion. The idea is to encourage blog readers to click on the trackback link and visit the other blog. As you can see, the number of blog posts and trackback links can grow exponentially. The problem with trackbacks is that they can be spammed easily, and there is no real authentication process to ensure that a trackback is valid.

Pingbacks are a method for Web authors to request a notification when somebody links to one of their documents. Typically, Web publishing software will automatically inform the relevant parties on behalf of the user, allowing for the possibility of automatically creating links to referring documents. Here is an example:

- You publish something in your blog.
- One of your blog readers sees this blog post and decides to leave a comment. In addition to having other blog readers see what they have posted, the commenter also wants to allow any fellow readers to comment on his or her blog.
- The blog reader posts something on his or her blog and links back to your blog.
- The blog reader's blogging software automatically sends a notification telling you that your blog has been linked to and automatically includes this information about the link in your blog.

Although they are very similar, there are differences:

- They use different technologies to communicate.
- Pingbacks are automated, while trackbacks are manual; pingbacks will automatically find hyperlinks within a blog posting and try to communicate with those URLs, whereas trackbacks require you to manually enter the URL that the trackback needs to be sent to.
- Trackbacks send the comments while pingbacks do not. Trackbacks typically send only part of your comments to entice the reader into following the actual links to read the entire blog or blog entries.
- Pingbacks appear as links only. Trackbacks appear as links with content or comments.
- Trackbacks can be faked, spoofed, and spammed. Pingbacks are not easily faked.
- Trackbacks provide the reader with a preview of the content on the blog, whereas pingbacks do not.

Free Blog Software

There are two major players who offer free blogging software. They are Blogger and WordPress. Here is a close look at each:

Blogger (www.blogger.com)

Blogger is entirely free. It is a basic and effective way to start a blog. Blogger, which was started in 1999, was bought by Google, which has improved the overall functionality of the site.

Blogger uses standard templates to get you started with an attractive site right away without the need to learn HTML. It also allows you to edit your blog's HTML code whenever you want, and you can use custom colors and fonts to modify the appearance of your blog. The simple drag-and-drop system lets you easily decide exactly where your posts, profiles, archives, and other parts of your blog should live on the page. Blogger also allows you to upload photos and embed them in your blog.

Blogger Mobile lets you send photos and text straight to your blog while you are on the go. All you need to do is send a message to **go@blogger.com** from your phone. You do not even need a Blogger account. The message itself is enough to create a brand new blog and post whatever photo and text you have sent.

You will not find a simpler free option for creating a blog than Blogger. It is perfect for casual bloggers or personal blogs; however, if you want to use your blog for business, you may wish to choose WordPress or invest in blog software that you can host on your site.

WordPress (http://wordpress.com)

WordPress is a free, open-source blogging application. It is fully featured and fairly simple to install. If you prefer, you can have it hosted on the WordPress servers for free. WordPress boasts outstanding features that will give you control over most aspects of your blog without being overcomplicated and difficult to use.

While originally being a blogging platform, WordPress is now a full-fledged CMS system with a robust selection of features for online users trying to build an online presence.

WordPress has features for user management, dynamic page generation, RSS and Atom feeds, customizable templates and themes, password protection, the availability of plugins to enhance functionality, scheduled postings, multi-page posts, file and picture uploads, categories, and email blog updates. It is as powerful and feature-rich as most commercially available blogging applications. You should install it on your existing Web servers if they can support it, but as an alternative, you can host it free on WordPress.

There are many other free blogging applications you can use as an alternative to Blogger and WordPad or Blogger. The following list contains some of the best in the blogosphere:

- **Movable Type™ (www.movabletype.org):** Movable Type is powerful blogging software that is free to download and install on your own Web servers. The advantage of Movable Type is that you have full control over the design of your blog; however, you provide the support since you are hosting it. Extensive documentation is available, and there is significant user-based support.

- **LiveJournal™ (www.livejournal.com):** You can use LiveJournal in many different ways — as a private journal, a blog, a discussion forum, or a social network. It is not recommended in use for a business, organization, or cause.

- **Blog.com (http://blog.com):** This platform is also free and supported by advertisements.

Introduction to RSS Feeds, Atom, and Syndication

RSS and Atom are XML-based file formats that provide you with an easy way to syndicate your blogs to your readers. These feeds provide your readers with all recent content posted to your blog, with links to each content page. By subscribing to feeds, your customers are automatically notified whenever new content is posted. They can also use newsreaders to read your updated content along with any other feeds they may subscribe to, all in one place.

RSS and Atom-powered blogs are the most effective way to keep the lines of communication open with your audience and site visitors. They will support all of your goals, such as customer interaction, acquiring new customers, improving customer relations, selling products, and promoting your goods, services, or business/organizational philosophy.

Email can be time-consuming, ineffective, and challenging due to spam blockers and filters that prevent even legitimate subscriber emails from reaching their intended targets. Syndication helps generate new business by effectively marketing directly to your subscribers. It is free and simple to use. Both of the free blog applications featured in this book, Blogger and Word-Press, automatically include the capability to create RSS or Atom feeds.

The concept is very simple. You publish blog posts on a regular basis, and people want to read your blog posts. It may be time-consuming for individuals to navigate to your blog to read the latest post. To simplify things for your readers, you can syndicate your blog posts to everyone who has subscribed. As you publish blog posts, they appear on your blog and are also sent out in an XML formatted file — either RSS or Atom — to your subscriber or syndication list, and they are automatically delivered to your subscriber's "reader."

Typically, the reader is an email application, or it is built into the Web browser. To find a free reader to download, peruse the list at **http://blog space.com/rss/readers**. As you publish new posts, they are automatically sent to the subscribers. The subscribers then open your feed in their reader and browse your new blog posts. They do not even need to be online to do this. A perfect example is for individuals who travel often. They subscribe to various blog RSS or Atom feeds, and the information is delivered to them as soon as it is published. They can then browse, read, and reply to these new blog posts offline and maximize the use of their time when they do not have Internet connectivity, such as during air travel.

Web feeds eliminate all of the concern with email subscription-based delivery. With RSS or Atom, there is no spam, no viruses, no phishing, no identify theft, and no opt-out process. They are safe and simple to establish, send, and receive.

You must have a reader in order to subscribe to a feed. Internet Explorer, Microsoft Edge®, Google Chrome™ and Mozilla Firefox include the ability to accept feeds. Enter your blog URL into the Google Database quickly at **http://blogsearch.google.com/ping**.

There are many free RSS or Atom feeds you can subscribe to. Think of a topic, and it will have an RSS or Atom feed. Since your blog software creates the feed for you, there is no reason not to have your own RSS feed. While there are dozens of readers and syndication services to choose from, stick with what you know, and use either your email client or your browser as your reader.

When you subscribe to feeds, you are usually asked how you want them delivered, such as in the example below, where you can choose from Mozilla Firefox's "Live Bookmarks," Outlook, Yahoo!, and Bloglines. In this example, "Live Bookmarks" is chosen.

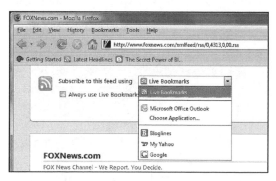

You are asked how you want to store the data from the subscription:

Your subscription to the feed is effective immediately, and it brings in all the recent posts you have subscribed to for you to review. You simply pick which ones are of interest, and you can view them. In this example, there is a subscription to the headline stories from Fox News. You would click on this "Live Bookmark" to obtain the latest top news stories from this site.

You can find RSS or Atom feeds in directories and search listings and through search engines. You can even specify parameters in your subscriptions to deliver only content that has relative keywords to your search parameters.

Feedburner™ is often recommended. Feedburner, a service of Google, is the leading provider of syndication services for blogs and RSS feeds. There is a free version of Feedburner and a professional version, which you must pay for. You can find Feedburner at **http://feedburner.google.com/fb/ a/myfeeds**.

To use Feedburner, you simply type in your blog URL and follow the on-screen prompts. You set up your feed, and it provides you with your Feed-burner URL. You can enable tracking and statistics options on your feed. A step-by-step walkthrough is provided to insert the code on your Blogger blog and you can add the code as a text widget in WordPress. There is no reason not to create an RSS or Atom feed; it will help you increase your audience base and allow you to consistently send all blog posts to your sub-scribers. Best of all, the process is completely automated, seamless, and free.

Creating a Blog With Wordpress and Blogger

As we already discussed, two of the most popular blogging websites are WordPress and Blogger. Let us now take a look at some of the basic nuances of these two platforms and understand how you can fully leverage them to your benefit.

WordPress claims to provide the best blogging system on the Web. WordPress is installed on a Web server, which either is part of an Internet hosting service or is a network host itself. The first case may be on a service like **http://wordpress.com**, for example, and the second case is a computer package **http://wordpress.org**. It includes various features such as plugins and templates in order to provide flexibility to the user for superior customization.

As on January 2015, among the top 10 million websites, WordPress has a staggering share of 25 percent in the market (**http://wordpress.com**). It is vastly used on the Web at more than 60 million websites. WordPress is immensely popular within the blogging community. It is by far the most powerful and customizable application with many available plug-ins. Just as with Blogger, WordPress is simple to set up and can be set up as a blog or a website.

WordPress has a wide variety of built-in features. This includes pre-designed blog templates that let you change the look of your blog with dozens of professionally designed themes. You can switch between themes instantly with just a click of a button, as with Blogger. WordPress also lets you customize your blog code using CSS, and it includes a system that allows you to categorize and tag your posts while you write them — this is another feature shared with Blogger.

WordPress also includes a spell check option, previews, autosave, photos, and videos. You can upload your own photos or easily include images from other services such as Flickr® or Photobucket®. You can also embed videos from places like YouTube or Google. An online spell checker makes it easy to proof your posts. As with Blogger, you have the ability to preview your blog post before you publish it, and your draft posts are automatically backed up while you write.

WordPress allows you to have a completely public blog, a blog that is public but not included in search engines, or a private blog only members can access. WordPress also provides you with an integrated stats system that gives you up-to-the-minute stats on how many people are visiting your blog, where they are coming from, which posts are most popular, and which search engine terms are sending people to your blog. This is a feature that is not available in Blogger.

You will find that automatic spam protection is one of the best features of WordPress. WordPress uses Akismet™, the world's best comment and trackback spam technology, to block spammers from leaving spam comments on your blog.

If you are ready for more features for your blog, you can actually import your entire blog from sites like Blogger, TypePad®, and LiveJournal into WordPress. You can also easily track follow-ups to your comments. WordPress created a special page that notifies you so you can track these follow-up comments, even if they are on other blogs.

What sets WordPress apart from Blogger and most other blog applications is the availability and ease of adding widgets to your site. WordPress defines widgets as "tools or content that you can add, arrange, and remove from the sidebars of your blog." You can add widgets to your sidebar by simply dragging and dropping. Widgets add functionality, design, and interactivity. With WordPress, you can also create Web pages, not just blog pages. You can even create an entire website, using your blog as one of the pages on your site.

All WordPress blogs support RSS, while Blogger supports Atom. WordPress creates feeds in RSS format and allows people to subscribe to updates on your blog using services like My Yahoo!® or Bloglines™.

Blogger is a platform provided by Google. Blogger is free and includes free Web publishing tools used for blogging. This allows for multi-user blogs where events are arranged in accordance to their timeline. It was originally developed by Pyra Labs, and was then bought by Google in 2003.

All of its blogs are generally hosted under the sub-domain "**blogspot.com.**" After integrating Picasa into blogger, Google facilitated photo sharing on their blog. Blogger has launched mobile applications for users with mobile devices. Users can post and edit blogs; they can also share photos and links on Blogger through their mobile devices. With the power of Google backing Blogger, it is a very good choice for a free and easy Blog.

Creating a blog in WordPress

Step 1: Type **https://wordpress.com** in your browser to navigate to WordPress:

Step 2: Click on the "Start a Blog" icon and then click on the "Get Started" button:

Step 3: In this step, you can customize your blog by selecting a theme.

Step 4: Select a domain of your choice. This step may take some planning and thought, as this is the most significant step of all. It is the first impression on your reader and should reflect your brand, product or name. It should be specific and relevant to what you are going to write in your blog.

You can even include a keyword to help it stand out among searches; for example, Atlantic Publishing Company may choose "AtlanticPub." It helps your blog to be in coherence with the insider tactic of the searching algorithm. You can use a provided domain name, buy a domain name or map an existing domain name. The latter options have fees associated while the first is provided at no cost to you.

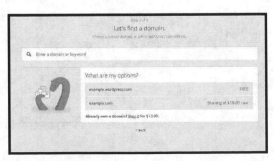

Step 5: Create your account. You have options for the free account or upgrades, which have more features but cost money. WordPress will use your user name as part of your domain name; in the example, this would be **brucecbrownblog.wordpress.com**.

Simply follow the steps and you will have your completely free blog available in minutes. You will receive a confirmation email that contains your account information along with helpful links, frequently asked questions, and other information to help you access, update, and publish to your blog.

Begin by clicking on the "My Account" link and the "Edit Profile" option to start customizing your account. Update the basic information such as name, profile, and password. You are now ready to start customizing your blog. Although it takes only a few minutes to actually create the blog, it most likely does not yet have the final look and feel you desire.

Step 6: Get started and customize your blog. In this "My Site" window, you can post to your blog, customize your layout, update your profile, add images, and much more.

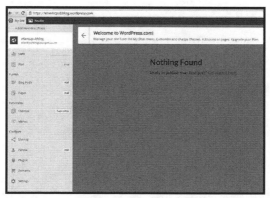

On the left side of this window you will see all of your control panel functions (statistics, themes, blog posts, menus and configuration options). You can immediately start to post blog entries, which are each searchable through Web browsers. Blog post are entries listed in reverse chronological order on the blog home or the posts page. A URL for a post includes the date the post was published like **http://blogname.wordpress.com/2008/11/30/post-title**.

Pages are static and are not listed by date. Pages do not use tags or categories. A typical URL for a page looks like this: **http://blogname.wordpress.com/page-title**.

In the "Reader" section, you can follow your favorite blogs similar to how you bookmark your favorite websites. Sharing information from other relevant blog sources helps you build brand confidence as you can share other articles and information regarding your products and services. That is all there is to creating a blog and starting your own blog entries and sharing your blog URL. In all, it takes little more than five minutes to create a 100% free and easy to use blog that is highly customizable. If you get tired of a theme or layout, you can change the entire look and feel with a few mouse clicks.

Under the "Privacy" link, you will want to ensure that you have selected the options for your blog to appear in search engines and public listings in WordPress to ensure maximum visibility.

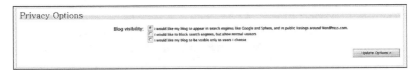

Click on the "Presentation" tab to begin the process of selecting a site template and adding widgets and extras to your blog.

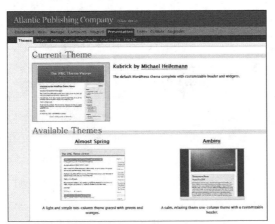

Go through each tab to customize your blog to your desired settings. You have a great degree of flexibility in choosing the final appearance of your blog. Simply drag and drop your desired widgets into the sidebar of your blog. For widgets that require customization, click on the blue customization tab within the widget in your sidebar to modify the settings and preferences.

The "Manage" link lets you manage your blogs, uploads, imports, and exports; it also lets you delete individual posts. The "Comments" tab allows you to search, view, edit, and delete comments from your blog.

The blogroll is where you can add your favorite blogs or relevant blogs that have content your audience may be interested in. Maintaining your blogroll is a great way to increase your audience. As you can see below, this process is very simple.

You can also create and indicate which specific categories each blogroll listing should be listed under by selecting it when you add the new blog listing. If you need to change anything later, just click the "Edit" link to change any of your information, links, or category selections.

The "Write" feature is what you will use to publish blog posts. This is much more robust in features than Blogger. You can use pre-edited HTML formatted text or format on the fly in the entry form. You can attach images, include trackbacks, and upload files, slideshows, or videos. WordPress saves every 60 seconds, and you can also save drafts for later publishing to the blog.

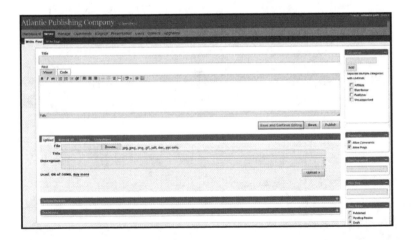

The "Dashboard" is the main control panel for your blog. You can publish posts, view comments, edit your site, change preferences, and edit your template, layout, widgets, and extras.

Establishing an RSS feed with WordPress is simple. Navigate to your dashboard, click on the "Presentation" link, and then click on the "Widgets" tab. Drag one of the "Text" widgets to your sidebar and double-click on the blue lines in the text box to open the parameters feature.

In the parameters, enter your title and RSS link in the format below. Replace yourblog.wordpress.com with your actual blog address, such as **atlanticpub.wordpress.com**, and replace **imagelocation.com** with the location of your RSS image icon:

<a href="http://yourblog.wo*on.com/rss.png">

Save the changes and your RSS subscription feed will appear on your blog. You can use the same HTML code on your website to create a signup link for your RSS data feed.

It is recommended that you spend some time on the discussion forums, help files, and other readily available resources. There is a wealth of information available, as well as an abundance of widgets you can use to customize and enhance your blog. At this point, your blog has been published, and several posts have been published. All that is needed now is to link the blog with your website and start promoting it.

Creating a blog in Blogger

First you need a Google Account. As you read in this book already, you should have a Google Account for many of the features and services that

Google offers including Google Web Analytics, Google Merchant Center, and Google Shopping.

Step 1: Type the URL **www.blogger.com** in your search bar and then sign in with your Google account.

Step 2: On the left side of this home page, click on the new blog button and a menu pop-up will appear for you to create your new blog:

Google screenshots © Google Inc. Used with permission.

Step 3: Enter the desired title of your blog and select the template of your choice. Carefully choose an address that represents your blog. This name should act as keyword for further searches on Google's search engine. In my case, I created a blog titled "Guide to Awesome Wines" and chose the URL **awesomewines.blogspot.com**. If the URL you choose is not available, it will notify you, and you will have to select another one. Click "Create Blog" to continue. You can also purchase a domain name for your blog, or you can stick with the free URL Blogger provides you.

Google screenshots © Google Inc. Used with permission.

Step 4: Customize the Blogger Dashboard according to your needs, and start posting your blog entries. You will see that Blogger provides you with statistics, the ability to easily create new blog entries, and the ability to modify the layout and template with the click of a mouse. You can share blog entries through Google+, as well. You can easily make new blog posts, and there is a "view blog" button on the top so that you can view your actual blog on the Web. You can review all comments by followers. You will find Blogger very simple to use. Most features are self-explanatory and are based on your personal preferences. You can customize most items and add page elements, images, links, and text. You will find the entire process to be very simple and self-explanatory. The average person can create a robust blog in less than five minutes with no blogging experience.

Google screenshots © Google Inc. Used with permission.

You can engage in campaigns to grow your audience with Google AdWords:

Grow your audience

Whether you're looking to bring in new readers or keep them coming back for more, AdWords can help your blog get more visibility.

Start now   Learn more

1 Create your ad
Start by writing an ad that tells people about your blog. Next choose the search terms that will make your ad show in the Google search results.

2 People see your blog on Google
If the words people type in Google match your keywords, your ad can appear above or next to the search results.

3 You get more readers
They click your ad and go to your blog. Best of all, you only pay when they do.

Google screenshots © Google Inc. Used with permission.

You can easily change your template, layout, and many other features as well as add, remove, and edit gadgets on your blogs. Gadgets are "add-ons" which you can use to customize your blog. Examples of Gadgets are Google AdSense, Wikipedia, Calendars and many more third party options. You can also customize your "mobile" blog, which is automatically created for you by Blogger. You can enable email notifications so you are emailed every time a new blog post or comment is created on your blog. Similar to Wordpress, it takes just a few minutes to create a 100% free and easy to use blog that is highly customizable.

Lastly, Blogger supports syndication feeds for your website. Syndication means that when you publish your blog, Blogger automatically generates a machine-readable representation of your blog that can be picked up and displayed on other websites and information aggregation tools. The setup within Blogger is very simple; you should click on the "Site Feed" link to specify your feed parameters. You can specify "full" or "short" to syndicate the full blog text, or truncate the first 255 characters.

Blogger supports Atom, which is a syndication format or "feed" for your blog. When a regularly updated site such as a blog has a feed, people can subscribe to it using software for reading syndicated content called a "news-reader." To create the Atom feed in Blogger, simply log into your Blogger dashboard. Click on "Settings," then "Site Feed." Here you can turn your site feed settings to off, short, or full. With new Blogger accounts and templates, your feed is automatically displayed on your blog unless you turn it off.

People like using readers for blogs, because it allows them to catch up on all their favorites at once and avoid navigating to multiple websites. It is delivered spam-free. There are many newsreaders that support Atom.

Spend the time to customize your blog through the settings control panel. Some features you will want to turn on and customize may be under the "Comments" tab, which lets you specify whether to turn backlinks and word verification on or off. Allowing word verification is a critical step in preventing spam posts from hitting your blog through automated blog systems. Help is readily available by clicking the "Help" link on any page.

How to Write a Blog

There is an art to blogging effectively. You really do not need to have any special skills in writing to write blogs. You do need some education if you wish to create and write *effective* blogs — you are not writing the next great novel.

Lose your audience, and your blog is useless. This list is certainly not complete, and is in fact dynamic, based on the type of blog, topic of the blog, target audience, and the "attitude" of the bloggers who are posting comments on the blog. That said, this is a helpful compilation of the best techniques to help you write effective blogs and become a master blogger.

Content

Your blog content is the most important factor in your blog. It is the central point of interest for anyone visiting your blog and forms the crux of how you plan to develop your blog.

Of course, the key question is, how do you determine what good content is? There is not a simple answer, since it depends on the type of blog, the intention of the blog, the target audience, and the experience of the bloggers. A good blog entertains, enlightens, captures interest, fascinates, sparks debate, and inspires conversation. A blog needs to be unique, invigorating and useful. There are many, many blogs in the blogosphere. You need to be unique or create your own market niche in order to gain an audience.

Remember that users are going to your blog to be entertained, educated or enlightened. You will want to decide early on which of those three purposes you are looking to fulfill, but the best blogs tend to accomplish all three purposes in varying degrees.

You need to define what your target audience is after, design it with content that addresses what your target audience wants, communicate it effectively, and reach out to your readers. Give them what they want, and they will be back. A little research on your target audience can go a long way. Seek feedback and make changes to your blog accordingly. Your readers know what they want, so deliver it to them. One of your challenges will be to establish a unique blog when using free blog software, such as Blogger, since it is not as customizable as some of the higher-end commercial products.

Writing guidelines

Your blog needs to be relevant and on topic. A professional blog or interest blog is very different from a personal blog, which might meander about based upon daily experiences and not necessarily for business purposes. A professional or special interest blog is written for an audience on a particular subject be it something as broad as gardening tips to the development of a specific product.

Keeping your blog on topic is critical in preventing you from going in directions that may cause you to lose your core audience. Followers and subscribers to an interest or professional blog are interested about information related to their specific interest of that specific topic and will feel that their attention is being wasted if you keep going off topic.

Keep the topic on track, and encourage others to share opinions, thoughts, and opposing views where possible to keep the blog engaging and interesting. Interject humor and wit when you can. Blogging is not an art form. It does not require a graduate level education. Try not to overthink it; keep a sense of humor and do not patronize your readers.

Here are some guidelines to help you establish your blog:

Inform your readers

You must convey knowledge about what you are posting. Be factual, accurate, and professional. Ensure that your blog is clearly written and there are no spelling or grammar errors.

Differentiate between fact and opinion

If your post is based on fact, then clearly present the fact. If it is your opinion, be sure to make it clear that it is your opinion only, and is not based entirely on fact or corporate policy.

Be timely

Blogging can be time-consuming, but you need to present timely information for it to be of value. Dated information will indicate that your blog is not timely, and it will ultimately become irrelevant.

Punctuality is important

You need to have periodic blog updates, and you need to stick to that schedule. As your blog grows in readership, your audience will look forward to your scheduled blog posts. Do not disappoint them by failing to stick to your schedule. Be realistic with that schedule; do not announce daily updates if you cannot stick to it. Do not lose your audience because your communication is lacking.

Be straightforward and simplistic

Keep your blog entries clear, easy to read, and easy to understand. Keep it brief, but not too brief. Get your point across quickly using a minimal number of words. Long posts can lose your readers and get off-topic. Short blog posts may not contain enough information to be of value. Learn the magic length for your blog and try to stick to it. You may have more success keeping your blog posts shorter and breaking them into multiple posts to capture increased readership through your RSS feeds and in search engines. RSS expands your blog like a spider web by pushing your blog out to your subscribers as you post entries.

Use keywords

Include related keywords in both the title and content post of your blog entries. Do not overload your keywords to the point that your blog post becomes nothing more than a string of unreadable keywords. Use them in natural sentences. To increase your visibility, you need to develop thorough content that is keyword-enriched and captures the both the reader and the search engines.

Post often

The frequency of your blog posts also affects search engine rankings and visibility. Update your blog on a regular, frequent basis. This not only develops and increases your audience, but it also helps you with search engine rankings.

Spelling counts

It reflects professionalism and attention to detail. Make sure you read what you post before you publish.

Be patient

You may think your blog is exciting, but it takes time for people to find it, and even more time to cultivate your audience.

Express your opinion

Although you do need to be careful about posting your blog opinions, your audience wants your personality, thoughts, and feelings — so express them.

Use links

Links are critical. Link where possible to other Web pages that are relevant to your blog post. Link to websites, other blogs, books, articles, and news.

Have a great title

Titles attract attention. Make them capture the essence of your blog post. Good titles also drive your overall readership. Most people scan Web pages and only stop when something catches their eyes. If your titles do not attract attention, you will lose potential blog readership.

Keep it organized

Organize your posts for clear readability. Keep sentences short, and use spacing or bullets to organize thoughts. Use bullets and white space to maintain easy readability.

Be consistent

Consistency is important, especially as you win over audiences by adding your unique personality or interjections into your blog posts. Keeping your posts consistent is important in sustaining audiences.

Be clear

Jargon and acronyms are bad. Do not use them. You may understand them, but others may not. Write in clear, captivating, and descriptive tones. While following the length rules, give enough verbal signals in your descriptive words to "paint the picture" in the reader's mind. By providing enough detail to capture the imagination, you draw in interest and avoid monotone, colorless one-line entries.

Take a risk

Write outside of your comfort zone about topics you have an interest in, want more information about, want to learn about, or want to offer your opinion on. If you only write about your specialty, you will get bored, and your blogs will get boring and one dimensional.

Be tough

Your opinions and blog posts may be your opinion, or your company position on issues, but there will be opposing thoughts and opinions. Do not take them personally, and do not worry about negativity. It comes with the territory.

Commenting

There are some specific guidelines you can follow when posting comments that will help you build a reputation and improve your professionalism as a blogger. Write respectfully and intelligently, and support your comments. In the blogosphere, reputation is everything.

Your blogs will be read by a wide variety of individuals. Some will seek you out for potential partnerships, to purchase products, and for marketing ventures. You never know who will read your blog, so follow the guidelines of professionalism. This is critical for corporate blogging.

The key is to provide useful, factual information so that, over time, it becomes clear to other readers of the blogs to which you post that you know what you are talking about. In general, it is a good idea to keep your posts short and on point.

Here are some general commenting guidelines:

- Keep your comments short and simple.
- Keep your comments relevant, professional, and on topic. Blog administrators will purge offensive material, personal flames, and other inappropriate content. When using someone else's material, give them the appropriate attribution.
- Sign your comments. Include your email address, website URL, and blog URL.
- Provide quality comments that add substance and meaning. Fluff or generalized two-word entries are of no value.
- Promote your blog, business, and website in your blog posts by either providing a URL and brief description or embed it naturally into the blog comment so readers can have the option to follow the link if they wish to visit your site and obtain more information relative to your blog comment.
- If you have nothing useful to add to a blog, do not add anything.

Blogging Tips, Hints, and Tricks

Here are some basic rules to follow to help you to achieve the success you desire.

Know your niche: Understand that a reader may be intrigued by your blog's domain before they actually visit your blog and read your blog entries. Your domain name is your very first impression upon your blog visitor. If you have a niche, product, or unique service, be sure that you focus on that from your domian name to your blog posts and keep a streamlined approach to your blog. All too often, well-intended blogs go off in so many different directions it loses its identity and purpose. If your blog becomes highly vague and covers too many topics, readers will get confused, lost and quickly lose interest. Your niche is your charm, if you provide your reader a daily dose of creativity pertaining to your blogs ideology, then you will continue to add new readers to your blog.

Blog keywords: Millions of blogs are on the Internet, but only a few appear in the first page of search engine results. This is often because most do not understand search engine algorithms. Search engines look for keywords within your blog entries. Use keywords in your blog and blog entries that align with the central purpose of your blog. Choose the keywords wisely to achieve better search engine results.

Creative and relevant content: Content is king. Relevant content is paramount to everything you have in your blog. Content should be framed in a simple, easy to understand language, which helps to grow followership. Support blog's content with images that best align with its purpose. An image is worth 1000 words, so use images to enhance the look, feel, and overall functionality of a blog. Content should be specific to a topic and it must be creative. Your content uniqueness differentiates you from other, similar blogs.

Identify your target audience: This is similar to other marketing strategies, where you should know your customer market and segment. Prior to writing blog entries, you should understand that the best blog is not always an exceptionally articulated blog, so cater to your audience.

Social media: Promotion is key to the popularity of a blog. Promote your blog across different platforms. You will draw many readers to your blog from social media outlets.

The Benefits of Blogging

Here are some potential benefits of a blog. As a reminder, you can create a blog in less than five minutes and it is absolutely free.

Income potential: In addition to using a blog to draw in potential customers, clients, and shoppers, you can use your blog as an income source through paid advertisements. You can use Google AdSense, which is built into Blogger, through an AdSense Gadget.

Name and brand recognition: Blogs can generate a continuous stream of information to promote your business name and brand. For no cost, you can "push" highly searchable, keyword-enriched content onto the Web to grow your business and increase your name and brand recognition with minimal effort.

Blogs can be a fun and creative outlet: Get in touch with your creative self. You must capture interest to draw in readers and keep them coming back. With your own blog, you have ultimate creative control over the content. You can post on your own schedule. You will have direct communication with your target audience, so you drive the topics and discussions.

Blogging & Spam

Just as spam is a huge problem for email, it is a growing problem for blogs. There are two major categories of blog spam. They are:

- Bogus blogs, or spam blogs. These are designed purely for spamming purposes by launching spam attacks through viral methods.

- Comment spam, when spam comments are inserted into legitimate blogs.

Spam blogs are also referred to as "splogs," a combination of the two words. According to Blogger's help pages, spam blogs "cause various problems, beyond simply wasting a few seconds of your time when you happen to come across one. They can clog up search engines, making it difficult to find real content on the subjects that interest you. They may scrape content from other sites on the Web, using other people's writing to make it look as though they have useful information of their own. And if an automated system is creating spam posts at an extremely high rate, it can impact the speed and quality of the service for other, legitimate users."

The spam blog problem has continued to grow despite efforts to stop it through IP blocking and word verification fields.

Comment spam contains links to one or more websites, which are usually also irrelevant, inappropriate, or purely spam-centric websites. Combating spam blog entries is time-consuming, frustrating, and a growing problem. While most blog software has built-in tools to combat comment spam, they are not foolproof. Spammers use automated software applications, robots, auto-responders, and other techniques to spread spam throughout the blogosphere. The secret to defeating — or at least minimizing — spam in your blog is to employ the tools of your blog software and host to their fullest potential. Just like with email, you may not stop all content spam, but you can certainly minimize it. Spam is not a reason to quit blogging; it is simply an annoyance you will have to deal with.

Chapter 13

Unlocking the
Secrets of eBay

One of the best ways to market your small business is by utilizing eBay. An eBay store can dramatically improve the visibility and sales of your product, as well as drive traffic to either an already existing website or a physical store or business. There are many advantages to advertising and selling products on eBay, as well as many ways this e-commerce giant has made the selling process an easy and effective way to promote and expand an already existing business.

With over 150 million users, eBay is an incredible opportunity to gain valuable business and product exposure. This can be achieved through creating an eBay store, learning to effectively list items, and building a business following and email list through the visibility an eBay store can create for your business.

The eBay website also features a simplicity that does not require Web design or intensive development. Creating a basic eBay store only takes a few minutes; it is very simple to do and this means that your business will be up and running in minutes. Some businesses get their start on eBay, while many businesses that already have their own website or physical location use eBay as a tool to reach even more potential customers on a daily basis. Under Armour® has a large retail presence, which includes platform stores as well as a very robust online store. Under Amour has an eBay store, which lets them sell their products directly through eBay, greatly expanding their market presence.

Opening an eBay Store

The first step to using eBay to advertise and market your business and ultimately sell your products is to open an eBay store.

In order to open a store, you must first set up your eBay seller account. You will do this from the eBay home page, where you should choose the option to sign up for a business account rather than a personal account. Compared to a personal account, this offers a broader range of tools to monitor and manage your account and sales.

Standard seller accounts are designed for those who will be selling an occasional item or who only wish to make purchases through their eBay account, whereas the business account is designed to be adapted to a broad range of business needs. Signing up will require a business name, business address, phone number, user name, and password. It will also require that you register a payment method, which can either be a bank account, a PayPal account, or credit card information.

In order to open an eBay Store, which is the next step for a business owner after signing up for an account, you must verify your account through Paypal as well as register a credit card with your account. To simplify the sign up process, it is best to take care of registering both of these types of payment methods immediately. I strongly encourage you to open a Paypal account for your business, as this greatly simplifies the payment process with eBay.

Choose your account type

One of the benefits of creating an eBay store rather than utilizing the basic business account is cost effectiveness. An eBay store has monthly fees, but offers a reduction in fees for listing each item compared to a basic seller account, which charges fees for every single item you offer.

There are several levels of eBay store subscriptions, which include Basic Store, Premium Store, and Anchor store.

The best way to choose which store is appropriate for a new user is to determine how many products you wish to list and then calculate which plan minimizes the overall monthly cost of utilizing the platform. A basic store costs $19.95 a month and allows for 200 free item listings; a premium store costs $59.95 and allows for 500 free item listings; an anchor store is $199.99, but allows for 2,500 free listings. The choice of which store is appropriate varies greatly on the amount of items one plans to list. For example, if one is listing only 230 items on average, a basic store might be the best choice. You are also able to upgrade your subscription at any time.

Fees	Basic Store	Premium Store	Anchor Store
Monthly subscription	$19.95/month	$59.95/month	$199.95/month
Yearly subscription (1 year term required)	$15.95/month	$49.95/month	$179.95/month
Unlimited insertion fee credits for auction-style listings that end in a sale (exclusions apply†)	⊘	⊘	⊘
Discounted fixed price insertion fee	20¢	10¢	5¢
Discounted auction-style insertion fee	25¢	15¢	10¢
Lower final value fees	4%-9%	4%-9%	4%-9%
Number of free fixed price insertion fee listings* (per month)	200	500	2,500

Another benefit of the eBay store is that it also allows you to arrange your items and store pages in a way that is visually appealing and effective to customers, in the same way one might design the homepage of an individual website. Sellers can arrange their items into categories as well, as the store allows up to 300 categories and even subcategories for your items.

An eBay store also allows users to manage and promote their business via more in-depth features and tools. For example, when one opens an eBay store, they are listed in the eBay store directory and will receive a personalized Web address to direct buyers to their store. They will have the ability to list featured items on their store, use advanced tools to manage sales, and have advanced options to customize their store display, previously referred to as an eBay storefront.

Premium and anchor stores also include eBay's Seller Manager Pro, which features additional useful tools. These include the ability to create bulk listings, more effectively manage inventory, automate listings, create monthly profit and loss reports, and display product success ratios based on monthly sales. This can be an excellent tool for high volume sellers, or for small business owners who hope to expand to be selling more products via eBay. You can also promote your eBay store on your website, social medial site, or blog.

Open your store

To open your store, eBay provides you with a very easy-to-follow tutorial, which is available at **www.ebay.com/gds/How-to-Design-a-Custom-eBay-store-FULL-TUTORIAL-/10000000008283781/g.html**, **http://stores.ebay.com/MiloDesign/StoreTutorial.html**, or through a YouTube video at **https://www.youtube.com/watch?v=-Rhvc8wqNDM**.

Creating Your Storefront

Another key to effectively utilizing the eBay store is to create a well-designed and eye-catching storefront that will impress future and current customers; you can think of this as very similar to the homepage on your website — first impressions count. The storefront represents the business, products, and services, and can be used to create a level of professionalism that will give you the credibility you need to positively impact customers. The eBay storefront has three main components: a billboard, a store description, and featured items.

Billboard

The billboard is a visual image that is at the top of the store, and can range from something as simple as a photo that relates to the business to a customized company logo. eBay requires that billboard images be 1200×270 pixels, and that the image be created by the seller or that the seller has the rights to use the image.

Some ideas for using this space are to display a logo banner, to display visuals of promotions you are running, to display business specials, and to display dynamic photos that create excitement around your business. You can also add a logo of 150x150 pixels beside your billboard image, if you choose.

Store description

The store description is where a business can briefly outline the purpose of their business and their product line or services. In this area, you can describe what you sell, why your product is unique, how long you have been in business, or your area of expertise.

eBay gives some tips on what to include in this section:

- Use words in your description that you think people might enter when they search for a product. For example, if you specialize in wrist watches, state that you sell "wrist watches" rather than "timepieces." A more straightforward description will improve your Store's chances of being found by interested buyers.

- Make sure your description accurately represents your Store. Filling your description with product or brand names that you do not usually have in stock (known as "keyword spamming") will frustrate buyers and actually cause your Store's placement in search results to decline.

- Use a Store theme that includes your Store description in the header (for example, the "Classic Left" theme), because this increases your chances of appearing in search results.

(Tips courtesy of eBay: **http://pages.ebay.com/help/stores/contextual/ store-description.html**.)

Featured items

Featured items are listed items that are placed at the top of the store. The featured items default to listings that are ending soonest, but can be changed to highlight the best of what a company has to offer or the most commonly purchased items a business has in stock. They are arranged however the seller deems appropriate.

Consider these featured items, which are similar to the display window in a physical brick-and-mortar store. This is where a business can show items that will draw potential customers in to browse all the other items in their inventory.

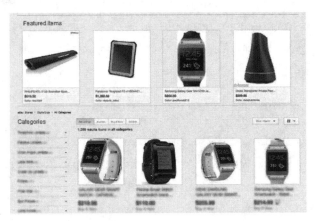

Other elements a store includes are categories, a search bar where customers can search for specific items within your listings rather than eBay as a whole, and a follow button, where customers can bookmark your store to return later. Sellers can also add a Subscribe to Newsletter feature here as well to develop an email list, which we will discuss later.

Creating Effective Listings

While the storefront is important to consider, item listings are just as important. The storefront is all about driving traffic so potential customers will see your items. On the other hand, the item listing is about creating a drive to purchase that item, and can also be used to drive traffic back to the storefront or to a business website.

There are quite a few elements to an item listing to consider. These include title, item description, images, pricing, shipping methods, return policies, and selecting an appropriate category, which are described in further detail below.

Title

The title of your item is quite possibly the most important thing to consider, as the words you choose to describe your listing will determine whether the eBay search engine favors your item, therefore making it visible to potential bidders. The title is also your opportunity to pre-sell your item to customers and is your first opportunity to make your listing stand out.

Some tips on effective titles include:

- Do not use ALL CAPITAL LETTERS

- Be descriptive, but utilize short listing titles. Feature keywords that customers are likely to search for. EBay Search engines penalize listings with excessive words that are not popular, while favoring those that feature keywords that are searched for more often. For example, *Digital Nokia 3600 Camera with Case* is actually more likely to be featured in a search than *Digital Nokia 3600 Camera with Black Leather Carrying Case Great Product.*

- Do not use "salesy" words in the title; eBay search engines penalize words like "wow," "cheap," "deal," or "look," and your items will get less visibility. Customers do not search for these words, and they tend to discourage rather than encourage potential buyers, as they come across as gimmicky. Use good basic descriptions and titles that you would personally search for.

- Do not misspell keywords. The quickest way to not be found in the eBay search engine is to misspell an important word in your title.

- Do not use excessive punctuation. Using punctuation decreases search visibility and is visually distracting to potential buyers.

- For an additional fee, which varies depending on the listing type, sellers have the option to include a subtitle. I recommend only using subtitles if there is useful information that might encourage a customer to click on an item. You may also experiment with listing similar items with and without subtitles to see which generates more sales, and whether this is cost efficient. Listing Analytics are one way to do this, which are discussed in a later section. It is normally not worth the extra fee for subtitles; however, eBay may offer this as a free promotion, so feel free to use them if they are offered at no cost.

Item description

This is the text area on your listing where you are able to describe your item in more detail after a potential buyer clicks on your listing. There are many ways to effectively utilize the item description. The following are guidelines for creating the best possible use of this space.

- Use eBay features to format text color, size, and spacing. In the past, an effective way to create the description in your item listing was to use HTML code to create your descriptions by creating an item description in a Web Page Designer (such as Dreamweaver) and then to copy and paste the HTML code into the description block in eBay. While this method can still be utilized, eBay now offers a more rich ability to edit item-listing text, which allows one to change font, color, size, insert line spacing, and images. It is also important to note that while HTML may still be used to create more extensive visuals in an item description (or to insert tables), eBay search engines now tend to favor item listings which do not utilize extensive HTML code, so one may want to consider only utilizing this when necessary.

- Do not use flashing icons, images, and text that distract the viewer. A clean, simple interface is best to sell your products. I recommend you only use white backgrounds for any descriptions pages.

- Be sure to include all relevant information. Be detailed in your description and always include elements such as color, size, brand, and condition.

- Include benefits or product features. In addition to describing physical attributes and features, this is the space where you have the opportunity to describe why a customer should buy this product. Try to describe why your item stands out above similar listings, including what makes it a great purchase.

- Utilize item description to describe the excellent customer service you offer. After describing your item, this space can also be utilized to describe another thing that makes your item stand out — that you back it with amazing customer service. Feel free to use this space to describe how you ship items in a timely fashion, have free shipping, how you respond quickly to customer inquiries and concerns, or anything else about how you do business that makes you stand out.

- To increase search engine visibility, always include the title as the first line in your item description, and repeat keywords that customers are likely to search for. This makes your item more likely to receive visibility on Google or other relevant search engines.

Pricing and listing duration

Whereas eBay started as an auction only website, now there are two main ways to price your items on eBay. One of these is the traditional auction style with bidding, and the other is fixed price where purchases are immediate.

Auction style items have a starting bid, which should be the lowest price possible as bidders on these items are generally looking for a bargain. Starting bids of just a few dollars are more likely to generate interest than items that are listed near the retail value. In most cases, bids for low starting items produce more interest and bids, which increase visibility of these items, and they will typically sell above the expected final bid amount. Auction items can be listed for 1, 3, 5, 7, or 10 days, with a fee for 10 day auctions that varies depending on the listing. Seven day auctions are recommended, as they give the item a chance to draw attention. On auction listings, much of the interest will be generated in the last day or two of the listing, as this is when buyers expect to get the best deal by snatching up an item right before the auction ends.

Another option on auction style items is that one is able to set a reserve price, which is a hidden price that if users bid below they will not win the auction. It is generally discouraged to set a reserve, as these discourage bidders who are looking to get a deal. Buyers will assume that with a reserve, they will not get as good of a deal, and therefore are more likely to ignore these items. However, a reserve price does protect one from selling items below the desired profit.

Fixed price items are listed in the same way items might be listed on a traditional e-commerce website, with a set price that does not change. The lowest fixed price for an item is 99 cents. Fixed price items tend to sell slightly worse than auctions. They are only recommended if one has an item that sells well or if you are a well-established store that offers your items for a fixed price on another website, such as Amazon, and you want to keep your pricing consistent. For drumming up business, fixed pricing is risky. However, one of the benefits is that while auction style listings can only be listed up to 10 days, these listings can be up to 30 days.

Buy it now is another price option that falls somewhere between a traditional auction price and the fixed price, and is added onto auction style listings. This is also referred to as the BIN price, which is a flat price a bidder can purchase the item for before it receives any bids. This offers buyers the opportunity to snatch up an item that is listed as an auction item, and is especially attractive to bidders willing to pay a higher price in order to guarantee that they get this item. Buy it now is a price that is in addition to the auction. One should be thoughtful in establishing a Buy it now price, as too low a price could suggest that the value of the item is not high, but too high a price might discourage eager buyers who might have been an easy sell if the BIN had been a few dollars less. Items with lower BINs gain more visibility in eBay item searches. Some ways to determine an appropriate BIN are to research the BINs of other similar items, and set yours somewhere in the middle, at a price that would still garner a desirable profit. BIN prices must be 30% more than the starting bid price of an item.

Images

Another important thing to consider when listing an item on eBay is the images that display the product. Below are some tips for creating effective images for listings.

- Photographs of images should feature a plain, white, or uncluttered background. This will make sure that the background does not draw attention away from the product. This can be achieved in a variety of ways, including photographing in front of a white wall or sheet, or utilizing photo editing software that clears the background of an image.

- Use photos that show the item from a variety of angles and use close-ups to show relevant details, textures, and features. Think of what a potential buyer would look at if they were looking at this item in the store. What details would they examine? What would they be looking for? Take photos that give potential bidders a clear visual of exactly what they are getting.

- Use more images for greater effectiveness. Items with more images receive better visibility as the eBay search engine features these items, so even if one or two pictures are sufficient to display the item's features, consider utilizing more photos.

- Use photos that are clear. Avoid photos that are blurry or pixelated. Some ways to do this are to use a high quality camera to take your shots. Smart phone cameras have advanced to the point that they are acceptable for images, and the eBay app lets you create listings on the fly from your smart phone, iPad, or tablet.

- Utilize a tripod to avoid shakiness or unnecessary motion.

- Use high-resolution photos. eBay images feature a zoom option in which users can take a closer look at photos to examine details, so use images that are over 800 pixels per side to allow this feature to be used by potential bidders. This creates a feeling that they are able to look at the item as they would in real life.

- Consider the lighting. Do not use flash, as it will create shadows and glare. Take photos of items in well-lit areas and use lighting that does not distort the view of an item, and that highlights the details of what you are selling.

- Compare your photos with other sellers and other e-commerce websites. You want your item photos to look professional in order to communicate to potential bidders that you are an experienced seller who is detail oriented and will provide them with great service.

- When appropriate, create a greater impact with video. If you have an item that is more impressive when it is being used, you may want to include a video or a link to a video on your item listing to make it stand out. This is, of course, in addition to using photos, and should not be used as a substitute for using still images to display the item on your listing.

Shipping methods

There are three options for shipping on eBay: free shipping, fixed shipping, and calculated rate shipping. While choosing a shipping method is often a matter of preference, there are several important things to consider, as the choice of shipping can both increase sales and increase or decrease profit.

Free shipping will attract customers, as they see this as a better deal. However, when one utilizes this option, the price of shipping must be considered against the profit, as the shipping will be covered by the seller and not the buyer. It is therefore important to consider how much this item would cost to ship, and factor in the weight of this item and the cost of its delivery to various locations. Free shipping is best used for small, lightweight items, or on items where the shipping represents a small percentage of the overall profit. Items that offer free and expedited shipping will also feature a "Fast 'N Free" stamp and a boost in search visibility.

Fixed (or flat rate) shipping is recommended after free shipping in most cases, as it both allows the potential buyer to know how much his item would cost including shipping, and also allows the seller the most control over shipping costs. However, one should be cautious and make sure to utilize a shipping rate that is fair, or it will discourage bidders, especially as frequent eBay users are wary of shipping rates that seem unfair or are notably above what the item would cost to ship at a rate calculated by weight. One way to do this is to use flat rate boxes of varying shapes and sizes which are often available for free from USPS, UPS, and FedEx.

Calculated shipping does not offer the seller any benefits, and requires use of a postal scale prior to listing, so generally flat rate is a better option. However, there are exceptions to this. An example of a time when one may need to use calculated shipping may be when selling media (such as books, DVDs, and magazines), which many bidders will purchase with the knowledge that these items can be shipped at very low rates utilizing USPS media mail.

It is also not uncommon to get a request from a potential bidder on eBay requesting a different shipping option than the one you have listed, especially if they are a seasoned buyer who knows they may save a dollar or two by switching to economy shipping or shipping via a different service.

While this may create an inconvenience, it may be worth it to honor those requests as the potential for a repeat and loyal customer often outweighs the cost or time required to adjust shipping methods.

Another beneficial shipping option to consider is combining multiple items, which increases the likelihood that a buyer will purchase more than one item from you. This can be used with both fixed and calculated rates, and changed under the general shipping setting on your eBay account.

Shipping promotions where one receives a percentage off by selecting the shipping service of your choice can also be created. This can be beneficial in multiple ways, as it both creates the impression with a customer that they are saving money, and it streamlines your shipping process. This can also be created in a similar way using the shipping settings on your eBay account.

For larger items that are targeted to a specific location, one can select "Local Pickup." Additional options are available for selling vehicles through eBay Auto.

Delivery time and carrier options

Sellers have control over what delivery times and carriers they ship with. Offering expedited shipping is beneficial as it both increases the likelihood that someone will purchase an item and gets the item ranked higher via the eBay search engine. One can choose from USPS, UPS, and FedEx and will have a variety of delivery time options.

It is important to be realistic about your ability to do timely, daily shipments. If an item is not shipped on time for an expedited purchase and arrives later than anticipated, a buyer may be dissatisfied and give poor feedback, which will negatively effect sales and negate the benefits of offering expedited services. It is also important to note that utilizing eBay to print shipping labels can greatly reduce shipping fees, as can ordering free shipping supplies through eBay, as both USPS and UPS have partnerships that offer reduced rates for sellers who use these services.

International shipping

There are pros and cons to consider that are dependent on your business as well as the type of items you are selling. Some thoughts to consider are:

- Are your items likely to be damaged if shipped long distances?
- Do you wish to reach a global market with your product?
- Can shipping internationally increase your sales reach and your potential profit?

You also may think of international shipping from a marketing perspective. If you acquire bidders from outside the country, you are potentially creating international exposure for your business with very little marketing effort.

EBay offers varied options for international shipping. One can choose to ship their items to the international shipping warehouse and let eBay cover any additional responsibility or one can choose to take care of international shipping themselves, through the global shipping program. Shipping to the international warehouse simplifies things, as one is only required to calculate national shipping rates and decide between standard shipping options. Once the item reaches the warehouse, any damaged or lost goods will be covered by eBay rather than a potential loss to the seller.

Return policies

Buyers generally have the most confidence with sellers who have the most liberal return policies. This assures them that they are going to be taken care of if the item does not fit their needs or does not match the description in the listing. It creates a greater sense of safety for online purchases in general.

One thing to note is that with the eBay return policy, if you offer a return, the customer can return this item for any reason within 14 days, which does increase risk for the seller. However, these risks are outweighed by the benefits, as sellers with returns not only get better ratings but are also eligible to receive a "Top Seller" award, which will increase their overall sales and visibility. We will discuss how to receive a Top Seller award in depth later on.

Selecting a category

When you list an item, you choose which category it will be listed in. One way to figure out what category is appropriate is to search for similar items and see which they are most commonly listed in. You also get an additional option to list the item in multiple categories for a small fee, which may increase visibility, especially if your item fits well into two diverse categories.

Using eBay Seller and Marketing Tools

Once your business has mastered the basics of selling on eBay, you can begin to utilize some of the additional features of the site to streamline and create increased levels of productivity. These tools can help promote your business both inside and outside of eBay.

Both eBay and third party service providers offer great options that make listing easier, especially if one is listing many similar or identical items. eBay Seller Manager Pro offers the option to save a template for future listings, which can then be preloaded, altered, and relisted more efficiently than creating a brand new listing from scratch. It also offers the option to preset a schedule for automated listings of repeat items.

There are also options to set an item to automatically relist if it does not sell, and to relist an item after it sells if one has many of the same item in stock. Third party automated listing services expand on this by offering image hosting for storing photos, management of multiple eBay accounts, image galleries, and inventory management functions.

EBay newsletters and mailing list features

Recognizing that email is an effective marketing tool for creating repeat customers, eBay has simplified the process of acquiring a mailing list and creating a newsletter for sellers.

One can create a "Sign Up For Newsletter" button on their homepage through their storefront account settings, which can be customized with a message to future subscribers explaining the benefits of signing up for the newsletter. When potential buyers browse your storefront, they can choose to subscribe to this mailing list, which creates a huge potential for future marketing.

Try to list several reasons why signing up for the newsletter might be beneficial, including sale prices, new items, and exclusive deals. Once you build a list, eBay also features templates that aid in creating effective email marketing and newsletters to create great emails to draw in buyers. This can be found in the "Marketing Tools" section of account settings, under "Email Marketing."

There are several templates to choose from, designed for a variety of business types and visual preferences. You then choose a message as well as featured items, and this email will be automatically sent to everyone who has subscribed to your storefront. This will act to draw buyers back to your store, specifically ones who may have been considering a purchase at a later date.

A great strategy for utilizing the newsletter is to greatly reduce the price on one or two items, and to bring customers back who will then look at your other items. This will increase traffic, leading to a greater likelihood that other potential buyers will see your storefront and will be interested in your listings, creating a snowball effect of future exposure and sales.

Promoting individual items

One of the easiest ways to drive eBay sales is through the use of eBay's promotional listing services. The first way to do this is through listing upgrades.

Listing upgrades can be purchased individually or as a value pack, and fees vary depending on the starting price of the item. Upgrades allow you to further customize the visual appearance of your item when it appears in a search listing, allowing you to have more control over when you list your items. It also allows you to list items in multiple categories, all of which may increase visibility.

Some other upgrade options are to list your title in bold for a small fee, Gallery Plus, which displays a gallery view of your photos in the search list, the subtitle option, and an image upgrade option to allow you to list beyond the standard 12 images.

Another specific route is to use eBay Promoted Listings. In addition to individual item upgrades, this service provides a boost in item exposure for a small fee. This puts your items, and therefore your business in front of more customers. Promoted Listings can be set up through your Marketing Tools under Account Settings. You can use promoted listings to promote up to 30% of your items or 500 of your items, whichever comes first.

When creating a Promoted Listings campaign, the seller chooses a percentage of the item profit they are willing to commit to the advertisement, and this fee is only charged if this item sells via a click on the promotional ad.

Go to the Marketing Tab on your Seller hub and locate the promotions category in the left navigation panel. This will pull up a promotion screen that will list any active promotions you are running and will allow you to create new promotions. You will be asked to decide which category you want to use for the promotion, define your offer (this is where you decide how much to give off), and then select the individual items to include in the promotion. You set a promotion date range, and you are done. Shorter promotions tend to do the best, as these create a sense of urgency and compel buyers to act.

Promotions will be displayed on the storefront as well as on the listing of each eligible item above the photos. Other featured items that are included in the promotion will be displayed below your item description. When a buyer checks out, they will be reminded of the promotional discount in order to encourage them to add an additional item to their cart.

One thing to note when creating a promotion is that customers tend to be more reactive to percentage off discounts rather than dollars off when the items are smaller in value. Larger items on the other hand may benefit from using a dollar off promotion, as $30 off a $200 purchase sounds greater than 15% off, even though the amount is the same. The promotions page can also show you how each promotion performed, so over time, you can get an idea of which promotion styles are the most effective.

Building collections

A collection is a group of related items that eBay users have created that usually revolve around some sort of theme, brand, or function. For example, a user may create a collection titled Exotic Home Décor that features imported furniture and home decorations, or a collection around a specific type of electronic, accessory, or collectible item. Users can post comments, share collections, and follow the eBay user that created the collection.

This may also bring those browsing directly to your storefront. If used in the right way, these collections can be great tools to promote your items. Consider creating 5-10 collections that feature a wide variety of items related to your business, and then include a couple of your listings. Some other tips for creating effective collections are:

- Choose items that have quality images. Use the same rule of thumb you would for your own listing images, and avoid blurry, poorly shot, or unprofessional/amateur looking photos.
- Use a descriptive and clear title that is an accurate preview of the collection.
- Write comments for each item you include, which are allowed to be up to 2000 characters.
- Consider sharing your collection on social media.

Managing positive feedback

When someone makes a purchase or a sale on eBay, they have the option to leave feedback. Creating a positive impression with your buyers and maintaining great feedback ratings is key to using eBay to grow your small business. Users can leave a positive, neutral, or negative rating, as well as a comment.

Positive feedback is worth one point, neutral is worth zero points, and negative feedback results in subtracting one point. There are also more detailed rates that range from zero to five stars. These involve categorical feedback. The questions a seller is asked when giving detailed feedback are about accuracy of listing, seller communication, shipping time, and shipping charges.

Ways to increase the likelihood of five-star ratings include:

- Having incredibly detailed listings. Make sure to not omit anything in the item description that might confuse a buyer; utilize images, and be thorough.

- Respond to all messages and inquiries in a timely fashion. eBay users are notorious for asking many questions, and they expect personal responses. Be warm and friendly. This type of personable communication is one of the reasons people choose eBay businesses over other big name e-commerce websites. When your buyer receives a thoughtful response from a real person, it will not only help your ratings, but will boost your likelihood of loyal return customers.

- Ship the items within 24 hours, either using the pre-print labels through eBay shipping affiliates, or make sure to enter shipping and tracking information for your shipments within the same day the auction ends or item is purchased.

- Do not overcharge on shipping. There is a temptation to make a little extra by charging a dollar or two more, but buyers are savvy and will recognize when they are being ripped off on shipping. Provide the most beneficial and cost efficient shipping method to your customer and work with them if they request regional shipping or media mail rates on eligible items.

- Ship on time and make sure to enter the tracking information in a timely manner. Sellers receive an automatic five-star rating if they enter tracking information within 24 hours of the item selling and delivery confirmation shows the item was delivered within the time window specified.

Another way to reduce the likelihood of negative feedback is to include contact information for your business, a note that you wish to provide excellent service, and a way for customers to reach you in order to resolve any issues. This allows the customer the chance to reach out to you if they have an issue before they give you a bad rating, and a chance for you to resolve that issue in a way that pleases the customer. Not only is this a way to reduce the likelihood of a bad review, but if you provide amazing service, even if the customer was initially displeased, they may be so impressed that they provide positive feedback or even return to make a purchase because they trust that they will be taken care of in the future.

EBay SEO and the "Best Match" Feature

SEO is key to using eBay to market your small business. The more you figure out how to be effective in your use of SEO, the more views and therefore purchases your items will receive. Some things to keep in mind when focusing on SEO are keywords, the proper use of barcodes (UPCs & ISBNs), and creating focused content. These will contribute to your visibility on eBay as well as your ability to be found through other popular search engines like Google or Bing.

When users search for an item on eBay specifically, their search results are automatically sorted and listed in order of something called "Best Match." Best Match is ranked based on a number of factors, relevance to users search term, items popular with buyers, value to buyers, listing completeness and quality, listing service terms (including returns and shipping), and seller feedback and history.

Understanding the Best Match function is incredibly important for maximizing listing visibility. Best Match ranks items using an algorithm referred to as the Cassini search, but generally as a seller, understanding each factor and designing your listings in compliance is the easiest way to get great listing visibility. Here is some information on how one can improve their Best Match ranking & overall SEO for items.

Title relevance

As discussed previously in the description of creating an effective title, titles should include key words and no extraneous words that customers will not be searching for. At least three keywords should be in your item title. However, be sure not to keyword spam, as eBay searches are sensitive to this and will flag your item and push it down in the search list.

Keyword spamming is the practice of inserting unnecessary amounts of keywords that a seller believes will boost their items search rating. For example, writing "Shoes Shoes Shoes" in your title may seem like an easy way to trick the search engine into believing that these are more relevant to anyone searching using the word shoes, but will ultimately be interpreted by the search engine as keyword spamming and will backfire. It is likely that your item will be flagged and pushed down in visibility on Best Match.

Item description

Your item's description is the most valuable tool for creating search engine friendly listings. While your primary goal is to describe the item you are selling to your eBay audience, here are several ways to use your description to its fullest:

- **Create great content.** Describe your item in as much detail as possible, using between 200 and 300 words of visible text in your description. Keywords should comprise about 5% of your text, so in this amount of words, you are aiming for 10 to 15 keywords. Search engines are unlikely to pick up on anything beyond a certain length, so unless you have necessary information to include that may help you customers make a decision to buy your product, writing overly lengthy item descriptions is ineffective.

- **Avoid invisible copy or hidden HTML text.** Search engines cannot pick up on this, and it may harm your rating if it is flagged as inappropriate/excessive.

- **Use a variety of fonts, sizes, and text styles.** Create headers with bold or italics. Use varying font sizes as long as these look crisp and are not too small to be read. We recommend using between 12 and 16-point fonts, and while the font style can vary, make sure the font you are using is incredibly easy to read. Cursive and fancy script fonts may appear elegant, but if your seller cannot read the description, they will move on to the next item.

- **Include links.** Add links to other products and to your eBay Store in your item description. However, do not use item descriptions to link to external websites, as this often violates eBay seller policies. Using welcoming but less pushy phrases is most effective, such as "check out my other items" or "visit my store." You can then use your storefront to link back to your business website if you so desire.

- **Listing completeness is one of the easiest ways to assure your item is ranked high in Best Match.** Listings that have incomplete portions, blurry photos, or no photos are penalized. Make sure each portion of your item is filled out thoroughly. If your category asks for "brand," for example, and your item does not have one, instead of leaving this blank, select "other." This will assure all portions of your listing are complete for a better ranking and increased visibility.

Listing analytics tools

Listing Analytics are a set of tools that help you review key metrics of your listed items and can be incredibly helpful in learning how to adjust your items or your store.

One must first subscribe to the "Listing Analytics" under their account settings in the "Applications" section. Once you have subscribed, you are able to review your performance using these tools at any time. To review the listing analytics of an item, you can search by item keywords or by a specific item.

Listing Analytics will show all the performance data of this item, including rank, format, impressions, clicks, click-through rates, sold items, sell-through rates, watchers, and sales. Below are some definitions for these key terms.

- **Rank** is how the item is listed amongst other similar items with the same keywords or title. A lower number is better, as this means your item is being seen more than competitors with higher rank numbers.

- **Format** simply denotes whether this is a fixed or auction style item.

- **Impressions** are the number of times your item shows up to potential buyers who are searching for that item.

- **Clicks** are the total number of times a potential buyer has clicked on your item title and visited your item's page.

- **Click-through rates** are the number of impressions divided by the number of clicks and can give a user a good idea of whether the title and main photo are creating interest or not. If you have a relatively low click-through rate, you may want to consider how your item is presented in the list; consider changing the title, the main photo, or both.

- **Sold items** are the total number of sales.

- **Sell-through rates** are a ratio of sales divided by clicks. Where click-through is a good way to assess whether an item is selling based on its appearance in the search list, sell-through is a better way to gauge whether the item is selling based on the description and page. If an item has a low sell-through rate, you may want to reconsider how you have presented the item in the description, whether you have enough photos, or if there is missing information that a customer may require in order to feel confident purchasing this item.

- **Watchers** are the number of people who have clicked the "watch this item" button on your listing description. Watching an item means a potential buyer gets notifications when this item is going to end or if the price is lowered. Watches can be a way to gauge interest, but generally, having many watchers on an item is not necessarily an indication that the item will sell. This is because many people watch hundreds of items, but may only purchase one or two, and may simply be bookmarking some of them because they are great products but are not necessarily committed to a future purchase.

- **Sales** are the dollar amount associated with this item. For example, if the item sold for a rate of $50 and the sold item rate is 4, the sales would be $200, because the total profit from this item was 4 × $50.

Promoting Your eBay Store

There are also a variety of ways to promote your eBay store outside of eBay. These include using social media and blogs, print marketing materials, and promoting to existing customers through existing email lists.

Social media and blogging

There are a variety of social media platforms one can use to promote any e-commerce business, and utilizing these to drive traffic to your eBay store will increase your potential for sales. One of the key things to consider when dedicating time to social media promotion is which of these platforms your customers are most likely to use. Given the broad range of social media platforms, it may be impossible to commit enough time to effectively hit all social media platforms to promote your presence on eBay. It is instead a good idea to attempt to predict which of these platforms your customers are most likely to utilize, and concentrate on those.

Facebook: You can create a fan page for your business where you post links to new eBay listings. This can be set up through your main account by going to **www.facebook.com/pages** and clicking on "Create A Page;" you then follow a fairly straightforward set of directions. This is not unlike setting up a personal profile, other than that it will request you to share details about your business.

Be sure to share relevant and interesting content, or your posts will seem like spam and not draw interest. For example, find articles related to what your business offers, and share these. Ask compelling questions that will engage readers.

Do not use your personal profile to promote eBay listings, as this will seem unprofessional and most likely be ineffective. Fan Pages were designed for business and promotion for this exact reason.

Cross promote by inviting existing customers to like your page via email or the eBay newsletter feature. Invite Facebook users to follow you on eBay.

Include a link to your Facebook on your store's website and in print materials; list both Facebook and eBay. People may be more likely to add your page on Facebook, which feels less committal, and then end up browsing eBay and purchasing a product as a result of your posting links to your listings and store.

Twitter: Create a business specific twitter username. You do not want to tweet your customers details of your personal day, nor are they interested in this. Treat social media very much like you would anything else; keep business and personal matters separate. Tweet product links as often as you like.

Search twitter hashtags to see what people who are discussing things relevant to your business are interested in. This can be a way to draw people to your account and it can also be a great way to explore how these trends apply to Facebook.

Invite already existing customers to connect with you. Then, tweet news about your promotions and listings. Include your Twitter username in eBay newsletters and emails.

Use twitter to research trends in your area of business expertise, and find engaging articles or information to share via other social media accounts. Use this to draw interest and then pull people back to your storefront.

Create eBay discounts for people who re-tweet posts about your promotions. For example, "15% off for RT of this post."

Blogging: Use a blog to write about information relevant to your business, and link posts to eBay items, sales, promotions, and your storefront. Use keywords and blog tags to drive traffic to your blog content and then back to your business.

Do not limit yourself to these three examples; you can use these basic techniques on any social media platform. Be sure that you have a following on whatever platform you choose, and be sure to refer to Chapter 10 to see the demographics on what kind of audience each platform has.

Creating coupons

Another great way to utilize social media and external Web sources to promote your business is to offer something called a "codeless" coupon. These are sales that potential buyers are only eligible for if they visit your store through a link you offer them.

The great thing about offers like this is that they make the customer feel special, because they are somewhat exclusive offers that are not visible on your general eBay store. You can create a codeless coupon through the "Marketing" section of your account tools, similar to how you set up other promotions for your items. Select "codeless coupons" under the promotions section on the left toolbar. Then, select a minimum (this can be a quantity or amount). You will then be prompted to create inclusion rules. In other words, does this coupon apply to your entire store, just one category, or to specific items? You can also create exclusion rules, which allow you to to apply it to your entire store except one category, for example.

After this, you will create the text to describe the sale to customers who would get this coupon. For example, "$20 off a $100 purchase of cell phone accessories, excluding Apple brand products."

After this, you will set a schedule for the coupon. You can choose to have the promotion start immediately or at a later date. Then you are able to select an image to go with the promotion. Choose a great image, as this is your chance to add excitement about this special deal you are offering.

Becoming a "Top Rated Seller"

The Top Rated Seller status on eBay is more than just a flashy label. There are a multitude of benefits to earning a Top Rated Seller rating, and it is best to aim for this rating from the launch of your eBay store.

Some of the benefits of this rating include getting ranked higher in searches and therefore more potential exposure and sales, and the customer confidence that is automatically achieved when they see the Top Rated Seller icon on each of your items and on your storefront. You also qualify for a 20% reduction in selling fees and USPS commercial discounts, which can add up quickly if you are selling and shipping items at a high volume.

How do you earn the Top Rated Seller status? There are sales requirements, shipping requirements, and transaction defect rater requirements. A seller must be active for 90 days before becoming eligible; this is so that eBay knows that their performance levels are consistent. They also must have at least 100 total sales in the most recent twelve-month period, and $1000 of sales in that time period. These can be earned in the first 90 days to make the seller eligible.

EBay also looks at fulfillment, or whether items are being processed and shipped appropriately. A seller must enter tracking information for all their shipments within one business day, although this excludes weekends and holidays. This is calculated not from when the item is bid on or when it sells, but from when the buyer actually completes their payment. There also must be shipping information for each additional item, even if these were shipped together. In this case, a seller would just enter the same tracking number for each item.

The third thing eBay looks at is transaction defect rate. One stars, two stars, three stars, neutral, or negative general feedback are considered "defective" by eBay standards, as are returns because the item was not as described, or any eBay guarantee case opened against the seller. Seller cancelled orders are also considered defective, as these generally mean the seller listed something that was not available, and is potentially damaging the reputation of the eBay selling community. Only 2% of transactions can be defective in order to qualify for the Top Rated Seller status. In order to have your Top Rated Seller status featured on your item listings, you also must have both a 14-day return policy and offer one business day handling on items.

Becoming a "Power Seller"

Not to be confused with the Top Rated Seller status, the Power Seller program is a different ranking system, but is also incredibly beneficial for growing one's business.

While Power Selling is mostly based on raw sales, numbers, and profits, Power Sellers must meet all the same requirements as a Top Rated Seller, have larger volume, and have impeccable customer service.

The bare minimum to become a Power Seller is to have $3000 in sales in the last 12 month period, as well as having only a 1% defect rating. Power Sellers are ranked in levels, with a bronze, silver, gold, platinum, or titanium status. Bronze is the beginning level, $3,000 or 100 transactions. To reach silver, a seller must jump to $36,000 or 3,600 transactions, gold is $120,000 or 12,000 transactions, platinum is $300,000 or 30,000, and titanium a whopping $1.8 million or 180,000 transactions.

Power Sellers receive the benefit of being able to have one-on-one consultations with an eBay representative to plan their business, receive unpaid item insurance which covers the relisting fees and any other fee losses if a buyer does not pay for their purchase, deeper shipping discounts, and promotional offers through eBay. Power Sellers may also get access to new features first as well as opportunities to participate in beta research of new marketing options. However, the top benefit of this is that Power Sellers get bumped to the top of the search, driving future sales and traffic.

Peak listing times

Another thing to consider when using eBay to market your small business is when you are going to list your items. It may seem unimportant, but listing items at times of peak traffic can create huge profit increases.

Peak visitor time on eBay is Sundays, as this tends to correlate with the least busiest day of the week for most people; however, Monday and Thursdays are also considered ideal. This is when they are most likely to sit down and browse eBay. Another thing to consider is what time zone you are likely to get the most traffic from. If your items sell on the US West Coast, for example, do not list them when it is too early or too late in the day for people to be online, because you have listed according to Central Standard Time. Make sure you are thinking of both time zones and your target demographic. Fridays are generally considered to be the worst days to list items on eBay, because people make plans to go out and are not paying attention to their phones or computers.

Using eBay guides and tutorials

Another useful feature that eBay has included on their site is the section with Buyer and Seller Resource Guides which are written by buyers and sellers. These are informative guides written by sellers for sellers and for buyers. They are full of easy to follow tips from seasoned eBay users, and may include topics that relate to your specific business. One of the reasons sellers write these is because eBay is a community, and they realize that in writing a guide, they may garner support from other sellers and therefore drive traffic. Sellers also often enjoy sharing the knowledge they have acquired as they have grown their business on eBay.

There is also the option to write your own buyer guide. These are useful for bringing customers to your store, especially if you have an expertise in the items you are selling and can offer information that makes selecting and purchasing easier for a potential buyer. For example, if you sell eyewear, you may write a guide on selecting the proper shape or size for one's face, or if you sell printers, you could write a guide on selecting the perfect printer for one's home or business.

The eBay website also offers tutorials in the form of videos and webinars, including videos on everything from holiday sales, to international sales, processing returns efficiently, and listing optimization. EBay radio is a streaming podcast service through eBay that also offers tips, tricks, and strategies, and can be useful to learn new ways to expand your business once you have mastered the basics.

Past audio is also archived for a greater amount of potential resources. All of these can be found in the seller resource section of eBay. Given the easy to use nature, the millions of users, and the endless potential of ways one can utilize eBay, the possibilities to advertise are potentially endless, as is the growth you can see if you continue to adapt your eBay store and listings, hone your skills, and aspire to reach as many customers as possible.

Chapter 14

Business Directories

W hen you are trying to promote your online or traditional brick and mortar business on the Internet, you will want to ensure that your business is listed in as many places as possible so that you have a better chance of reaching as many people as you can, and even more importantly, provide all possible resource avenues for them to reach you. You need to connect with a lot of potential customers before they become actual customers and you generate sales revenue from them.

Business directories can be found all over the Internet; in a sense, they are typically nothing more than search engines combined with Web-based white and yellow page services. The primary purpose of business directories is simple. They exist to help you find products, services, companies, jobs, and people.

Typically, the listing is free. Business directories, such as SuperPages and Yellow Pages can help send traffic to your Web pages, no matter what type of business you have. Directories place a listing of your business, product categories, website address, and other pertinent information into a consolidated listing that many people browse each day. Often times, people are looking for exactly what you are selling or the services you are offering, and they can locate you through a business directory.

You can find Web business directories that are specific to location, products or services, or by random selection. I highly recommend that you have your business listing in a variety of business directories so that you increase your chances of being noticed by Web visitors.

The following is a list of some of the more popular business directories that you can find on the Internet:

- **www.yellowpages.com**
- **www.business.com**
- **www.europages.com**
- **www.business-directory-uk.co.uk**
- **www.hoovers.com/free**
- **https://local.yahoo.com**

There are many more online business directories from which you can choose. An Internet search using any search engine will yield you many results, however, the business directories can provide more detailed information about a particular company or organization.

The Internet is a vast network where anyone can do business, exchange information, get an education, or search for any kind of data that they can imagine. With so much potential at your fingertips, it is important that you take advantage of being part of B2B Web communities, or, in some cases, B2C Web communities.

There are many different B2B Web communities on the Internet in which you can take part, and if you cannot find the right community for you and your business, you can build your own community. B2B is often used to describe websites that sell goods or services to other businesses. These businesses are serving other businesses as opposed to consumers.

The difference between a B2B e-commerce website and a B2B Web community is in the type of information and degree of functionality that is offered. A B2B Web community is a full-service centralized clearing house of data, which presents content such as news, industry analysis, email, purchasing, an industry-indexed search engine, trading exchanges, electronic storefronts, and career information, just to name a few.

A B2B Web community is a community that exists on the Internet much like a big virtual marketplace that centers on a specific topic, product, service, or other bits of information. Other functions that the B2B Web community can provide for you and your business are:

- Search engines within your product or service category
- A place to trade industry information
- A place to join discussion groups about your specific business
- A way for you to find out what the market value is of the products and services that you are selling

All of these elements combined are ways that you can improve your knowledge of the business, or industry, in which you are involved so that you can become more successful as a merchant.

The Internet is ever evolving. When I wrote the first edition of this book, Facebook, Twitter, Instagram, Pinterest, and LinkedIn did not exist, nor did social media. Blogs were a new and evolving trend, and selling products online was still in the infancy stage.

Today, we have modern e-commerce websites that dominate the market such as Amazon and eBay. You can shop from your computer, tablet, iPad, iPhone and every other brand, make, or model of smart phone.

I never envisioned that in under two years, you could shop for virtually anything while you were eating lunch. The most recent online sales volume from Amazon should tell you that more and more people are using the Internet for shopping, finding dining options, looking up product reviews, finding price comparisons, and virtually everything else, let alone all of the social media options available. Use available tools to promote and market your site. For example, if you are in the hospitality or tourism industry (restaurant, hotels, or travel), you should be keenly aware of TripAdvisor and Yelp; put extra emphasis into obtaining great reviews and providing personalized feedback to your customers. This is just an example of the many available social media and other outlets that you can use to boost the reputation of your business, ensure that you are easily found, and have rich information about your business that is relative and useful (hours, menus, prices, and features).

Using the Internet to advertise for your online or traditional business is all about using the right technique, having confidence, planning for success, and harnessing the power of tools that are available to you at little or no cost. Set clear, definitive goals, and strive to reach them. Promote your business through every avenue possible — most of them can be free and take little more than a time investment.

When you establish a web-based presence, you open the door to a world of potential customers, with minimal overhead and maximum return on investment. Times have changed, and so has this book. I have presented the best Web design techniques, tips, and hints to optimize your website for maximum search engine visibility, discussed website automation, and explained how to increase the amount of traffic that your website receives each day. This new addition adds a wealth of new information related to blogs, social media, email marketing and pay-per-click marketing opportunities. I am confident that you will find this book to be a useful reference as you grow and expand your online presence.

Take an organized approach to your online promotion and marketing; go one step at a time, slowly expand your brand, and develop a solid business plan for success. An organized, systematic approach will serve you well and yield tremendous results, all at little or no cost to you. I hope this updated revision to my very first book has helped to both educate you and arm you with the tools to grow your website and achieve unprecedented levels of success with your online ventures.

I highly recommend you build a quality reference library to assist you with your overall online promotion and marketing plans. While there are plenty of excellent books on the market, I definitely recommend you add the following to your library. All are available through Atlantic Publishing Company at **www.atlantic-pub.com**.

The Complete Guide to Google Advertising —Including Tips, Tricks, & Strategies to Create a Winning Advertising Plan

Are you one of the many who think Google is simply a search engine? Yes, it is true that Google is the most popular search engine on the Web today. More than 275 million times a day, people use Google and its related partner sites to find information on just about any subject. Many of those people are looking for your products and services. Consider this even if you do not have a website or product. There are tremendous opportunities on the Internet and money to be made using Google.

Google has created numerous marketing and advertising products that are fast and easy to implement in your business today including Adsense, Adwords, and the Google APIs. This new book takes the confusion and mystery out of working with Google and its various advertising and marketing programs. You will learn the secrets of working with Google—without making costly mistakes. This book is an absolute must-have for anyone who wants to succeed with advertising on Google. This book teaches you the ins and outs using all of Google's advertising and marketing tools. You will instantly start producing results and profits.

In addition to the extensive research placed in the book, we spent thousands of hours interviewing, emailing, and communicating with hundreds of today's most successful Google advertising experts. This book contains their secrets and proven successful ideas, including actual case studies. If you are interested in learning hundreds of hints, tricks, and secrets on how to implement effective Google marketing campaigns and ultimately earn enormous profits, then this book is for you. ISBN-10:1-60138-045-3 • ISBN-13:978-1-60138-045-6 • Item #9781601380456 • $14.95

Online Marketing Success Stories: Insider Secrets from the Experts Who Are Making Millions on the Internet Today

Standing out in the turmoil of today's Internet marketplace is a major challenge. There are many books and courses on Internet marketing; this is the only book that will provide you with insider secrets. We asked the marketing experts who make their living on the Internet every day—and they talked. Online Marketing Success Stories will give you real-life examples of how successful businesses market their products online. The information is so useful that you can read a page and put the idea into action—today! With e-commerce expected to reach $40 billion and online businesses anticipated to increase by 500 percent through 2010, your business needs guidance from today's successful Internet marketing veterans. Learn the most efficient ways to bring consumers to your site, get visitors to purchase, how to up-sell, oversights to avoid, and how to steer clear of years of disappointment.

We spent thousands of hours interviewing, emailing, and communicating with hundreds of today's most successful e-commerce marketers.

This book not only chronicles their achievements, but is a compilation of their secrets and proven successful ideas. If you are interested in learning hundreds of hints, tricks, and secrets on how to make money (or more money) with your website, then this book is for you. Instruction is great, but advice from experts is even better, and the experts chronicled in this book are earning millions. This new exhaustively researched book will provide you with a jam-packed assortment of innovative ideas that you can put to use today. This book gives you the proven strategies, innovative ideas, and actual case studies to help you sell more with less time and effort. ISBN-10: 0-910627-65-7 • ISBN-13: 978-0-910627-65-8 288 Pages • Item # 9780910627658 • $21.95

The Ultimate Guide to Search Engine Marketing: Pay Per Click Advertising Secrets Revealed

Is your ultimate goal to have more customers come to your website? You can increase your website traffic by more than 1,000 percent through the expert execution of Pay Per Click Advertising. With PPC advertising you are only drawing highly qualified visitors to your website! PPC brings you fast results and you can reach your target audience with the most cost effective method on the Internet today.

Pay per click, or PPC, is an advertising technique that uses search engines where you can display your text ads throughout the Internet keyed to the type of business you have or the type of products you are promoting. Successful PPC advertising ensures that your text ads reach the right audience while your business only pays for the clicks your ads receive!

Master the art and science behind Pay Per Click Advertising in a matter of hours. By investing a few dollars you can easily increase the number of visitors to your website and significantly increase sales! If you are looking to drive high quality, targeted traffic to your site, there is no better way than to use cost per click advertising. Since you only pay when someone actually clicks on your ad, your marketing dollars are being used more effectively and efficiently compared to any other advertising method.

By 2010, online marketers will spend $7 billion on PPC advertising (JupiterResearch). Thousands of companies will waste precious advertising dollars this year on ineffective or poorly organized PPC campaigns. There is an art form to this method of advertising, and that is what this new book is all about. In this book we show you the secrets of executing a successful, cost-effective campaign.

The key to success in PPC advertising is to know what you are doing, devise a comprehensive and well-crafted advertising plan, and know the relationships between your website, search engines, and PPC advertising campaign methodology. This groundbreaking and exhaustively researched new book will provide everything you need to know to get you started on generating high-volume, high quality leads to your website. This new book will teach you the six steps to a successful campaign: Keyword Research, Copy Editing, Setup and Implementation, Bid Management, Performance Analysis, Return on Investment, and Reporting and Avoiding PPC Fraud.

In addition, we spent thousands of hours interviewing hundreds of today's most successful PPC masters. This book is a compilation of their secrets and proven successful ideas. Additionally, we give you hundreds of tips and tricks to ensure your website is optimized for maximum search engine effectiveness to drive business to your website and increase sales and profits. In this book you will find actual case studies from companies who have used our techniques and achieved unprecedented success. If you are interested in learning hundreds of hints, tricks, and secrets on how to implement Pay Per Click advertising, optimize your website for maximum search engine effectiveness, develop a cost-effective marketing campaign, and ultimately earn enormous profits, then this book is for you. ISBN-10:0-910627-99-1 • ISBN-13:978-0-910627-99-3 • Item #9780910627993 • $ 9.95

The Complete Guide to Email Marketing: How to Create Successful, Spam-Free Campaigns to Reach Your Target Audience and Increase Sales

Researchers estimate that by 2008 email marketing revenues will surpass $1.8 billion annually. Are you getting your share? According to Jupiter Research, 93 percent of U.S. Internet users consider email their top online activity. Email is a fast, inexpensive, and highly effective way to target and address your audience. Companies like Microsoft, Amazon.com, Yahoo, as well as most Fortune 1000 firms are using responsible email marketing for one simple reason. It works! And it generates profits immediately and consistently!

In this groundbreaking book you will learn how to create top-notch email marketing campaigns, how to build stronger customer relationships, generate new qualified leads and sales, learn insider secrets to build your email list quickly, deal with spam filters, and the optimum days and times to send your emails.

You will have step-by-step ways to:

- Build your business quickly using responsible, ethical email marketing,
- Leverage your current website, using auto responders
- Write effective email advertising copy
- Develop newsletters
- Write winning subject lines
- Get high click-through rates
- Format your messages
- Put the subscription form on your site
- Use pop ups
- Use single or double opt-in subscriptions
- Increase the response rate of your offer dramatically
- Format your email so that it will be received and read
- Choose between text or HTML email (and why)

- Reduce advertising expenses
- Have measurable marketing results with instant feedback
- Automate the whole email marketing process

In addition, we spent thousands of hours interviewing, emailing, and communicating with hundreds of today's most successful email marketing experts. This book contains their secrets and proven successful ideas, including actual case studies. If you are interested in learning hundreds of hints, strategies, and secrets on how to implement effective email marketing campaigns and ultimately earn enormous profits, then this book is for you. ISBN-10:978-1-60138-042-5 • ISBN-13:1-60138-042-9 • Item #9781601380425 • $14.95

How to Open and Operate a Financially Successful Web-Based Business (With Companion CD-ROM)

With e-commerce expected to reach $40 billion and online businesses anticipated to increase by 500 percent through the year 2010, you need to be a part of this exploding area of Internet sales. If you want to learn about starting a Web business, how to transform your brick and mortar business to a Web business, or even if you're simply interested in making money online, this is the book for you.

You can operate your Web-based business from home and with very little start up money. The earning potential is limitless. This new book will teach you all you need to know about getting started in your own Web-based business in the minimum amount of time. This book is a comprehensive, detailed study of the business side of Internet retailing. Anyone investigating the opportunities of opening a Web-based business should study this superb manual.

While providing detailed instruction and examples, the author teaches you how to draw up a winning business plan (The Companion CD-ROM has the actual business plan you can use in MS Word), basic cost control systems, pricing issues, legal concerns, sales and marketing techniques, and pricing formulas. You will learn how to set up computer systems to save time and money, how to hire and keep a qualified professional staff, meet IRS reporting requirements, plan sales, provide customer service, track competitors, do your own bookkeeping, monthly profit and loss statements, media planning, pricing, and copywriting. You will develop the skill to hire and fire employees without incurring lawsuits, motivate workers, apply general management skills, manage and train employees, and generate high profile public relations and publicity. You will have the advantage low cost internal marketing ideas and low and no cost ways to satisfy customers and build sales. Learn how to keep bringing customers back, accomplish accounting, do bookkeeping procedures and auditing, as well as successful budgeting and profit planning development.

This manual delivers literally hundreds of innovative ways demonstrated to streamline your business. Learn new ways to make your operation run smoother and increase performance, shut down waste, reduce costs, and increase profits. In addition, you will appreciate this valuable resource and reference in your daily activities and as a source of ready-to-use forms, websites, and operating and cost-cutting ideas that can be easily applied to your operation. 978-1-60138-118-7 1-60138-118-2 Item #9781601381187 $14.95

The Secret Power of Blogging: How to Promote and Market Your Business, Organization, or Cause with Free Blogs

Blog is short for weblog. A weblog is a journal (or type of newsletter) that is updated often and intended for the general public. Blogs generally represent the personality of the author or the website. In July 2006 the Pew Internet & American Life Project estimated that the US "blog population has grown to about 12 million American adults," some 8% of US adult Internet users. The number of US blog readers was estimated at 57 million adults (39% of the US online population).

If you have a product, service, brand or cause that you want to inexpensively market online to the world then you need to look into starting a blog. Blogs are ideal marketing vehicles. You can use them to share your expertise, grow market share, spread your message and establish yourself as an expert in your field, for virtually no cost. A blog helps your site to rank higher in the search engines. This is because Google and the other search engines use blogs because of their constantly updated content.

Tiny, one-person part time businesses use blogs as well as companies like Microsoft, Apple, Nike, General Motors, Amazon, and Yahoo!. Most Fortune 1000 firms are using responsible Blogs and Blog marketing as well as advertising on blogs for one simple reason — it works! And it generates profits immediately and consistently. In addition many blogs earn additional revenue by selling advertising space on their niche-targeted blog.

In this new groundbreaking book you will learn how to create top-notch Blog marketing campaigns, how to build stronger customer relationships, generate new qualified leads and sales, learn insider secrets to build your readership list quickly.

In addition, we spent thousands of hours interviewing, emailing, and communicating with hundreds of today's most successful Blogging experts. This book contains their secrets and proven successful ideas, including actual case studies. If you are interested in learning hundreds of hints, strategies, and secrets on how to implement a highly effective blog marketing campaigns and ultimately earn enormous profits, then this book is for you. • 978-1-60138-009-8 • 1-60138-009-7 ITEM #9781601380098 • $14.95

Word of Mouth Advertising Online & Off: How to Spark Buzz, Excitement, and Free Publicity for Your Business or Organization-With Little or No Money

Word-of-Mouth Marketing, "WOMM" as it is commonly known, is the least expensive form of advertising and often the most effective. People believe what their friends, neighbors, and online contacts say about you, your products, and services. And they remember it for a long, long time.

Word-of-mouth promotion is highly valued. There is no more powerful form of marketing than an endorsement from one of your current customers. A satisfied customer's recommendation has much greater value than traditional advertising because it is coming from someone who is familiar with the quality of your work.

The best part is that initiating this form of advertising costs little or no money. For WOMM to increase your business, you need an active plan in place and do what is necessary to create buzz. If your business is on the Web, there are myriads of possibilities for starting a highly successful viral marketing campaign using the Internet, software, blogs, online activists, press releases, discussion forums and boards, affiliate marketing, and product sampling. Technology has dramatically changed traditional marketing programs. This new up-to-date book covers it all.

This all sounds great, but what is the catch? There really is none, except you must know what you are doing! This groundbreaking and exhaustively researched new book will provide everything you need to know to get you started creating the "buzz" — free publicity about your product or service whether online or off.

In this easy to read and comprehensive new book you will learn what WOMM is, how to get people talking about your product or service, how to get your customers to be your sales force, how to get WOMM to spread quickly, how to automate WOMM, how to create a blog, create awareness, and how to amplify it. The entire process is covered here: marketing, dealing with negative customer experience, writing online press releases, creating a customer reference program, bringing together a fan club/loyalist community, naming VIPs, using flogs (photos), and spurring evangelism among influential people. Included are tactics that pertain especially to non-profits, including reputation management.

In addition, we have gone the extra mile and spent an unprecedented amount of time researching, interviewing, emailing, and communicating with hundreds of today's most successful WOMM marketers. Aside from learning the basics you will be privy to their secrets and proven successful ideas.

Instruction is great, but advice from experts is even better, and the experts chronicled in this book are earning millions. If you are interested in learning essentially everything there is to know about WOMM in addition to hundreds of hints, tricks, and secrets on how to put WOMM marketing techniques in place and start earning enormous profits, then this book is for you. Item # 9781601380111 $12.95

How to Open & Operate a Financially Successful website Design Business: With Companion CD-ROM

According to a 2007 survey by Netcraft, there are more than 108 million websites worldwide. Every website needs to be designed. The Pricing & Ethical Guidelines Handbook published by the Graphic Arts Guild reports that the average cost of designing a website for a small corporation can range from $7,750 to $15,000. It is incredibly easy to see the enormous profit potential.

Web design businesses can be run part- or full-time and can easily be started in your own home. As such, they are one of the fastest growing segments of the Internet economy. This new book will teach you all you need to know about getting your own website design business started in the minimum amount of time.

Here is the manual you need to cash in on this highly profitable segment of the industry. This new book is a comprehensive and detailed study of the business side of website design. This superb manual should be studied by anyone investigating the opportunities of opening a Web design business and will arm you with everything you need, including sample business forms, contracts, worksheets and checklists for planning, opening, and running day-to-day operations, plans and layouts, and dozens of other valuable, time-saving tools that no entrepreneur should be without.

While providing detailed instructions and examples, the author leads you through finding a location that will bring success, drawing up a winning business plan (the Companion CD-ROM has the actual business plan that can be used in MS Word), buying (and selling) a Web design store, pricing formulas, sales planning, tracking competitors, bookkeeping, media planning, pricing, copy writing, hiring and firing employees, motivating workers, managing and training employees, accounting procedures, successful budgeting, and profit planning development.

By reading this book, you will become knowledgeable about basic cost control systems, retail math and pricing issues, website plans and diagrams, software and equipment layout and planning, legal concerns, sales and marketing techniques, IRS reporting requirements, customer service, direct sales, monthly profit and loss statements, tax preparation, public relations, general management skills, low and no cost ways to satisfy customers and build sales, and low cost internal marketing ideas, as well as thousands of great tips and useful guidelines.

The manual delivers literally hundreds of innovative ways to streamline your business. Learn new ways to make your operation run smoother and increase performance. Shut down waste, reduce costs, and increase profits. Business owners will appreciate this valuable resource and reference it in their daily activities as a source for ready-to-use forms, websites, operating and cost cutting ideas, and mathematical formulas that can be easily applied. The Companion CD-ROM contains all the forms in the book, as well as a sample business plan you can adapt for your own use. Item# 9781601381439 $29.95

The Complete Guide to Writing Web-Based Advertising Copy to Get the Sale: What You Need to Know Explained Simply

Since the advent of the Internet and since more and more people are making purchases online, writers have had to adapt to composing copy for the Web. Contrary to what many people think, writing for the Web and writing for print are not the same and involve very different skill sets. Instead of struggling to find the right words, copywriters should read this new book from cover to cover to discover how to write sales-generating copy.

The Complete Guide to Writing Web-based Advertising Copy to Get the Sale will teach you how to make your copy readable and compelling, how to reach your target audience, how to structure the copy, how to visually format the copy, how to forget everything you ever learned about writing, how to pull in visitors, how to convince visitors to buy, how to outline and achieve your goals, how to create a customer profile, how to create a unique selling position, how to include searchable keywords in the copy, how to convert prospects to paying customers, and how to compose eye-catching headlines.

In addition, you will learn about the trends in Web-based advertising; the categories of advertising; the important information that needs to be included in your copy, such as what you are selling, what sets your product apart from the competition's, where you are located, what makes your product affordable, and why you yourself would buy the product; writing in the inverted pyramid style; the do's and don'ts of Web-based advertising; and key phrases to incorporate in your copy. We will also provide you with some common mistakes to avoid and tips for writing, revising, and proofreading.

By incorporating the principles in this book, you will take your Web-based advertising copy from boring to brilliant, while boosting your sales and increasing your customer traffic. Item# 9781601382320 $12.95

Internet Marketing Revealed: The Complete Guide to Becoming an Internet Marketing Expert

Internet Marketing Revealed is a carefully tested, well-crafted, and complete tutorial on a subject vital to Web developers and marketers. This book teaches the fundamentals of online marketing implementation, including Internet strategy planning, the secrets of search engine optimization (SEO), successful techniques to be first in Google and Yahoo!, vertical portals, effective online advertisement, and innovative e-commerce development. This book will help you understand the e-business revolution as it provides strong evidence and practical direction in a friendly and easy-to-use self-study guide.

Respected author and educator Miguel Todaro has created a complete introduction to Internet marketing that is instructive, clear, and insightful. This book is the result of several years of research and deep professional experience implementing online solutions for major corporations. Written in an instructive way, you will find fundamental concepts explained along with detailed diagrams. Many short examples illustrate just one or two concepts at a time, encouraging you to master new topics by immediately putting them to use.

Furthermore, you will find a variety of teaching techniques to enhance your learning, such as notes, illustrations, conceptual guidance, checklists of learned topics, diagrams, advanced tips, and real-world examples to organize and prioritize related concepts. This book is appropriate for marketing professionals as well as Web developers and programmers who have the desire to better understand the principles of this fresh and extraordinary activity that represents the foundation of modern e-commerce.

Finally, you will learn and understand why big and mid-size corporations in North America have redistributed more than $15 billion of their advertising budgets from traditional promotional activities to Internet marketing initiatives. Discover why online users spent more than $112 billion last year (U.S. and Canada) and how you can be part of this successful business highway that is redefining the future of the world's digital economy. Item # 9781601382658 $15.95.

Online Marketing Success Stories: Insider Secrets from the Experts Who Are Making Millions on the Internet Today

Standing out in the turmoil of today's Internet marketplace is a major challenge. There are many books and courses on Internet marketing; this is the only book that will provide you with insider secrets. We asked the marketing experts who make their living on the Internet every day — and they talked. Online Marketing Success Stories will give you real-life examples of how successful businesses market their products online. The information is so useful that you can read a page and put the idea into action — today!

With e-commerce expected to reach $40 billion and online businesses anticipated to increase by 500 percent through 2010, your business needs guidance from today's successful Internet marketing veterans. Learn the most efficient ways to bring consumers to your site, get visitors to purchase, how to up-sell, oversights to avoid, and how to steer clear of years of disappointment.

In addition, we spent thousands of hours interviewing hundreds of today's most successful affiliate marketing masters. This book is a compilation of their secrets and proven successful ideas. Additionally, we give you hundreds of tips and tricks to ensure your website is optimized for maximum search engine effectiveness, which will drive business to your website and increase sales and profits. You will find actual case studies from companies who have used our techniques and achieved unprecedented success. If you are interested in learning hundreds of hints, tricks, and secrets on how to implement affiliate marketing, optimizing your website for maximum search engine effectiveness, developing a cost-effective marketing campaign, and ultimately earning enormous profits, this book is for you. Item# 9781601381255 $15.95

Amazon Income: How Anyone of Any Age, Location, and/or Background Can Build a Highly Profitable Online Business with Amazon

The Internet affiliate program industry is one of the largest and fastest growing digital revenue generators in the world, with more than $65 billion in total income brought in during the 2006 fiscal year. It is because of programs like Amazon's Associate program, which has been around for more than a decade, and allows casual, every day users of the Internet to install widgets and links on their websites that link back to Amazon products. Users like you can earn commissions of up to 15% on products that your website visitors purchase when they visit Amazon. With the world's largest online retailer as a potential source of income, you can make generate endless streams of income as a result.

No matter where you are from, how old you are, and what your background is, you can build and run a highly profitable business with Amazon. This comprehensive book is written to show you exactly how to do so. You will learn every detail necessary to complete the transformation from casual Internet user to Amazon guru in just a matter of weeks, making unfathomable amounts of money by selling Amazon products, your own products, starting a store, promoting outside projects, and making referrals.

In this book, you will learn how the Amazon business model works and how much money they will pay you in multiple different ways. You will learn how to build a traffic funneling website with dozens of free tools such as blogs, podcasts, videos, and social networks that will allow you to increase the number of visitors you can send to Amazon in no time for minimal investment. You will learn how to take advantage of the brand new Amazon Kindle program and its revolutionary take on digital distribution of books and newspapers. You will learn what you can do to start your own store in the Amazon Marketplace, selling products at set prices to anyone in the world in much the same way you could on eBay with substantially more freedom.

Learn how to publish your own books on Amazon with little to no investment and use the features Amazon provides such as Search Inside and digital distribution to reach more people faster than you could anywhere else. In addition, learn how you can take advantage of multimedia services on Amazon such as Advantage that allow you to publish your own music, videos, and professional titles around the globe. Learn how to use Amazon Connect effectively to promote your products and reach potential customers and how Amazon provides dozens of additional methods by which you can advertise your products without outside investments.

You will learn how to choose a niche to market towards and what you need to create in your website to make your visitors more willing to click your links and purchase the products you are promoting or selling on Amazon. Hours of extensive research and interviews with the top Amazon associates and independent authors has given us countless pieces of advice that will ensure your marketing and promotion methods allow you to generate traffic, promote products, and convert sales at a rate that will help you build a successful business in no time. If you have been looking for the resource that will undoubtedly help you break free of the shackles of your job and start working from home, this guide is that resource and Amazon is your ideal income source. Item#9781601382993 $14.95

The Small Business Owner's Handbook to Search Engine Optimization: Increase Your Google Rankings, Double Your Site Traffic...In Just 15 Steps - Guaranteed!

The Small Business Owner's Handbook to Search Engine Optimization is ideal for small business owners who want to learn an efficient and effective process for dramatically improving their website's search engine rankings and doubling their site's monthly unique visitors. Guaranteed! Stephen Woessner, of the University of Wisconsin-La Crosse Small Business Development Center, is a search engine optimization (SEO) expert. But more importantly, Woessner has owned four businesses and understands the significant time and cash constraints faced by business owners every day. Because of this, Woessner placed increasing efficiency and effectiveness at the core of the 15-steps allowing a business owner to maximize results in as little time as possible.

A business owner does not need to know technical skills, like Web programming, to be successful at SEO. Instead, business owners will rely on their marketing skill and the ability to think like their customers and prospects, versus an ability to write HTML or other form of Web programming. Business owners will learn how to select keywords that are proven performers, blend the keywords into site content, boost site popularity, and more. Woessner explains with precision how business owners can use SEO to achieve measurable results. This practical and tactical guide includes a free SEO toolkit and other valuable resources that will help business owners increase the return on investment generated by their websites. Business owners will also receive a detailed blueprint with specific checklists to follow throughout the 15-step process.

Lastly, this book can also serve as an excellent resource to business owners who are considering outsourcing their SEO work to a third-party. Developing a working knowledge of the 15-step process will make any business owner a more informed consumer. This book is also an ideal resource for marketing and advertising agency professionals who want to expand their services and need to develop a proficiency in SEO as efficiently and effectively as possible. Item #9781601384430 $9.95.

Google Income How Anyone of Any Age, Location, and/or Background Can Build a Highly Profitable Online Business with Google

Google is the largest Internet company in the world. In the 2006 fiscal year, they managed to generate more than $6 billion in profit and more than 90% of that income is generated through the use of their advertising program AdWords, a program that paid out more than $3 billion in the same year to advertising partners. The opportunity to make money with Google is so great that entire companies have been built around working with the search and advertising giant and if you are properly situated, you can tap into that market and start generating your own massive profits.

There are dozens of ways to start making money with Google and because of its digital nature, anyone can do it from anywhere in the world. This book leaves absolutely no stone unturned in cataloging for you every possible method through which you can generate and maintain steady income streams through the world's largest search engine.

Starting with a fundamental discussion of why your online business is different from any form of business ever run in history, you will learn everything you need to know to use Google to create and run your business online. Google's ample supply of tools in the form of Google Base will allow you to list, promote, and sell products that will provide you the foundation of a solid business and this book will walk you through the process of utilizing that service.

You will learn how to utilize Google Base to list a single item at a time, or to create an entire store front. You will learn how to tap into Google's API and create your own high quality, customized storefront that is unlike anything you have worked with before. Learn how to use your own XML and spreadsheet files for quick product descriptions and a streamlined interface while taking advantage of Google's dozens of different posting categories such as Housing, Vehicles, Services, Jobs, and Vacation Rentals.

You will learn how craft a winning listing, utilizing the right balance of carefully selected information, well placed imagery, and the right target audience. You will learn how to optimize your postings to work in tandem with your websites and to rank highly in Google's most up to date search algorithm. You will also learn how to start implementing Google's swarm of services such as YouTube, Blogger, Orkut, and Gmail to promote and build your business across multiple social and interactive Web platforms, drawing traffic and attention from every corner of the Web.

With the help of Web and business experts and many in-depth interviews, we have compiled chapter after chapter of advice that will guide you through the process of understanding the inner workings of Google's business and advertising opportunities, as well as how you can best market your business within those tools. A special chapter is included to guide you through the tricky labyrinth of mistakes that can actually hurt you when selling and marketing through Google, ensuring that you consistently make the most of your postings and marketing efforts. For any business, new or old, looking to the Internet as a tool, this book is an essential resource to help you make money, take advantage of Google's countless resources, and stay on top of the multibillion-dollar e-commerce industry. Item#9781601383006 $15.95

Marketing in a Web 2.0 World - Using Social Media, Webinars, Blogs, and more to Boost Your Small Business on a Budget

Social networking started as a small idea that was novel but not necessarily viable to making money or promoting business. But, then a major change occurred. Starting in 2003 and continuing through 2007 and 2008, sites like MySpace.com and Facebook.com have exploded to become two of the biggest, most powerful social networking hubs on the Internet and the two single most powerful marketing tools at many business owners' fingertips with more than 350 million combined accounts between the two. Providing unparalleled, technologically enhanced means to reach demographics in ways that was never before possible, businesses small or large can reach their target audience quickly and effectively through social networks and sites and yours can be part of the revolution with the right tips.

In this book, a map to huge success in marketing and promoting your business is provided that, without you needing to spend nearly any money, will allow you to take your business to all new heights. You will learn how the social Web and the various social networks that make it up has fundamentally altered how the Internet is used as a marketing tool, allowing businesses to reach out and touch their target demographics like never before. You will learn how to recognize and start optimizing to reach those demographics and how to fundamentally understand how they use the social Web and what they use it for. You will find out how the social Web became a business resource, first for musicians and then for Fortune 500 companies. Details about Facebook and MySpace as the two biggest sources of potential new customers along with why this is not a fad, but is a fundamental shift in how business should be done will be laid out in great detail.

Dozens of individuals have been interviewed for this book, providing their expert opinions on how the social Web has developed and what it will mean for the future of business marketing and promotion. You will learn how the perspective of marketing firms in major companies across the world has changed and how viral marketing is now the buzz word of the industry. You will learn how to utilize videos and podcasts alongside topnotch Web copywriting to reach your target audience and most importantly you will learn where experts see the future of the industry going so you can get a head start on the next big shifts in technology. For any business or individual with a big dream, this book is a must have – showing you how to take advantage of the top new business technology in more than two decades. #9781601383174 $14.95

eBay Income: How ANYONE of Any Age, Location and/or Background Can Build a Highly Profitable Online Business with eBay

EBay has changed the way products and services are purchased all over the world. Daily over 1.5 million online customers and providers log on to bid and sell virtually anything that can be bought or purchased. In 2006 eBay sellers are estimated to post $22 billion in sales. There are businesses earning $1 million a year selling products on eBay today. It is estimated that more than half a million people make full-time incomes just with their eBay business. EBay also allows you to run a business that requires no advertising costs. This expertly written new book will show you how to take advantage of this business phenomenon and arm you with the proper knowledge and insider secrets. Filled with actual examples and antidotes from real eBay entrepreneurs, this book is as engaging as it is informational.

EBay is a level playing field — it does not matter how old you are, what nationality or income level, whether you own a business now or not, what your background is, or where you are located. Start making money on eBay today!

The book starts with a complete overview of how eBay works. Then you are guided through the whole process of creating the auction and auction strategies, photography, writing copy, text and formatting, managing auctions, shipping, collecting payments, registering, About Me page, sources for merchandise, multiple sales, programming tricks, PayPal, accounting, creating marketing, merchandising, managing email lists, advertising plans, taxes and sales tax, best time to list items and for how long, sniping programs, international customers, opening a storefront, electronic commerce, buy-it now pricing, keywords, Google marketing, and eBay secrets; everything you will ever need to get started making money on eBay! ISBN-10: 0-910627-58-4 • ISBN-13: 978-0-910627-58-0 288 Pages • Item # 9780910627580 • $9.95

How to Build Your Own Web Site With Little or No Money The Complete Guide for Business and Personal Use

Websites are an essential tool that every business must have in today's economy. Only 15 years ago, you could count the number of websites in the world with five or six digits; today there are between 15 and 30 billion active websites and millions more being added every day. Creating a website can be a great way to market a new product, promote your business plan, promote yourself, or simply share a few details about your life with the world.

The cost of creating a website has risen right alongside the number of websites created though and many people are nervous about being able to utilize this revolutionary medium without breaking the bank. This book has been created for just such people, outlining for you in perfect detail everything you need to know to create a traffic attracting website, while spending little or no money at all. There are countless resources available, and when you put them all together, they provide a complete toolkit that can make anyone a top notch website in no time flat.

You will learn how to buy a domain name and host your website for less than $15, with no additional fees charged to your account. You will learn how to use open source software like Wordpress, Joomla, and Mambo to create a platform on which you can build anything you want. You will learn how blogging has made website creation easier than ever and how sites like Squidoo, Facebook, and MySpace allow you more freedom to build traffic and draw more attention to what you are advertising at any given time.

You will learn how to use common software to edit and tweak your websites and how to read the basic code that all websites are created in. In addition, an entire chapter is devoted to teaching you how to promote your website and draw traffic to it, without spending a dime in the process. You will learn why information is the most valuable asset on the market and how you can become an expert in a niche of your choosing, making money to cover any fees associated with your website.

With the added resource of hours of interviews with Web professionals you will learn which free resources not to use and which ones to outright avoid, as well as how to find and install open source modules and tools to enhance the look and feel of your site. You will learn where you can find copyright free images to use on your websites and how to get free copy that will draw traffic and entertain your visitors. You will learn how to keep a free website from falling into the traps the major search engines set to stop spam and ultimately how to leverage new friends, business contacts, and interactions out of your website. If you are now, or have ever, considered starting your own website before, this book will map the way for you. Item#9781601383044 $19.95

Glossary

Above the fold: A term borrowed from print media; refers to an ad that is viewable as soon as the Web page arrives. You do not have to scroll down (or sideways) to see it. Since screen resolution can affect what is immediately viewable, it is good to know whether the website's audience tends to set their resolution at 640 by 480 pixels or at 800 by 600 (or higher).

Accessibility: The degree that a website can be accessed by people with disabilities.

Ad: For Web advertising, this is almost always a banner, a graphic image, or a set of animated images (a GIF) of a designated pixel size and byte size limit. An ad or set of ads for a campaign is often referred to as "the creative." Banners and other special advertising that include an interactive or visual element beyond the usual are known as rich media.

Ad impression: This occurs when a user pulls up a Web page through a browser and sees an ad that is served on that page. Many websites sell advertising space by ad impressions. Also referred to as an ad view.

Ad rotation: Ads are often rotated into ad spaces from a list. This is usually done automatically by software on the website or at a central site administered by an ad broker or server facility for a network of websites.

Ad space: This is a space on a Web page that is reserved for ads. An ad space group is a group of spaces within a website that share the same characteristics so that an ad purchase can be made for the group of spaces.

Ad stream: The series of advertisements viewed by the user during a single visit to a site.

Ad view: A single ad that appears on a Web page when the page arrives at the viewer's display. Ad views are what most websites sell or prefer to sell. A Web page may offer space for a number of ad views. Also referred to as an **ad impression**.

Affiliate: The publisher/salesperson in a partnered marketing relationship.

Affiliate directory: A categorized listing of affiliate programs.

Affiliate forum: An online community where visitors may read and post topics related to affiliate marketing.

Affiliate fraud: Bogus activity generated by an affiliate in an attempt to generate illegitimate, unearned revenue.

Affiliate marketing: Revenue sharing between online advertisers/merchants and online publishers/salespeople, whereby compensation is based on performance measures, typically in the form of sales, clicks, registrations, or a hybrid model. Affiliate marketing is the use by a website that sells products of other websites, called affiliates, to help market the products. Amazon.com, the bookseller, created the first large-scale affiliate program, and hundreds of other companies have followed since.

Affiliate merchant: The advertiser in an affiliate marketing relationship.

Affiliate network: A value-added intermediary providing services, including aggregation, for affiliate merchants and affiliates.

Affiliate software: Software that, at a minimum, provides tracking and reporting of commission-triggering actions (sales, registrations, or clicks) from affiliate links.

Animated GIF: A GIF file that is animated or has motion.

Apache: A popular Web server.

Bandwidth: A measure of how fast data can be transferred between two computers.

Banner: A form of a graphic image that typically runs across a Web page or is positioned in a margin or other space reserved for ads. Banner ads are usually Graphics Interchange Format (GIF) images. In addition to adhering to size, many websites limit the size of the file to a certain number of bytes so that the file will display quickly. Most ads are animated GIFs since animation has been shown to attract a larger percentage of user clicks.

Behaviorally Targeted Advertising: A method of compiling data on Web visitors, such as surfing history, gender, age, and personal preferences, to later target them with tailored ads.

Beyond the Banner: This is the idea that, in addition to banner ads, there are other ways to use the Internet to communicate a marketing message. These include sponsoring a website or a particular feature on it, advertising in email newsletters, co-branding with another company and its website, contest promotion, and, in general, finding new ways to engage and interact with the desired audience.

Blacklist: Lists of URLs identified as spam URLs and therefore eliminated from comments and trackbacks on a blog.

Blammer: A blog spammer.

Blaudience: The audience of a blog.

Blawg: A blog about the law.

Bleg: A blog or blog post consisting of a request to readers of the blog for ideas.

Blego: The self-worth of a blogger, as measured by the popularity of their blog; a combination of the words "blog" and "ego."

Blog: Short form for weblog. This is a public website with posts or entries ordered, most often, with the most recent first. Blogs generally represent the personality of the author or reflect the purpose of the website that hosts the blog. It also means to maintain a blog by posting text, links, images or other content using blogging software.

Blog client: An application that allows a blogger to post, edit, format and perform a variety of functions for a blog or blogs without launching a browser.

Blog Digest: A blog whose purpose is to summarize other blogs.

Blog feed: The XML-based file into which blog hosting software embeds a machine-readable version of a blog to allow it to be syndicated for distribution, often through RSS and Atom.

Blog hopping: To jump from one blog to another.

Blog mute: Someone who only occasionally blogs.

Blog roach: A commenter who rudely disagrees with all posted content.

Blog site: The online location of a blog.

Blog: This Allows a blogger to blog the entry they a reading.

Blog troll: A blogger who wants attention.

Blogathy: This refers to the following sentiment: "I don't want to post today and I don't care."

Blogger: A person who creates and posts to a blog.

Blogger bash: A party for bloggers.

Blogger.com: A popular, free blog hosting website.

Bloggies: Annual blogging awards.

Blogging: The act of posting on blogs.

Blogiversary: The anniversary of a blog's founding.

Blogography: The profile section of a blog, usually containing a biography of the blogger.

Blogoholic: A blogger addicted to blogging.

Blogophobia: Fear of blogs and blogging.

Blogopotamus: A very long blog article.

Blogorrhea: An unusually high volume output of articles on a blog.

Blogosphere: The Internet blogging community. The collective content of all blogs worldwide.

Blogroll: A list of blog links, usually placed in the sidebar of a blog, that reads as a list of recommendations by the blogger of other blogs.

Blogsit: To maintain a blog while the blog's original or primary author is not available (comparable to pet sitting).

Blogsite: A website that combines blog feeds from a number of different sources including non-blog sources.

Blogsnob: A blogger that is unwilling to acknowledge comments on a blog from anyone outside of his or her circle of friends.

Blogspot: Hosting service for blogs operated by Blogger.com.

Blogstipation: Writer's block for bloggers.

Blogvert: A blog ad.

Blogvertising: Advertising that appears on a blog.

Blooger: Refers to a blogger acting like a teenager or in an otherwise immature or boorish manner.

Booked space: The number of ad views for an ad space that are currently sold out.

Brand, brand name, and branding: A brand is a product, service, or concept that is publicly distinguished from other products, services, or concepts so that it can be easily communicated and usually marketed. A brand name is the name of the distinctive product, service, or concept.

Branding is the process of creating and disseminating the brand name.

Browser: Software is used to view and locate websites on the World Wide Web.

Caching In: Internet advertising, the caching of pages in a cache server or the user's computer means that some ad views will not be known by the ad counting programs and is a source of concern. There are several techniques for telling the browser not to cache particular pages. On the other hand, specifying no caching for all pages may mean that users will find your site to be slower than you would like.

Campaign: This consists of one or more Ad Groups. The ads in a given campaign share the same daily budget, language and location targeting, end dates, and distribution options.

Cascading Style Sheet (CSS): A technology used to control the presentation and layout of a Web page.

Click: A click is when a visitor interacts with an advertisement by clicking on it.

Click rate: The click rate is the percentage of ad views that resulted in click-throughs. Although there is visibility and branding value in ad views that do not result in a click-through, this value is difficult to measure.

Click stream: A click stream is a recorded path of the pages a user requested in going through one or more websites. Click stream information can help website owners understand how visitors are using their site and which pages are getting the most use. It can help advertisers understand how users get to the client's pages, what pages they look at, and how they go about ordering a product.

Click-through: This is what is counted by the sponsoring site as a result of an ad click. In practice, click and click-through tend to be used interchangeably. A click-through, however, seems to imply that the user actually received the page. A few advertisers are willing to pay only for click-throughs rather than for ad impressions.

Client-side: Applications or software that are downloaded and run by the user's Web browser rather than on the Web server.

Co-branding: Co-branding on the Web often means two websites, website sections, or features displaying their logos, and thus their brands, together so that the viewer considers the site or feature to be a joint enterprise.

Co-branding: Co-branding on the Web often means two websites or website sections or features displaying their logos (and thus their brands) together so that the viewer considers the site or feature to be a joint enterprise. (Co-branding is often associated with cross-linking between the sites, although it is not necessary.)

Common Gateway Interface (CGI): Technology that lets a Web browser communicate with a program on the Web server.

Content Management System (CMS): A collection of tools designed to allow the creation, modification, organization, and removal of information from a website.

Conversion rate: The percentage of site visitors who respond to the desired goal of an ad campaign compared with the total number of people who see the ad campaign. The goal may be, for example, convincing readers to become subscribers, encouraging customers to buy something, or enticing prospective customers from another site with an ad.

Cookie: A small text file downloaded to a user's computer that can be used to track user activity on a website or to store user information about a visitor.

Cost-per-action (CPA): What an advertiser pays for each visitor that takes some specifically defined action in response to an ad beyond simply clicking on it. For example, a visitor might visit an advertiser's site and request to be subscribed to their newsletter.

Cost-per-click (CPC): The amount of money an advertiser will pay to a site each time a user clicks on an ad or link.

Cost-per-lead (CPL): This is a more specific form of cost-per-action in which a visitor provides enough information at the advertiser's site (or in interaction with a rich media ad) to be used as a sales lead. Note that you can estimate cost-per-lead regardless of how you pay for the ad; in other words, buying on a pay-per-lead basis is not required to calculate the cost-per-lead.

Cost-per-sale (CPS): Sites that sell products directly from their website or can otherwise determine sales generated as the result of an advertising sales lead can calculate the cost-per-sale of Web advertising.

Cost-per-thousand (CPM): Cost per thousand ad impressions; an industry standard measure for selling ads on websites. This measure is taken from print advertising. The "M" is taken from the Roman numeral for "thousand."

Creative: Ad agencies and buyers often refer to ad banners and other forms of created advertising as "the creative." Since the creative requires creative inspiration and skill that may come from a third party, it often does not arrive until late in the preparation for a new campaign launch.

CTR: Click-through rate. The cost of one click-through for a banner ad.

Demographics: Demographics are data about the size and characteristics of a population or audience; for example, gender, age group, income group, purchasing history, and personal preferences.

Domain name: A unique name that identifies one or more IP addresses.

Double opt-in: A message is automatically sent to the person who has been signed up for a mailing list, asking whether they want to be added to the list. Unless they actively reply positively, their name is wiped from the list, and they never get another message.

Download: The transfer of files from a remote machine (web server) to a user's machine.

E-commerce: The process of buying, selling and transferring money through the Internet.

Expression Web: A Web page authoring application from Microsoft.

Extensible HyperText Markup Language (XHTML): This next-generation language uses the same expressions and basic code as HTML, but also complies with the XML standard. It will help you to create websites that contain more features, functionality, and flexibility than ones created using HTML.

File size: The amount of space that a file takes up when stored on disk measured in bytes, kilobytes (K), megabytes (MB) or gigabytes (GB).

File transfer protocol (FTP): The most common way of transferring the files from one computer to another across a network.

Filtering: The immediate analysis by a program of a user Web page request in order to determine which ad or ads to return in the requested page. A Web page request can tell a website or its ad server whether it fits a certain characteristic, such as coming from a particular company's address or that the user is using a particular level of browser. The Web ad server can respond accordingly.

Firewall: Software to protect networks from unauthorized access.

Flame: To post a hostile comment or personal attack on a blog.

Flame war: A series of flames going back and forth on a blog.

Flash: A vector-based, multimedia technology that can be embedded in HTML pages; this is typically in the form of animations. The entire website may be developed in Flash.

Flickr: A digital photo sharing website and Web services suite.

FrontPage: A Web page authoring application from Microsoft.

GNU Image Manipulation Program (GIMP:) An open source graphics creation and manipulation application.

Google bomb: To intentionally insert words or phrases into as many blogs as possible to increase the ranking on the Google search engine.

Graphic Interchange Format (GIF): A popular image file format.

Group blog: A blog maintained by two or more bloggers.

Harvesting: Using automated scripts known as "bots" to identify the correct syntax of email addresses on Web pages and newsgroup posts and then to copy the addresses to a list.

Hit: The sending of a single file.

Home page: The first page a user sees when visiting a website.

HyperText Markup Language (HTML): The language of the Web. Web pages are written in HTML.

HyperText Transfer Protocol (HTTP:) The protocol used to transfer Web pages on the Internet.

Impression: According to the "Basic Advertising Measures" from FAST, an ad industry group, an impression is "The count of a delivered basic advertising unit from an ad distribution point." Impressions are how most Web advertising is sold and the cost is quoted in terms of the CPM.

Insertion order: An insertion order is a formal, printed order to run an ad campaign. Typically, the insertion order identifies the campaign name, the website receiving the order and the planner or buyer giving the order, the individual ads to be run (or who will provide them), the ad sizes, the campaign beginning and end dates, the CPM, the total cost, discounts to be applied, reporting requirements, and possible penalties or stipulations relative to the failure to deliver the impressions.

Internet: A worldwide collection of computers all connected together to form a large, growing network.

Internet Information Services (IIS): A Web server created by Microsoft.

Internet Protocol Address (IP Address): A unique number

assigned to each machine connected to the Internet to uniquely identify it.

Internet Service Provider (ISP): An entity that provides users with connectivity to the Internet.

JavaScript: A client-side scripting language used to create dynamic Web pages. JavaScript should not be confused with Java, the full featured programming language.

Joint Photographic Experts Group (JPG or JPEG): A popular image file format.

"Junk" Email: Email messages sent to multiple recipients who did not request it and are not in the right target audience.

Keyword: A word or phrase that a user types into a search engine when looking for specific information.

Keyword Matching Options: There are four types of keyword matching: broad matching, exact matching, phrase matching, and negative keywords. These options

help you refine your ad targeting on Google search pages.

Keyword Searches: Searches for specific text that identifies unwanted email.

Link: An object on a Web page that connects the user to another section of the page, the website or the Internet. Links are normally a different color to stand out from the rest of the text on a page.

Linkbaiting: Writing good content with the sole purpose of getting it linked from multiple sites.

Linux: An open source operating system.

Lurker: A reader of a blog who never comments.

Macintosh (Mac): The Apple computer.

Mark up: The process in which text and other data is converted into Web pages by using HTML tags.

Maximum cost-per-click (CPC): With keyword-targeted ad campaigns, you choose the maximum cost-per-click (Max CPC) you are willing to pay.

Maximum cost-per-impression (CPM): With site-targeted ad campaigns, you choose the maximum cost per thousand impressions (Max CPM) you are willing to pay.

Media broker: Since it is often not efficient for an advertiser to select every website it wants to put ads on, media brokers aggregate sites for advertisers and their media planners and buyers, based on demographics and other factors.

Media buyer: A media buyer, usually at an advertising agency, works with a media planner to allocate the money provided for an advertising campaign among specific print or online media — such as magazines, TV, or websites — and then calls and places the advertising orders. On the Web, placing the order often involves requesting proposals and negotiating the final cost.

Meta tags: Hidden HTML directions for Web browsers or search engines. They include important information such as the title of each page, relevant keywords describing site content, and the description of the site that shows up when a search engine returns a search.

MP3: The file extension for MPEG. They can be embedded into a website to provide audio.

Newsgroups: Topic-specific discussion and information exchange forums open to interested parties.

Non-permission marketing: An email message which is or appears to be sent to multiple recipients who did not request it, even though they may be in the right target market

Open source: Programs that allow the source code to be distributed thereby allowing programmers to alter and change the original software.

Opt-in email: An email containing information or advertising that users explicitly request (opt) to receive.

Page impressions: A measure of how many times a Web page has been displayed to visitors. Often used as a crude way of counting the visitors to a site.

Page requests: A measure of the number of pages that visitors have viewed in a day. Often used as a crude way of indicating the popularity of a website.

Page view: A common metric for measuring how many times a complete page is visited.

Paid search: The area of keyword, contextual advertising; often called **pay-per-click**.

Paint Shop Pro Photo X6: A powerful graphics application.

Pay-per-click (PPC): In pay-per-click advertising, the advertiser pays a certain amount for each click-through to the advertiser's website. The amount paid per click-through is arranged at the time of the insertion order and varies considerably. Higher pay-per-click rates recognize that there may be some "no-click" branding value as well as click-through value provided.

Pay-per-lead: In pay-per-lead advertising, the advertiser pays for each sales lead generated. For example, an advertiser might pay for every visitor that clicked on a site and then filled out a form.

Pay-per-sale: Pay-per-sale is not customarily used for ad buys. It is, however, the customary way to pay websites that participate in affiliate programs, such as those of Amazon.com and Beyond.com.

Pay-per-view (PPV): Since this is the prevalent type of ad buying arrangement at larger websites, this term tends to be used only when comparing this most prevalent method with PPC and other methods.

Permalink: The unique URL of a single post on a blog, used when anyone wants to link specifically to a post rather than to the most recently updated page of a blog.

Photoshop: The industry standard graphics application.

PHP: Hypertext Preprocessor (PHP): A server-side programming language designed for Web programming.

Ping: Used to notify other blog tracking tools of updates, changes and trackbacks.

Pixel: The smallest point of light that a monitor can produce.

Portable Networks Graphics (PNG): A lossless, compressible file format for images on the Web.

Post: A single unit of content on a blog, usually consisting of at least a title and text. A blog is made up of a collection of posts.

Post scheduling: Using blogging software to write posts and schedule them for publishing in the future.

Practical Extraction and Reporting Language (Perl): A server-side, interpreted programming language commonly used with CGI.

Proof of performance: Some advertisers may want proof that the ads they have bought have actually run and that click-through figures are accurate. In print media, tear sheets taken from a publication prove that an ad was run. On the Web, there is no industry-wide practice for proof of performance. Some buyers rely on the integrity of the media broker and the website. The ad buyer often checks the website to determine the ads are actually running. Most buyers require weekly figures during a campaign. A few want to look directly at the figures, viewing the ad server or website reporting tool.

Relational Database Management System (RDBMS): A database management system that allows data arranged in a tabular form to be related to data in other tables via common fields.

Reporting template: Although the media must report data to ad agencies, media planners, and buyers during and at the end of each campaign, no standard report is yet available. FAST, the ad industry coalition, is working on a proposed standard reporting template that would enable reporting to be consistent.

Return on Investment (ROI): The bottom line on how successful an ad or campaign was in terms of what the returns (often sales revenue) were for the money expended (invested).

Rich media: Advertising that contains perceptual or interactive elements that are more elaborate than the usual banner ad. Today, the term is often used for banner ads with popup menus that let the visitor select a particular page to link to on the advertiser's site. Rich media ads are generally more challenging to create and to serve. Some early studies have shown that rich media ads tend to be more effective than ordinary animated banner ads.

Rich Site Summary (RSS): A method of describing news or other Web content that is available for "feeding" (distribution or syndication) from an online publisher to Web users; also called Really Simple Syndication.

RSS aggregator: Software or service that automatically check a series of RSS feeds for new items on an ongoing basis, making it possible to keep track of changes to multiple websites in real time through one application.

RSS feed: The file that contains the latest updates to an RSS-equipped page.

RSS publisher: A Web server that publishes RSS feeds for retrieval by aggregators and RSS readers.

RSS reader: An application that reads many RSS feeds on behalf of one or more RSS subscribers.

Run-of-network: A run-of-network ad is one that is placed to run on all sites within a given network of sites. Ad sales firms handle run-of-network insertion orders in such a way as to optimize results for the buyer consistent with higher priority ad commitments.

Run-of-site: A run-of-site ad is one that is placed to rotate on all non-featured ad spaces on a site. CPM rates for run-of-site ads are usually less than rates for specially-placed ads or sponsorships.

Screen reader: Software that reads the content of the screen aloud to a user.

Search engine: A special site that provides an index of other website addresses listed according to key words and descriptions in the original page.

Search engine marketing (SEM): Promoting a website through a search engine. This most often refers to targeting prospective customers by buying relevant keywords or phrases.

Search Engine Optimization (SEO): Making a website more friendly to search engines, resulting in a higher page rank.

Secure Shell (SSH): A secure way of transferring information between computers on a network.

Server side: Programs that reside on the server and that a user can interact with through the CGI or more directly through the Web server.

Spam: An unwanted email message sent in bulk to thousands of addresses to try to advertise something.

Spam posts: Messages posted to an email discussion group, chat rooms, or bulletin boards that are "off topic" or are distinctly promotional.

Spambot: A program designed to collect, or harvest, email addresses from the Internet in order to build mailing lists for sending unsolicited email.

Sping: A ping sent from a splog to make recipients think content has been updated.

Splash page: A splash page is a preliminary page that precedes the regular home page of a website and usually promotes a particular site feature or provides advertising.

Splog: A blog composed of spam.

Sponsor: Depending on the context, a sponsor simply means an advertiser who has sponsored an ad, and by doing so, has also helped sponsor or sustain the website itself.

Syndication: The distribution of a news article through an RSS or Atom feed.

Targeting: The purchasing of an ad space on websites that match audience and campaign objective requirements.

Trackback: A protocol that allows a blogger to link to a post, often on other blogs, that relate to a selected subject. Blogging software that supports Trackback includes a "TrackBack URL" with each post that displays other blogs that have linked to it.

Trackback ping: A ping that signals a blog's server that a post on that blog has been commented upon.

Trackback spam: Sping sent by means of the Trackback system.

Unique visitor: A unique visitor is someone with a unique address who is entering a website for the first time that day (or some other specified period). Thus, a visitor that returns within the same day is not counted twice. A unique visitor count tells you how many different people there are in your audience during a specific time period, but not how much they used the site during the period.

Universal Resource Locator and Uniform Resource Identifier (URL and URI): A string of characters used to identify a resource on the Internet. Commonly called the domain name.

Unix: An operating system commonly used for Web servers.

Upload: The process of moving files from a local computer to a remote computer.

User session: A user session is someone with a unique address that enters or reenters a website each day (or some other specified period).

View: A view, depending on the context, is either an ad view or a page view. There can be multiple ad views per page views. View counting should consider that a small percentage of users choose to turn the graphics off (not display the images) in their browser.

Visit: A visit is a Web user with a unique address entering a website at some page for the first time that day (or for the first time in a lesser time period). The number of visits is roughly equivalent to the number of different people that visit a site.

Web Accessibility Initiative (WAI): A W3C initiative aimed at improving the accessibility of the Web.

Web Content Accessibility Guidelines (WCAG): A set of guidelines to make a website accessible.

Web design: The selection and coordination of available components to create the layout and structure of a Web page.

Web designer: A person who designs Web pages.

Web developer: A person who performs programming for a website.

Web server: The computer (and software) that hosts a website.

Weblog: Longer, alternative word for a blog; an online diary listing thoughts on a specific topic, often in reverse chronological order.

WebPlus XD2: Website Maker A Web page authoring application from Serif.

Website: A collection of Web pages available on the World Wide Web through a Web server.

White lists: Guaranteed delivery of known good addresses.

Wiki: A collaborative online environment that allows contributors and readers to add to a variety of subjects.

World Wide Web Consortium (W3C): Developer of specifications and guidelines for the Web.

Yield: The percentage of clicks versus impressions on an ad within a specific page.

Index